CHILDREN
of CRISIS

❇ BOOKS BY ROBERT COLES

CHILDREN
of CRISIS
A Study of Courage and Fear

ROBERT COLES, M.D.

with illustrations

An Atlantic Monthly Press Book
LITTLE, BROWN AND COMPANY • BOSTON • TORONTO

LIBRARY OF CONGRESS CATALOG CARD NO. 67-14450

10   9   8   7   6   5   4   3

00254   08   L2

The author wishes to thank the following magazines for permission to
reprint material which first appeared in their pages: *American Scholar,
The Atlantic, Contemporary Psychoanalysis, Journal of Nervous and Mental Disease, Massachusetts Review, Yale Review.*

Chapter X, "The Meaning of Race," appeared first in *Daedalus,* Journal of
the American Academy of Arts and Sciences, copyright © 1965 by the
American Academy of Arts and Sciences, and is reprinted here by permission.

ATLANTIC–LITTLE, BROWN BOOKS
ARE PUBLISHED BY
LITTLE, BROWN AND COMPANY
IN ASSOCIATION WITH
THE ATLANTIC MONTHLY PRESS

BP

*Published simultaneously in Canada
by Little, Brown & Company (Canada) Limited*

PRINTED IN THE UNITED STATES OF AMERICA

To the Children of a Coming South

And Moses sent them to spy out the
land of Canaan, and said unto them,
Get you up this way southward, and
go up into the mountain: And see the
land, what it is; and the people that
dwelleth therein, whether they be
strong or weak.

FOREWORD

THE SOUTH has had more than its fair share of analysis
these past years, and I am not trying to join the region's
defenders or critics with yet another book.

What I am trying to do is describe certain lives; specifically,
describe the way those lives have come to terms with the political
and social changes that have taken place in a particular region of
this country. I speak as a child psychiatrist, trained first in
medicine, then psychiatry, and finally one of its subspecialties. If
this book concerns itself with adults as well as children, its title
accurately reflects my chief professional interest — though obviously no one can study children too long without taking a look at
the people who nurture them, teach them, and on occasion fail
them terribly. The reader will learn that I started my work in
the South as an Air Force physician in 1958, and undertook the
work this book aims to present shortly thereafter. I still continue
to see a number of the children and families mentioned in these
pages. Our acquantance will soon have lasted a matter of ten
years. As some people put it, this is a "long-term study."

I am working under the assumption that there still is room —
maybe a corner here and there — for direct, sustained observation of individual human beings living in a significant and critical
period of history. By direct observation I mean talking with
people, listening to them, watching them — and being watched
by them. By sustained observation I mean taking a long time:
enough time to be confused, then absolutely certain and confident, then not so sure but a little more aware of why one or

another conclusion seems the best that can be argued, or at least better then any other available.

There is another qualifying word to the kind of observation I have attempted; it has been clinical, in the twin sense that I am a clinician and that I was looking at how children (or their parents and teachers) managed under stress; that is, abnormal and dangerous circumstances. The people I met had discernible cause to feel nervous, to develop a variety of symptoms in both mind and body. Whether they did so, and if they did how and when they did — such questions are reasonably the doctor's; while the psychiatrist, at least in this century, traditionally wants to know who chooses which kind of danger, and for what reason, known or unknown. What doctors and psychiatrists usually do not do is work with people who have no particular reason, interest or desire to see them — perhaps quite the opposite inclination. Medical students and psychiatrists in training are taught to understand the ways of disease, and then to heal pragmatically the illnesses that so often fail to follow the descriptions textbooks give to them. As a result, little if any medical or psychiatric attention is directed toward asking what exactly makes for survival under stress, for endurance, for courage against grim odds; indeed, for plain good health in contrast, say, to bad health and perhaps even bad "mental health," whatever that is.

Who is the "ordinary man," if he exists, and what does the word "normal" mean, if anything? What makes for persistence and stability in everyday people (not patients)? What really does bring about the mind's collapse? A threshold of suffering passed? A long-standing weakness finally exposed, or given a decisive chance to do its bad work? Should we in medicine consider the economic indices or environmental settings that are sometimes summoned in the abstract as "causes" of this problem, or "factors" in that? What does the child's mind make of the world — of politics, race and the facts of money? Why does one person make satisfied peace with the world, while another takes the world on and tries to change it in any number of ways? Social scientists have the job, the very necessary job, of documenting exactly what "outside" world it is — the time, the place, the culture and the society — that a particular child finds at birth and learns about as he grows. The clinician has always been interested in what goes on "inside" others — he himself being part of *their* "outside," their world. Presumably he is as qualified as anyone to go back and forth, to see how the two worlds (outside, inside) connect, blend, engage — words and images fail to describe the continuity between man's thinking and the world's state of affairs. In any event, there are encouraging signs that the traditional concerns (and obligations) clinicians have felt are widening; they want to apply their method of study — I hope not their categories of illness — to men and women who want and seek things other than diagnosis and "treatment."

So, what I have tried to pursue is a method of study (the clinical) and what I have tried to do is locate my body and mind where certain *citizens* are up against difficult times, so that their lives, like those of the sick, may have something to teach the rest of us. I have done this work knowing that every day the world changes, bringing new threats and promises to people. There is no keeping up with history, but I hope the record set forth here will be of some worth to future historians who find themselves interested in how a few Americans lived through a critical time in their lives and this country's development as a democracy. One thing is certain: no longer is the South's struggle a lonely one. It is an entire nation that has had to consider the special problems faced by Negro families, or look at what lies behind riots, or cries of "black power," or the new and fearful solidarity of whites that bears the ugly label of a "backlash."

In doing this work I have followed a direction pointed by others. When training to be a child psychiatrist I learned of Anna Freud's sensitive work with English children during German air attack, and later with children once in concentration camps, all done so simply, so directly and with a minimum of theoretical flourish. She has consistently championed a combination of observation and practical service; and her example will stand any investigator in good stead. I also met up with Erik Erikson's thought, with his consistent willingness first to know the human mind; then to see its everyday relatedness to the world, to social institutions, indeed to history itself; and finally to bind the known and the seen through a sensible (and tolerant) conceptual system.

In addition to such clinical and theoretical encouragement, I wish to acknowledge other help. My research in the South and later in the North has been supported by grants from the New World Foundation, the General Education Board of the Rockefeller Foundation and the Field Foundation first to the Southern Regional Council and then to the Harvard University Health Services. I have thus been permitted to give this research my full time and energy, without once being asked to justify or tamper with its purposes or style. I am grateful; but I fear I am also lucky.

Sections of this book have appeared elsewhere in shorter or expanded and different form. In Part One the first chapter was originally published in the *Massachusetts Review;* the second chapter first read before a divisional meeting of the American Psychiatric Association in Philadelphia (1964) and later published in the *Journal of Nervous and Mental Disease.* In Part Two a portion of chapter III was published in the *Atlantic.* In chapter IV "The Matter of Chocolate" draws from a paper read to the American Orthopsychiatric Association, then published in the *Journal of Nervous and Mental Disease;* in that same chapter "George and His Lois" first appeared in the *New Yorker.* In chapter VII a section from "Stay Home or Go to School?" appeared in *Contemporary Psychoanalysis,* and much of the last part of chapter VIII ("The Last Ditch") originally was published in the *Yale Review.* Finally, two chapters of Part Three have been previously in print: chapter IX in the *American Scholar* and chapter X in *Daedalus.*

Without the help of Kenneth Beach, Katharine Taylor, Vernon Eagle, Leslie Dunbar and Dana Farnsworth I could never have started and continued this work. I again thank them. I also wish to thank Peter Davison for his help as an editor, and Nancy Kane for her hard and loyal work with the book's manuscript.

Then, there are the people mentioned and described in the book, and others like them from the various cities and states of the South we lived in or worked in. I cannot mention them, only thank them many times for their kindness — and for what they have consistently taught me. I think they all would want me to conclude any list of acknowledgments with my wife Jane's name. In home after home, and in schools too, she accompanied me. Much more, though, she made the work possible for me and for the children. One of them, a six-year-old girl in New Orleans, put it this way when I came to see her alone: "Next time come with your wife, because it's not the same when she's away." Yes, indeed.

In a real sense this is also a foreword to work in progress. Perhaps no one needs to be reminded that the problems faced by the people mentioned in this book are shared in one way or another by many other Americans, in the South and elsewhere. What I learned as I came to know one family after another was that individual families share problems, just as regions and nations do. Many of the children I observed in Southern cities have cousins whose parents are migrant farmers, or share-croppers, or "mountain folk" from the Appalachian hills of Virginia, North Carolina or Tennessee. Then, there are the cousins — not only Negroes, either — "abroad," in Chicago, New York or on the West Coast. When I finished the main, everyday part of my work with Southern children attending desegregated schools, I moved my concern to some of those cousins. I started looking further into the lives of migrant farm children, tenant farm and mountain children, and eventually the children of Northern cities who must also face social isolation, segregation, desegregation — in brief, the dislocated, hard living that is still America's gift to some of its young, regardless of race or ancestry. In future volumes — there seems no end to crisis in this world — I hope to tell of them and have them speak their own thoughts.

CONTENTS

(Children's Drawings between pages 50–51)

THREE: COURAGE and FEAR

PART ONE

METHOD

I

THE SOUTH

I CAME to the South a New Englander, not only by birth but with over a quarter of a century of living and growing up. At the end of a psychiatric residency I was called to Mississippi to serve my required two years in the military as a doctor, in this case as the chief of an Air Force neuropsychiatric hospital. The Air Force is a memory, but the South has become a real, a fresh part of my life. At first it was a region that I cared little to know, in fact it took me from several assignments I would have preferred. It has become one whose continuing pull upon my mind and heart prevents me from staying away for very long.

It is easy to categorize and give names to experiences once we are done with them. It is often sad that we do, because the effort takes away much of their original and spontaneous character. I suppose we need to try — it helps others understand, and makes us feel less anxious because more in control of our fate. As I look back at the past years in the South, I recall how easily I slipped into its very distinctive life and how pleasant I found that life to be. Only now do I stir anxiously at the thought of just how long (weeks turning to months) it took me to develop the dim awareness that became the vague uneasiness which marked a change in my thoughts and habits while living there.

One way of putting it is that I was a white, middle-class professional man, and so I easily fitted into that kind of Southern society. Only gradually did I begin to notice the injustice so close at hand, and as a consequence eventually take up my particular effort against it. (There would be those various categorical "stages" in such a development, ranging from faint glimmers to horrified, full recognition.) In the South, of course, anyone who begins to discover "injustice" in the world is in fact noticing the existence of a caste system wherein Negroes have an inherited position in a social organization which both needs them and yet notices their skin color before any individual attainments or accomplishments.

I think the major conclusion that I now draw from my first stay in the South is less one of deliberate accommodation to its social evils than of intense preoccupation with a brief but demanding interlude in my life — a new kind of job in a new location. The world cries out with its innumerable trials and horrors — the betrayal of human life, made cheap and stripped of its dignity, in every nation. The very nature of the human mind forces us to limit our interests and compassion, or else we drown in their diffusion and our own extreme pain.

In any event, toward the end of my second year South I was interrupted one day on a bicycle trip along the shore of the Gulf of Mexico by the sight and sound of a vicious battle. To this day I can remember my mind working its way toward some comprehension of what was happening, fighting its way through its old attitudes for a moment, then slipping back to them in relief. I saw a scuffle, and at first I wondered why people would want to behave that way. For a few seconds, I suppose, my lifetime — and I don't think only mine — was recapitulated: its innocence, its indifference, its ignorance, its sheltered quiet, its half-and-half mixture of moral inertia and well-intentioned effort. For a while I could only see *people* fighting. I heard shouts and cries. Some nasty and vulgar words fell upon my ears. I recall thinking for a moment that it was a Sunday, a beautiful Sunday; and it was a shame that people could be so mean-spirited and irreverent on Sunday, on any day, on such a clear, warm morning in early spring. I pedaled faster; I almost had the scene out of sight; but I can remember today slowing down, hesitating, only able to stop by lifting my body from the seat of the bike, by using my dragging, scuffing feet. I let the bike lie on its side, and stood still.

Not only was there a fight, but among the people I could see several *women*. A woman screamed that a man had smashed her watch and stepped on her glasses. Before I saw that she was a slender, middle-aged *Negro* lady, that he was a young, athletic *white man*, I felt the sympathy and horror that the weak share with the weak against the powerful. With that feeling I also knew for a moment that I would not easily be able to go to the woman's aid. In another flash, however, I realized I could justify my reluctance: it was a *racial* incident; the truth of what was happening was that the people were not simply people, the men and women not simply that.

I can still feel myself standing there, benighted, frightened, seized with curiosity, suddenly quite restless. I was not morally outraged. I did not want to join in the Negroes' protest for equal access to that essentially useless, shallow bit of seashore. Eventually, I simply wanted to go away; and I did. Riding home I condemned *all* the antagonists — for fighting, for choosing to fight for such absurd stakes, for being the kind of people who *would* fight. I am not now very proud of those minutes. Yet if I forgot them, I would be even more ashamed.

That night I worked in the emergency ward of the base hospital, a duty which fell on each doctor with unnerving regularity. I had come to know the local police quite well during those evenings; they were on call, too, and we shared the long stretches of dark silence in that small town. The incident I had inadvertently witnessed was very much on the minds of both policemen, and their insistent talk about it made it impossible for me to forget it. We had never before mentioned the subject of race, but not, so far as I know, out of self-conscious or fearful avoidance in any of us. I liked those two policemen. They were kind, polite and quite intelligent — considerably more so than many I had met in similar situations in certain Northern hospitals.

Like the event itself, I recall the first words: "They'd be dead now if it weren't for the publicity they get these days," followed by an avowal from his companion that "They will be if they try it again. We're never going to have mixing in this state." They had been talking with me; suddenly I felt them talking *to* me — *at* me. Their voices tightened. They spoke as crisply as a Southern drawl will permit — the honey in it had crystallized. They seemed aloof, yet fiercely determined to make their feelings clear to me, to the others nearby — now I realize to themselves. I found myself slipping into a psychiatric posture with them, noticing their defensive anger, their accusations — diffusely directed at history, at Northerners. I decided that *they* were afraid, but I really didn't know why. I said little in reply. I wondered how men so strong, so appealing, so sensible could be aroused by an event I had managed to put out of my mind. Then a patient came in, and I was strangely glad to see him. His minor infection kept me exceptionally busy. If he hadn't been there . . . I remember thinking that I would not have told my friends that I had seen the "swim-in." I saw their mood, observed their tension, felt their resentment, sensed their irritability, and feared my own involvement in any of them. Psychiatrists, of course, learn to watch for the unreasonable, avoid entanglement with the irrational. I imagine it was handy for me to be able to call upon such professional practices.

By morning we had talked of town news, the fishing and shrimping, the new shopping center going up, the meaning to the area of a projected increase in the population of the air base. That dawn we left, friends to one another as before. During the next weeks I continued with my usual tasks of work and play; but something had taken place. I can recollect, for instance, picking up the Jackson and New Orleans papers, reading in them of the coming probability of school desegregation in nearby New Orleans. It was well before the fateful day of its start, but the New Orleans papers were bitter and the Jackson papers almost incredulous. Somehow that news didn't manage to slip by me the way some news does, out of the impossibility of keeping totally abreast. It wasn't simply my reading, however, that was being affected. I started noticing where Negroes lived, where they didn't; where they were in evidence, where they were not; how they behaved with white people, and white people with them.

This new consciousness took root over several months. I find it hard to do justice to whatever growth and consolidation of feeling may have occurred during those months, because to think about that time now often invites in myself a certain scornful disbelief — that I could have lived so long under such a clearly oppressive social, political and economic system, only to have been so blithely, so very innocently unaware of its nature. Yet I was.

Today there may be other problems than blindness facing many people living in the South. Large numbers of people in the region have awakened to the racial problem, and many of them, like me, must be freshly sensitive to the limitations which all human beings discover in their involvements and sensitivities. As if that were not enough, many probably are also coming to know that strong commitments push and tug at one another with their various demands, so that new kinds of indifference — even arrogance and hate — can follow old blind spots or prejudices. For example, there is the fighter's need to shed himself of much of the ambiguity of life, to sacrifice perspective, kindheartedness and even, at times, good judgment to the interests of the hard battle. When I look back at my first days there I am glad that I came to know the South as I did; but I also feel torn and paralyzed when I think of those times too long. I enjoyed one kind of life then, and that kind is gone for me.

Of course the South has always had its moments of paralyzed nostalgia. Nostalgia can be for anyone a valuable way to avoid the terrible strain of the present by forsaking its reality in favor of the more pleasant world of memory. There is a painful ambiguity to Southern life: the genuine beauty of the landscape, the very real tradition of generosity and neighborliness, the long-standing sense of persecution, moral as well as economic, at the hands of powerful and hypocritical Americans from other areas. Effective protest, even against many open and declared social evils, does not always easily find a voice; and segregation in the South has hardly been considered anything but inevitable for both whites and Negroes: each in their own way have known for generations the futility or risks of trying to change so awesome and peculiar a social system.

The protest I witnessed at the seashore in Mississippi showed that whatever balance it had taken to keep a way of life from being seen as a social evil was beginning to be upset. Not only was the protest no accident, but the restraint of the town's police was no accident either — whatever solemn excuses they offered for it. The South was feeling the swift encouragement (and consequent fear) of a chain of events connected to world history as well as our own nation's. My life is no "average white Southerner's" (hopefully none of our lives submit to approximations like that), and I am not sure that sit-ins such as I saw that day affect the majority of the South's white population as they do many of us who live elsewhere. Yet I think most people of the South — Negroes and whites alike — have experienced some of that same surprise I did, a jolting flash when one kind of world begins to collapse, another begins to appear, and it all becomes *apparent.*

My work of the past years has been to study what happens to people in the midst of such social changes, how they relinquish their old ways and take up new ones, how, that is, they manage the various stresses and exertions of doing so. I shall never know how those Negroes and whites felt whom I saw that day on the Gulf Coast of Mississippi, but I think I have some fair notion about how others like them have felt in equally tense if not so vicious encounters — the children in desegregated schools in Louisiana, or in Georgia, where I lived for two years; the sit-in students from all over the South, and the whites who have been confronted by them; some leading segregationists, whom I came to know over a good number of months; and most recently, some sharecroppers and migrant workers, the poor of both races whose hands harvest our cotton and food for little enough reward indeed.

Doing such work has required so much travel throughout the region that I know much of it better than any part of the North where I have lived. Even before I started studying some of the problems in the South, however, I had become somewhat sensitive to it through the astonishing contrast there with all that New England taught me to expect from nature and people. The very names of the towns were surprising. Some were familiar enough, but there are special preferences, too, such as the Greek and Roman names given to town after town in state after state: Rome in Georgia, Mississippi and Tennessee; or Sparta in Georgia, Tennessee and North Carolina. The ancient city of Carthage on the Gulf of Tunis is no more, but of fourteen cities which carry on its name over the world, six are in the South. There are other names less classical but in their sum a story of the region: Laurel, Enterprise, Liberty, Eufala, Senatobia, Natchitoches, Yazoo, Magnolia, Opelouses, Amite, and the Fayettevilles and Waynesboros, telling of flowers, ideals, Indians, and the French or English who lived there or came to do so.

The South's difference from the rest of the nation depends upon more than villages named in honor of Indian tribes or patriots to be celebrated. The South is not only its history, of those towns, of slavery, of rebellion. The skin feels the bouts of winter warmth, and must live with the heat in summer, dry in Atlanta, steamy in New Orleans; for heat *is* the South, and the weather is indeed kinder in winter and fatiguing in the summer.

Whole theories of human nature have centered themselves on climate, and most often they seem single-minded or excessive, except for a moment in February when a soft wind rises from the bay and comes into Mobile, and with it a warm sun which brings out azaleas and high spirits both; or a time in midsummer when the damp heat in Louisiana has gone on long enough to make nerves already worn thin become frayed beyond recovery.

The earth, too, is special, much of it red with copper. The growth is different; tropical plants and palm trees, the famous wisteria and symbolic magnolia. The water is particularly abundant and rich in its variety: wide rivers, their tributaries weaving through the entire region, and the still smaller bayous, and canals, and the swamps with the mist over them. Lakes are everywhere, and much of the oceanside shows a tropical green band when it touches the shore.

The people have their own ways, too — their words, their food and stories, their kind of churches and praying. It's been noted so often, but an outsider like me coming from Northern or Western cities is surprised at first by the very few names that are not Anglo-Saxon; those names, of course, shared by Negroes, who are not simply confined to ghettoes as they are so predominantly in the North, but are everywhere. They take care of homes and often live near them; they work in stores, gas stations, office buildings, and on the farms which still dominate the area; they cultivate and harvest crops, sharing in some of the profits in exchange for land and house, or moving from state to state to wait for harvests and gather them.

White and Negro alike, the people are, I suspect, church-going beyond all others in the nation. The land seems covered with churches, and their denominational variety is astonishing. Revivals are common, and strict tithing by no means rare. The Bible is read literally in many towns throughout the section, which is still rural, strong on family and unashamed patriotism. Many whites have not yet surrendered their intensely suspicious regional and national pride, and many Negroes have till now found no reason to let go of the apathy and dependency, the alternation of good-natured frolic and sulky aloofness which characterized for so long their lack of pride in both themselves and their condition. Both races share some of the social forms of the society — the expressions like "Y'all come back," said frequently out of meaning as well as ritual, or the food, like pecan pie, grits and okra, which come upon any visitor fairly soon and which one "favors" or is "partial to."

The federal roads are coming in, television with its widespread news and "culture" is everywhere, and national loyalties have always contended with local ones. The region, though, for good and bad has had a stubborn power, not only in its social and economic system, but in its history, its earth, its language and literature. Certainly what I have described about the South's particular nature is familiar to most of us, and has been repeatedly described before. I had read those descriptions and "knew" their message before going to live there. Yet the experience of those differences of living and thinking made for a sharper kind of awareness in me of the very real effect of those differences on the outsider who comes to live there as well as the lifelong inhabitant of the section. Too much can be made of these "local" variations; but then too little significance can be granted them in an age that recognizes perhaps rather exclusively the grossest kinds of political and economic power, or dwells with a certain preoccupation upon the unqualified sovereignty of early childhood experiences.

My work has been concerned with changes in Southern life as it moodily breaks with the past. For well over a generation a "new South" has been anticipated and hailed, but its arrival is now certain. As I walk through Atlanta or Charlotte the people can be seen in all their hurry, dressed out of New York, their office buildings as new, ugly and efficient as those in other "growing" sections. The airports are the same boxes of never-ending buoyant music, and the runways as hungry for jets as all others. Yet Southerners have resisted as well as yielded to and even welcomed our modern nearness to one another. In studying the adjustment of white and Negro children (and their parents and teachers) to school desegregation I have learned to expect just that unusual blend of affection and reserve, accommodation and resentment which characterizes not only racial relations as they change in form and substance these days, but the South itself — recasting itself, but in its own fashion.

No one interested in the individual as he encounters a society in swift transition will be bored by Mississippi or the Carolinas. Some of the South's people hurt and exploit others, but the region itself has been ruthlessly exploited over the generations. Many of its people are poor, ignorant and capable of an absurd kind of defensive chauvinism, but many are sturdy, hardworking and kind people, so that as a whole every bit of Faulkner's vision seems sound. For all the shrill and resentful voices there have been many silent warriors in hopeless causes, many silent sufferers reduced to poverty and defeat; and now their descendants fight against hateful mobs and the mean conditions of life which generate them.

These past one hundred years have not been a pretty story, and distress has not fallen upon one race alone. The kind of political tyranny practiced by whites over Negroes has gained little for large numbers of whites, and the saddest part of studying whites hating Negroes by forming mobs or being nasty to them in schools, or sharing their fate on the collapsing farms of the region or in the flow of migrant farmers which travels through it each year, is how very treacherous that "psychological satisfaction" of racial superiority has really been to the lives of those who have sought nourishment from it, and sometimes almost it alone.

A nation within a nation, emerging from years of exile and hardship, the South's people today are showing individual dignity and courage as well as fear and desperation. Today, when some of us wonder whether our social order is in fact becoming drab and lifeless through its ability to make many of us fearfully similar and compliant, the South still clings to its almost biblical struggles between those willing to risk and dare and those anxious to flee and hide. Perhaps out of no special virtue except its own tragic history, the people there are fighting one another with an intensity and consistency which is rare indeed in our country.

The protagonists have been ordinary people, but all of them have found themselves in a place and a time which have given heroic and symbolic proportions to their struggles. I am thinking, in this connection, of a white woman in New Orleans whose four children, with only a very few others, defied the mobs attempting a total boycott of an elementary school in opposition to one little Negro girl. Why did this woman, deeply of the South, not by any means committed to "integration," hazard her life, the lives of her husband and children? I was in the company of those who tried to find the answer; a reporter, a sociologist, a psychiatrist, each of us worked at our common curiosity about human nature and its motives. I think we were all baffled — perhaps because we were all eager for the categorical solution, afraid of the clumsy, undefined, paradoxical flow of life and its events which may, in fact, be the truth of it.

Again and again — I talked with this woman over a period of two years — she came back to her only reply: she hadn't *planned* to dispute the angry, threatening crowds; she didn't think she was actually in favor of desegregation when all the uproar started; perhaps she was now, though; but she had always believed in education for her children, and she also felt a deep loyalty to the South's tradition, as she put it, "of good manners."

One day she was at her most open, and most persuasive: "My heart is divided, and at the worst of it I thought we'd die, not just from dynamite, but from nervous exhaustion. I wasn't brought up to have nigras at school with me or my children. I just wasn't. . . . If I had to do it over, I wouldn't have made this system, but how many people ever have a say about what kind of world they're going to live in? . . . I guess in a sense I did have my way with those mobs. But I didn't plan to, and we were near scared to death most of the time. . . . People blame the South for the mobs, but that's just part of the South. If I did right, that's part of the South, too. . . . They just don't know how a lot of us down here suffer. We didn't make all this, we just were born to it, and we don't have all the opportunity and money down here that they do in the North. . . . I told my children the other day that we're going to live to see the end of this trouble, and when we do I'll bet both races get on better down here than anywhere else in America. . . . Why? Because I think we're quieter down here, and we respect one another, and if we could clear up the race thing, we really would know one another better. . . . We've lived so *close* for so long. . . ."

A full transcript of what this woman has said at various times tells more than any comments from those who have heard her. She is not alone in her courage. The South is filled with an underground of sly liberals in the midst of situations hardly likely to support their efforts. It is filled with a tradition of solid, dignified Negroes and ashamed, confused whites, enough of both so that it would take a bold man indeed to separate and weigh their respective suffering. It is also, however, filled with bitter, spiteful whites and fearful, apathetic Negroes, some of them capable of exploiting their own people or demeaning them.

Perhaps nowhere in America is there so much that is good and bad about human beings so clearly in evidence. Few would want to keep the region's special virtues at the price of its outrageous faults. Yet, it is a beautiful land to see, and its people in their guilt and distress may have a good deal to teach us all. The United States as a whole has known little frustration and defeat for some time. The South has lived intimately with both, and it may have some wisdom to offer from that experience. This is surely a time in our national life when we need any help we can get about how to live properly and sensibly in the face of prolonged uncertainty, ambiguity, and even the frustrations which come from not winning every battle in every war. The South has not only seen the gloomy and tormented side of man's destiny; it has seen it and known enough of it perhaps to realize also the redemptive promise and power in human suffering. Sorrow may be fated, but to survive it and grow is an achievement all its own.

II

OBSERVATION
AND PARTICIPATION

PSYCHIATRISTS can study the relationship between the individual and society in a number of ways. Certainly the Yale study by Hollingshead and Redlich[1] or the work of the Cornell group in Manhattan[2] and Nova Scotia[3] represent one kind of research: carefully planned and controlled, highly systematic research that follows a scrupulous methodological design, itself often the product of social scientists from several disciplines, including statistics. Such studies, occurring under the sponsorship of medical schools and sometimes implemented through various field trips, reflect the increasing substance and capability of what is now called social psychiatry. Yet, long before this term became one to describe a new subspecialty, some psychiatrists worked with delinquents, alcoholics, drug addicts or prisoners in need of rehabilitation. They did important, socially oriented work, including a lot of very good and important research, and they did it in child guidance clinics as part of their regular programs in clinical and child psychiatry and psychoanalysis.[4]

When I was taking my training in child psychiatry, and trying to understand what caused some of my young patients to become delinquent, was I embarking upon psychiatric research into social issues? If so, I doubt I ever considered moving from observation of delinquency to participation in its various forms. Later, however, studying another social issue, the sit-in movement, I found it hard to decide how much of what I was studying I ought to take part in or share. The special problems that thus come up in the social psychiatrist's research must even be compared to the everyday problems that confront the clinician treating patients with the most "private" or idiosyncratic complaints. How often do we only "observe" our patients? How much ought we to get involved with them, participate with them in the sense of seeking to know and join in their feelings or activities? No one yet knows a final answer to such problems. It is helpful and important to remember that, particularly when one sets out to obtain information from people who are not patients at all.

In the South I have been studying individuals under continuing social stress. Before I went South my interest was in the stress exerted by severe physical illness upon the minds of children.[5] I was in psychiatric training during a severe epidemic of poliomyelitis in Boston, just before the Salk vaccine came into widespread use. I became interested in how a group of paralyzed individuals managed such a cruel strain suddenly thrust upon them. In time my study of the first fateful weeks of their adjustment settled into a more specific concern with how the children among them came to terms with their variously handicapped bodies. I was by then taking my training as a child psychiatrist, and in the course of this training I worked with delinquents, with boys in a unit attached to a juvenile court and with girls as consultant to an "industrial" school for those who were severely troubled and most often called "antisocial."

All of those interests I left to go to Mississippi; and all of them, as I look back, I picked up again while there. I began to realize that right before my eyes human beings were facing severe stresses, this time caused not by a virus but by a society going through a hard time of change and conflict. Would it somehow be possible to learn about the lives — the attitudes, hopes and fears — of those human beings?

In sum, my life interests intersected with a situation that freshly stimulated them. Next, I had to translate "interests" into "research." I had to determine whether an *occasion* for research and a *motivation* for it would be supplemented by two other necessary conditions: a *purpose* that would make the effort worthwhile, and the *possibility* that work could actually be done so that some clinical information would eventually be gathered.

I decided that there was every reason to study individuals facing desegregation in the South; in contrast, that is, to desegregation as a "process" or a "problem." Historians document the accidents and misfortunes that plague the region. We call upon political scientists and economists to explain not only the development of slavery but the substantial failure of emancipation to measure up to its promise. Depending upon our taste, either novelists or sociologists (or both) clarify for us the special and sometimes intricate pattern of customs, taboos and myths that can be observed from Virginia to Florida, from Savannah to Amarillo. Yet, what of the individual people who have lived and do live in the midst of history, and under the political, economic and social conditions that prevail in the South? Ought we not learn how particular and various Southerners think and feel about the rather obvious troubles and even dangers they face — inadvertently, reluctantly, angrily, or because they feel the necessity? Black and white, old and young, rich and poor, people by the many hundred thousand stand by and in a number of ways react as laws and customs change, indeed as our strongest *region* — its separate identity is all of a kind in American history — accepts and resists those changes.

How are we to know what those people truly feel — deep down? For that matter, is the question an important one? Some say that how Southerners are inclined to vote is all that makes any political difference in their attitude; consequently what polls and questionnaires can obtain from them is quite enough. Yet, the violence, unrest and uncertainty that continue in the region in spite of a number of political and legal breaks with the past argue for a closer look at the day-to-day effects of a fast-shifting social system on the minds of its various (and representative) members.

My job has been to learn what I can about individuals contending with a continuing series of social crises. I brought with me a particular kind of training — the child psychiatrist's — and my purpose was to put that training to use as effectively as possible under conditions rather unlike those usually obtaining in clinical practice. In her most recent book[6] Anna Freud once again has emphasized the importance of direct observation in clinical work. In nurseries or schools, as well as hospitals or clinic offices, children require close watching and hearing. Adults, too, deserve to be given the broadest attention (admittedly busy) doctors can manage. The borderland between what doctors call "mental health" and what most everybody recognizes as "mental illness" has not been charted, though there are enough theories and phrases to make it seem otherwise. Anna Freud asks that we stop to look around a little and in the meanwhile frankly acknowledge our theoretical and methodological difficulties.

I cannot emphasize too often that desegregation in the South means a variety of efforts under a variety of conditions. Any psychiatrist who plans to study the South as a region whose social conflicts affect its people's emotions must first know how many Souths there are. One South is small mountain communities with few Negroes and a long history of much casual integration. One South is fertile Delta land with its rich, flat and sunburnt alluvial acreage covered with cotton and the thousands upon thousands of Negroes who pick it — they make up a large percentage of the population, and they are segregated from birth to death by a yet untouched array of habits and customs.

The South is also "Northern-bought," relatively young, self-consciously progressive Atlanta with its new factories and the branch offices of many national firms. It is the old and relaxed part of New Orleans, full of a distinctive Creole pride and a certain European scorn for the American, Anglo-Saxon, puritan parishes to the north, always pressing hard with their penniless, rural whites. The South is failing farms and the frustrated impoverished local towns in their midst, or it is the Piedmont area of the Carolinas, full of textiles, fine roads and bustling cities. There are the steel mills of Birmingham; there is old aristocratic Charleston; there is the still-preserved nineteenth-century gentility of Savannah; there are desperately poor hillbillies and sharecroppers in Tennessee or Alabama; there are toeholds of the Appalachian Mountains (and culture) in Georgia or Virginia; and there is Florida, a haven not only for the rich, but for the poorest in the land, in the persons of thousands of migratory farm workers.

Perhaps the most enduring part of the South is its distorted, stereotyped image, alive in millions of American minds because of ignorance, vengeance, fake piety and moral hypocrisy; but also because of genuine horror and compassion aroused by the most terrible (and all too true) deeds. If we cannot here discuss fully the contradictions in the South's tradition, or the wide variations in its life and forms of livelihood, we must at least insist upon their existence. For when people talk about desegregation in the South, they mean several kinds of social change occurring in several kinds of society, each change affecting only certain people, and in characteristic but different ways. Even now, with new and strong laws, casting a vote may be more difficult for a Negro *landowner* (let alone farmhand) in Mississippi than getting elected to the Georgia legislature is for a Negro businessman or civil rights worker in Atlanta. The degree of tension aroused when a Negro enters a formerly all-white school has fluctuated widely, even within a city as well as between cities. It has varied not only with social and economic factors, but according to the quality and intentions of the newspapers, the wishes and behavior of the civic and political leadership, the police and school officials. A psychiatrist looking at individuals facing desegregation will see how "private" thoughts and feelings come to terms with all those public forces; and the daily influence of public forces upon the minds of people simply cannot be called (as is often the case) "superficial."

We have heard — often from people with vested political or legal interests rather than psychological ones — that segregation is an emotional problem, its causes buried deep in the hearts and minds of not only whites but Negroes. A Negro child in New Orleans remarked to me in 1961: "The teachers, they say it's inside us, that's where all the trouble is and the mean words, they come from people with bad hearts; but it's outside, too, because they're all the time around, the people shouting at us, and they fired my daddy from his job yesterday."

What *was* happening to that Negro child both in school and in her mind? What made her white assailants finally take their angry opposition to the streets? While they did that, why did other white people refuse to join them — or even take the little girl's side? My job was to *reach* that girl, reach people in the crowds that heckled her so persistently, reach those who would never join a crowd, or would fight those who did. What do all these individuals think and feel — about race, about one another, about the contemporary world that is theirs to contemplate, accept, reject or on occasion change? Are they influenced significantly by their past lives, their family background, the quality of their childhood, the nature of their early or recent experiences, illnesses or achievements? Again I have to fall back on a child's words, this time an older one, a white youth speaking to me in Atlanta: "I sometimes wonder why it's *those* nigras who came to be at school with us, and if it had been others whether it would have gone differently this year. The same goes for us. What if a few of us hadn't taken the side of the nigras? I'm not saying they stayed here only because we did; but it made it easier for them because we did, and if they had been totally alone, it might have been the straw that broke their backs."

Youths like him are not patients, and so if I was going to meet them I could not ask them to come see me in a hospital or an office. I had to become what anthropologists call a field worker, I had to seek out people at home, in schools or on streets and talk with them at their convenience.

There were young schoolchildren of six or seven and their families, and there were older youths of fifteen or sixteen and their families. There were the men and women who taught them, often enough under the most difficult of circumstances. There were college students who protested segregation through sit-ins or "freedom rides," and there were those they confronted: store-keepers, voting registrars, the police and jailers. There were white people who chose to protest the dominant ways of their society. (Almost every town in the region, even in deepest Alabama and Mississippi, has had its isolated, usually silent but sometimes fearlessly outspoken advocates of political and economic equality for the Negro.) There were grown Negro citizens, sacrificing what little they owned in time and money to work for their race's destiny. Finally, there were passionate segregationists: picketing, meeting in "white councils," gathering at times in outraged and violent crowds. I had to find these people, then somehow bring it about that they would want to talk about themselves, and be heard.

The school boards of two cities, New Orleans and Atlanta, selected the first two groups of Negro children I met by choosing small numbers of them to start "token" desegregation. In 1960, four little Negro girls entered two white elementary schools located in the eastern section of New Orleans, near its industrial canal. Each school was surrounded largely by people who work in factories or smaller shops, many of them recent arrivals from the farm and plantation country of Louisiana or nearby Missis-sippi. As in many sections of New Orleans, "sophisticated" pat-terns of urban housing segregation, so common in the North, did not yet obtain in either of the neighborhoods surrounding the schools; indeed the little Negro girl who entered by her lonesome self one of the two schools lived within easy sight of white houses, on the very block of her street.

The story of what happened to these girls and "their" schools is a matter of history: mobs; the constant threat of violence; the international attention of news reports and television; the intervention of federal marshals, needed to escort the children to school; the near emptying of the schools, with an almost total boycott in one school, a completely successful one in the other for the remaining six months of the first school year, and in the second year only a handful of white children in both schools. What happened to these four Negro girls also happened to the very few white children (and their families) who braved the mob's anger to remain at school. (At one point there were about five or six of these children, in later months some two dozen.)

It is these children we first started interviewing: the four Negro girls, five of their white classmates, their families and their teachers. In later years we saw other children in New Orleans. They were white and Negro; they were less grimly harassed under desegregation; they were small children who initiated and experienced desegregation under tension but without street mobs or vandalism.

The names of the Negro children were a closely kept secret; it took considerable effort to learn who they were and to reach their families. The help of the lawyer who was handling their case in federal court was necessary. The weeks involved in arranging my first visit to the four homes showed me from the very beginning that I would be talking with people virtually driven underground by fear and the experience of terror. Though in many Southern cities the first Negro children going into white schools have had a bad time of it, these families in New Orleans — remember the year was 1960 — suffered a particularly grim fate. Their children were small (unlike the high school youths in Little Rock, Arkansas or Clinton, Tennessee) and they were in the "deep" South, the first there to enter elementary schools. Mississippi was a scant fifty miles away, nor is Louisiana itself the same — in its history as well as its geography — as Tennessee or Arkansas.

The four families had very much drawn together. They were in psychological fact a closely bound group, although there was a split in that three of them were involved with one school and the fourth with another. The three sets of parents met daily to take their children to school and escort them home. All four families were encouraged by neighbors, honored at local banquets by their communities (not given publicity in the press of the "other world") and specifically encouraged by a middle-aged woman who in many ways became their leader, a very kind and maternal one.

She was our guide. She took us to the houses, introduced us and clarified our intentions to the hesitant families. Without her we would have been refused, and with her there was still quite enough uncertainty and awkwardness — television sets kept on and tuned at high volume, people hiding but listening in nearby rooms, nervous ingratiation or unrelenting silence similar to the long familiar behavior felt to be white people's due while working in their homes or offices.

Not once were we offered a glass of water during those first visits, although later food and drink almost became a plentiful hazard. When we came alone on the fourth visit fear reasserted itself with constant references to our missing Negro guide. I know that for anthropologists such a course of events is the natural, preliminary essence of cross-cultural fieldwork. As a clinician I had certainly become accustomed to the initial nervousness of the patient (in contrast, that is, to the doctor's, as he also struggles to comprehend the complaints and symptoms at issue). Yet, the one thing a physician at work can assume is his patient's presence, his reason and his decision to arrive on medical territory, whether the hospital or the private office. In contrast, I was asking people —

fellow American citizens — to give me their time and confidence when they had no reason to want me, trust me or welcome me — quite the opposite. They were not ill, though the streets of their city were filled with disorder. As for my visits, the lady who first took us on them put it this way as I prepared to go alone: "They never have had a white man come to them, except to take something away. A few come to the door, to sell insurance or demand some money, but they never go inside, to stay and talk, and especially to ask questions. (Isn't that what you're going to do eventually?) So I think it'll be tough on you and on them, but if you have the time, maybe it'll be fine later. You never know, these days, with all the changes. This might be another one for them, that they'll take in stride like the rest."

In Atlanta my wife and I had to reach ten Negro families on our own initiative, with persistence again required. Ten Atlanta youths had the doubtful pleasure of finding their names, addresses and pictures in the local paper. What this meant to them — despite the city's honorable and impressive intention to avoid the mobs that had plagued New Orleans — was the immediate onset of constant harassment: phone calls at all hours of the day and night, threatening letters, pressures upon the parents' employers. As in New Orleans we came up with the same panicky reluctance to receive white visitors regularly — particularly in the midst of a crisis, and without a friendly guide or observer.

We met the members of our first family through a white minister who knew them, at his church, where they had come to a meeting. We asked to visit their home. They hesitantly agreed when assured by the minister of our good intentions. They were poor people, very poor, and thoroughly surprised that we did come, after all. There were no chairs for them, let alone my wife and me. Awkward silence was interrupted by remarks which did not seem to catch fire into conversation. We stood there, shuffling and anxious. Finally I told them of my nervousness, and asked if I might sit on the floor — which I then did by their permission. I started telling them about myself, my life and my interests. After what seemed like an endless monologue — my wife later assured me it was about five minutes long — I stopped and the sixteen-year-old boy's mother said, "We will pray for you and make a way for you." They did. They agreed to start seeing us every week. They even helped us meet the other families.

Once in contact with these families in Atlanta (1961–1962) we visited them weekly, sometimes daily, as we had those in New Orleans. We continued our work in New Orleans on regular visits there several times a month. In both cities we visited white families as well as Negro. We were brought to white people as we were to Negroes, through helpful ministers or schoolteachers.

We traveled widely those years over the South. While we followed the children in Louisiana and Georgia for several school years, we also came to know more briefly their counterparts in states like Arkansas, Tennessee and North Carolina — and later, Alabama and Mississippi. A necessarily devious but surprisingly effective network of white "friends" led us to these children during the late 1950's and early 1960's. Thus, upon being brought to the home of one child in North Carolina by a young white teacher I was told the following by a Negro boy of eleven: "She's tops to us. Any friend of hers *has* to be a friend of mine, because she has proven herself to my people a million times over." I knew that underneath his protestations he had his doubts, and in a way was telling me to measure up in the future as well as relax then and there. Still, assertions can be taken at face value, too — even by those professionally interested in turning them upside down and inside out.

To meet strong segregationists required careful planning. Working inside of me in spite of my years in Mississippi were the distortions and misconceptions which Northerners have about the South; they see in the region a jungle of lawlessness and violence. Indeed, under certain circumstances, conditions may approach just that; but so long as particular irritations or provocations are not present (they can involve racial customs and they can fast swell into emergencies) the region has been and still is "quiet" and "law-abiding." (That the price of this is a rigid caste system is another matter. Many people outside the South mistakenly see its recent violence as a way of life rather than what it is: a direct challenge to a way of life.)

Working in favor of getting us relatively convenient access to militant segregationists was the fact that in periods of racial conflict people's tempers are aroused, their guilts mobilized, their fears alerted, their anger made all too available. Despite my ignorance and fright, despite the possibility of arousing in the people I wanted to meet severe distrust or hostility, I eventually found a path to many of their homes. I did so in several ways. In New Orleans I observed the mobs assembling each day and began talking with those participating in them. After a while I felt free enough with certain people to identify myself and my interests. I told them that I was a physician interested in how people managed under the kinds of difficulties then in progress. In several cases I met people quite willing (as a matter of fact, anxious) to talk about their attitudes and feelings, even to let me talk with their children and get to know them as I did those children in the desegregated schools — by playing games with them, drawing with them, asking them questions. I approached and in several cases came to know quite well white Southerners in situations like that in New Orleans, where they were demonstrating or protesting some "integrationist" advance.

Another and very important part of my work has involved the sit-in movement. I have been interested in who joins it and why; how those who join manage to survive and work, to succeed or — in their own estimation — fail. Again, it has not been a matter of interviews directly sought and obtained. For weeks upon going to see some of these students at their central office in Atlanta I was ignored or greeted with the slimmest of attention. I might have reason to see them, but they gave me clear notice that *they* had no immediate reason to trust me, even though my work was sponsored by an organization (the Southern Regional Council) well respected in the civil rights field. They did offer to put me to work though — stamping envelopes, doing errands, generally becoming one of them about their headquarters. I accepted gladly. I rarely wore a tie those days anyway, and I was near enough their age to enjoy what sociologists have called "participant observation."

As I look back I realize that the students would gladly have forgotten that I was a doctor and a psychiatrist if I had encouraged them to do so. I might have simply become one of them, a committed demonstrator; many professional men in their late twenties and early thirties have done so. I might, keeping my professional identity, have put it completely at their service and become a staff physician with total dedication to their daily needs. However, I could (and did) resolve to help them as much as possible while making it clear (without spelling the matter out needlessly) that I was involved in study as well as service.

It took several years for my "role" to be consolidated. Psychiatric emergencies, depression, anxiety states, psychoses as they rarely arose in the staff received my immediate attention, day or night; and I soon learned these students live by night. In the summer of 1964 I came with them to Oxford, Ohio, where they were confronted with the task of evaluating and "orienting" over five hundred college students for work in Mississippi. I worked with them the rest of the summer in the state, assisting in a variety of medical and psychiatric problems, but also continuing to interview certain students and estimate how they lived, worked and survived through the summer. In so doing there were times when I contributed little to them, but much to my own knowledge of their background, motivation and psychological adjustment.

Finally, I have visited a number of these youths in jail, where some of them have become quite disturbed out of long and sometimes hard and cruel confinement. Often it was surprisingly easy for me to gain entry into jail. In some cases the jailers and prison doctors were eminently fair and cooperative — either because it came naturally to them, or because they feared the repercussions of what one sheriff kept on calling "jail martyrs." Particularly when sedatives and tranquilizers were needed, I found no objection from any of the physicians I met.[7] There were, however, some jails I could not get near. I found out what went on inside them only when I had a chance to examine and treat youths who had left them. Their bruised, cut, infected bodies, their thoroughly shaken nerves showed once again how much freedom we have yet to win within the borders of our own nation.

Before we go on to the substance of this work, can any clarifying remarks be made about how a psychiatrist may best walk the tightrope of being both an observer and involved? A crisis generates new psychological tensions in people; it supplies fresh reasons for them to feel upset, and in some instances it arouses a need for medical or psychiatric help. Yet the doctor must beware of getting drawn too far into those "other" psychiatric problems — those beyond the ones that temporarily afflict people as the result of a crisis.

All along I somehow have had to strike a balance between *study* of the contemporary, as well as its antecedents in the past, and *treatment* of symptoms — some of them generated only by the present, some essentially recurrences from the past but triggered by the present, and some with a life of their own that largely ignores racial conflict. There seems to be no easy and universal rule to fall back upon in the face of the mind's stubborn and common resistance to a clear-cut division of psychiatric labor.

For instance, I spent five years visiting one family, regularly, then at occasional intervals ("follow-up visits"), and never felt myself a physician confronted with an illness. Yet, a family nearby presented me with quite another picture: both parents had a long history of medical and psychiatric difficulties, as did one of their children, though not the one I was primarily interested in getting to know. Eventually, under enough stress, that child also faltered. He became nervous and fearful — as indeed other children did who came from far more solid, less brittle homes. Though at one point or another I talked with all those children about their worries, I was more nearly the doctor with the child and the parents who were most nearly the potential patients. If you ask me how my behavior changed, how I slipped in and out of the roles of passive observer or active investigator, doctor, psychiatrist or child psychiatrist, I can only answer that I did: sometimes easily, sometimes with difficulty, sometimes with great bewilderment and embarrassment.

There is, of course, no law that prevents a doctor who has decided to be an observer from doing the following: prescribing medicine; remaining aware of the nature of his relationship with those observed and using that to their advantage, as indeed is done for patients in doctors' offices every day; and, finally, even making an explicit interpretation or formulation for others (as well as himself) along the way.

Since I have aimed to find out how individual minds (with all their past history) engage with contemporary change as it makes future history, it was perhaps inevitable (even desirable) that "treatment" sometimes contaminate the purity of the "research." Yet, I hope the reader will see that, regardless of who watched them, questioned them and recorded their voices on tape, the people I met have had a destiny of their own to fulfill — relentless, affirming, consuming.

The question of how generally valid or applicable research of this kind may be is not easily answered. It is an issue all clinicians must face; certainly Freud did so when he decided to make specific generalizations based on a few carefully studied cases. Yet can we even begin to speak about how private lives affect

and are affected by world events if we do not study a few such
lives at length and in psychological depth? How can we know
precisely what influences the adjustment of people exposed to
danger unless we get to know some of those people long enough,
and take a close enough look at the entire span of their lives? If
some people can sustain enormously taxing and vexing pressures
and fare well psychiatrically, as many of these families I have
studied seem to have done; and if other children, sheltered by a
generous social and economic fate, show evidence of a diversity of
mental symptoms, then what *does* cause mental illness? Perhaps,
at last, we can warn the middle class that money and power do
not guarantee what they seem to want so fervently: "mental
health." Perhaps we can assure the poor that "mental illness" is
not their problem.

How scientific is work done this way? We can go astray in
either direction: claiming much too much for it, or ridiculing its
lack of laboratory precision. The lives of the individuals I will be
describing scarcely lend themselves to experimentation. Even
when intensive analysis can be done, we must be very cautious
about transferring concepts useful in offices or hospital clinics to
homes where people live "normal" if stressful lives. I have, for
example, been asked about the "masochism" and "guilt" of the
Negro parents who allowed their children to go to desegregated
schools amid violence, about the "sado-masochistic" aspects of
nonviolent youth, about the "paranoid" elements in segregationists.

If we take careful histories we often find nonpsychiatric explanations for this man's involvement, or that man's survival and
style of behavior. Many Negro parents never realized what would
face them and their children when they allowed them to be
chosen (or choose themselves) for a role in school desegregation.
Many young students stumble upon "the movement"; others seek
it out. Segregation is a "way of life," a social phenomenon shared,
intensely shared, by whole towns and states.

By listening to people talk, by listening carefully enough, by recording their ideas and their fantasies and dreams, we can add the psychiatrist's insights to those of the sociologist, the anthropologist, the historian, the political scientist and the economist. We can ask whether, indeed, there are degrees of segregationist sentiment. We can look for the signs of illness in rioters. (If we do *not* find them we have at least learned something about the political and social causes of riots.) Finally, we can document the ways people handle stress and try to discover which seem to work best, which not to at all.

White informants kept me in touch not only with how *they* were responding to school desegregation but how the Negroes were. A Negro child, like anyone else, can tell just so much about himself, his thoughts, his daily behavior. The white children watched the Negro children narrowly, and they often saw things that Negro children did not see about themselves, or would not tell me, or "forgot to" tell me. Similarly, teachers and parents could tell me about children, just as children could report on the actions and feelings of the grown-up people they know so well. Segregationists could report on the effects of nonviolence, just as youthful demonstrators could recognize changes in white people who had disclaimed any willingness *ever* to change. Though "checks and balances" may seem crude laboratory standards, they were the best available.

One more comment is necessary in preparation for the coming pages. I must explain how hundreds of interviews became transformed into the particular descriptions offered in this book. Over a period of eight years I talked with these children and adults under a number of circumstances: at home; in school, and walking to or from school; at a basketball game, or in a restaurant; while a demonstration was going on; in jail; in a store, in a park, in an office. Sometimes the conversation lasted a few minutes and was interrupted by events beyond the control of me or the other person; sometimes the conversation lasted a half hour or an hour and the other person signaled for an end in the various ways we all do; sometimes I had to raise the white flag and suggest we continue another day; and sometimes — as in a Mississippi Freedom House — we talked all night, one student with me, or many students in a "soul session," with myself an onlooker or often enough a stirred participant.

Obviously there were times when the presence of a tape recorder — a useful tool that has become for many the present-day symbol of science and objectivity — was out of the question. There were times, however, when I was lucky indeed to have a machine that caught for me — in a crucial talk — every precious word and intonation. What was I to do with all those words, with the hundreds of interviews I recorded and later had transcribed, or with all the pages of notes and impressions I took? Obviously I had to read and edit the statements of others, and make sense of my own. More important, I had to extract what I thought to be the significant part of the material — as it is sometimes called. I had to weave together fragments and cut away at long monologues or dialogues. In each case I had in mind conveying to the reader what about that person, that life, that situation or problem, that series of interviews sheds light upon the central (and vexing) issue this book aims to examine: the relationship between individual lives and the life of a nation — where a crisis has come upon them both.

I have sacrificed much rich language, much strong dialect, in the interest of pulling together many years of acquaintance and conversation into a few coherent pages. I have sometimes ignored time by putting together sections from separate interviews. Part of me wanted to follow Oscar Lewis's[8] example and let the people speak without interruption. I have been able to do so only occasionally. As the title of this chapter suggests, I have not only observed, but often joined company with the people I have been studying. At times I have treated them as a physician and a psychiatrist. Particularly as a psychiatrist I have relied upon dialogue, upon what has gone back and forth, upon my own reactions and feelings. I am not writing this book to discuss the complexities of my relationships with the various people I have interviewed. I have done that in technical papers.[9] Here I am trying to give prominence to the lives of those people, to their involvements with the *world* — but there has to be the qualification: as I have seen and known those lives and involvements. I originally intended to keep myself rigorously out of the narratives to be presented here, but in a number of clinical conferences, in both Southern and Northern medical schools, I have been consistently urged to do otherwise. I want to share with the reader my mixed feelings on this matter. Again, the image of walking a tightrope comes to mind. Since the work itself has been done on the borderland territory of medicine, psychiatry, anthropology, history and political science, there is reason to wonder just how it ought be presented.

Perhaps I have made a mistake by putting some (by no means all) of these interviews into familiar (middle-class) grammar and sentence structure. I can only try to atone by keeping my own language free of *its* (professional) dialect, far less attractive to my ears than what I have often heard from Southerners of both races and all classes.

Finally, I have scrambled names, locations and revealing events, though in certain cases the unique historical situation initiated by some of the children I was observing makes any disguise difficult — and discretion especially important.

PART TWO

The CHILDREN of CRISIS

III

WHEN I DRAW THE LORD
HE'LL BE A REAL BIG MAN

IN recent years child psychiatrists have steadily increased their ability to understand what is happening in the minds of even their youngest or only remotely communicative patients. When Freud insisted upon the extreme relevance of childhood experiences to the lives of grownups he did so in a middle-class Viennese climate that held children either innocents in need of progressive enlightenment or devilish knaves whose mischief deserved every possible restraint and punishment. On a tide of free associations he and his followers carried virtually an entire culture backward to the life of the child's mind, and as a result the new profession of child psychiatry came into existence.

Within the psychoanalytic tradition his daughter Anna took the lead in giving the profession purpose and competence. In fact she turned the new interest in children to a continuing study of them; to a concern with childhood she added her concern for children.[1] Soon, in the twenties and thirties, the influential pull of psychoanalysis came to be felt by academic psychologists and anthropologists, so that children in all sorts of cultures eventually were watched,[2] while children in the Western world were observed, tested and measured as carefully as adult ingenuity permitted.

Once children became so significant to doctors or social scientists, ways had to be found to learn what was going on inside them as well as what they could or could not do at various ages. Direct observation was — and still is — championed by Anna Freud.[3] The psychoanalytically sensitive can discover in the "ordinary" or "random" behavior of children, be they in the nursery, classroom or clinic, a number of patterns and clues to what holds their attention and concerns them, or worse, troubles them. No tests or questionnaires are necessary, only watchful eyes and attentive ears. When such direct observation is coupled with conscientious interviews of parents and teachers, the child's behavior becomes reasonably well understood.

Yet those who treat children have a task rather different from those who study them. They have to not only find out what they can, but so reach and affect the child's mind that he no longer ails. The child must be helped to comprehend what bothers him, and he must then settle the problem so decisively that he no longer feels upset, or indeed shows any signs to the ever-watchful clinician that he may still be troubled "deep down." To accomplish that goal in young children of five or six, to exchange views with them, to learn what they feel, commonly requires in the doctor a willingness to abandon his reliance upon one of his chief assets in his work with grown-ups, or for that matter older boys and girls — the service of the spoken word.

In the case of very young children, say of six months or a year, by the nature of things the child psychiatrist will direct a heavy share of his attention to the parents, or those standing in for them by choice or necessity. Infants and toddlers who refuse food, develop unusually cranky dispositions, and in general show signs of poor emotional or neurological development that cannot be explained by the presence of a physical illness are babies responding to unduly apprehensive care, or worse, to cruel care or no care worthy of the name. As a result a generation of therapists have appreciated the value of holding the baby, playing with him and feeding him, so that what he does not obtain outside the office he at least consistently gets inside.[4] What must be communicated by the doctor at that age is solicitude and affection.

As children go into the third year their interest in play becomes quite reliable and developed, an obvious result of their increasingly organized and purposeful mental life; in brief, they have more going on within them that seeks engagement and expression with the outside world, both of people and things. During the thirties and into the forties child psychiatrists took increasing clinical advantage of that fact, harnessing toys and games to their investigative and therapeutic efforts — a development stimulated by the simple yet revolutionary psychoanalytic tenet that all behavior, however discrete or frivolous, makes sense and is likely to express something more (or other) than what is apparent.

In contrast, much less clinical attention has been given the drawings children so abundantly produce from three and four until adolescence.[5] For that matter, the grown artist has both confused and fascinated psychoanalysts. Freud looked closely at the lives of a number of them, but was careful to acknowledge[6] that what actually makes the artist, what separates him from others (non-artists whose lives and problems resemble his, or would-be artists who never seem to make the grade) is unaccountably nonspecific, i.e., not by itself derived from any necessary, particular — or at least presently obvious — kind of psychological experience or development.

A few psychoanalysts have continued to struggle with the twin problems of what makes for creativity, and what can be learned from artistic productions, be they ordinary or outstanding. Ernst Kris[7] gave close attention to those who paint and what they produce, and particularly demonstrated the revelatory nature of drawings and paintings done by the psychotic: illness finds its way to the canvas in both themes and styles of representation. Henry Murray[8] spent years perfecting the Thematic Apperception Test, an imaginative and practical way to take advantage of our everyday inclination to look at pictures and talk about them in ways that tell some truth about ourselves. With the development of the Children's Apperception Test boys and girls also could be asked to say what a series of pictures — photographs of drawings or paintings — meant to them.

Of course for several decades social, experimental and educational psychologists, or those interested in measuring neurological development, have used drawings in studying the attitudes children have, how competent and coordinated they are with their hands, or how they see themselves or others. Asking a child to draw himself, his parents, or simply a boy or a girl has become one of a number of ways to appraise growth, development, intelligence, and in some cases a patient's psychological status.[9]

In therapy, however, child psychiatrists often use toys and games rather than crayons and paints. Even in research the significant work done by social scientists on the child's growing sense of racial identity, his awareness of prejudice or his capacity to have it consistently, has involved the use of dolls and other toys coupled with questionnaires or a series of picture cards.[10] Such methods have the advantage of being standard, somewhat measurable ways to evaluate children and compare their feelings on one or another issue.

On the other hand, to ask a child to draw whatever he wishes to draw in order to learn about his racial attitudes, or even to request from a series of children that they each draw the same person, place or thing for such a purpose, is to court the subjective and the individually variable, usually thought of as the clinician's job. Consequently any "results" that emerge from that sort of endeavor must rest upon the validity of case histories, upon the cumulative insights of a very particular kind those histories may offer. In this regard, I am offering the analysis of many hundred drawings as evidence only of what they suggest to a child psychiatrist who has come to know those who drew them. I value these pictures for what they have told me about individual children, rather than children in general or children of one race or another. The fact that many other children, under certain social and historical circumstances, share feelings that these children have been willing to indicate with crayons and paint is probably a fair assumption. That is as far as I would care to take the matter of what scientific relevance this study has.

The reader is entitled to know why, how and where these drawings came into being, and who did them. As I have already mentioned, my work in the South studying school desegregation fell into three rather distinct categories: weekly (at a minimum) interviews with high school children of both races; weekly interviews with young children — from five to eleven — of both races; and periodic interviews with the parents and teachers of all these children. I was able to *talk* with the adolescent youths (say, in Atlanta) and the adults who taught them or were their mothers and fathers or grandparents. Young children, however, are often uninterested in conversation. They want to be on the move, and they are often bored at the prospect of hearing words and being expected to use them. It is not that they don't have ideas and feelings, or a need to express them to others. Indeed, their games and play, their drawings and finger paintings are full of energetic symbolization and communication. It is simply that — as one eight-year-old boy once told me — "Talking is okay, but I don't like to do it all the time the way grown-ups do; I guess you have to develop the habit."

Before I ever started my work in the South I had been interested in what the children I treated would tell me with crayons and paints — and chalk, for I always kept a blackboard in my office, and often a child would suddenly want to use it, then just as quickly apply the eraser to it. Because of my own interests I made a point of asking children whether they would like to sketch whatever came to mind, or indeed draw for me their home, school, parents or friends. Some did so eagerly, some reluctantly; some would have no part of my schemes for a long while, though in the course of treatment those who refused invariably changed their minds, as if they recognized that now they were able to let me know something once unmentionable and as well forbidden to representation.

I kept those files with me when I went South — a stack of drawings made by the middle-class children who make up the major population of a child guidance clinic and a child psychiatrist's private practice. When I started visiting the four little girls in New Orleans whose entry into the first grades of two white schools occasioned the strenuous objection of mobs and a boycott by most white children, I carried with me paper and crayons. From the very beginning I made a point of asking those girls to draw pictures for me: of their school, their teacher or friends, anything they wanted to draw. I also took an interest in the artwork they did in school, always a favorite activity for children in elementary school. There is no doubt about it, they learned that I was interested in their sketches, and without exception they have furnished me an increasing abundance of them over the years.

That same school year (1960–1961) a few white children trickled back to the boycotted schools, in spite of tenacious mobs that in varying strengths constantly besieged the two buildings. I began going to the homes of those children too, and I encouraged those children to draw as well as play games and talk with me. (They were five children from three homes.) During the second year of desegregation, from 1961 to 1962, I continued my studies in New Orleans and expanded them there (while also starting them in Atlanta) just as the city itself, by coming to some terms with its unruly elements, enabled its harassed schools to return gradually to normal. I started interviewing the eight Negro children who were added to the roster of pioneers; they went into three additional elementary schools. (I also expanded the number of white children I was seeing so that I could include their classmates.) All in all in New Orleans I was following up twelve Negro children and twelve white children that second year, as against the four Negro and five white children who in the first year were at one point the entire population of two schools.

In addition to those children I was seeing regularly and continually, I traveled widely in the South, spending a week or two in other villages, towns or cities where younger Negro children were initiating (and white children were experiencing) school desegregation. I lived for a while in Burnsville, North Carolina — a small, rural mountain village — and nearby Asheville, its metropolis. I spent several weeks in Memphis, and later I worked in Birmingham. Finally, in 1964, I divided three months' time between Jackson, Mississippi, and the little farming community of Harmony, near Carthage, Mississippi. In all these instances I tried to gain some impression of how children other than those I knew in New Orleans were managing the social and personal trials of desegregation. At times I felt rude and presumptuous asking children I scarcely knew to draw a picture of their school, a friend, eventually of themselves. Yet these children (and especially their parents) found it easier to draw than to talk; in fact I came to see that they expected me to ask them to *do* something, to test them in some way.

Television reaches across the barriers of race and caste, class and neighborhood, bringing our self-consciousness, our preoccupation with knowing and measuring the "normal" and "timely" in the child's growth and development, into cabins and tenements otherwise far removed from our national life. For example, I was astonished to find the mother of a six-year-old boy in an isolated Mississippi town relax visibly when I took crayons from my pocket, placed them on the paper of my clipboard and asked her whether her son and I might draw pictures together. "Son, the doctor is going to learn about you and find out how good your thinking is, like they say it has to be done on TV," she told the boy, and they both seemed able, finally, to comprehend my purposes. David drew eagerly, as if taking an examination at school, and his mother no longer worried so openly about just what the white doctor had in mind. "It's testing you're doing," she told me, answering her own silent questions aloud, "and I'm sure grateful for that, because David will do better in school if he knows what his mind is about."

In New Orleans, as the months passed by, a firm relationship between the children and me developed, so that our drawing and painting exercises became more enthusiastic and personal. I encouraged the children to draw whatever they wished. The troubles and joys of their lives gradually took on form and color, and so did their shifting feelings toward me. At times I tried to direct their attention toward one or another concern I had: how they regarded themselves; how they felt they were managing at school; what skin color meant to them, and to others in their neighborhood or the city; why the mobs formed, and to what purpose; how they saw themselves getting along with their white or black classmates; how they viewed their teachers, and how they felt their teachers felt toward them as children, or as representatives of a race or a group of people. (One white child brought me up short at the very beginning of my work by telling me she thought her teacher prejudiced toward her: "She wishes my daddy made more money, so I could dress better. She always talks about the nice kids she used to teach in the Garden District, and how good they behaved. I think she minds me as bad as the nigra girl.")

What have these children had to say in the drawings they have done these past years? Is there any reasonable way to categorize and classify their pictures so that the individual child's feelings are preserved, and yet more general conclusions made possible? I think the answer to the second question is yes, and I will try to show why by describing the interests and concerns these children reveal when they take up crayons or a brush.

Drawings and paintings can be compared in a number of ways: the use of color; the subject matter chosen; the child's command of form; his desire to approximate the real or his ease with whatever fantasies come to mind; his willingness to talk about what he draws and explain it, to expand upon its relevance or significance — for his own life or the lives of others around him. Moreover, anyone who has worked with children and watched them draw over a period of time knows how sensitively the child's activity and performance will respond to his various moods. One day's chaos on paper may give way to another's impressive order and even eloquence. The child's fear and shyness, his doubts and suspicions about adults, especially doctors or visitors to his home, are translated onto the canvas: little may be drawn, mere copying is done, or only "safe" and "neutral" subjects are selected. Often the child may say that he has absolutely nothing on his mind, or that in any event he does not know how to draw. Weeks later that same child may ask for crayons or pick them up quite naturally. What he said in the past is of little concern to him; at last he feels safe, or interested in exchanging ideas and feelings with his doctor, that older stranger who keeps returning to his home.

Any discussion of what a given child (or one of his drawings) has to say about racial matters, school problems or mob scenes must take pains to put the child's social observations, his prejudices and partialities, into the context of his home life. By that I mean to insist upon the young child's strong inclination to reflect his parents' views; but even more, transfer to the neighborhood his personal tensions and struggles, so that other children, not to mention teachers or policemen, take on a meaning to him quite dependent upon how he manages with his parents, brothers and sisters.

I am saying that each child's particular life — his age, his family, his neighborhood, his medical and psychological past history, his intelligence — influences what and how he draws. I am also saying that the way these children draw is affected by their racial background, and what that "fact" means in their particular world (society) at that particular time (period of history). My task in the analysis of these drawings has been not

only to understand them, but to learn to appreciate their significance in clinical work with adults.[11] Over the years I have
heard grown-up Southerners of both races recall their childhood
experiences, their "old" attitudes; but there may be a distinct
difference between the memories we have and the actual feelings
we once had (or didn't have but now claim to have had) years
ago. For that matter, it is often interesting to obtain the reactions
of a parent or a teacher to a given drawing. A mother in New
Orleans said to me once: "I looked at Mary's picture and all I
could see was that she didn't draw it as good that time as she does
others." The girl's teacher had this to say about the same picture:
"Mary had trouble keeping the drawing accurate. She must have
lost interest in it, and the result is a poor picture." Mary herself
had the following appraisal to make: "Maybe I tried too hard,
but it's a better picture than the easy ones I do." In point of fact,
for the first time she had tried (and struggled) to include herself
(and her brown skin) in one of the landscapes she usually did so
easily.

The first Southern child to put my crayons and paints to use
was Ruby. She and I started talking, playing and drawing
together when she was six years old, and braving daily mobs to
attend an almost empty school building. Upon our first meeting I
told Ruby of my interest in drawings, and she showed me some
she had done at school and brought home to keep. Over the years
she has drawn and painted during most of our talks, so that I now
have over two hundred of her productions. Many of the topics
were her choice, while other pictures were started in response to
my specific suggestion or even request. I would ask her to draw a
picture of her school, or of her teacher. I would ask her to paint a
picture of anyone she knew, or wanted to portray. I might ask her
one day to try putting herself, her brother or her sister on paper,
while on another occasion I might ask her to sketch a particular
classmate or schoolmate of hers. (For many months there were
only two or three of them, the children of the few whites who

defied the boycott. We both knew them, and each of us knew that the other spent time with them, Ruby at school and I in visits to their homes.)

For a long time — four months, in fact — Ruby never used brown or black except to indicate soil or the ground; even then she always made sure they were covered by a solid covering of green grass. It was not simply on my account that she abstained from these colors; her school drawings showed a similar pattern. She did, however, distinguish between white and Negro people. She drew white people larger and more lifelike. Negroes were smaller, their bodies less intact. A white girl we both knew to be her own size appeared several times taller. While Ruby's own face (Figure 1) lacked an eye in one drawing, an ear in another, the white girl never lacked any features (Figure 2). Moreover, Ruby drew the white girl's hands and legs carefully, always making sure that they had the proper number of fingers and toes. Not so with her own limbs, or those of any other Negro children she chose (or was asked) to picture. A thumb or forefinger might be missing, or a whole set of toes. The arms were shorter, even absent or truncated.

There were other interesting features to her drawings. The ears of Negroes appeared larger than those of white people. A Negro might not have two ears, but the one he or she did have was large indeed. When both were present, their large size persisted. In contrast, quite often a Negro appeared with no mouth — it would be "forgotten" — or she used a thin line to represent the mouth; whereas a white child or adult was likely to have lips, teeth and a full, wide-open mouth. With regard to the nose, Ruby often as not omitted it in both races, though interestingly enough, when it appeared it was in her white classmates a thin orange line.

Hair color and texture presented Ruby with the same kind of challenge that skin color did. So long as she kept away from brown and black crayons or paints she had to be very careful about the hair she drew. White children received blond (yellow) hair, or their hair would be the same orange that outlined their face — always the case with Negro children. Many people of both races had no hair. No Negro child had blond hair.

The first change in all this came when Ruby asked me whether she might draw her grandfather — her mother's father. It was not new for her to ask my permission to draw a particular picture, though this was the first time she had chosen someone living outside of New Orleans. (He has a farm in the Mississippi Delta.) With an enthusiasm and determination that struck me as unusual and worth watching she drew an enormous black man, his frame taking up — quite unusually — almost the entire sheet of paper (Figure 3). Not only did she outline his skin as brown; every inch of him was made brown except for a thick black belt across his midriff. His eyes were large, oval lines of black surrounding the brown irises. His mouth was large, and it showed fine, yellow-colored teeth. The ears were normal in size. The arms were long, stretching to the feet, ending in oversize hands; the left one had its normal complement of fingers, but the right was blessed with six. The legs were thick, and ended in heavily sketched black boots (a noticeable shift from the frayed shoes or bare feet hitherto drawn).

Ruby worked intently right to the end, then instantly told me what her grandfather was doing, and what he had to say. (Often I would ask her what was happening in the place she drew or what the person she painted was thinking.) "That's my momma's daddy and he has a farm that's his and no one else's; and he has just come home to have his supper. He is tired, but he feels real good and soon he is going to have a big supper and then go to bed."

Ruby's father at that time was unemployed. It was not the first time, though never before had he been fired simply because his daughter was going to one school rather than another. He tended to be morose at home. He sat looking at television, or he sat on the front steps of the house carving a piece of wood, throwing it away, hurling the knife at the house's wood, then fetching a new branch to peel, cut and again discard. He also suffered a noticeable loss of appetite — the entire family knew about it and talked about it. The children tried to coax their father to eat. His wife cooked especially tasty chicken or ribs. I was asked for an appetite stimulant — and prescribed a tonic made up of vitamins and some Dexamyl for his moodiness. I gave him a few sleeping pills because he would toss about by the hour and smoke incessantly. (In a house where eight people slept in two adjoining bedrooms with no door between them it seemed essential to do so not only for his sleep but the children's.)

I asked Ruby whether there was any particular reason why she decided to draw her grandfather that day. She told me she had none by shaking her head. She smiled, then picked up the crayons and started drawing again, this time doing a pastoral landscape (Figure 4). Brown and black were used appropriately and freely. When it was finished she took some of her Coke and a cookie, then spoke: "I like it here, but I wish we could live on a farm, too; and Momma says if it gets real bad we can always go there. She says her daddy is the strongest man you can find. She says his arms are as wide as I am, and he can lick anyone and his brother together. She says not to worry, we have a hiding place and I should remember it every day."

She was having no particularly bad time of it, but she was rather tired that day. By then she also knew me long enough to talk about her fears, her periods of exhaustion, her wish for refuge or escape. Only once before Ruby decided to draw her grandfather and a countryside scene had she mentioned her impatience with the mobs, her weariness at their persistence: "They don't seem to be getting tired, the way we thought. Maybe it'll have to be a race, and I hope we win. Some people sometimes think we won't, and maybe I believe them, but not for too long."

It took Ruby several more months to be able to draw or paint a Negro without hesitation or distortion (Figure 5). From the beginning I wondered whether it all was my fault, whether she was in some way intimidated by the strange white doctor who visited her, with his games and crayons, his persistent curiosity about how she was getting along. Though in fact I am sure she was, there is reason to believe that the pictures she drew reflected a larger truth about her feelings than the undeniable one of my somewhat formidable presence. Her mother had saved many of the drawings she did in Sunday school (all-Negro) before either desegregation or strange visitors came into her life, and the same pattern was to be found in them: whites drawn larger and more intact than Negroes; brown and black used with great restraint, just enough to indicate the person's race but no more. It was as if Ruby started drawing all people as white, then turned some of them into Negroes by depriving them of a limb or coloring a small section of their skin (she preferred the shoulder or the stomach) brown.

It seemed to me, then, that on my account Ruby had merely tightened up a preexisting inclination to be confounded and troubled at the representation of racial differences, not to mention the implications those differences had for how people lived. Eventually I asked her why she thought twice about how much brown she would give to a colored child. She was then eight, and we had known one another for two years. She replied directly: "When I draw a white girl, I know she'll be okay, but with the colored it's not so okay. So I try to give the colored as even a chance as I can, even if that's not the way it will end up being."

Two years later Ruby and I could talk even more openly. At ten she was still the outgoing, winning girl she always had been, though of course each time I saw her she was taller, thinner, a bit more composed, a little less the child. She wasn't very much interested in drawing any more. She preferred to talk. She and I looked over many of her drawings and at various intervals she made comments about them, much as if she were a colleague of mine. Almost in that vein I commented that her most recent work was less prolific but very accomplished indeed: "You didn't draw much this past year, but when you did the people were really alive and very accurately shown, and the buildings look as real as can be." She smiled and answered quickly: "I guess when you grow older you can see better, and so you can draw better. My teacher told me last week that my handwriting was getting better, too." A few minutes went by and I decided to persist with my comments on her artwork, this time with a bluntness I can only justify as feeling quite "right" and appropriate at the time: "Ruby, you know my wife and I were looking at your drawings last night, and we both noticed how differently you draw Negro people now, in contrast to the way you did years ago when we first started coming to see you. Do you think there's any reason for that, apart from the fact that you're now a better artist in every way?"

She paused longer than usual, and I began to feel in error for asking the question and nervous about what she might be feeling. I was scurrying about in my mind for a remark that would change the subject without doing so too abruptly when she looked right at me and spoke out: "Maybe because of all the trouble going to school in the beginning I learned more about my people. Maybe I would have anyway; because when you get older you see yourself and the white kids; and you find out the difference. You try to forget it, and say there is none; and if there is you won't say what it be. Then you say it's my own people, and so I can be proud of them instead of ashamed." When she finished she smiled, as if she had delivered a hard speech and was relieved to have it done. I didn't know what to say. On the one hand she was still the same Ruby I had known all those years; yet she now seemed grown-up. Her arms were folded quietly in her lap; her language was so clear, so pointed; and she somehow seemed both content with herself as she was and determined to make something of herself in the future. "Ruby is an exceptionally alert child," one of her teachers wrote on her report card a few days before Ruby and I had this talk. The teacher realized that her pupil had gone through a lot and had gained an order of understanding, of worldliness, that is perhaps rare in elementary school children, at least in more sheltered ones.

Ruby had for several years a classmate named Jimmie, a lively, agile, particularly freckled boy whose blond hair tended to fall over his forehead. She drew several pictures of him for me; he sat near her and they knew one another rather well. When I first asked Ruby to do a picture of any school chum she wished (there were only three at the time) she obliged with a painted picture of Jimmie that certainly did not ignore his hair and eyes (Figure 6). (I could not help contrasting the painting with one of a Negro boy [Figure 7] Jimmie's age and size she had done the day before.) "He is a good boy, sometimes," she said of Jimmie, adding the last word of qualification after a genuine moment of hesitancy. In point of fact Jimmie's behavior troubled her. One minute he would be attentive and generous, anxious to play games or even share food with her. Yet in a flash he could turn on her, and not just as one child will do with another. Ruby knew why, and could put it into words: "Jimmie plays with me okay, but then he remembers that I'm colored, so he gets bad." I asked whether he was "bad" at other times — fresh or spiteful simply out of a moment's impulse. She handled my question rather forthrightly, even with a touch of impatience: "Well, he's bad sometimes when he wants things his own way and someone won't let him get it; but I mean it's different when he gets bad because I'm colored. He can be my friend and play real nice with me, and suddenly he just runs and says bad things, and he even gets scared of me and says he's going to leave; but he comes back. He forgets, and then he remembers again."

Jimmie's parents had it no easier. Like him they could not establish in their minds a clear-cut set of attitudes toward colored people. When riots made their son's school attendance dangerous they kept him home. As the mobs achieved their purpose, a near-total boycott, the noise they made and the terror they inspired in passersby gradually subsided. A few white families sent their children back to the schools involved, some in direct defiance of the small crowds that persisted, others rather quietly, almost secretly, through rear doors or side doors. Jimmie's parents sent him back as soon as it was safe to do so openly. When I saw him come to the school, neatly dressed, carrying his lunch box, I thought the very spirit of sanity resided in him, and with him was returning to the deserted halls and classrooms of the building he so casually and confidently entered. There was something very open and calm about him as he walked along — and I guessed something refreshing, something unsullied, also.

As I came to know Jimmie and his family I realized how unfair I had been to the boy when I first saw him. I pictured him as Ruby's hope. In fact he returned to school in spite of Ruby because his parents did not want him to waste months of time learning nothing. When he first met Ruby he told her the facts rather explicitly: "My mother told me to stay away from you." Ruby told me what she had been told, then informed me that Jimmie had contradicted his own words only seconds later by asking her to join him in a game. "So I did" was her way of letting the matter drop.

When Jimmie and I started drawing together he made his feelings about Negroes rather clear: either they were in some fashion related to animals, or the color of their skin proved that if they were human they were certainly dirty human beings — and dangerous, too. I don't think Ruby ever knew the fear she inspired in Jimmie, nor did Jimmie have any idea how very much Ruby strived to portray herself with his features and coloring, as if then she could be less afraid of *him*.

When I asked Jimmie to draw his school as it appeared to him the very first day he came to enroll in it — before Ruby's presence caused its various afflictions — he drew a rather conventional brick building; he carefully emphasized its stucco character by covering the bricks with some yellow. There were no chimneys. The grass was uniformly green, and flowers were everywhere. The sun looked down on the almost bucolic scene with a smiling face. I have seen dozens of such drawings by children of Jimmie's age, though I did take note of his definite artistic ability and his very keen, even meticulous powers of observation.

For a while Jimmie drew pictures of his home, his parents, his friends and himself. He was particularly fond of landscapes, and once did eight of them in two weeks — each surprisingly different, though all dwelling upon trees, grass and water. When I first asked him to draw a picture of Ruby he looked at me quite in dismay and said he couldn't. I asked why. He now appeared cross: "Because I don't know what she looks like. I don't look at her close if I can help it."

I asked him whether sometimes he couldn't help noticing her. "Accidents happen sometimes, Jimmie, even when we try to do as we feel we should." He nodded, and allowed that he had managed a few glimpses at Ruby, and would try to draw her. He started to do so rather furtively, then somehow lost his nervousness, so that by the end he was the confident and scrupulously attentive craftsman and landscapist he always was — except, that is, for what he had done to Ruby (Figure 8). It was almost as if he had suddenly embraced surrealism. In the midst of a stretch of grass he abruptly placed her, without feet, legs inserted in a piece of land left strangely sandy and barren in contrast to what surrounded it. He made Ruby small, though her arms were larger proportionately than those he usually drew. She had only the thinnest line of a mouth (Jimmie usually was careful to show teeth and indicate lips by double lines) and pinpoint eyes. Her hair was frizzly black, yet curiously and inappropriately long. She was brown-black, much more strikingly so than Ruby's medium-brown complexion justified.

I asked what Ruby was doing in the picture. Jimmie said that he didn't know. I asked whether he could imagine something she might be doing, even if it wasn't apparent from the drawing. He thought about it for a few seconds, looking intently at what he had done and at the crayons. I saw his eyes fall upon a bottle of cola and some crackers. A second later he had his answer: "Maybe she is drinking a Coke and eating candy or something. My mother says niggers eat stuff like that all day long, and their teeth rot away because they're no good for you all the time." The sweet tooth he was learning to master only with difficulty Ruby somehow was permitted to enjoy, though he felt sure her day of suffering would come.

In time Jimmie was able to develop on paper the various (and conflicting) feelings he had toward Ruby and her race. He drew Ruby many times, at intervals upon my request and often because he wanted to do so, or felt that I silently wished him to do so. For many weeks she appeared only as a speck of brown or in caricature, sometimes both in one picture, usually on what he reminded me was *his* street (Figure 9). Jimmie had obvious trouble picturing her at all. He hesitated as he did at no other time. He told me that he didn't know what she looked like: "She's funny. She's not like us, so I can't draw her like my friends. Besides, she hides a lot from us." Whereupon I asked him where she hid. "She doesn't really hide. I mean she stays away sometimes; but if I say something, she answers me all right." I wanted to know whether he had any idea why Ruby might be keeping her distance from him and the others. He knew exactly why: "Well, she's colored, that's why." I reminded Jimmie that colored children lived nearby, and often played with white children. (In New Orleans large areas of the city are thoroughly mixed racially, and have been for generations.) He knew that, too: "That's different. It's on the street, not in school. My daddy says that on the street it's for everybody, but inside is where you have to be careful."

In fact he made a distinction at first between the classroom and the school playground. When I asked him whether he would draw a picture of Ruby at school he readily obliged, though invariably he put Ruby in the play area outside the building. Finally I mentioned what I saw him doing, and he scarcely hesitated before replying: "The teacher said it won't be long before we go back to normal. She said that if most kids still stay home and the people still make all the noise in front of the school, then they'll send Ruby away and the trouble will be over; she said Ruby still isn't a regular member of the school, but that we have to be polite, anyway." The yard, for him, was like a waiting room, and in one drawing he put a bench in it — in actuality there was none — and Ruby on the bench.

In time Jimmie took Ruby into the building he drew, and in time he regularly came to see her as an individual. Amorphous spots and smudges of brown slowly took on form and structure. Ruby began to look human every time, rather than, say, a rodent or a fallen leaf one day and a rather deformed human being the next. Eventually she gained eyes and well-formed ears. It took more time for her to obtain a normal mouth; and only after a year of knowing her would Jimmie credit her with the pretty clothes he often gave to other girls. In describing Ruby's speech after he had finished his pictures Jimmie for a long time tried his best to render a Negro dialect (or his version of one). His parents began enjoying such performances, and also hearing from him how "the nigra" was doing in school. *They* were changing, too — from calling Ruby a "nigger" to calling her a "nigra," and from wanting no mention of her at home to insisting upon information about her schoolwork and her general behavior. By the middle of our second year's talks Jimmie was forgetting himself and telling me in his own words and accent what Ruby might be saying in one of his productions.

Jimmie may have tried to ignore Ruby, he may have consigned her to anonymity, even to the indignity of a dot, or an animal-like appearance, but he never really overlooked the difference her presence made to his school. He showed how embattled it was by drawing a policeman here, a picket with a sign there. The demonstrators were drawn big and open-mouthed, their arms unusually beefy, their hands prominent indeed, a child's view of the shrill, stifling, clutching power they exercised over the school's population. As they gradually lost that power and began to disband, Jimmie pictured them as the smaller, less galling irritants they were becoming.

The school building itself took on a variety of shapes in Jimmie's mind and on his paper. At first it was a confusing, almost ramshackle building, its walls as flimsy and unreliable as the school's future seemed at the time. Slowly, though, Jimmie realized that — as he put it — "We're going to make it." Quite casually, without self-consciousness, he showed that he meant what he said. His school grew in size, each time looking sounder and more attractive for all the wear it was taking from its assailants. Eventually he allowed the building to dominate everything around it, from the shrubbery to the crowd of human beings who once impressed both him and Ruby with their persistence and assertiveness.

On occasion Jimmie would confine Ruby to her own section of the building (Figure 10), even as Ruby twice drew herself in the middle of a black circle, in turn within the building (Figure 11). Ruby told me each time that she meant to draw her desk, that the circle was her version of a desk. Though I never pressed the matter with her, I felt I could be more curious with Jimmie. I asked him whether he was assigning Ruby a permanent corner of the building. (It was, I thought to myself, always the corner under the chimney, and the chimney was always emitting noticeable — at the very least — or commanding billows of smoke, even on the warm spring days Jimmie did the pictures in question.) On the several occasions I questioned him on the matter he denied any such intention. Then one day he anticipated my renewed interest by letting me know *his* ideas on why he placed Ruby where he did: "She has to be in the same place, because she always tries to sit near the teacher, and if we take her seat she gets upset and says it's hers, and once she cried. So I keep her in the same place, and that's why." Since Jimmie often complained that his teacher talked too much and was moody, perhaps the chimney — in Jimmie's mind — was meant to symbolize his teacher (his disposition black, his talk mainly hot air) rather than racial conflict or the place of the Negro in this world. No matter what the doctor makes of a picture, there are often other possible interpretations. It is only after enough of a particular child's drawings have been seen that certain trends or directions in thinking (and representation) can be reasonably established — for *that* child, of course.

From the very start of our talks I asked Jimmie not only to draw Ruby but her parents and friends as well. He occasionally saw Ruby's mother when she accompanied Ruby to school, though I doubt he would have protested lack of acquaintance as an excuse for not attempting a picture. His first drawings showed that if he had to distort Ruby's appearance somewhat he had to caricature other Negroes far more grotesquely. Ruby's father would appear with enormous teeth and animal-like arms coming down to his feet. Her mother came out equally simian. On several occasions he put both of them in the same picture; they were above the ground and below a tree, a compromise Jimmie never elsewhere felt called upon to make. Quite the contrary, he always started his drawings with broad strokes of brown and green to indicate the land, then firmly placed his people and buildings upon it.

For Jimmie, Ruby's house had to resemble its occupants, even though he knew perfectly well where she lived and what houses looked like on that street (it was not far from his own). He labored long and hard on his own house, or his school, drawing the walls and windows, the doors and chimneys with increasing skill and refinement over the several years we met. For a long while, however, a Negro home had to be clearly seen as just that, some lines hastily sketched perpendicular to one another, always brown, often not quite fitting together, so that the homes seemed irregular and exposed, though always warm, for every one of them had a chimney stack and plentiful black smoke to justify its presence. It is not that Jimmie has a "fixation" upon chimneys or smoke. His own home often as not lacked both. No Negro home he drew lacked either.

He furnished other homes or his school with chairs and tables, even curtains, but not Ruby's house, or those of her neighbors. He piled Ruby's house and those nearby on top of one another, as if they were a jumble rather than a row of buildings. What is more, he denied them grass and for a long time he denied them the sun.

I remember so very well the day Jimmie let the sunshine fall upon those homes. It was, in fact, a rather cloudy and humid day, very much an autumn day in New Orleans. I could tell by the slower speed of his drawing hand that he was paying more attention to the homes he was "building." As we often did, he and I talked as he worked. I was drawing, too; sometimes Jimmie would assign a topic to me in trade for an assignment from me. He told me to draw the Lake Pontchartrain bridge. "You better get a lot of paper, because it's the longest bridge in the world," he warned me as we began. As we proceeded I realized that he himself would require more time than usual. He was doing an exceptionally meticulous job with Ruby's house and a nearby store. He finished the store first, and then told me about it: "Ruby goes there every day after school and gets herself a Coke and some potato chips, and sometimes she gets some extra potato chips to bring to school the next day. She gave us some yesterday; and I like potato chips better than almost anything except maybe dessert and candy, and maybe sometimes ice cream."

From the store Jimmie moved to the houses. Instead of brown he used red, and instead of hasty lines he slowly moved his crayon along, sometimes backtracking to broaden and strengthen what he had done. When the construction proper was over, the decoration began: a door, two carefully drawn windows, one with curtains, a chair, and outside some grass, a tree, three flowers, and finally a blue sky with the sun in it, shining directly over the new building.

When Jimmie had finished he turned to ask me how I was doing. I was still working on the bridge, and he offered to help me. After we had finished that we compared our work. Jimmie said he was tired: "That's a lot we've done. I want a Coke." (We always had one at a nearby stand.) I had noticed his drawing, indeed had watched him draw it. He knew that, yet he wanted to make sure I took note of what he did: "Did you see my picture?" "Yes, Jimmie, I did, and I liked it a lot. You did a real good job with the house." "Well, I tried to make it strong, like you did with the bridge. If a bridge isn't strong it could cave in, and then someone could get hurt. They could drown in the lake. And if a roof fell down in a house it would be the same." At that point we were ready to leave his living room for the street. I let him turn off the tape recorder — always a great pleasure for him — and carry it to my car. When we were outside we felt light rain beginning to fall. Jimmie was annoyed: "Why does it rain every time I go outside? I just drew the sun, but it didn't help any with the weather." Then he wanted to know whether New Orleans had any rivals in America for cloudy, rainy weather. I told him that I didn't know; but I liked the weather there, the semitropical quality of it. He did, too: "It may get cloudy and rain, but the sun comes out a lot, too; and when it does, you like it better, because you've missed it."

What both Ruby and Jimmie chose to draw or paint reflected the particular lives each of them lived. I once asked Jimmie whether he thought his friends saw things the way he did — whether, for instance, any of them might draw his school, his teacher, his classmate Ruby as he did. Once and for all he cautioned me against whatever inclinations I might have to generalize: "I don't know. Which one of them do you mean?"

I followed Jimmie's advice to the best of my ability as a clinician, so that in all I spent four years getting to know two-score children like him and Ruby in New Orleans and other Southern cities. Though each child had his own life — including his own quality of artistic interest and ability — there *were* certain patterns to be discerned in what these children chose to draw. Thus, Jimmie's drawings and Ruby's drawings resemble one another in the way all children's drawings do — the style, the sense of proportion, the preoccupations that change from year to year. If they also differ because Jimmie and Ruby are different artists, different human beings, the racial crisis they both witnessed and experienced served to draw them together by giving them a common experience, a shared number of difficult times together. Eventually that crisis influenced not only what they thought but what they drew. Other children in their school, their city, all over the South, have been similarly aroused and affected.

For the many I have known there can be no question that in the beginning they fear their white-skinned or dark-skinned classmates. Nor can there be any question of the very hard struggle they must contend with inside their minds as they try to sort out the hate and envy they have come prepared to feel toward one another, the curiosity, the interest, the confusion over the whole matter of black and white, bad and good, wrong and right.

The issue of what skin color means is already confronting the child by three, let alone school age. In my interviews with grown-up Negroes and whites their memories hark back to one event or another that marks a first awareness of skin color and its implications. Yet, as I have said, the memories of adults are no substitute for direct observation of what children themselves see and do. Some of the children I have come to know were three when I first started talking with them — they were the nursery school brothers, sisters and cousins of the older children I was visiting. All in all these children have lived in cities, towns and the countryside. They have ranged in age from three to ten. They have lived in rather comfortable homes or in very poor ones. They have been both white and Negro children, both boys and girls. What they all have in common is their American citizenship, their Southern residence and their Southern ancestry. Most were caught up, willingly or otherwise, in school desegregation; but I have worked closely with others, too — Negro and white children *not* going to desegregated schools, though obviously living at a moment in history when the subject has an unprecedented immediacy.

Every Negro child I know has had to take notice in some way of what skin color signifies in our society. If they do not easily — or at all — talk about it, their drawings surely indicate that the subject is on their minds. Like Ruby, many have trouble using black and brown crayons and paints. One three-year-old girl obviously avoided using those two colors in the pictures she made; instead, she used her fingers as if *they* were crayons. After watching her use green and orange, then rub her hand alongside them, I asked her what she was doing. She said, "Nothing, just trying to make a picture." Her mother, however, was nearby, and later she unabashedly explained it all to me: "She has been telling me on and off for weeks that she knows she can rub some of her brown skin off and use it for coloring. My two boys talked like that for a while when they were two or three and then they got over it. So I guess she will, too."

Negro children of elementary school age have not had enough time to set themselves straight about "why" they are colored and what that fact will mean for them in the future. Often they will try to deny the fact, or they will accept it so extravagantly that it is clear they are yet confused and troubled. Ruby abstained from browns and blacks; another girl of six I knew in New Orleans could scarcely use any other color. Her white classmates — like Ruby she was in a desegregated school — were drawn Negro, a touch of yellow here or there sometimes giving me the clue to their racial identity. For a long while I assumed that my whiteness — and my middle-class, professional whiteness at that — in some way made these children reluctant to color themselves brown or made them exceptionally anxious to color everyone brown. When I compared drawings done by the children for me with those they did with others, at Sunday school, even at the request of their older brothers and sisters or parents, I learned that what I found significant and revealing in their drawings had a consistency and persistence quite its own, quite independent of my presence.

Is it true, then, that the words "Negro" and "white" help distinguish the dreams and fantasies of children? That is, do children of each race draw themselves and those of the other race quite differently? At two and three have they very different ideas about who they are, who they will be, all based on a budding sense of racial identity? I would answer yes to those questions. Before he is born the Negro child's color is likely to matter a great deal to his parents. By the third year of life the child is asking the kinds of questions that ultimately will include one about his skin color. A mother of five children in Jackson, Mississippi, described it to me rather explicitly: "When they asks all the questions, they ask about their color, too. They more than not will see a white boy or girl, and it makes them stop and think. They gets to wondering, and then first thing you know, they want to know this and that about it, and I never have known what to say, except that the Lord likes everyone because He makes everyone, and nothing is so good it can satisfy Him completely, so He made many kinds of people, and they're all equal before Him. Well, that doesn't always satisfy them; not completely it doesn't. So I have to go on. I tell them that no matter what it's like around us, it may make us feel bad, but it's not the whole picture, because we don't make ourselves. It's up to God, and He can have an idea that will fool us all. He can be trying to test us. It's the favorite child sometimes who you make sure you don't spoil."

I asked her when she found such conversation necessary. "I'd say about two or two and a half," she answered rather quickly. A bit deferentially she turned to me and asked: "Do you think that's too early for children to know?" I said no, I didn't. I said that what she told me confirmed some of my own observations. She smiled, a little proud but still a little nervous. She wanted to pursue the matter further: "I know I'm right on the age; I've gone through it with too many to forget when it happens. But to tell the truth I never have been certain what to say. That's why I try to talk about God. No one knows what color He is. I tell the children that it's a confusing world, and they have to get used to it. You have to try to overcome it, but you can't hide it from the kids. When they ask me why colored people aren't as good as whites, I tell them it's not that they're not as good; it's that they're not as rich. Then I tell them that they should separate being poor and being bad, and not get them mixed up. I read to them from the Bible, and remind them that the Lord is a mighty big man, and what He thinks is not the same as what white folks do, or even black folks. He's bigger than all of us, I tell them, and I hope that makes them feel satisfied, so they don't dislike themselves. That's bad, not liking your own self."

Again and again I have heard mothers talk of similar struggles, and seen their children represent on paper those same struggles (and the "answers" to them they have been given or devised on their own). It is not that Negro and white children in the South have thoughts unlike those of other children. A thematic analysis of the hundreds of drawings and stories they have produced shows their kinship with all children. They draw their mothers and fathers, food and clothes, animals and trees. They show how sensitive they are to people: to what their parents say, or their teachers, or their brothers and sisters. They reveal the affections they have, and they also reveal the tensions, the conflicts and resentments that are inexorable and shifting, part of growing up, part of life ongoing. With only one or two exceptions these children were in no sense "sick." They had no symptoms, gave no clinical evidence of serious trouble with eating and sleeping, with nursery school or regular school, with family and friends. They did not come to see me in a clinic; it was I who sought them out because of their role in a social struggle. I had to remind myself of that fact constantly. (For that matter, even when — years ago — I treated severely disturbed children in a Boston hospital I tried to keep in mind the "healthy" side of their mental life, the strengths and abilities they somehow had mustered and consolidated in spite of the afflictions pulling at them and giving them — or those around them — so much worry.)

Sometimes I erred by becoming too much the investigator. When I did so, when I emphasized racial matters too much, when I seemed to be forcing a point here and there, the child or his mother often managed to bring me up short. One five-year-old colored boy had been unusually explicit in both his talk and pictures: he wished he were white, and that was that. He said so, and he drew himself so. When I asked him whether he thought he *was* so, he said no, he was colored, but there was little harm in wishing otherwise. I asked him whether he thought all colored children shared his views: "I don't know, I only know the ones I play with. We all say let's turn white, then we pretend it's done. But we know it isn't all the while. And a white boy, he told me in school one time that he plays 'nigger' sometimes with his friends, and they say they're black and pretend, and then turn back to being white."

Being black and being white is, however, a long-term affair, regardless of the mind's ability to make believe. Thus, while all children draw animals — indeed are quite interested in them — it is the Negro child who is often apt to call himself one of them with exceptional consistency. Negro children usually draw themselves and their friends as smaller than white children. In the stories they tell that involve the two races (based on the pictures they draw) the white child is almost invariably asking the Negro to do something, or having it done. Moreover, again and again I have been assured by Negro children that the Negro in the picture is smiling, or working hard at whatever task he has set upon. That there is anger and spite toward white people burning underneath is also discernible, though by no means are such emotions easily conveyed to other Negroes (even to the child's parent), let alone a white observer like me.

One Negro mother put rather well the feelings I have heard many others express: "I guess we all don't like white people too much deep inside. You could hardly expect us to, after what's happened all these years. It's in our bones to be afraid of them, and bones have a way of staying around even when everything else is gone. But if something is inside of you, it doesn't mean it's there alone. We have to live with one another, black with white I mean. I keep on telling that to the children, and if they don't seem to learn it, like everything else I have to punish them to make sure they do. So I'm not surprised they don't tell me more than you, because they have to obey me; and if I have to obey you and they have to obey me, it's all the same. Just the other day my Laura started getting sassy about white children on the television. My husband told her to hold her tongue and do it fast. It's like with cars and knives, you have to teach your children to know what's dangerous and how to stay away from it, or else they sure won't live long. White people are a real danger to us until we learn how to live with them. So if you want your kids to live long, they have to grow up scared of whites; and the way they get scared is through us; and that's why I don't let my kids get fresh about the white man even in their own house. If I do there's liable to be trouble to pay. They'll forget, and they'll say something outside, and that'll be it for them, and us too. So I make them store it in the bones, way inside, and then no one sees it. Maybe in a joke we'll have once in a while, or something like that, you can see what we feel inside, but mostly it's buried. But to answer your question, I don't think it's only from you it gets buried. The colored man, I think he has to hide what he really feels even from himself. Otherwise there would be too much pain — too much."

The task, then, is one of making sure the child is afraid: of whites, and of the punishment his parents fearfully inflict upon him whenever he fails to follow their suit. The child's bravado or outrage must be curbed. In my experience even two- and three-year-old Negro children have already learned the indirection, the guile needed for survival. They have also learned their relative weakness, their need to be ready to run fast, to be alert and watchful. They have learned that white children, as well as adults, are big, strong and powerful; and that such power is specifically related to the colored man's defenselessness.

In drawings such attitudes come up again and again. If the Negro child is alone in a white school his loneliness there is carried over to the other situations he draws. For example, I asked one Negro boy in Asheville, North Carolina, to select a neighborhood chum and any classmate he decided (in his school the child would have to be white), then place them both in a landscape the child was particularly fond of drawing for me. I said to him at the time: "Johnnie, I'd like to see how you fit the boys and girls you know into that countryside you like so much to draw." He obliged, showing a rather robust white boy near the summit of a mountain, and a rather fragile Negro one well below (Figure 12).

What Johnnie told me was happening in the picture he drew shows how a seven-year-old child can summon the sharpest, most outspoken fantasy without the slightest embarrassment. "Freddie wishes he were up top, like Billy, but he isn't, because there's not room for both of them up there, at least not now there isn't. They're not talking, they're just there. Freddie would be afraid to be on top. He wouldn't know what to do. He's used to where he is, just like Billy is. Billy is a big eater, and he has to have food with him everywhere he goes. So Freddie is getting some food for him from the farms and maybe he'll carry it up. But he'll come right down. He might get dizzy, and Billy would not like for him to stay there too long, because he might slip and get killed if the two of them were there when there's only room for one."

I wanted to know why Freddie was so small, why his arms were so much less than Billy's arms, and how they managed when they were together, up or down the mountain. "Freddie doesn't get to be so big, because he stoops over. He picks the crops and plows, so his back is bent, that's why; and his arms are bent for the same reason. But Billy, he can stretch when he wants to, and the air up there on top is real healthy for him. When they talk it's real hard, because they are far from one another, so they have to shout."

Did Johnnie think they both did well in school? "Well, I think so," he replied. Then he added: "But I'm not sure. Maybe Billy does better. He can talk better, so he comes out better in school, too."

How do boys like Billy look at boys like Freddie? White children in the South have a virtual field day attributing many of their own problems and struggles to Negro children. The segregated social system comes to bear upon children as well as adults, so that long before a white child goes to school he has learned that good and bad can find very real and convenient expression in black and white skin. Negro children are described as bad, ill-mannered, naughty, disobedient, dirty, careless, in sum everything that the white child struggles so hard *not* to be. Moreover, the white child's sense of his own weakness, loneliness — or angry defiance — are also likely to be acknowledged indirectly by being charged up to the Negro. Nowhere is this more obvious than in the drawings of young white children. While Johnnie was letting me know how he saw the world, a white classmate of his was doing likewise — and with the virtuosity, I felt, of a real draftsman.

Allan liked his ruler. He would never draw without it, and when he started he did so by putting the ruler on the empty paper, as if *it* would decide, he merely follow orders. Allan liked order and structure. He used the ruler to make sure that the walls of his buildings were straight, the pathways of his roads were direct, and the mountains undeviating from ground to summit. Even with human forms or trees he would use the ruler, rounding off his lines when necessary. Allan talked more than most children of seven, and one day spoke as follows about Johnnie's presence in school: "I guess he's okay. But if we had a lot more everything would get bad. The teachers wouldn't know what to do, and neither would we. Johnnie, he's not making any trouble, but he's different from the rest of us, and that's important. So he shouldn't be with us, anymore than we should be with him; because differences mean something." I asked him what differences meant. "They mean that one thing is one way and another was made different; and if they didn't have differences, then everybody would be confused, and they wouldn't know what's right and what's wrong to do."

Later he drew a picture intended to show me what he meant about Johnnie being different from himself. I asked for just that. I said, "Allan, could you *show* me what you mean? Could you draw a picture that shows how Johnnie is different — or is it because his skin color is different and that's it?" "No," he shook his head, "it's more than skin color, because if I get a sunburn, I get tan, but I'm still not like Johnnie."

In the drawing he decided to do a street scene. He drew a road, then buildings along each side. A few cars appeared. Then he turned his attention to the sky. After that he decided to control the movements of his cars by placing a traffic light prominently on one side of the road. Finally he drew Johnnie, leaning on the post that held up the light, turned red. On the other side of the street he populated the store windows with several white faces, and put one white man on the street, opposite Johnnie.

Now some of the details in this drawing were similar to others I have seen white children draw when they have in mind to show their social awareness, their realization that Negro children live a less hopeful or protected life. Thus, the sun was noticeably on the "white" side of the street, a side whose buildings were far bigger and sturdier than those on the "other" side. Red walls, orange windows, green grass and trees contrasted with the makeshift brown and purple lines of the buildings on Johnnie's side of the street. They had no grass or trees nearby. Moreover, clearly Johnnie was the less intact person, his features in less proportion, his body less carefully and sensibly constructed (Figure 13). It was all very familiar.

On the other hand, I thought the use of the traffic light rather unusual. It signaled a definite, commanding red. Allan told me that it was a major road he had drawn, and a dangerous one to cross. The red light was on, a warning to motorists that speed had its dangers. I asked him whether there was a green light some-times. "No," he said. "This is one of those red lights that goes on and off. It's to warn the cars not to go too fast, but it's a big highway, and *you're not supposed to cross over.*" Did that go for Johnnie as well as the others? Yes, he had no doubt about that. Nor did he think Johnnie in danger of confusion either: "He knows about the light; and he's so close to it that he can't very well forget it, can he?"

Allan is a very orderly boy. He is sensitive to what he may do, to when and where he may do anything, to the "stops" and "goes" of daily life — to be learned (and resisted) by all children. The longer I knew him the more I realized how neatly he had assigned the forbidden to Johnnie and others like Johnnie. *They* were the wrongheaded ones; they were unruly, even messy, disobedient, wild, unpredictable. Allan summarized it all very pointedly one day by telling me what was for him an unfor-gettable incident: "Johnnie dropped his ruler in class and he didn't even seem to care whether he got it back or not."

Allan and Johnnie, Ruby and Jimmie, the boys and girls I have known these past years have all had in common their childhood, their developing sense of themselves and the world around them. Each of these children has learned to identify himself, somewhat, by his or her skin color — learned so during the first two or three years of life. What they have learned about their skin has been but the beginning of what they will learn. Yet, when they finally know what color they possess and what color they lack, they know something more than a few facts; they know something about their future. As one little Negro girl in Mississippi said after she had drawn a picture of herself; "That's me, and the Lord made me. When I grow up my momma says I may not like how He made me, but I must always remember that He did it, and it's His idea. So when I draw the Lord He'll be a real big man. He has to be to explain about the way things are."

IV

THE STUDENTS

IN 1964 an outbreak of articles — and two good books[1] — commemorated the tenth anniversary of the Supreme Court's reversal of its own doctrine (*Plessy v. Ferguson, 1896*) that "separate but equal" schools in the South are permissible. The decision was historic, and it certainly helped clarify at least this much to the South: whatever the nation had sanctioned before, it no longer was possible for the United States to condone by law the more obvious institutional bulwarks of a split, race-bound social system.

A decade showed that federal laws yield sometimes. But what do they yield to? A number of answers have figured prominently: the hesitations of those charged to enforce them; the nervy assurance of those who make a business (or a political success) of disobedience; the incredulity of people accustomed (if not devoted) to a way of doing things, a way of getting along with one another; the fear and inertia of the poor, the fear and pride of the well-to-do, the fear of the black, the fear of the white, and everywhere in everybody the hate and suspicion that accompany fear.

In the fifties we heard "never" in the South, and for years I've seen people wear buttons with that word alone on them. I have even seen those buttons on parents whose children were going to desegregated schools. So "never" can become "never, but sometimes." We were told that segregation lives and grows in the heart: no laws can undo what people have to undo for themselves, by a change of heart if not mind. Changes in behavior or habit come last.

Yet, inevitably federal law spread from the border states through the wavering hill country of Tennessee to the key cities of the Old Confederacy. Regardless of what most whites said they wanted, the courts ordered what most Negroes dared not believe they would get: a token, a sign, a beginning of desegregation.

In 1958 when I lived in Mississippi, I recall going to a medical meeting held in one of the motels on the Gulf Coast. A doctor was just recovering from the shock of Little Rock, only to hear that New Orleans was, as he put it, "next." He was beyond anger, and a bit of the doctor was in him when he spoke: "One by one the schools are taking a turn for the worse. This desegregation is spreading from city to city, and we can't seem to stop it. I think it'll destroy our schools." At that time, with a history of mobs and violence behind us, and still more to come, he seemed to me an unlikable but not so hysterical man.

Some day — will it be in this century? — a social historian will be able to assess the very substantial progress toward school desegregation made all over the South. Even with new laws and sympathetic Presidents the numbers of Negro children at school with whites seems destined to be relatively small indeed during the second decade since 1954; and a dual school system still exists, almost solidly intact in many towns. Meanwhile there are those few Negro children who press hard for their rights, while others they know (often brothers and sisters or friends) fall back in anger, boredom, indifference or outright scorn. Who cares about whites? Who wants to be with them, anyway? Who wants to risk *anything* for them, merely to study at their side? There are also those white students who have yet to begin or complete their "adjustment" to the disaster, the unpleasantness, the confusion, or to the curious, arresting, interesting, even exciting and welcome change.

I cannot report on the academic and emotional fate of the many hundreds of children, Negro and white who have attended desegregated schools in the South. There have been spectacular "successes" and terrible "failures." Negro children have overcome awesome odds — white children have overcome generations of hate; or Negro children have slipped and stumbled, sometimes unexpectedly, while white children have been found so wanting of decency, so nakedly insensitive, that the matter of exactly who *is* poor and deficient in this country stands open to question.

1.   *The Matter of Chocolate*

There is more to tell about Ruby, whose drawings we have already discussed. She was born in December 1954. She entered this world in a sharecropper's cabin at the hands of a cousin who in the words of the child's mother "knew about children getting born." She was a warmly welcomed first child. Her father, in his early twenties, had just returned from the Korean War, where for wounds received in combat while risking his life to save a white soldier he received a Purple Heart. Her mother was nineteen when she married, and the same age when she became a mother. The parents had known one another as children, and grown up together in a hot, sleepy Mississippi town whose existence was confirmed only by several stores, a post office and a gas station. For miles in all directions from the town the rich soil of the Delta stretched, and both their families had worked its soil, picked its cotton, for generations.

"Farm work is all I knew before I got into the army," was this military hero's summary of his education and occupation. He barely knew how to read and write, had attended school only cursorily until twelve, then simply worked at farming. It was fortunate for him that in the army he learned how to repair automobile engines because on his return home he married and started a family but was quickly confronted with the joblessness of a shrinking rural economy. Some of his brothers took to the nomadic if familiar life of migrant farm-workers. His mechanical skills prompted him to choose New Orleans. ("I figured I knew how to make cars work, so I could take on the city.")

The young couple brought their baby daughter (six months old) to the city, and soon were settled in its eastern industrial slums, an area whose worn shacks on unpaved streets seemed impressive to two people whose rural homes were hardly more than primitive cabins. "I got a good job in a station through a cousin, and we just lived along real quiet like" was the way the father summarized their lives before the crisis of school desegregation. By then, the year 1960, they had two more girls and one son, and Ruby's mother was expecting a fifth child.

The question has often been asked of me, and particularly by my psychiatric colleagues: Why did these parents consent to let their children face the ugliness and danger that occurred in desegregating the New Orleans schools? Ruby's mother at first replied tersely, "We just did." After months of our visits she talked much more openly. Her several answers basically showed that little calculation or sleight-of-hand was involved in the decision. She had no burning ideological zeal, no secret desire for prominence or profit. They had never expected the trouble they met. If they had, they would never have begun. Ruby's father once said, "We agreed to sign for Ruby to go to the white school because we thought it was for all the colored to do, and we never thought Ruby would be alone. . . . We thought she'd be going with hundreds of them."

If they had applied out of naïve faith and quiet hope, their first surprise, that their daughter would be alone, was quickly followed by their second, that she would by her mere presence at the school occasion an uproar which would plague them for months. Indeed, the grim historical facts of the kinds of pressures brought to bear upon this child of six when she started school are a matter of public record. Riots greeted her arrival there, and a boycott soon followed. Daily crowds, abusive and taunting, hailed her for many months. For a long while she had a classroom and teacher to herself. At one point there were only four fellow students, so nearly complete was the white boycott on her account.

I first saw Ruby when she was facing her worst time in the first grade, and I have continued to see her on occasion ever since then. During those years she emerged from anonymity to international notoriety, then slowly saw her fame disappear, so that in one of our recent visits she could talk about my departure this way: "I told my daddy I miss the people from before that came. . . . Are you coming here for my promotion next year, too?"

What she missed was the excitement and attention she had received, which could now perhaps be seen as pleasant. She had never been "sick," no matter how lamentable some of her experiences, but she had become frightened and anxious, and she had suffered private worries unknown to the world which watched her on television and saw her in newspapers. Despite the noise and disorder outside, her work in school was good and her attendance regular. For a while it was her parents who were most severely tested. Her father lost his job, and he and his wife feared for their lives. Their families in Mississippi were afraid of lynching. Yet they were strong and stubborn people — to be alive is an achievement when one grows up in the unspeakable poverty and toil that were theirs — and they managed. The father obtained a new job, not from a white man this time. Neighbors rallied round them and guarded their home. Significantly, they drew close to their children, but not anxiously so.

Ruby slept well, studied well at school, played regularly after school and developed only one symptom — a puzzling one for her parents, who ate hungrily and heartily if not healthily. One day at the height of the tension her mother described it for me this way: "She doesn't eat the way she used to. Ruby was always a good eater. Now she stays clear of a lot of foods and she won't eat unless we all eat with her." They assumed she had lost a bit of her appetite because of the strain she faced, and in a general sense they were correct. Ruby for a while had to eat alone at school, and she had been leaving her lunches untouched, hiding them in various spots of the near-empty building. When she joined her few white schoolmates at lunch she ate with them hesitantly, enough so that they noticed it. Slowly she relaxed at lunch, but only because she was very careful about what she took to school to eat. At home she ate listlessly, and never alone. Once she had sought snacks constantly and with scant discrimination; now she was fussy.

On several visits I asked Ruby about her appetite, and she replied that it was "good" or "pretty good." She seemed unwilling to pursue the matter, but glad to share a Coke with me. One day I again asked about her appetite. Her mother had been particularly worried — "I went and got her some vitamin pills today to keep her healthy." After being questioned, she was silent for a few seconds, then looked at our doll house nearby. I asked her whether she wanted to play with it. She nodded with obvious relief and enthusiasm. Ruby and I had spent considerable time with this set, or with crayons and paints. The set included Negro and white dolls and a house for them. We were arranging the house's furniture when I asked how her schoolwork was coming along. She replied "okay," then volunteered that "they're still there." They were, I knew, and still pretty nasty. "They tells me I'm going to die, and that it'll be soon. And that one lady tells me every morning I'm getting poisoned soon, when she can fix it." She paused a moment, then added, "Is it *only* my skin?" I wasn't sure what she meant. I asked her, "Is *what* only your skin, Ruby?" She did not answer. She picked up her teacups and asked me whether I wanted some tea. I said yes, and we made some. While brewing it we talked about the kinds of cookies we'd have with it, and then she volunteered that her sisters consumed large numbers of cookies each day, but not she. Had this always been the case? No, she told me, and I knew that her parents had said the same. I had known her long enough to recall her sweet tooth on earlier visits, and its indulgence in the very chocolate cookies (Oreos) she now steadfastly refused.

Ruby and I had been talking quite regularly about her school experiences. She told me she had especially disliked eating there alone, although she didn't mind being alone with her teacher. In fact, she regretted in certain ways the slow return of white children to "her" school. On each of my visits she would give me the tally: "Two more came back." Talkative about such matters, Ruby became quite silent about any discussion of her appetite. Her parents were the ones who were concerned, and they described their concern to me one day as follows: "She don't eat the way she used to, and she only eats what's hers alone, and she won't share from our food." Further questioning revealed that the girl was largely rejecting freshly prepared food and favoring packaged and processed food, especially potato chips and Cokes. She had always been drawn to fried and mashed potatoes, pork chops, cookies and ice cream, and now would have none of them. She was reluctant about peanut butter and jelly sandwiches, once her favorite. She shunned greens even though formerly she had not.

Before discussing Ruby's food habits and home life further, we may indicate what happened to her when she left home each morning and approached the school. Any one who cared to "hear" could learn what this girl was told every day as she approached school. "You little nigger, we'll get you and kill you," was a commonplace. Some of the language is unprintable. But one comment is both printable and important. Spoken in a high-pitched but determined voice, its words were always the same: "We're going to poison you until you choke to death." Its speaker was always the same. In the midst of so much abuse, this threat sounded relatively mild. Watching Ruby coming to school I felt that *all* the rebukes, all the fierce tongue-lashings, were to no avail. She came with federal marshals at first and later with her mother, and would invariably march rather firmly and stolidly right into the building. She rarely looked at her accusers, though even the slightest of hurried, backward glances from her shoulder sent each of them into excited pitches of slander. One seemed to compete with another for the child's attention.

Those backward glances I was to learn in later months were specifically directed and significant. Ruby had been told to ignore the crowd, and she told me for some time that she did: "I pays no attention to them. I just goes in." But she *was* paying attention to the one who threatened her death by poisoning and choking. She had asked her mother whether that lady owned a variety store near her home, the same variety store, white-owned, that had refused to sell Ruby's mother food when the trouble about school desegregation first started. Of course, the woman was not the one who owned the store, but the associations in Ruby's mind might be put together as follows: A woman tells me I'm going to be poisoned. It is dangerous anyway, going to school. I can't get candy and cookies and my family can't buy other food from our old store — we go to a supermarket now. Of course, I'm familiar with threats about food; that is, being told that if I'm bad I'll be punished by missing meals or getting indigestion. My mother has told me I'll choke on some of my bad words, and she has also kept me from certain pleasant foods when I've been fresh or cruel with my sisters and brother. So I'd best be circumspect. And since I'm not sure about how good and how bad I am, and since I seem to be having a rather bad time of it and therefore may well *be* "bad," I'm worried enough to have lost a good deal of my appetite, and to fear punishment — from that lady outside the school building, and from my parents, too, who say they are not worried but must be, what with all those threats.

At first Ruby's food habits changed without her family's knowledge. She simply pretended to eat her lunch, but left most of it untouched, either discarding the food or leaving several days' total in her desk, to be later done away with in secret. By the time this behavior was apparent to her teachers and the few white children in the school, her parents *had* begun to notice a definite fall in her appetite at home. They also found themselves questioned about what poison is and how it works.

"She keeps on asking me, 'Is it only my skin?' and I tells her that if she was white there'd be no crowds there. Then she'll ask if we'll all die if they gets poison to our food, and I tells her that's foolishness . . . I tells her nobody's going to get our food like that, but I can see she don't believe me all the way." These recorded words helped to discover what was happening. They describe Ruby's fears and her mother's awareness of them. "Is it *only* my skin?" was a question Ruby asked many times of her parents and of me. The origins of the question are in both public and private matters, a twin derivation that must be emphasized.

What Ruby meant when she asked this question of her family, and of me in our talks and play, was that she comprehended her exposure to harassment and wondered about its causes. She is a Negro; she knows that and could hardly help knowing it during those months. There are restrictions and penalties associated with her racial condition; she knows that and has been taught them. No, she cannot go here or sit there. No, her race's people do not ordinarily appear on television programs or in movies. Yes, she would probably never finish school, because money is short, expenses high, her family large and opportunities very few. Yes, most of her race are poor, and menially employed. You will remember that Ruby drew white children strong and able-bodied; Negroes undersized, even stunted. Her doll-house play also showed that she knew the facts of her future life: who was always mistress and who had to be servant. Nor was it all sketched and played this way merely for my benefit. Her mother daily confirmed and enforced what her children knew, what they *had* to know as they grew older and left their backyards to face the world of school, buses and shopping centers.

Yet, Ruby is also a girl in a particular family, and now the eldest of six children. She was a growing girl of six years when she was told every day that she would die from something she ate. Her symptomatic reply of appetite loss and sharp sensitivity to categories of food and food technology reflected her awareness of her social and racial vulnerability. But her question, her play and talk, showed that she vaguely expected *other* punishment, or knew of *other* causes for worry or guilt.

Once she told me she had been punished that day for striking her sister hard enough to fell her. Her mother had lost her temper and punished her with a "good" whipping. Ruby told me that her mother had said words to this effect: "We're letting you off easy and often these days, because we know you're under a strain at school; but there are limits." I asked Mrs. Bridges later what had happened and she replied, "Ruby has always got on bad with Melinda [eleven months her junior]. She bosses all the children too much and they gets angry; so I have to punish her — even now when I know she's getting it bad at school . . . but two bads won't make Ruby a good girl."

Ruby, then, was learning to be a good girl, a rather conventional task for one of her age. Her envies, her feelings of rivalry toward others in her family, are not unusual. She is a girl of sound mind and body, a lively, rather perceptive child whose drawings and frolic show imagination even as they indicate the normal anxieties and fears of a growing child. Were it not for the intersection of her childhood with a moment of our country's history, her difficulties at school or with her family would not be under discussion.

Anna Freud's work during the Second World War[2] demonstrated that tensions in the family engage with public tensions; that is, the adjustment of children to the various hardships of war depended to a considerable extent on how they managed with their parents, nurses or guardians. True terror can invade and destroy the happiest home; but an unhappy home can be crushed by the merest discomfort.

Ruby's home life seemed basically sound, and her family stable. As a girl of six, she was fast learning the rights and wrongs of her world, shaping her conscience to reflect what her family urged. The crisis of school desegregation became involved in this development, its perils and punishments fitting in with her prior guilts. Her mother had threatened her often with no supper if she persisted in wrongdoing — hitting her sister too hard, failing to obey a command or request. Now segregationist mobs were telling her she might be hurt, poisoned and killed. One member of that mob, impelled by reasons within her own life, kept telling Ruby of poison in her lunch or supper, forging in the child's mind a link between home and school, between the child's personal conflicts and this public struggle which found her a sudden participant.

Small wonder that Ruby developed temporary symptoms and asked her fearful question — one stimulated by racial conflict, but also related to her psychological development and the quality of her family life. Small wonder, also, that with slow improvement in the city's crisis and continued growth on Ruby's part, she is now a normal, even lusty eater. "Lord, she eats the table up now," has been her mother's consistent report to me in recent years. Ruby is now saying goodbye to childhood, and her school is quietly, fully attended on a desegregated basis.

Eventually attending that school with Ruby was the child of a woman who once vowed the contrary, not only for her own child but for all other white children. Mrs. Patterson withdrew her son Paul from the third grade when Ruby entered the school, and he went without schooling the rest of that year. The following year Paul attended a private school specifically, abruptly and furiously organized for the white children "dispossessed" by the Negro child. The next year the boy's mother bowed to the inevitable. To abide by her principles would cost more money than she could afford. The public school was a better school, a nearer school, a free school, and now hardly boycotted. Her boy wanted to go back there. She agreed, saying like others I was interviewing, "There's only a few of them in our schools now, anyway. The real ruin will be for the next generation, when they flood us unless we get them all to go North."

For that matter, as language went this woman's was mild for a member of the mob that bothered Ruby. Moreover, part of her threat to Ruby was one she hurled at her own children. If they misbehave she threatens to choke them. I have heard her use the expression commonly enough to indicate that for her it has the meaning of a serious spanking. Her children do not seem overly frightened by the threat. She is a cooperative informant, and I visited her and her sister and two of their children for the same length of time I saw Ruby. I saw and heard her on the streets, angry and shouting. I was introduced to her there, by a minister who knew her well.

There is no question that this woman fears and hates Negroes, and there is also no question about her generally suspicious personality. She is poor, now in her very late thirties, with little education (eighth-grade) and perhaps too many children as well as a wayward, fickle, heavily drinking husband. Most of all she is tired: "I have enough to do just to keep going and keep us alive without niggers coming around. They're lower than our dog in behavior. At least he knows his place and I can keep him clean. You can't ever do that with them. They're dirty. Have you ever seen the food they eat? They eat pig food, and they eat it just like pigs, too."

When she is weary she becomes surly, and underneath it all very sad and very frightened. She is struggling to manage herself and her large family in the face of poverty, ignorance, social isolation (like Ruby's parents, she comes from a farm in nearby Mississippi) and virtual abandonment by her occasionally employed husband. She herself is an obese woman, plucking candy from cheap assortments during every visit I made. Her five children are as old as nineteen and young as four.

She has had no history of contact with a psychiatric clinic. One of her children is mildly retarded and mildly spastic, and has been followed by one of the free clinics in the city. Her other children are "normal"; that is, they appear to have no symptoms warranting referral to a child-guidance clinic. One boy was a bed wetter until fourteen, but seems without major emotional troubles now. He is rather tough and laconic, very much like his father. Her husband has bouts of heavy drinking, at irregular intervals, which are followed by pious sobriety. He is a guarded, aloof man, possibly very paranoid under his stylized silence or episodic drinking. Yet, he seems less entangled with racism. He will sneer at "niggers," then shrug his shoulders and sit back, saying nothing, or very little. His silence is often his wife's cue for a bitter remark about the lowly nature inherently attached to Negro skin. One of her complaints is that her husband cares very little for the education of his children. Another is that he is not suitably aroused by the perils of the Negro advance into the white world. I have never heard her directly attack her husband's character or habits of drink and work.

Mrs. Patterson does, however, complain about her own life, even as she can complain about Negroes. Her life is cheated and impoverished, and she feels at times lonely and hard-worked with little hope of an end to either condition. Her feelings emerge in remarks like this: " I have to do the best I can with little help from anyone, and I'll probably die young doing nothing else."

There is no very special reason why this woman joined a mob and said what she did while its member. When I asked her why she joined she replied with conventional hatred for Negroes, not unlike those of other people who never have joined mobs. She was undoubtedly influenced by the attitude of her city, its hesitant police and politicians; that is, by the fact that there *was* a mob, that one was allowed to form and daily continue its actions. She is not a psychotic woman, and when reality changes, as it has over these past three years, she makes her ideological and practical adjustment to it. She now defends *her* right to *her* school against the claims of "the niggers." The same Negro child no longer bothers her as before.

As for her choice of threats for Ruby, they surely bear some relationship to her own problems. Feeling her own life frustrated and empty, she could only want to poison another's, *but* as a devout Baptist she could only allow herself to express such despair and rage at a Negro. She, who ate chocolates so passionately, who was so lonely herself, would poison a lonely chocolate-brown girl. The need for a public scapegoat could not be more clear. Yet, the history of her life shows that for her, unlike some, the possession of a *public* scapegoat is no compulsion. Deprived of the outlet of the mob, she goes on, her family goes on, strained, tense at times, but law-abiding.

In a sense the chocolates Ruby came to shun and the chocolates one of her hecklers craved were a symbolic link joining their fears. Ruby once told me I could choose vanilla cookies because I was white. I have often heard Negro children and adults similarly attach importance to the white or brown color of food, clothes, even furniture. Ruby at the height of her difficulties was all *too* Negro. She avoided reminders and "reinforcements" as the poisonous threats she believed them to be.

Her taunter of each morning ate chocolate cake and candy to soften her feelings of desolation. Listening to Mrs. Patterson then and listening to her again and more closely on tapes it becomes clear that Ruby's isolation as a Negro expressed this woman's sense of her own condition. She shouted at the Negro girl because she was moved to cry out and protest her own fate. What she called the Negroes she feared herself to be; what she saw in that Negro child was herself, unhappy and isolated. She wanted that part of herself to die, and in one of those "moments" which allow people like her "expression," she said as much with her threats toward Ruby. Indeed, the transcripts of her associations during our conversations — the trends in our talks — reveal again and again her mind's unwitting connection of frustration and loneliness with chocolates, with worthlessness, with Negroes, with Ruby.

2. *Tessie*

"Tessie was the first Negro child to step into that white school. There were three of them, 'the three little niggers' they were called, but Tessie stepped into the building first. I saw it with my own eyes, and I won't forget it, you can be sure. That night I said my prayers, just as I have for over sixty years, but I added something. I said, 'Lord, you have started giving New Orleans your attention, at last. The whites are screaming at Tessie and me, but that's because they know You are watching; and they're mad, because they know they're bad, and they'll soon be punished, soon now that You've decided to take a hand in our lives here.' That's what I said, and some more, too — because I had to repeat myself, I was so happy. The way I see it Tessie and I can be cursed every day, and it will only mean we're nearer our freedom."

Tessie's grandmother lives alone in a little house next door, alone except for a frisky mongrel dog. Tessie is an only child, and an only grandchild. Spot is her dog, boarded with her grandmother for the convenience of Tessie's mother, who is very neat and resents Spot's untidy habits. Tessie lives in a new, small ranch house of yellow bricks and pink shutters, with firm, waxed hardwood floors, and a kitchen fitted with electric appliances.

Her grandmother's house is older and her grandmother is a casual housekeeper. On my visits, papers and old magazines always lay about — I saw newspapers telling of Hoover's victory in 1928. A stack of old records stood like a piece of furniture beside a new phonograph that could not possibly give life to their hymns and ballads. Newspaper clippings were stuffed under table mats or left shamelessly on a bureau beside two combs and some perfume. The bureau was in the living room and the old lady once saw me notice that fact: "I keep meaning to have my son move this old thing into the bedroom, but there's no real room for it, and you know how it is, you get used to things as they are." Though she had saved papers for a long time, she had specifically clipped them only during the past two years. The scissors she used were handy, sharing space on a coffee table with an ash tray. "I used to use those scissors for my sewing," she told me with a faint smile, "but then it seems I stopped sewing so as to worry about Tessie and cut pictures of her from the papers."

At six Tessie was a prying child. She liked to poke her way through a mess and create a new one. She could not do so at home, where everything not only had its place but kept it. The grandmother would justify her ways to the grandchild: "I've taken care of so many homes that I don't have much energy to keep my own so precious clean." She would walk about, half closing drawers that were half opened, in no way really contradicting her apology to Tessie with the flurry of activity. "That's what got me, cleaning all those homes for thirty years, and then seeing what my son's little girl had to go through." She was a very well spoken woman. She used good words, and put them into forthright sentences: "I never went much to school, but my favorite lady taught me while I worked for her. She used to have me eat lunch with her, and she'd give me worthwhile things to read and help me in my pronouncing. It was never the same after she died. She was a lonely woman, but she had real character, I'll tell you. Maybe we don't have people like her anymore, and that's why Tessie has to hear those terrible things on her way to school."

She heard them with Tessie. Often she accompanied her to school when her daughter-in-law had to have a rest from the heckling mobs. She was a handsome woman, tall and straight, with long, pure-white hair braided neatly on top of her head and large dark eyes set in a light-tan face. She was a bit stout, but it was a hard, muscular kind of heaviness collected slowly over the years rather than the fat of gluttony. "I'm supposed to lose some of my weight, but I can't do without my grits, and I can't give this child ice cream without taking just a little for myself. Tessie and I eat grits before going through those mobs, and we eat ice cream after we come home from them."

Her life, and the lives of her only son and his wife and their only daughter, had been very difficult from the fall of 1961 until well into 1963, when she remarked to me: "I haven't seen a crazy letter in two months. They must have decided we're going to live." They weren't always sure they would live, she and her granddaughter. Tessie's parents felt that without Grandma they all might have *lived* — I think they had their doubts about that, too, but never could admit them to themselves or anyone else — but none of them would have really survived the fear and tension. It wasn't just her extra house and land, and having another person around, it was what Tessie called her grandmother's "gumption." I thought the two homes did seem like an enclave at times as I watched grandmother and grandchild leave their territory to walk to a nearby public school through curses, spit and brandished fists, through biceps tightened, tongues pointed and mouths filled with what the old woman called "unpleasantness," demeaning her and the little girl pitilessly, confronting them daily with terror and the need somehow to make terms with terror. "I said I'd sooner die than show them one ounce of fear," Tessie's grandmother told me one afternoon, the child nodding along, staring in devotion at the lady. "Some days I thought we were going to die, but it was a test, going by them to get our rights, and the worse it got the more certain I was that we could outlast them."

In front of their homes were ditches, and beyond them a dirt road. "The colored don't get good streets with cement on them as easy as the white," Tessie once informed me. It was one of her few spoken references to racial matters. In winter the street became soft and impassable for cars; summer turned it from mire to baked clay. "Daddy said he would make our own road one day, but that was because his car was stuck. When summer came he forgot." I think Tessie was wrong; her father impressed me as a man who never forgets anything. He is a large man, three inches over six feet, wide-chested and muscular. He is a college graduate. He speaks excellent English. He reads widely in magazines and paperbacks, particularly on world affairs and recent history. He works in the post office, sorting letters all day. His mother said that he wanted to be a lawyer, but getting him through college taxed her to the point of exhaustion. "There wasn't any more money in those days."

His job in the post office gave him some security when Tessie entered the McDonogh 19 school in mid-November 1961. At first he was the one who took his daughter to school and picked her up. They followed him there, followed him home, and followed him to work. "They told me they were going to picket the post office, and they flooded us with mail, telling me they were going to kill all of us, or they'd be getting me on my way home from work." He even sorted some of his own mail, some of the threats on his life. His wife stopped reading the letters, and wanted to tear the phone from the wall. He wanted to read the letters and for a while wanted to listen to the voices on the phone. He even started talking more himself, his wife and mother recalled. He was fighting again: they put it that way, as if he were back in the army.

Tessie's mother is a thin woman of medium size with a noticeably oval, dark-brown face. She has wide eyes and exceptionally long lashes covering them. Sometimes when speaking of her daughter's experiences at school, she would close her eyes for a few seconds but keep on talking. "I try not to go beyond each day. The way I look at it, if you can get your strength up for the present, the future will take care of itself. It was my mother-in-law who was best with Tessie though. I cry too easily." She had wanted her daughter to go to a desegregated school, but she also acknowledged that she worried about the strain of it upon both her daughter and herself. "The truth is," she said quietly one day after talking about how she felt when she answered abuse with silence, "I might have taken Tessie out, returned her to a Negro school. I held firm because my husband held firm, and we both held firm because of Tessie's grandmother. My husband and I were angry and scared, but she never gets scared, and if she gets angry only she knows it; and she understands the whites. She's lived and worked with them. We haven't."

She and her husband were young. Unlike many Negroes, in the old tradition of New Orleans, they did not live near whites. They had long ago withdrawn into an all-Negro neighborhood. In many ways they had tried to insulate themselves from the white world, and for a long time had never been much impressed by their mother's intimate knowledge of that world. It was a knowledge, they felt, that stemmed from a kind of peonage, and they wanted no part of it. "My mom still wants to know what's going on in the white world," was the way her son James put it, "but a lot of us younger Negroes didn't much care for a long time. Then the Supreme Court decision came, and we realized we had to come out from our shells, and once and for all fight our way into the white world. It was a good thing people like her were there to help us. You need to know the people you're trying to get with, and you have to know the enemy, too, I guess."

"Can you imagine a more confused three years of school for Tessie than these three?" her grandmother asked me when Tessie was promoted to the fourth grade. Her grandchild and two other girls of six had been the only pupils at school during their entire first year. Everyone else had boycotted. "I guess it wasn't segregation and it wasn't integration, they just had the whole school building for themselves. I kept on telling Tessie, she'd never have it as good again, all that building and teachers to herself and everything. Take advantage of the white man's mess, because it'll work for your gain, that's what I said to her when I thought she needed a little helping word here or there."

When the boycott was partially broken the second year, Tessie learned to live with a few white classmates. As her grandmother told it, "That was a big thing for the girls, counting how many whites came back to school. They gave me a day-by-day accounting. I would know all their names and what they would say every minute of the day." Finally, after a pleasant year in a school of about twenty, their school was decreed a Negro school; however, as "integrated" students, in contrast to all their Negro neighbors of like age, they were transferred to another white school, for the third year of what some brochures, advertising the city's assets, called "quality education."

It was no great blessing for the three girls to leave McDonogh. In their new school they were alone in a mass of white children. They found the sheer numbers of children strange, and they found the attitudes of some of the older children, the fifth and sixth graders, decidedly unfriendly. In a sense, they also saw themselves leave the stage of history, disappear into the crowd, left with their memories — of newspapermen, cameras, federal marshals and letters from all over the world.

"Tessie was always quiet, so she kept quiet during all the troubles. The teachers never quite knew what she was thinking, and it bothered them a lot. They couldn't help feeling that if she talked more she'd be in a safer state of health. They worried about how brave and silent she was." Her grandmother followed that description with her own attitude: "I tell her that it doesn't make any difference what you say, or if you say anything. It doesn't even matter if it's easy or hard for you at school. It's *going* to be hard, sometime or other it's going to be hard in this world, and Tessie girl, you'd just as well start getting used to it now."

Tessie was indeed a silent child, a deep, thoughtful child, I felt. With paper and crayons and with some games, she could give expression to what she felt and thought about the world around her. She liked to draw, and she put a great deal of time and energy into her efforts. When the drawings were completed she wanted to keep them, holding them in her room for weeks, looking at them, sometimes decorating her walls with them, and eventually giving them silently and shyly to me. She knew she was telling me something about herself and giving me something of herself. I thought that it was helpful for her to give her fears and hopes some expression, to put them into pictures. She could give representation to her tormentors, to her dread of their vengeance, to her feelings of weakness, to her natural wish to escape, to be a little white girl living a less turmoil-filled life. By keeping the drawings with her for a while, she could confront them when she felt able to, and eventually allow them to settle in her mind as the fantasies they were. Then, the master of their contents, she could hand them over to me. "I know it's scary sometimes going to school," she told me one day, "but not as scary as what I can dream up. So I told Granny that as bad as they make it for us, the stronger I'll get, because I'll beat them to the punch by imagining it even worse than it is, like I did with that picture I drew the other day. Remember?"

As a small girl Tessie wanted her own way in many matters. She was a fierce, stubborn child. When she was four and five she would often have tantrums. Her parents had wondered what would happen were she ever in a fight at school. They knew only too well the intense willfulness in their child. Curiously, she seemed more contained once she started school under the watchful eyes of the mobs, more contained at home as well as at school. "She stopped her tempers once she started McDonogh," her grandmother reported. "Maybe she was outgrowing them anyway, but maybe the dangers on the way to school made her a better child all around."

I saw Tessie much less frequently when she was in fourth and fifth grades. I was studying the psychological adjustments of migrant farm-worker families, and none of those families came near New Orleans. Several times a year, though, I make a point of coming back to visit her and some other children like her I know in Louisiana; and I always try to see her on "promotion day." It is her favorite day of the year. Her grandmother bakes a "promotion cake" for her, and each year I receive a card from both of them asking me to come celebrate "Tessie's Day."

In June of 1965 she was promoted to the sixth grade. I noticed then how very tall she was becoming. It is in her blood to be tall, I know, but I was surprised to see such growth in a child not yet in adolescence. I told Tessie that and she replied: "It's because you go away, then come back. If you stayed, you wouldn't notice me growing, then I'd just be Tessie, not tall Tessie." She added very quickly, "It's that way at school now, too: everything goes fine with the whites until I get sick and stay home. Then, when I come back to school, it takes them a day or so to get used to me, all over again. They look at me as if I was a stranger, then the next day it's all forgotten and I'm glad, because they know me again." As reprimands go, I thought that one tactful and kind.

In the summer of 1965 I spent some time in Mississippi, as I had the previous summer, working as a physician attached to some civil rights groups in the state. I knew Tessie's grandmother had an elderly sister in one of the Delta towns; indeed, I had often promised to visit her. Tessie's grandmother felt I would never do so on my own, and so wrote me a letter asking whether I would accompany her one day on such a trip.

A few days after I received the letter we went — Tessie, her grandmother and I. It was the last week of summer for Tessie, and school was to begin, as Tessie put it, "in exactly nine and a half days and a couple of hours." I had driven to New Orleans, so that they could drive north with me to the small town near Greenville, Mississippi. It was a hot, humid day, but my rented car was air-conditioned. Tessie was excited about that, delighting in the cold flow of air upon her hands. Not her grandmother: "It keeps the world out. You don't know what's happening out there, and you get the shivers just like in December. So what the point is I don't know." Tessie was sharp in her reply: "It's making progress, Grandma. You can open the window and have both kinds of weather; not too hot and not too cold."

We drove along, Tessie concerned with the car, her grand-mother with the landscape. As we passed the cotton fields the old lady estimated the condition of the crops. When the small airplanes that spray the fields came in sight, she explained their purpose to us, and also told us what used to be done, by her daddy and his daddy and over the generations, "world without end," as she put it. We saw the choppers at work, and we saw the miracle of those new chemicals — no weeds, but good cotton growth.

As we approached Greenville the girl became particularly alert. She wanted to see the Mississippi upstream, before it gets to New Orleans. The old lady kept pointing out plantations to her, telling her of relatives who had worked them, who still do. The girl showed no interest. She punched the buttons of the radio, and when they did not respond because of the distance we had driven, she used the band selector, slowly moving it along until she caught noise, then turning the volume up so that none of us could talk or even do anything but notice rather than hear the radio's music or talk. The girl made her point one time: "Grandma, it's better to listen to the songs than work in those fields, don't you think?"

"No, I'm not so sure," was the reply. Then we both had to listen, because Grandma wanted to tell us about living in the country and working on "the white man's acreage" and going into the white man's house and "carrying those trays of food to him" and "doing the dusting" so that "his dust comes off on the dark man, and he can be clean and the colored are the ones with the dirt." Finally, tired and a bit self-conscious, she said yes to Tessie: "You're right child, it *is* better to listen to the radio; except that you can't do that all day long. You have to eat and sleep, and get the money to pay for the radio, and that's why I want you to see what it was like for us in the old days. Now my sister, she's still in those days. That's the truth."

We came to her sister's home, an old, weather-worn shack, like many I've seen, like many that have been described before. The sister was five years younger than Tessie's grandmother, yet she looked not simply older but grotesque. She was thin and toothless. I noticed how unkempt she looked, perhaps because of the contrast to her sister's appearance that day. Tessie and her grandmother had dressed as if we were going to church. Seeing them I had even thought of wearing a tie, but had been dissuaded: "We just want to give our clothes a good time, don't we Tessie child?" Now I felt awkward; and I judged the three of us in a way cruel.

The sisters were distant with one another. I thought my presence might be responsible, and tried discreetly to leave. Neither would have it. The sister wanted me to see *her* grandchildren, whereupon Tessie made it clear she would not allow that without a fight. She told me she was "carsick," though we had been out of the car and on firm Delta soil for a half an hour. For a few minutes I talked with her, asking her questions about her symptoms; then I suggested we *both* see her cousins.

We did so, and enjoyed ourselves. Several were as old as Tessie, though it soon became clear they would be no threat to her. They were poorly dressed, and far less educated. They were painfully shy not only with me but with Tessie, whose fame they knew quite well. "Tessie knows everyone important," her cousin Martha told me, looking at me both coyly and nervously, as if I were one of those people. After a few minutes Tessie was actually holding court: answering questions, telling stories, hushing one child, encouraging another to tell about her life at school.

I was anxious to talk with a five-year-old girl who was attending one of the local Head Start classes, preparatory to entering school that fall. (I was actually in Mississippi, among other reasons, to do just that, speak with children in the various Head Start programs.) The little girl wanted very much to tell about the numbers and letters she was learning, the colors she could identify, the drawings she now could do. Tessie listened for a few minutes, then seemed to become irritable and glum. She was tired. She wanted to rest. She wanted to be with her grandmother. Where would I spend the night? With them? It was late. It was time for supper. Let's go see Grandma.

I had to go into Greenville to see some friends. I knew I couldn't eat supper with Tessie and her grandmother. It was enough strain for *them* to spend the evening there. The two old sisters clearly did not get along — and had not done so in the past. My arrival and Tessie's had come as a surprise; Grandma had sent a note saying *she* would be coming sometime late in August. So I left, promising an early return the next day for our trip back.

They were both waiting at nine in the morning, alone. Their hosts, all of them, were in the fields harvesting. We drove over to see them, to say good-bye. Babies were near their mothers playing quite happily with one another. Children were helping their parents at work. The old great-aunt of Tessie's was bent over, picking. We talked very briefly, perhaps for a minute. The sisters embraced and kissed, and each wished the other Godspeed. By nine-thirty we were headed south.

Tessie reached for the radio. The air-conditioner was now working so well we had to open the window slightly — as Tessie's grandmother put it, "to calm down the artificial cold." Tessie had trouble with the radio. "I can't find anything I like," she said. Then she added, "But I'm still glad to be in this car, going home." She pulled at one of her fallen socks and then gazed out the window at the cotton fields, as one by one we passed them by.

About a minute later her grandmother spoke — in reply to Tessie, in reply to her own thoughts: "Tessie child, I'm glad, too. I only wish we had room in our home for my sister and her kin. But that day maybe you'll see. I know I won't. I never thought I'd see as much as I have these past few years; and you mustn't be a hog about seeing." Tessie gave her a lingering look, and knew enough not to reply. About a minute later she turned to me and asked when we would be back in New Orleans. "I miss station WDSU in New Orleans. They talk friendlier to you than the stations in other cities do."

3. *Pioneer Youth: John Washington*

"We once were slaves, but now we have to free our country as well as ourselves," said a Negro minister to his flock in the summer of 1961. His church is in Atlanta, Georgia, and in the words of one parishioner, "it is a hard-praying one." It is also an old and a new church: the red-brick building housed a congregation of white Methodists for many years; but the neighborhood around the church had changed recently, and with it the character of worship practiced in it. "We're Baptist sometimes," the minister had explained to me, "but sometimes we're just ourselves. We takes the Bible at its word, and goes off on our own kind of original praying." Most of his flock were new to the city, and their rural ways of worship did indeed persist in that church: passion and severity, heaven and hell, sin denounced ecstatically. It was a hot, terribly humid day, but everyone was immaculately dressed in clothes never worn except in church. They listened attentively, nodding often and occasionally shouting their assent to one point or another made in the sermon. It was a sermon meant to bolster the spirit of a community set to accomplish part of its liberation; school desegregation would take effect the coming week. Sitting in the church was John Washington, a youth of fifteen who was to be one of ten students (in a city of a million, a state of several million) to lead his race out of its special schools and into those shared by the rest of the community.

After the church service had ended, I was at a loss to see how John would be able to live up to his avowedly solid faith during the time ahead. For one thing, he himself seemed bored and restless during the rather long time of singing, reading and listening. Moreover, I had been in Negro churches better led, more neighborly and warm-hearted in atmosphere.

Yet, whatever I felt, in our first interviews John emphasized to me his reliance upon religion, and predicted his ability to survive — through faith — whatever dangers and pressures he was soon to face. "If it gets rough, I can always pray and go to church, and that will calm me down real fast" was the way he once put it. He spoke quietly and slowly, as if he was needing and gaining strength from his own words.

John was born in South Carolina in the early summer of 1946, the fourth child of Joseph and Hattie (Turner) Washington. His grandparents grew up in the homes of people once slaves — all of his ancestors worked on cotton for generations. His parents took pride in telling me that theirs was the first generation free enough to raise children who would never see a slave. John's birth was attended by his aunt, one of the younger sisters of his mother. His parents were sharecroppers, and until the Second World War had been having an exceedingly hard time of it. Their yearly income had never been more than two hundred dollars. They lived in a cabin at the edge of a large plantation; the cabin still stands, occupied by Mr. Washington's younger brother. He now averages about a thousand dollars a year for farming cotton and tobacco. The land is rich and seemingly inexhaustible. Several times I visited the farm with John — after I had known him for two years — and we both noticed the curious presence of shabby, makeshift living quarters amid abundant wild flowers, heavily cultivated land, and well-fed animals — hogs, chickens, even a goat.

John's father never left that farm until he was drafted to fight in the war. He had his basic training in New Jersey, then went to Europe where he served as a cook for troops fighting in France. He says that he will never be able to forget the sight of men dying in war, but he counts his time in the army as the best and most influential period of his life: "I never had it so good. I ate food I never dreamed I could, even in battle; and I had a good bed and real fine clothes. I saw the world outside, and I figured I wouldn't stay a 'cropper' after that."

He didn't. He came home for a year and tried resuming his earlier life. He had married a nearby girl when she was fourteen, he sixteen. When he was drafted at twenty they had three children. His wife Hattie very much wanted to remain in South Carolina. Her large family lived only a few miles away from his. They were all part of a community. If they were poor beyond description, essentially illiterate and almost totally isolated from the social, cultural, political and economic life of the nation, at least they knew it in their bones; and so they feared the risks and burdens of leaving one another as well as a life both familiar and communal, whatever else it was not. Some, of course, had left, even before the war. Each family had its son or daughter, cousin or neighbor "abroad," in the Southern or Northern cities.

Hattie finally agreed to leave, to emigrate, but not until John had been born in his grandmother's cabin. Her husband Joseph had agreed to wait for the birth. Hattie had hoped that by the time their new child had arrived, Joseph would change his mind about moving. Instead, he was more determined than ever. Their fourth child was their first son; he was given his paternal grandfather's name. Mr. Washington wanted a job in a city. He wanted schooling for his children, particularly his new son. He wanted to go northward, to Philadelphia or New York. His wife persuaded him to compromise on Atlanta. "I felt safer going to Georgia since we had to go at all," she now recalls, "and if it was to do again, I'd still rather be here than up there North." She didn't like cold weather, snow, distance from her family, large cities or the way people get along in them — shunning one another, making her feel lonely. In Hattie's town white people spoke to her on sight, asked after her. Hattie knew Negroes had a much tougher life to live, but she wasn't sure that moving from one place in America to another would solve *that* problem. To this day she feels this, her own version of the Southerner's pride. She accepts the higher standard of living she now has in the city, and the new-found rights she has there — to vote easily, to ride anywhere on the bus, to walk into any store without worrying whether she will be arrested for doing so. Yet, she also will say nostalgically: "I'd sooner have an outhouse and all the land we had than live like we do here, crowded together, even if the plumbing is good." Another time she remarked that, "We knew white folks by their names and they knew us; and when we met we were real cordial to one another. Now it's everyone strange to everybody else, and it don't make any difference what your color is, people will let you die in the street before helping you. My granddaddy had his life saved by a white man, on a road right near our house. Now fancy that here."

In Atlanta young John began to grow up. Six months after he was born his mother was again pregnant. John eventually was to have seven brothers and sisters. Two brothers followed him, and two sisters followed them. This steadily increasing family settled at first in the outskirts of the city, where Mr. Washington obtained occasional employment as a dishwasher in a restaurant, then as a handyman in a service station. When John was two his parents moved into the neighborhood they now call their own. They have since lived continually in the same apartment, the five sisters in two bedrooms, the three boys in another, the parents in the living room. In addition there is a kitchen. For the entire Washington family — including the relatives in South Carolina and a few north in Chicago — this apartment represents the highest standard of living yet achieved. It is heated, has electricity, is not rat-infested, has running water, and though poorly furnished and crowded in comparison to the way most Americans live, it is by no means unattractive, because Mrs. Washington is a neat housekeeper.

John's childhood, as a matter of fact, was a fairly strict one. His mother, I eventually learned, had a breakdown shortly before the family moved to Atlanta. John was a few weeks old. She became despondent and her mother took care of the baby. She turned to the local minister and to a rather intensive reading of the Bible for support. She recovered upon moving to Atlanta, but since then describes a definite change in her personality: "I used to be easygoing, but since we had to be on our own I've been careful to be good and do things right. I turned to religion so that we would survive, and I've tried to instill the Word of God in all my children, and sometimes I think even my husband may get it."

I found her at times suspicious and preoccupied with religion. As her remark indicated, she and her husband have not always had a good time of it together. He is a very heavy drinker, enough so to be considered an alcoholic: he can't quite live with or without liquor. After two years of visiting the family and interviewing young John, I learned from him what he himself had only recently learned from his oldest sister, that when he was three, following the birth of his youngest brother, their mother had left for several months, hospitalized for "mental troubles." Mrs. Washington later talked very briefly about the episode: "I don't remember much. I know I got low, and they gave me electricity, and I got pulled back."

From what I could observe and gather from her response to my questions, she still has her moody times. How much they influenced John during his childhood is hard to know. He was breast-fed until "over a year" old, even while his mother was upset. His grandmother also cared for him then, in South Carolina, and for a month in Georgia. At about three months his mother was alone with him; she was still shaky psychologically.

Later, when his mother's illness required hospitalization, his grandmother again cared for him.

John was rather strictly toilet trained, in contrast to the way his three older sisters were reared. A very interesting change fell upon him and all the other children who followed him; they were rigorously and even punitively made to respect what was essentially a new — and I would imagine fearful — routine for their parents as well as them. In our first discussion of the subject Mrs. Washington noted that, "In the country we didn't much worry, except for the difference between the house and the trees, and that they has to get to know the difference. But in the city we knew we had to watch out in the apartment. The white owns it, and we just made sure the kids took care of theirselves right off."

It became clear to me — though very slowly — that not only plumbing (sink, running water and radiators) was new to John's parents when they moved with him as a baby to the city. We often forget what a perplexing and intimidating event it may be for people to leave the secluded poverty of sharecropper cabins for city living: its crowded streets, with their cars and rules of traffic, its noisy anonymity. John's strict upbringing reflected in some degree the guarded adjustment his parents were making to Atlanta. His mother put the matter this way to me once: "If we had stayed on the farm, I wouldn't have been so hard on John when he was little; but his daddy and me had to be more careful of what we did and what the children did, living in a new place where the rules are different — and for a long time you don't know what they are."

So far as John's parents, older sisters and past teachers can recall, he was not a particularly outstanding boy, either at home or in school. His appetite as an infant and child was normal. He grew normally, suffered the usual childhood ailments. At school he started out hesitantly and without distinction, but gradually gained ground, so that in the sixth grade he was one of the three or four leading students in his class. He always excelled in sports, whether in his neighborhood or at school. His parents proudly attributed his agile manner, his athletic excellence to the rural, farm boy "soul" in him. "John was born on a farm," his mother once reminded me, "and that's where his soul got fixed. He can run and jump because that's what you do when you live where we did. People say he's so strong, and his muscles are so good, but we're not surprised. He carries my daddy's body, and he'll hand it down, too — if the city don't take it out of him, somehow."

Whatever value both parents put on a limber body, they matched it with emphasis upon the worth of education. Amid the talk we hear these days about "culturally disadvantaged" Negro children, I think we tend to overlook the fact that Negroes — not only those from the skimpy Negro middle class — have had a widespread interest in education, though to be sure it has necessarily been education of a special kind. Negro colleges are scattered all over the South. Negro seminaries seem to be everywhere. Negro boys have aimed for teaching or the ministry as commonly as white boys have hoped to become lawyers, doctors or businessmen. By Northern white standards many of the schools and seminaries are weak indeed. We may, today, scoff at state-supported A. and M. (agricultural and mechanical) colleges as part of the "Uncle Tom" tradition that started with Booker T. Washington and is only now ending. We may be dubious about the endless educational courses and credits taken and achieved by the thousands of Negro teachers in the South's segregated schools — all leading so often and ironically nowhere but to further spiritless, flawed learning. Yet, such efforts have at least enabled the hopes and ambitions of Negro people to find some outlet, however small, during a period in history when nothing else seemed at all possible.

For example, Mrs. Washington wanted a future for her children, and even though she doubted its realization, she constantly invoked it as a possibility. Not only did she want her first son to be a teacher; she told me that her grandfather had wanted her father to be a teacher. When today we observe the aimlessness and apparent inertia of many Negroes, we may be seeing people who once had ambition, but have forsaken it.

John entered school at six, and for several years was a rather ordinary pupil. His favorite subjects were geography and history, to which he apparently brought considerable imaginative effort. His fifth-grade teacher gave him a book of travel adventures by Richard Halliburton as a reward for excellence in written reports on such subjects as "wheat" and "cotton." Mrs. Washington saved them and I have read them. They are neatly written, with pictures of cotton fields and sharecroppers working in them. As a matter of fact, John as a young boy was once told by his mother that such pictures showed the kind of life he might be living, had his parents not moved to Atlanta: "I told him that he has cousins working at cotton, and would you believe it, he said no, it wasn't so. He was six or so, and he believed we had always been in Atlanta; and every time we took him to see his grandfolks he wanted to know why *they* had left the city to work so hard in the fields."

John had some trouble with arithmetic when first introduced to multiplication and long division, but slowly mastered both. He also tended to talk or whisper in class enough to earn B's and C's in conduct. He was never known to have any psychological troubles. He has always had a lusty appetite ("he'd eat us poor if I didn't tell him there isn't any more left"). He never had trouble sleeping; and generally — from what his parents and former teachers say — he was obedient at home and school without turning obedience into the compulsion of uncritical compliance.

John entered junior high school (and adolescence) at twelve. He took up with a girl in his class, a rather attractive and quiet girl who then dreamed of being a nurse, and afterward became one. John continued to see her over the years, though they became "old friends" rather than courting friends. I noticed that they drew closer together — at his behest — when he faced the ordeal of desegregation.

He became involved in that ordeal quite casually. He was a tenth grader in one of the Negro high schools in Atlanta. He had been thinking of quitting school, as many of his friends had been doing with increasing frequency. He fought with his parents over this, and the considerations at issue tell about his home life. His father, as I mentioned, had been drinking for many years, but until John was about ten had managed to confine his intake to weekend bouts. John remembers as a child that his father would simply disappear, sometimes coming home for brief periods, sometimes lying down to sleep in hallways or alleys and then being picked up by the police and jailed, dried out and returned home, or brought to his family directly. However, he generally kept sober during the week, and kept his job out of jeopardy. About the time John entered high school his father's controls weakened; he insidiously began weekday drinking. Mrs. Washington apparently saw what was coming, and obtained work at a nearby factory where she helped assemble children's toys. She called upon her religious faith more than ever at that time, and attributes her job to divine intervention: "I saw him going for the bottle worse than ever, and I prayed to God for guidance. He told me to go and find a job, and let it be between Him and my husband, what will come from the drinking. So I looked, and I found one, and it's a good job, too."

The older sisters took care of the younger children. John became a kind of father to them, something he himself once readily described: "My sister Mary and I have sort of been mother and father to my younger brothers and sisters, especially the sisters, because they're young enough to need us." With this in mind, John wanted to leave school, find work and establish his position as the chief breadwinner of the family — its most reliable man. His mother, however, objected. She feared her son would take after his father if he didn't consolidate his own life, educationally and professionally. His father, too, objected to John's leaving school; so much so that he stopped drinking for the few weeks the decision was in balance.

Largely for those reasons — the various fears of his parents — John stayed in high school, and obligingly set to work studying harder than ever before. Listening to him talk about it several years later, I felt he must have been relieved to see his own struggles and decisions act to stabilize his family. In a way, he achieved his purpose without quitting school.

When the city of Atlanta and the state of Georgia yielded to a federal court order requiring a start toward school desegregation, they chose to begin with the last two years of high school. John was a sophomore at this time and like all his classmates was confronted with the choice of applying or not for transfer the next year to a white high school. The school board would then act upon the applications, selecting the children it judged suitable to make the move.

My experience in city after city of the South has taught me to expect no set pattern for the kinds of children who have taken on the leadership in school desegregation, nor any pattern for the criteria inposed by school boards in selecting them.[3] Many Negro parents would not allow their children to face the dangers involved: some because they were poor and afraid that they would lose their jobs; some because they were comfortable and unwilling to risk the loss of that comfort; some because they were (and are) so fearful of whites, or hate them so, that they would not want their children exposed to them even if they were assured it wasn't dangerous.

School boards in Southern states have not always shown a consistent interest in trying to select the students whose abilities would augur well for making desegregation work. In many instances the age of the child and his place of residence were the only considerations observed. Indeed, often the school boards regarded themselves as under legal attack, and accommodated themselves minimally, and only under court order. Frequently they would agree to desegregate, and announce that fact publicly; later on they set a time for those who wished to apply for transfer. In Atlanta a large number applied when they learned that the eleventh and twelfth grades of several white schools would be open to them.

John decided on impulse to request a transfer. Like his friends and classmates, he had been paying particular attention to what he once called "race news." He was eleven when the Little Rock crisis occurred, and remembered it vividly. He later told me that he would "never forget that if I live to be one hundred. I was walking every inch with those kids." In 1960, just a year before Atlanta faced its crisis, New Orleans had been the scene of more riots, in a sense worse than any before them in duration and intensity, let alone the vulnerability of the children involved. John had particularly worried for the young children — he had a sister of seven. "I kept on picturing her going through it, and I figured if she did, I'd walk beside her; and just let anyone try anything."

Walking home one day with his friends, he heard some say yes, they would, some say no, they wouldn't think of going through mobs or sitting through insults at a white school. John recalls the atmosphere and conversation as follows: "We were just kidding around, like any other time; only that day it was about integration and what we would do now that it was coming to Atlanta. We kept on daring one another and teasing each other. My friend Kenny said he was going to do it, regardless; and the girls let out a big cheer and hugged and kissed him. Then Larry called him a fool. He said we would be giving up the best two years of our lives for nothing but trouble. He meant the end of high school, and the dances and football games — everything you hope for when you're beginning high school. Well, we most of us said we would do it — I think more to be the hero before the girls. Then they fell to arguing just like we did. My best girl then was Betty, and she told me she would sign up if I would, but we had to promise we both meant it to one another. I can still remember the bargain. She said, 'No joking' and I said, 'No joking,' and that was it. A week later we went down singing to get the forms and apply. I didn't even tell my folks until it came time to get their signatures, and that was where the trouble started. They said no, sir. I tried to tell them we were all going to do it, but it didn't cut any ice with them. Momma started praying out loud, and quoting the Bible to me about getting into heaven by being poor, and if I tried to go to school with whites and rise up, I'll probably lose my soul. And Daddy told me I'd get myself killed, and they'd get him to lose his job, one way or another. For a while I thought I was out of the running before I even started; and a lot of my friends had the same trouble."

In a sense the week of struggle for his parents' signatures became a real time of intimacy and discussion between the three of them. It was also a confrontation of the generations, the past incredulous at what the present seemed to expect as its due. John heard from his parents stories of experiences which they themselves had long since "forgotten": accounts of terror, humiliation and repudiation which had formerly been handed down from parent to child as an inheritance, to be told and later relived. John was particularly moved by his mother's insistence that his generation was the first to be spared the worst of it — the constant possibility of lynching, the near-total lack of hope, the daily scorn that permitted no reply, no leeway. To be free of that, to be safe from night riders, to have steady work, to be left mostly alone, all that seemed enough. "They wanted me to be glad I could walk on the sidewalk," John summarized their conversations, "because they used to have to move into the gutter in their town when a white man approached them. But I told them that once you walk on the sidewalk, you look in the windows of the stores and restaurants, and you want to go there, too. They said, maybe *my* children, and I said *me*, so that my children will be the first really free Negroes. They always told me that they would try to spare me what they went through; so I told them I wanted to spare my children going through any mobs. If there were mobs for us to face, we should do it right now. And besides, I told them they were contradicting themselves. My mother always brags about how wonderful the farm life was, and my daddy says he thought the city would save him, and it drove him to drink, so it's too bad he ever left South Carolina. Suddenly, though, all the truth was coming out." When I asked him how *he* explained their opposing sentiments he replied briefly — and for me his words are unforgettable — "I guess people can believe different things at different times."

As he persisted they relented. Eventually they gave their reluctant, apprehensive endorsements. They apparently were proud as well as filled with foreboding as they signed their names, itself not an easy task for either of them. John must have sensed their pride. He described an unexpected rise of sentiment in himself as he watched his parents sign their permission: "I think I got more emotional over that than anything else that happened; even more than walking in the building the first day."

Before walking into any school building for white children he would have to meet the standards of school officials worried about how to implement an uncongenial court order in the face of an uncertain and fearful population. John expected to be one of hundreds of new Negro students. He may have been dimly aware that no Southern city had yet taken more than a handful of Negro children to start desegregation, but neither he nor his friends ever gave much thought to the likelihood that only a few of them might be chosen. To some extent they believed — and correctly — that their city was determined to secure their safety. That belief, that faith, helped these children forget or "overlook" some of the possible dangers in the future. John put it to me quite concisely one day several weeks before those dangers actually started coming to his attention: "I try not to think about what's going to happen when school starts. I just go from day to day. We never thought it would be a picnic, but we figured we'd just take what comes, and then we could have stories to tell afterward."

John was interviewed, along with many of his friends, by school officials who were trying to make their choices more rationally and thoughtfully than some of their counterparts had done in other Southern cities. John realized during the interviews that a quiet and sincere presence was wanted, that an inflammatory or argumentative one was feared. He was asked by the school system's deputy superintendent how he would manage insults and even attacks upon himself. He replied that he would ignore them. If anyone threatened to injure him or interfere with his activities, he would call for help from others, namely his teachers. He was pointedly asked whether he would strike back if hit. He said he would not. He was asked why. He said he would only be inviting worse injury by doing so; he would, after all, be outnumbered, literally a thousand to one. I asked him, on hearing him tell of this exchange, how he expected to maintain that degree of almost fearless restraint. My question was: "John, in your own mind — apart from what you told them in the interview — do you think you would act that way if one or two boys pushed or shoved you, and called you names?" He replied: "That's where my daddy is right. He told me a long time ago, 'The only way a colored man can win is to fool the white man into thinking he's won.' I don't think that's always right, but it has to be like that until we get strong enough to make it even steven."

John was chosen, one of ten in a city of a million. He was surprised and quite disappointed rather than honored to learn that he and a girl he casually knew would be the only two of their race to enter the large "white" high school near his "old" one. Again he made light of his worries by speculating that since they were so few, none of them would be allowed to enter at all. In fact, one of the girls selected for another school soon decided to forego her chance. She took stock of the threats and dangers about to begin and decided they were too much for her.

John did not seem to falter. I talked with him all that summer, and was myself a bit unnerved at his day-to-day calm in the face of harassment by phone and mail. Unlike the children of New Orleans, Little Rock or Clinton, Tennessee, that year, John would never face a mob. Yet, John could not have known that he would be spared; and so he experienced — somewhere out of sight — a long summer of anxious waiting.

During that time I talked with him two or three times a week, and finished gathering my general medical and psychiatric impressions of him — his past health, his way of getting along with himself and others, the history of his family, his interests and activities, his hopes, any of his difficulties he cared to remember or talk about. John's general health had always been good. His mother recalled that he suffered the usual childhood diseases, including an episode of colicky stomach when he entered school at age six. He had experienced occasional headaches in the past few years, but no other symptoms. John was not reluctant to talk about his father's alcoholism. He did so with a mixture of sympathy and anger. His mother's biblical preoccupations also upset him. As she gave vent to her warnings of sin and redemption, all the children kept a respectful silence until she stopped, then tactfully resumed their activities. In contrast, John himself had no trouble with drinking, no biblical preoccupations. He did not smoke. He had never had any trouble with the law. By his own description, he was "an ordinary teen-ager."

For three summer months he awaited his role in desegregation. He worked at cutting lawns, emptying trash, helping his father by substituting at the gas station, or selling Cokes at local baseball games. I saw very little evidence of anxiety in him. He did become concerned with his "strength," and accordingly set himself a routine of exercise. His sister asked him whether he was worried about trouble in the fall, and he impatiently denied it. He had noticed he was short-winded on occasion, and that alone was the reason for his exercise. I was on the lookout for "trouble," but his appetite held up; he slept well; he seemed to his family quieter and more relaxed than usual.

The week before school started, the threats on his life, on his family's life, reached their terrible and bizarre peak. The telephone calls came in round the clock, angry voices talking of dynamite, alarmed voices talking of "racial amalgamation," plaintive voices urging John to reconsider his ill-advised decision "before it is too late." His parents — and especially his older sisters — wanted the phone changed. A city detective watching their home advised them to change their number. John would not hear of it: "I'm going to have to get used to that, so we might as well start now." Such a response showed how firmly and stubbornly he was girding himself. As I look back — and only in retrospect can I see it and say it — his willingness to take on the constant irritation and heckling of the telephone calls foreshadowed his future capacity to deal with similar episodes in school. At the time I failed to understand why he wouldn't let his family follow their inclinations and the advice of the police department. Oversensitive as I was to the possibility of incipient neurotic illness under stress, I failed to recognize this youth's desire to have his preliminary struggle with the enemy on "home territory," and win it.

On the first day of school he was escorted and driven to school by city detectives. I watched him walk up to the door of the high school, heavily guarded by police, the students and teachers waiting inside for him, and wondered how he felt, what he was thinking, and whether in fact he had any words to describe those seconds. Everybody else seemed to have words: national and local political leaders, reporters, observers, all noted how important it was for a Southern city to initiate school desegregation without violence. There was none.

Certainly the white children and their teachers felt themselves in the presence of history; and so did John. He told his mother later that he said a prayer she long ago taught him as he left the police car; when that was finished, still walking toward the school, he looked quickly at the building and thought of words he had heard from his grandparents as a boy: "It's going to get better for us, don't you ever forget that." Approaching the front door, he thought of the classroom and pictured the students sitting, waiting for him to enter, and then watching him as he did.

They were doing just that, watching closely, and would continue to do so for two years. They stared at him and looked away from him. At the end of the first class some of them heckled him. A few days later he found insulting words scribbled on his books. Some of the students tried very hard to be friendly, though most of them kept an apprehensive distance from him. He, too, watched apprehensively; but he also worked hard in school, studied earnestly at home, and took things as they came each day.

During his two years in a desegregated high school I kept trying to learn how he managed to cope with the constant strains. I kept careful track of his moods, particularly so because I became puzzled at his altogether remarkable composure in the face of various social provocations or intellectual hurdles. In the first place, he was woefully unprepared for the transfer academically. He had prepared himself for unfriendliness, but not for the long hours of homework required to catch up with, not to say keep abreast of, his fellow students. Meeting these problems daily and a host of others he had never expected, he survived and — I came to see — flourished. I had a hard time understanding why.

I did note his increasingly guarded and circumspect behavior as it spilled over from life at school to life elsewhere. Even at home he walked more carefully, spoke a bit more slowly. He seemed less relaxed, less willingly outspoken and humorous.

These were times now when his appetite diminished; he picked at meat once gobbled, played with French fries once almost swept into his hungry, growing body. His mother and sister bought steak they couldn't afford to strengthen him, fight his loss of interest in ordinary food. He wanted only to be left alone, to study.

He sought out some academic help; he went to see a professor at the Negro college he would someday attend. He told me then that he was worried about his math and his French. Yet his tutor told him that his math seemed good, that he was doing his homework correctly. His French teacher in his "old" high school made the same observations about his work in French. Still, he did not seem appropriately reassured by them, or by his good grades as they started coming in. I saw that as evidence of tension, of an increasingly brittle determination that was costing him a high price in humorless rigidity and lack of perspective.

He didn't sleep as well as he once had. He had dreams, on occasion remembering fragments of them to tell me because he (and I) thought that studying dreams was my job. He also told me about his ordeal and that of his white classmates; for he saw that they, too, were having difficulty in reconciling their past expectations of Negroes with his particular presence.

There are two special moments worth mention here. In a way, each tells the story of what happened to John during those two years — how, to some extent, he survived as handily as he did. The first involves the one dream he did remember fully; the only one, in fact, he ever related to me in careful detail and worried seriousness: "I was walking to school, and was stopped because some railroad tracks were there and a long train was going by. I tried to get across the train, because it didn't seem to be going too fast; that is, I tried to leap across the connections between the cars. I know you can't, but in the dream I was staring at them as the only hope to get across, because the train seemed to stretch on and on in both directions. Well, finally the train did pass by so that I could get to school; but it stopped, with the last car right near me. I saw a lot of children on the car; it was like a platform, like in a campaign, where speakers speak from. They were colored children; I think they were maybe seven or eight, and I think one might have been my little sister. Then I saw some grown-ups. Then more and more of them came out from the car, and they came off it, toward me. They were colored, too. They had on suits and ties, I think. One of them was my French tutor [from his former Negro high school] and I think I saw my granddaddy, but I'm not sure. Then I got nervous, because I knew I had to get to school, and I was afraid I'd be late. So I started to move on, and suddenly I saw a huge hole in the road; it was a kind of pit, and I could see my momma and daddy in it. It was mainly their faces I saw, as big as life, just staring there. Then I woke up, and I was clutching the sheet. Boy, was I glad to be in bed. I really felt it had all happened. I went to school this morning, and I had to catch hold of myself near the railroad tracks. I thought I'd see that pit and fall into it. I've never had a dream stick with me like that."

The dream had obviously been upsetting to him, though he could make no sense of it. He had the dream several months after school desegregation had begun; indeed, he was well along the year, and well past the worst tension he had experienced in those first few awkward weeks. He had learned "how to behave"— at least his teachers felt so. I realized that he had his own doubts and fears, though at first I didn't know exactly what this dream told about them. About fifteen minutes after he had told me the dream (and I told him that I didn't know what it "meant") he came forth with two details to it that he had forgotten: "There was something else that just came to me. One of the boxcars on the train said Southern and Gulf Limited; and I think I saw Warren Sands near the pit. He seemed to be standing there, smiling. I think I was glad he was there or something — that was just as I woke up. I must have been afraid I would fall in there;

and maybe Warren was there to rescue me." Warren Sands is a white youth. He was a classmate of John's, a friendly boy, active in student government, one of the first to come greet him and talk openly with him several weeks after school had begun.

Then I asked John what *he* thought the dream "meant." He shrugged his shoulders and replied, "Beats me. The only thing I could make of it was that it showed I'm nervous about getting to school." His next comment was about Warren: "I don't know how Warren got into it. He's just a classmate of mine." In point of fact Warren was not *just* a classmate, and John himself had made that quite clear to me. I said nothing, because he wanted to talk next about his troubles with French, a foreign language which — as he was putting it then —"must have been invented to give trouble to people studying it." Yet, his main trouble, from his teacher's viewpoint, was not his ability to study the language, but his hesitation at speaking it in class. There were "conversational hours," the one time John was forced into a social setting by an academic routine. He was embarrassed, and very shy about taking up with anyone in French. Several white boys had tried talking with him, to no avail. He balked on his words. The teacher had sensed the awkwardness right off, and had frankly been unable to deal with it except by talking with John herself. On those occasions his French came to him easily. It was, however, a weekly ordeal for him and the whole class.

John and I never talked about his dream that year, though I think our talks generally helped him — and me — put some of his feelings — and my own, too — into explicit language. The following summer I asked him whether he remembered the dream, and he did; it was one that somehow lingered, stayed in his consciousness. He still couldn't make much sense of it; he called it "a sign of the strain I was under then." I had, of course, come to the same conclusion; but a few weeks after I heard that dream, I saw John face a strain in real life (and talk about it afterward) that gave me some concrete idea what the dream may have meant to him.

John and I went to a basketball game at his high school. The opposing team was from a school not yet desegregated. John as the only Negro in the audience attracted attention from the visitors by his mere presence. Indeed, a good part of the audience eventually paid more attention to him than the game. After the game, as we started leaving, one heckler after another confronted us. They had also seen the game, and now that it was over they turned their attention to John. Their language was awful, their behavior threatening. Were it not for quick action by hastily summoned police, there might well have been a riot. I was quite alarmed, and afterward sad and very angry. John was astonishingly steadfast during the episode, and rather composed afterward. I had known him for several months by then, and so I felt free enough to say what I did: "I don't know how you can take that sort of treatment; I really don't." He smiled, and looked at me as if he understood my problems and would try to help me as best he could. In a moment he did. He started with gentle criticism of me: "You don't know how I can take it because you haven't ever *had* to take it." He paused, "You see, when I grew up I had to learn to expect that kind of treatment; and I got it, so many times I hate to remember and count them. Well, now I'm getting it again, but it's sweet pain this time, because whatever they may say to me or however they try to hurt me, I know that just by sticking it out I'm going to help end the whole system of segregation; and that can make you go through anything. Yes, when they get to swearing and start calling me 'nigger' I think of the progress we're making, I'm making, every minute; then I know I can take even worse than we had tonight. I saw much worse happen to my momma and me when I was eight or nine, and we were shopping, and a woman decided she belonged ahead of us in a line in a store downtown. She slapped my momma, and momma didn't do a thing. I got so angry I kicked the lady and shoved her; so she called the police and soon the whole store seemed after us. The worst of it was that I got the beating of my life from my parents for doing that. You see, we just grow up to take it. But not you, you don't have to, and that's the difference."

When John had graduated from high school and I was trying to make sense of his two-year experience, I kept on returning to those two events, his dream and his virtual "speech" to me (and at me) after the basketball game. The dream told of his struggle going to school and being at school, not only with hecklers but with those who became kind to him (like the white boy whom he belatedly remembered to be in the dream) only to make him feel that he was turning his back on his own people. He felt a traitor trusting and accepting the friendliness of white people. Several times he could frankly tell me how hard it was for him to respond to some of the genuine respect and affection shown him by white students at school.

I suspect he also felt accused by his own people for the increasingly conscious desires he felt to leave their company, to spend his time with white people, even to be white. After we had known one another four years he told me that some of his friends in college deny ever having thought of what it was like to be white. I no longer record our talks on tape, but he spoke words to this effect: "I would never have admitted to you two years ago that I wished I was white when I was at school with whites. I never really could admit it to myself. The thought would cross my mind, and I'd try to forget it as quickly as it came."

John could also show signs of exhaustion and depression; he could summon a level of self-criticism far more severe than any censure I ever saw him direct toward others. He did not get depressed that night at the basketball game — I think taking me to task helped prevent it. At other times, however, he became weary, sulky, gloomy and unable to heed easily what he had assured me was the persuasive voice of his past life, reminding him at all times that he must not retaliate, that he must endure insults in silence.

John was particularly unhappy during the last months of his final year of high school. He knew he had done a good job, but he also knew it was time to say good-bye to friends he wished he had known longer and whom he realized he would never see again. He had studied hard and been rewarded with consistently high marks, despite inadequate preparation for the academic burden. In his senior year he decided to attend a local Negro college. Even though he was tempted mightily by the prospects of going North to an Ivy League school, he was also afraid of the prospect, and he admitted that he was perhaps tired of the strains that go with desegregated education — the self-consciousness and constant girding of oneself. Were "things different," were he from another home, he might have welcomed a continuation in college of such mixed blessings and hurdles. Beneath the surface lay other problems, though — the troubling fragments of his home life and the attention they demanded from him. His older sisters were leaving home for marriage; his father was sick, his mother rather worn. In a sense his crisis had been theirs, and they had all prospered under it; for their lives had found a real, tangible and significant purpose. That accomplished, John felt he could not simply walk off. Perhaps his family would eventually learn to need him less, but he felt that he and they both were not yet ready for his departure from Georgia.

As it turned out, he was wise to stay in Atlanta. His father's drinking became worse, though it had improved while the family was under the pressures of John's critical situation at school. His mother, too, declined into a condition of chronic, spiritless fatigue. John both studied and looked after his younger brothers and sisters as well as his parents. They had all supported him; he now worked at helping them.

As I have watched John grow from a youth to a young man, and reflected upon his capacity to endure the simple trials not only of growing but of growing in a home such as his, of growing while a student in a white school, while taking a leading part in an important social change, I have found the limits of my own particular professional training rather severely defined.

John, after all, came from a very grim home, psychiatrically speaking. Both parents have serious mental disorders, the father at the very least a heavy drinker, the mother at the very least subject to distracted, suspicious fits of not very coherent religious preoccupations. John's childhood was characterized by poverty and what we now call "cultural disadvantage." He had a mediocre early education. When he decided to apply for an education at a white school he was not deeply or specially involved in the civil rights struggle. He belonged to no organization working for desegregation. He was not "enlisted" or encouraged to seek an application form; it was almost a matter of a moment's whim, a teen-ager's dare, a response to the company he kept, to their collective teasing of one another — fear and desire blended into a challenge.

Yet, this rather "ordinary" youth survived handily two years of an academic schedule far more burdensome and severe than any he had ever been taught to expect or endure. He also survived the daily loneliness and fear of his special position at school. Finally, he survived the ugliness and nastiness of threats, foul language, even some shoves and pokes in the corridors and corners of the school and in the streets nearby.

What accounts for such durability, such a hardy spirit against such odds? Where did John find his strength? Is his case an exception that proves nothing? It certainly is not an unusual story. John's life is not unlike many others I have encountered in Little Rock, Arkansas, in Clinton, Tennessee, in Asheville, North Carolina, in New Orleans, Atlanta and Jackson. Many of these pioneer children have not been hand-picked or particularly able and bright — not natural leaders, chosen for that reason to lead their race into white schools. Whatever has enabled them to get along as well as they have is no mysterious and rare gift of intellect or "personality development."

John's family life — seen by itself — simply does not explain his capacity to deal with the problems confronting him while I knew him. What, after all, in his childhood, in the personality of either of his parents, can account for this boy's sound mind, his strong will, his competence in the face of a stiff academic challenge, his survival in the face of a severe (and threatening) social challenge? His mother received a diagnosis of paranoid schizophrenia when in a mental hospital. His father, as I have said, is an alcoholic. Were John's case presented at a clinical conference, few psychiatrists would deny the ominous quality of a "family history" such as John's — unless, that is, we called upon Erik Erikson's work in showing the many influences, public as well as private, that combine to make us what we are.[4]

In point of fact, John — and his brothers and sisters — had learned both the melancholy and the strength in their mother's personality. She is full of doubt, hesitation, anxiety, vacillation, religious fanaticism — yes, all of it and upon occasion more. She also can be a stern, tough woman, and a very determined one. She can pray and sing; what is more, she can dissolve many of her tensions in prayer and song, in faith and in hard work. When John was under pressure he could fall back on her ability to wave aside pain, concentrate hard on the intense moment — and the distant future's promise.

Likewise John could fall back on some of his father's characteristics as well as find them a burden. His father was more to him than an "alcoholic" or an illiterate, unemployed, "severely disturbed" man — what I regret to say people like me all too often have to say, and *only* to say, about men like him. To weigh the "effects" of Mr. Washington's illiteracy (or alcoholism) on his children, we must concede right off that different effects (from parental behavior) can emerge at different times in a child's life, in anyone's life. I am convinced, for example, that in his worst (that is, most fearful) moments, John drew upon some of his father's capacity to shrug his shoulders at the world, to avoid looking at it too clearly. John shrugged off cannily the useless baggage of anxiety a fear-ridden world gave him. He had *reason* to do so; he had a *chance* — to become more than he ever was by making all that he was somehow work, and work not only for himself but for everyone he knew, for history.

Finally, John received attention and honor, from others — and himself, too. The tough side of his personality, the stubborn, crafty, inventive qualities that poor and persecuted people often develop simply to survive, found an event, a challenge that could draw upon them — make them qualities that could guarantee success rather than, as before, keep chaos at arm's length.

John went on to college, to do quite well there. "That high school became my life," John told me the day after he graduated from it. It was his answer to my curiosity about "what enabled him to do it." "That school glued me together; it made me stronger than I ever thought I could be, and so now I don't think I'll be able to forget what happened. I'll probably be different for the rest of my life."

4. *George and His Lois*

He and all like him were being punished. He wasn't sure why, but he knew the time had arrived, a time of suffering. When he talked about it he emphasized his despair with a firm shake of his head. A husky, muscular boy, George was once plain fat, I learned from old pictures shown me. Just under six feet, he carried himself well and struck me as big, regardless of particular measurements. He walked in long steps and his feet came down hard on the floor. As a child he was blond, but now he had medium-brown hair cut close to his scalp. His eyes were blue, the pale sort that makes the pupils stand out especially black. He spoke well. His sentences were somewhat terse, but they came out nonetheless in a soft, native Georgian accent. He was a bright and ambitious boy. He did well in school and he played football well.

George wanted to be a lawyer. When he went downtown in Atlanta he saw lawyers walking the streets or coming out of modern office buildings. He told me one day that he noticed their suits, heard their voices — full of influence, of law and commerce. He wanted to leap across his own years to be like them.

His father, Walter Simmons, sold insurance; but not very much of it, so he had to collect premiums, too. Many hours every week he went to Negro homes. He rang the bells, stood outside or moved just slightly inside, took the money and handed back a receipt. Sometimes, beyond a greeting and a farewell, he would comment on the weather. He was familiar with "the colored" and understood them. He insisted upon that rather like a teacher essentially uncertain about a pupil, but trying to forget his doubts: "They're fine. I don't have anything against them. I know them. I've been in their homes. Every day I go and talk with them. They trust me. I can go through any one of their streets and they know me. They say hello to me; a damn sight more than the fancy liberals can say. Those people, those liberals, they don't even know what a nigra home is; and they're not going to find out either. All they want is the nigra's gratitude and his vote. It's a fad with some of our white people. They think they're sophisticated, because their Northern friends have come down here and told them it's the smart thing to do. I'm not against nigras. I just want us here and them there. If that's being against niggers [he did that, slipped from "nigra" to "nigger" unpredictably] then I'm against them. I still say I'm more for them than some of their so-called friends are."

Mr. Simmons comes from a small town in the south of Georgia. He grew up poor, "farm-poor" he once put it. He graduated from high school only because he was a tough and determined boy; three sisters and two brothers did not. After we knew one another for several months he admitted that one of those brothers takes an active part in the Klan.

To Mr. Simmons anyone who joins the Klan is ignorant rather than malicious; and so for a long time he pitied his brother and worried about George's future. He wanted much for his son. He wanted him to be educated, so that he would never ride about in white robes, swearing and "behaving the fool." He wanted the boy to rise, to find a place in the city's growing life, to become a lawyer or a businessman. He was essentially a modest man, yet he felt he had gone far. His accomplishments now served as a launching pad for his son, though suddenly the boy's last year of high school seemed in jeopardy. Even his college career might be affected. They had no money for private schools like many of the so-called integrationists in the city: "We're taking it on the chin for them. They send their children away, and *then* they support integration. Their children will go to college anyway, integration or not. It's our schools that will be damaged." He talked as if he and some of his neighbors were as long-suffering and abused as the Negro.

Mr. Simmons is a tall man, white-haired before his time, well-built and trim for his late forties. He doesn't drink, but he smokes a pack of cigarettes a day. He watches his diet very carefully; both of his brothers have had coronaries and have been warned against fats.

He keeps his family in a pleasant house. He seems ashamed of it, comparing it to heavily eaved Tudor homes a few miles away. In fact his house is impressively decorated with comfortable yet proper furniture. Mrs. Simmons takes care of that. She is a breezy, amiable, plump person, of medium height. She has light-blond hair, touched slightly by gray. She storms into a room, taking it over with an improbable walk, toes always pointing outward and other parts of her body revolving around several axes. When sitting she fastens her hands upon her chubby arms, often pinching or rubbing them as she talks. Her voice has a forceful high pitch to it — perhaps she was meant to be a Northern dowager — as well as the inevitable drawl. "I think you've talked long enough, so I just thought I'd come in for a minute and have you all take a breather with some refreshment," would be her way of joining us and then never for a moment leaving.

She had always felt sorry for dark people, and now she resented their ingratitude. She had grown up with them; indeed, they had cared for her and loved her. She knew that most of them didn't want to do what a few of them were now planning to do: threaten her and her son and others. She had talked with her maid. She had talked with her mother's maid, who was her old nurse. Both of them confirmed what she knew: a small "element" was ruining things for everyone, black as well as white. She couldn't understand how all this trouble had come upon her family and the city of Atlanta. She disliked her husband's bitter remarks about her native city. It wasn't the "Northern-bought city" he claimed it to be. She was as much Southern as he, and her family *came* from Atlanta. They saw it burn and they helped rebuild it. No one was running Atlanta but Southerners, and most Atlantans were as much against letting a Negro in a white school as she was. Yes, they were doing it. What else *could* they do? She would turn to her husband and remind him that they had lost. Somehow they had lost, a war and then a series of legal battles. He would slouch a little when she started reminding him of it all, episode after episode. He would fall back before her historical fire, then he would rise to remind her that they hadn't lost. For seventy-five years of American history, until very recently, they had won. Why surrender now? She had no reply. After all, she never meant to get into politics or history. They are subjects for men. She turned to serving the coffee.

The boy listened, and found it hard to stop either of his parents once they had started. He waited silently, but appeared to side with his father. Perhaps after desegregation began he would be able to join their conversation, and add to it the strength of his unique experience. Two were coming to school with him; two he did not want there. He had nothing personal against them. They would probably try to be nice enough. They would smile and try to please. It was all of them, from all over the South, who bothered him. They were trying to push their way where others didn't want them, where they themselves didn't really want to be.

Before school opened George was filled with anger, confusion, and self-reproach: "We deserve it, because you get what you ask for in this world. I don't blame the few nigger kids who are going to come over to our schools, though I have no use for them because they're spies, paid by the NAACP. It's us I'm blaming, because I don't believe that we have to do this, and I don't believe it's right to do. People say we have no choice, but we do. We can make sure those two don't have a picnic. They've got a few surprises coming."

He spoke like a trial lawyer during some of our talks. He was not simply relating information but aiming to persuade me. I could not fail to notice his genuine sense of being victimized. Nor have I ever been able to forget the curious mixture of warmth and sly indifference in his talk about Negroes: "I've grown up with them. I was taught my first lessons by them. I can remember walking beside our maid Martha. I can picture her even now. She left when I was five and they went North. My father gave her a long lecture and she said she wanted to stay but her husband wanted to leave, because he had a brother up in Chicago someplace. They tell me that I cried when I heard she was leaving and wouldn't be coming back; but I don't remember anything of that. I do remember that we got another one, but she only stayed a few weeks, because she used to steal liquor and drink while she worked, or something; it isn't really clear to me. Then we got Beatrice, and she's been with us ever since. She comes here five days a week and stays with us and cleans and she helps with some of the cooking. I'll bet I respect her and like her more than the Yankees do in New York or the other cities. I've been up there; we went there one summer. I never saw people pushed around the way niggers are in Northern cities. We haven't a slum in the South to compare with their Harlem. Take Beatrice, she doesn't want integration. She's happy with what we have, and she said she'd never go North. She irons my shirts and cooks breakfast, and she sits and sips coffee sometimes when I eat, and then we talk like real close friends. I just don't see how her children would ever come to our school. I don't see how Beatrice would have any respect for us if we let them. She'd lose all use for us. I think she'd think we're getting soft in the head or something. That's what people don't know up there, how we get along with our niggers." He turned plaintively earnest and continued with a long description of what his land and his forebears had suffered from carpetbaggers: the blood spilled, the tears poured, the unfairness of history. If his argument was a recital of clichés, they were clichés that aroused strong emotions in this young, busy, intelligent boy who was about to enter his last year of high school and prepare for college.

Of course, George was not always serious about Negroes. He could relax and show another kind of mood: "I do believe that it's going to be proved more funny than anything else in the long run. I think we'll have to go along with this until we've shown the rest of the country how silly it is. They've been turning on us and shouting, 'Love Your Niggers.' The joke is, we do, but not in the way they want. Eventually they'll find the truth out, that we live with them and love them. In the North they read about them and *say* they love them, until they get too close, when they start hating them real good. To be honest, I just don't think they're suited for our schools. Take Beatrice. I used to explain things to Beatrice. I would tell her what the newspapers said. (She can barely read, even though she's had eight years of schooling.) I would point out a place on the map to her, and the next day she just forgot everything, the news and the cities on the map. Of course, maybe she's smarter than we are. What difference does it make, knowing what's going on in Europe or Asia? Beatrice is earthy. She knows about people, not geography."

Negroes or no Negroes, George came to his high school that September; and so did two Negro girls. He told me that no one wanted them. Well, maybe a few did — he would turn statistician and hazard an estimate of one or two per cent. In the first weeks of school he could find only one boy who was really "soft on niggers," and that was because his father was a Northerner who had come South with a new factory. The boy was willing to say out loud that he didn't care one way or the other about desegregation. "He'll learn to keep that opinion to himself though," George noted, and then went on to say why: "When he's face to face with how we all feel he'll know enough to go along with us." George didn't plan to be violent. He would never try to attack the two girls — or the boy. He thought the girls would soon leave of their own accord when they began to realize they were truly unwanted. As for the boy, his attitude was totally unrepresentative. The whole affair was an unnecessary misunderstanding that would soon be cleared up by determined aloofness on the part of white students and teachers.

George did well in school. He always had, and the final year would be no exception. He was consistently on the honor roll, and in English compostion he led the entire senior class. His speech was ordinary, sometimes going beyond that to show a spontaneous eloquence. On paper he had a knack for good phrasing, and often his teacher told him how much she enjoyed his themes. He also excelled in French, a dubious distinction to his father, who distrusted foreigners and suggested that science or mathematics might be more "useful." In his reply the boy made a commitment: lawyers had to know words, even foreign words.

For that matter, one of George's first surprises was "her tongue." The Negro girl spoke well, "better than you would expect," he said. He listened to her so closely, she took so much of his attention, that he decided one day she was a distraction. He began ignoring her. To do so required also ignoring his parents' curiosity. His mother wanted to know what she wore. His father asked whether she talked "nigger talk." He attributed her neat appearance, her tasteful clothes, her quiet, well-spoken manner to the fact that she lived near white people and had been influenced by them. The "other one" — as he called her to his parents — was not in any of his classes; but he saw her around, and she was a tough-looking girl. Her face was sour; she never seemed to smile. The one in his class did though. He didn't like that smile; he was unnerved at the way it came across her face whenever someone was nasty to her. He could understand that she was anxious, but her apparent good humor confused him: "She's as tense as can be; I can tell. She sits around with no one to talk with, and you can see her worrying about what's going to come next. I've seen her eyes moving back and forth. She tries to see what's happening around her, but she's afraid to move her head and look. If she did she'd see us looking right back at her. You can feel the tension in the room; it's so thick you can almost cut it. The teachers are as nervous as anyone. We can tell by how they watch us and get excited at any noise we make. They're afraid we're going to start something. She's really brought a police state with her; she comes with detectives to school, and now the school is enforcing every little rule and regulation to protect her. Maybe that's why she has that silly smile on her face. She knows we're suffering too."

Smoking had always been forbidden at school, but the students had been able to do it in off moments and places without much interference if they were reasonably discreet. Since law and order were so emphasized during those first weeks of desegregation, all laws had to take on new force. "You'd think *we* were the criminals instead of those two," he told me on the third day of school, with what seemed to him unimpeachable logic. He went on with his description: "She ruins every class she's in. We're not the way we used to be. Everything is so silent a lot of the time, and we're wondering what will be the next move. One or two sit near her, but mostly she's surrounded by empty seats, and no one will work with her in the lab, so the teacher helps her out. We don't know whether we'll have our regular graduation picnic and dance, or whether she's going to ruin everything. You look forward all those years to the last one, and then you get tough luck like this. I don't know what we did to deserve this."

Two weeks later he felt more relaxed. He and his friends had been a furtive but successful bother to her. His closest friend had pried a message into her locker saying "Go Back to Africa." George didn't think he would have been able to do that, though he admitted feeling the urge, and he certainly could understand the deed. Then he reconsidered. He could imagine himself doing precisely that, though it would depend on the girl: "To be honest, I think I might if we had one here like I can imagine us getting if this continues. Then I might go ahead and try it every day."

Two months after the year had started he was talking about the end of the year. He was looking at college bulletins more than his high school books. About that time in the course of a discussion about colleges he turned and asked me where I thought Lois would go. He had called her by her first name, and he wanted to know about her future — simply because he was curious. I knew that Lois had not yet made up her mind, and told him that. He knew better though. She would not want to go on with integrated education. How did he know that? Well, he didn't *know* it; he surmised it, he gathered it, because he saw the hard time she had at school. He wasn't really sorry for her, but he wasn't really against her either. He spoke neither kind words nor harsh words. George thought lawyers evenhanded above everything else, and he was beginning to demonstrate that he could command the tone of a neutral observer in talking about Lois.

I remember an afternoon in early December when he lost that impartiality. One of the Negro transfer students, not one in his school, had returned to a Negro school, amid considerable public speculation about the hazard and burden of being one of two or three Negroes in a large white school. George backed his governor to the fullest: "I think he's right. She's being used by the NAACP like all of them are. If she wants to go back on her bargain with them because she's sick and needs a rest, that's her right, without the niggers pressuring her to stay. They're not really interested in how colored people live anyway. All they want is power for a few of themselves." His governor said that he felt the health of the girl was more important than any other consideration, and George agreed. He was quite angry at the NAACP; they were responsible for the girl's troubles. He moved from her to Lois: she wasn't happy as she probably imagined she would be in a white school. It was nearly Christmas; the year was half gone and she was still all alone. He thought the strain was beginning to tell: "She's not as smiling as she used to be. She tries hard to find a reason to smile, but there isn't any, and so she sits there most of the time pretending to read or write. I can tell she's not doing either, though. She spends too much time on a page, like you do when you're wanting to read or fill up an empty piece of paper but can't, because your mind just won't concentrate." He was right. Their descriptions matched perfectly; hers, of the refuge she sought in books and her inability to read them; his, of how he could see that her eyes were not moving with lines of print, but hiding and pretending.

By early spring — and in the South that is in February — he was becoming rather protective of Lois. She was "our nigger" as against the other girl, whom he judged much less attractive and intelligent. He could talk about the obvious ability Lois showed in all subjects with little envy or bitterness. "She's smart, there's no getting around it. She holds back on revealing *how* smart because she's afraid it'll get us jealous or make us mad. But I don't begrudge her good marks; they're the only thing she's got to hold onto right now." He was now aware of how hard it was for her, and how tenacious her staying powers were. He was willing to allow her any satisfaction and support she could find in what he now comprehended to be a dogged effort.

Near Eastertime George talked about vacations, not only his but the one Lois obviously needed. Yet, would a vacation really help her? He smiled when he guessed that she would probably miss her white friends during that week. In fact she had stayed out of school for a few days before the holidays and *they* had missed *her*. They played games of mock recrimination and accusation during her absence: "We kidded one another. I told my friends they would have to pay for the sins they committed against Lois. We agreed we were probably too hard on her. You can't blame her for integration. She's as much a victim of it as we are. We all know that."

Lois wore a new dress when she returned to school after the vacation, and they all remarked that it must have been an Easter present. George asked his girl friend Ann whether it was an expensive dress, and teased her by comparing it with her clothes: "I told Ann that she had better watch out; Lois is getting more attractive by the day. I know a couple of guys who keep calling her house up. They disguise their voices and ask her out on a date. She's as polite and friendly on the phone as she is here at school. She doesn't hang up on them. I listened on an extension once, and she said, 'No, thank you,' or something like that, and I could tell in her voice she was smiling. Then we waited and so did she. There was a long pause, and finally we hung up. I don't want to do that again. I felt sorry for her. I felt bad about it." A minute later, while we were discussing what a sense of humor can do for people under stress, he had a reminder for me: "It was only a joke we pulled, the phoning. I think she must have known it. We didn't swear at her, like some have, and besides, she likes her laughs."

When Lois made the honor society George was both pleased and scornful. She certainly didn't deserve it. How could anyone ever compare the high marks she received in a Negro school with those given in a white school? Yet, he also gave a surprising and moving account of how inadequate many Negro schools are: in books, in laboratory equipment, in suitable classrooms, "in everything." He continued by letting me know that in the past Negroes had no exposure to education of any kind: "Most of them were in one kind of slavery or another for fifty or seventy-five years after the Civil War. Even now they're mainly poor. I'll bet over half of them today still can barely write their names and read the paper." So, all things considered, he did not want to deny Lois her membership in the honor society. Let her have it — to help her keep going.

One day in April she dropped her lab notebook in the corridor and before he could think about it he had picked it up. One of his friends ridiculed him, and called him a traitor. The friend didn't quite mean it, but he was surprised and angry at what George did. How could George possibly want to do anything like that? George tried hard to explain the unexplainable. He hadn't *wanted* to do it; he had just done it, without a thought, a plan or a wish. If he had it to do over, he would not — though he had to admit a certain affection and pity for Lois. She was a lonely girl; white or black, she was lonely. He reminded his friend what it was like for her every day of the year. Shouldn't they go easy on her, even try to be nice to her? Negroes and whites are different, whites superior and Negroes inferior; but *Lois* — she should be allowed to finish the school year in peace.

The friend was glad that George had talked to him, because like George he had not been without secret sympathy for Lois. He confessed to George that recently he had let her go before him. He stood aside and treated her like a lady as they both approached a door, and then he looked around nervously; if seen he would be known to everyone as a "mixer." Fortunately no one did see him; or perhaps no one cared. Only a month or two earlier pointed rudeness to Lois in just such situations was a virtual necessity.

They admitted to one another their surprising sympathy for the girl. They agreed that her ability to shake off insults was both curious and impressive. How does she do it? Could they, under similar circumstances? George thought the answer was no. He asked his father what he thought. He disagreed. Wasn't George also under a strain? Black and white together suffered when the "unnatural" was forcibly done. It was as hard for whites as Negroes, this mixing of the races. Indeed, it is harder to comply reluctantly than push one's way in because it is thought the thing to do.

In any event, George began to feel openly sorry for Lois. Once or twice, when he thought they would be unobserved, he risked a smile at her. She smiled back, making him embarrassed and angry at her. "I could feel myself in a bind," he said later, "because I wanted to say something, maybe hello or something, but I didn't dare. I just looked at her and tried not to show any reaction."

He was not always so modest about his ability to handle difficult situations. He was proud of his strenuous activity in class, in sports, in the school's social life; and he was rewarded for it by being admitted to the college of his choice, one of the best in the South. His parents asked what his friends would be doing after graduation. It was too bad about one of them, who wanted to go to college but had no money at all. It was too bad about another, so smart in many ways, yet not able to apply his gifts to conventional study. He should be more than a skilled laborer or a struggling white collar worker — but today there is no avoiding it, the future is made and sealed in the present. It was too bad also that one of George's old girl friends was "aiming low," for a nursing career. Women should go to college these days; it is absolutely necessary. If they had a daughter she would go. By the way, what was *Lois* going to do, now that she had a "white education"?

Lois was going to college, to a local Negro college. She hadn't told any of her classmates, but a teacher had asked her, so she told him, and he relayed the news to the many students who had asked about her future plans. When George told his family about Lois's plans, they were happy. They approved of her choice, and of her for making it. She *should* go to college. There was an enormous need for Southern nigras to improve themselves. Whatever their capacities, they should try to fulfill them. George's parents sometimes became angry at all niggers, but they didn't really mean "the good ones" who worked well, or the bright ones who wanted to educate themselves, or their "real" leaders, who understood Southern ways. Now Lois, she is a leader. One day she will lead other nigras in their struggle for learning. She was no integrationist, no agitator. She had made a mistake by letting herself be "used" by them, but all in all she had held her head up, and not caused any trouble. She was going to finish the year successfully, and they were proud of her, and glad she had chosen a first-rate Negro college. She was "too smart" to attend a white college. She was too discriminating to keep trying for "the impossible," races side by side, "and not even caring." In sum, she had learned how whites feel. George did not disagree with the praise lavished on Lois, but he did have the final word on the subject: "I think we've probably learned how she feels, too." After he said that, his mother asked whether anyone wanted a Coke. Then his father wondered what kind of summer job George could find.

In May school was almost over for the seniors, yet they did not know whether the traditional picnic, dance and banquet would survive the presence of a Negro classmate. There were no rules to follow except those they themselves made. They could move their picnic from segregated state land to a federal park; or they could try to arrange their dining where Lois might join them, in the school cafeteria rather than a segregated restaurant. (All the city's restaurants were segregated at that time.) Finally, they could do nothing new. They could insist upon having what other seniors had always had; and that is what they did. "The problem of Lois," as I heard it called at that time, was solved. As George and his friends told me, she was probably happy, too. How could she ever go to a dance with white people? Certainly no colored boy would take the risk of escorting her.

The graduation ceremony was another matter. Most of the students still refused to sit near Lois in class or walk near her in the halls, just as outside of school they continued to shun Negroes on buses or in stores. However, if anyone was to graduate someone would have to sit beside Lois or near her, in full public view on a large stage which would hold all of them up to the proud inspection of their families. Since tradition required that they walk onto the stage by pairs, one of them would even have to accompany Lois in the walk from the rear of the hall to the platform. Lois herself had no interest — or none she cared to mention — in any of the social activities that preceded graduation. For that matter, she was willing to accept her diploma in the solitude she had come to know so well that year. Nor did her family care very much about the graduation exercises; they would cherish memories of their daughter's barest survival rather than any happy time she had. Like Lois, they simply wanted an end to the ordeal.

George came home one day and relayed to his mother the rumor that the exercises were being changed. While it had occurred to him that a white person would have to walk beside Lois, he had concluded that Lois was entitled to that honor, just as they deserved a ritual as old as the school itself. Lois had been with them all year. They at least ought to accept her as a fellow senior, like them about to graduate. Graduation day was the last day. No one would mind walking and sitting beside her. He wouldn't, or he didn't think he would. Perhaps he would be mocked; but he doubted it. Even so, after he had thought about the possibility, he said that he didn't care. He felt sure that many in his class would support and even admire him for doing it: "You know, we never asked for that girl, and we still don't want nigras with us in school; but I think it's over for us now. We're about to go to work or college. I'll have them with me in college, right here in Georgia, so it's a fact of life I've got to live with. I don't like the other one, and I might not walk beside her, but I'd walk beside Lois any day, and I'd volunteer to do it. I've been talking about this thing with my friends, and more of them than you might expect are pretty respectful of old Lois." (That's what they had been calling her in a friendly way for several weeks, "old Lois.") "She's taken a beating, and we've done it to her. At least *I* admit *I* have. I slipped one of those notes into her locker, I admit it now — despite what I said before. I felt bad about it even then, but I thought it was right to do — and I thought if I didn't go along, I'd be in bad shape with my friends. You see, now that it's over, we're all telling one another how we *really* felt back in October or November. She has more friends now than she'll ever know. It's been easy for her lately. A couple of guys work with her in the lab, and I sat beside her myself the other day and thought nothing of it. I even sat near one on the bus the other day. I didn't like that much because I felt everyone staring at me. A lady across the way said something under her breath, and I heard it; but I really didn't care. After a while no one even seemed to be noticing anything."

In fact the usual marching order was changed. The children walked in alone, along both sides of the hall, rather than together down the middle aisle. Two girls agreed to sit beside Lois. George felt both disappointed and spared: "I would have liked to volunteer to sit near her, but I've had second thoughts too, and it's just as well."

The day after graduation George remembered his final day in high school: "We were all standing around there, the last time before graduation that night. It was the final rehearsal we were scheduled to have. Then somehow she was just standing there alone, looking sad though she still had that smile. I think a couple of girls just felt sorry for her or something. They walked up to her and started talking, and before you knew it they were exchanging autographs. (We were all doing that anyway.) Soon a few more came up to her, and then a couple of guys started laughing at them, and calling them 'nigger lovers,' but no one moved an inch or stopped talking with Lois, and just about everyone around suddenly joined in and told the guys to shut up and leave. You might have thought Lois was some big star or something, because I'd say about twenty people asked her for her autograph or wrote in her book. I went over and I asked her if I could write something — exchange autographs — and she had that same old smile and said yes. I wrote 'Best wishes' and signed my name. I didn't know what else to say. I looked at what a few of my friends had written; they wrote too many apologies to suit me. I felt bad about it all, what she went through, but I couldn't bring myself to say so. I think I was right, just wishing her the best politely. I told my mother about it when I came home, and she agreed. She said that the chief virtue of the South is our politeness. She said we've never been against individual nigras — the South has taken care of them better than any other part of the country. Dad agreed, and said it's up in the Northern cities where they're really segregated and no one cares anything about what happens to them, while down here we live close by one another, but we get the bad name anyway. In fact my father said that the day will come when this country sees worse things happen in New York or Chicago than the South has ever seen; and then there may not be girls like Lois up there, and the white students, they may *never* change."

Later George showed me what Lois had written in his book. Each letter was very clearly formed and all of them were pressed close together to spell out "Good luck. Lois." There was another Lois in George's class, but in our talks years later George has never forgotten which Lois wished him well without signing her last name.

THE STUDENTS 139

5. *The Negro Family*

The father of one Southern Negro youth who was among the first and very few to enter the white schools of his state is a college graduate who majored in sociology, then went on to be a minister. He is an unusual father, the head of a very strong and stable family; perhaps when all things are considered the very strongest that I studied. His concern for his family is apparent, and has been successfully transmitted to his children, all of whom are at once sturdy and sensitive.

Yet the son who went to a white high school fared rather poorly compared to several others whom I frankly expected not to last at all. They did last, and so did the minister's boy; but he was more visibly upset than they, and often he openly talked of calling an end to the entire struggle. He resented leaving a well-protected, well-appointed home. He missed what he left because there was so much to it. He himself once described his dilemma this way: "I wasn't brought up to face all this kind of trouble. Some of the others, yes; they've been fighting all their lives just to keep going, but not me. My mother and daddy, they brought us up to work and study, and get along nice and easy with people — the way they do. So it's a shock, leaving home to find people swearing at you, and not even being able to talk to them, to ask them why they're saying what they are."

The minister lives in a very respectable and dignified neighborhood; I suppose it could be described as anything from "Negro upper middle-class" to "black bourgeoisie." He is a forceful man, and a frank talker. In time he admitted to me that he turned to the ministry to make a living: "I studied sociology because I was interested in it, but I didn't think I could get a job as a sociologist. When I was in college there weren't that many things a Negro *could* become. Teaching and the ministry were the two big fields, or the post office. I decided on the ministry because I was interested in moral problems, and I knew I could find work as a preacher."

He is a Methodist, a "socially concerned" one he says, in the tradition of his church. For years he has sponsored a summer retreat for young couples, dedicated to family life and called "The Family As a Career." In 1961, when I first met him, he told me something about its purposes: "We try to strengthen the confidence of young husbands and wives. They are mostly religious people, but they don't know how to put their faith, their beliefs to work. Even though they come from good homes, they're not sure how to *start* a good home themselves. We have discussions, and we bring in outsiders — other ministers, professors from Atlanta University, like sociologists or experts in education and child development. There aren't too many around, but we get everyone who *is,* and we've even had one or two whites come talk to us, the liberal kind that aren't afraid to do so. (You never know when the police might hear of it and decide to intervene. They take a chance, those whites, and we're especially grateful to them.)

"I think our retreats have been a good thing. We've done it long enough to hear people talk about the effects. They feel they become better parents, better fathers and mothers. We've strengthened family life around here, and that's as important as desegregation or anything else."

The next year, 1962, I was a good deal more comfortable with him. His son's troubles had become a major problem for him — and in a way for me, too. More than with any other child I was then seeing I had to lend what support I could to the boy and encourage him to talk about the hard time he was having. In a curious way, the very favorable influences in his life had ill prepared him for the stresses he was encountering every day. His parents had most of all taught him to speak his mind, to talk with others and share his feelings with them. He had gone to good camps — one of them up North and interracial — where he met like-minded children from somewhat similar families. Now he was also at school with middle-class children — presumably the kind he would be able to approach with some ease. Instead they were grim-faced and unfriendly, while he was becoming fearful and unable to study. What is more, the Negro girl who was his ally appeared to be stronger — or tougher — than he.

"I don't know. She gets it as bad as I do, but she's a fighter, and she doesn't let things bother her. She won't even *talk* about what's happening. She tells me that she doesn't want to hear about it; there's enough to do just getting by the next class. I don't know why I'm going through this, voluntarily. It can't be right to put up with pain, when you can avoid it."

We talked, and talked. He was afraid to confide in his parents. He knew that they were hopelessly conflicted. They wanted him to last it through — as parents, as Negroes, as ordinary, decent citizens. They also felt guilty and afraid — that he was doing it all on their account, that he would be hurt in body or mind, even that they would also be hurt, by gunshot or dynamite. Here was one situation where I could stand in their stead, and help a boy by talking with him; because for him such conversation was a very familiar and necessary way to handle tensions from within — and now, without.

In 1962 I was invited to talk at the minister's summer retreat, and I reluctantly did so. I recall two days of discussion on the family — this time, for the first time, on the Negro family. In his initial address the minister had an explanation: "You may wonder why we're talking about the *Negro* family, and not family life in general, as before. I think we have gone through a real crisis these past months, all of us in the South and in Georgia. The Negro has seen that he cannot overlook his race anywhere, even in the public schools. I think that also goes for the home."

At the time I thought much of the talk empty and boring, saturated with clichés and pieties that seemed to lead nowhere. Yet later in reading over the typed tapescript of the minister's concluding remarks I found the following comment: "Our homes have been vulnerable the way no other people's have been. We were never even allowed homes until a very few years ago. All of us have pictures of our slave ancestors. How can we compare *their* lives to the lives of other American grandparents or great-grandparents? Those of us here have overcome all those obstacles. We have somehow built a tradition for family life where none existed before, and none was allowed before. However, most of our people are still too poor, too confused to know where to begin, or how. We need help in helping them. We need the government, and the good will of white people; but most of all we need ourselves, especially people like us. The strong among our race must give to the weak; and what we must give is our strength, so that their families will be able to take that strength from us and build with it, and most of all hand it down to their children."

It was rhetoric, I suppose; a minister's rhetoric. Certainly I didn't pay much attention to it then. In later years, during my follow-up visits, I saw more of the son than the father. I watched a boy become a man, and develop a strong interest in his race's origins. (He is now studying in Africa.) I last met the father in 1965, and quite by accident we stumbled into the following conversation, which I put down here almost word for word.

The minister had asked me whether I was finding any difference in the new Negro and white children I was starting to observe in the North. "No, not yet. They seem to be very much like others I've met down here."

"I would have thought there might be some difference," he responded, a bit wearily. "It's such a different world for our Negro children from year to year. I can barely recognize it myself. This year we've even stopped our summer retreat. We don't think it's right to go *off* and contemplate, when what is needed is our presence among those who can't contemplate because they can barely stay alive from day to day."

"I guess you're doing what the President said has to be done: trying to strengthen the Negro family, rather than talk about it."

"Yes, in a way that's what we're doing. But I don't like that talk about 'the Negro family.' It singles us out unfairly. Look at the white middle-class, and all its divorces and instability."

"I agree, but do you think the President or Mr. Moynihan wanted to single out the Negro that way, or for that reason? Weren't they simply saying what you've always said, what all the civil rights leaders have said — that the Negro has been oppressed, and paid a price for it?"

"I don't know what they meant to say, but most Negroes I know took it the other way around. They want what is *due* them, rather than pity and sympathy. They think that if you have to make people look *bad* or broken up before you can get the country to give them what they should have by right, then that's the same old racism and segregation at work."

"Yes, again I agree, but there has to be a *political* solution, some approach or plan that will catch the interest and concern of the nation. Most people are too comfortable to care about a lot of things that need doing. Don't you think that the Moynihan Report was done in order to collect all the important facts together, and offer them to Congress, to the courts, in a manner that would get action, get results?"

"No, I don't. I rely on what my son says more than my own thinking, to tell the truth. He's the coming generation, the next father of a family in *our* family. He feels insulted. He says all our worst points were brought up, and so once again the country has the image of the poor, shiftless Negro — or nigger."

"I'd like to ask your son whether the issue is what *image* the Negro has among certain people or what *facts* the Moynihan Report essentially wanted to stress: unemployment, faulty welfare practices, the disorganized home life that goes with social and economic insecurity?"

"That's not what we're arguing about. We know Negroes have suffered, and we know how a lot of our children have to grow up. We just don't believe that our *family* troubles should be emphasized; particularly when everyone has family problems, and the divorce rate among whites is almost thirty-three per cent. We want the *causes* of our troubles licked, not the symptoms paraded up and down — which always happens to us, anyway. You yourself told us many times that you were seeing a lot of strength in our children. Look at what some of our Atlanta families went through; and in Little Rock and New Orleans it was much worse. Is that a sign of a weak family?"

"No; but I never meant to say that because some Negro children and their families acquitted themselves well under fire, the Negro family as a rule is strong. As you know, some of these children have lived very sad and upsetting lives, family lives. They survived a crisis — a lot was going for them in *that* crisis — but in many ways they are still hurt, or limited, or whatever word you want to use. (I think any word used will get *someone* in trouble, and get somebody angry, because tempers are short during a time of change, like now.) Perhaps that is it: the Moynihan Report with its emphasis on the Negro family's disintegration (or 'deterioration' or whatever) struck close enough to a painful truth to arouse protest, particularly when it didn't seem likely that the report would be followed by action — the action you feel is necessary."

"I agree. I think if we knew that the Congress was going to vote the billions we need to clear up slums, or even would give us more protection against snipers down here and slum landlords up North — then we could have overlooked a few people seeing us in a bad light. We're used to unfair treatment, but we're tired of it, too; and each time we get it now, we're going to yell, or know why we're not yelling."

"Then you don't object to what Mr. Moynihan said, but what

you were afraid would — or in this case would *not* — come of what he said?"

"Well, I object to the way some of our politicians treat one of the most serious moral problems in our history. They always talk like ministers, like me, but they behave like heathens. They don't lead us, they try to manipulate us. I think that if the President told the people what he wants and what the Negro needs, rather than what's wrong with the Negro family, then he could get it."

"I'm not so sure. American politics doesn't work that way. I think the President's advisers were trying to do just what you say they should do — and you see to what effect."

"I don't know what they were trying to do, but they sure put salt on open wounds, instead of coming to us with the first aid we need."

"I guess I'm defending them and their purposes. I suppose to some extent I can do that, not being a Negro and not feeling as sensitive about some of these matters."

"You beat me to the punch. I think we have to be sensitive. First of all, we *are*. Second of all, it's about time we were *more* sensitive. When I think of all I didn't worry about years ago, including the Negro family, I feel ashamed. We used to have those summer retreats, but did we ever worry about the Negro family then? Not really, only about ourselves, as individuals."

"Then Mr. Moynihan may have helped you do some thinking, just as the whole civil rights movement has helped you — and him."

"Yes. To be honest though, we need action. I have a friend who teaches sociology up North, and he wrote me the other day, asking why we always *discuss* the Negro, and do so little to change things. Now that's from a man who has discussed the Negro all his life."

"The Moynihan Report was a call for action."

"It was a call to white people. It didn't speak to Negroes."

"I disagree. It spoke to Americans. It was written by a politician, in the best sense of the word; in *your* sense of a good politician. He wanted change, or action."

"You don't see how we feel, reading those headlines, about our badness, our weakness — again."

"I disagree. I see how you feel, but I guess I can't feel as you do. We keep on coming back to that."

"Yes. We do; and all over the country people will, for a long while, I think."

V

THE TEACHERS

1. *Teaching the Teacher: Miss Lawrence*

ALABAMA is her native state. She is a high school teacher, a middle-aged, buxom woman whose blond hair has effectively concealed some white for several years. She teaches English, and considers herself a hard teacher, determined to enforce grammatical rules and correct imprecise language. Though not very trim, she is neat. With her clear complexion and her hair worn nicely waved and cut fairly short, she presents a fresh appearance. She favors colorful dresses, too; when my wife complimented her on one of them she explained that the world is dreary enough, and so every little bit of "glow" counts. If there is any underlying sadness in her, it is well hidden.

Though she lives alone in Atlanta, she has several brothers in Alabama and a sister in Mississippi, all with children; and she is an adoring aunt. She admits to favorites among her four nephews and three nieces, but she manages to keep all of their pictures in her wallet.

In class she is thoroughly impartial. She combines her harsh demands in composition with a usual willingness to let the children write about anything they desire. She encourages her children to read widely. If her reputation is to be believed, she is popular but strict. A pupil said to me, "Miss Lawrence, she makes everyone work hard, but she's a nice lady, too."

Miss Lawrence went to college in Atlanta, and started teaching there upon graduating. She liked teaching in high school because she liked awakening minds, with whom she could converse and share many of her own thoughts and feelings. She particularly liked teaching juniors and seniors in high school. She could send young people into the world more sensitive and thoughtful. Sensitivity concerned her; she used the word often. She called it "the chief virtue" and she worked hard for it in all of her pupils by correcting their errors and pointing out the many shades of meaning in the books they read. "This is your last chance," she told every graduating class, "your last chance to learn English well, to be sensitive to its possibilities." As a result, a tradition had grown in the school: she was called "Last Chance Lawrence."

Years ago she had gone North to get some additional education herself. More recently she had studied at a Southern university. In both cases Negro graduate students were in attendance. She never cared much about political affairs. She would scan the paper very lightly, picking up the gist of the news but not getting into it. She preferred to read short stories, even at breakfast. While others became increasingly involved in the issue of desegregation as it was slowly fought for many years of her life, she kept her attention on Galsworthy and Dickens. She was a Southerner, though. She had never liked Northern cities. They were big and rude places, and frankly — she was shy about saying it — she found the Northern Negroes harsh and discourteous, a poor comparison to their Southern relatives. She had gone through a crisis or two in the North about race and she had learned from the experience, but she was grateful for the quiet and civility of the South: "I learned a lot about Negroes while in the North, but I think the South has some lessons in personal dignity to teach the rest of the country."

What she had learned in the North had not come so easily. She left Georgia for the North because she was an educated, sensitive Southern lady who wanted to do graduate work in education.

Negroes were her last concern when she arrived in New York City. She was interested in her courses and in the city's cultural life. She lived in a graduate dormitory. She found it convenient and in addition she felt sheltered from the unfamiliar and sometimes overpowering ways of the city. She had her own room and shared a bath with several others on her floor.

"It may seem strange to you," was the way she began to tell me about an episode of her life that had happened long ago, fourteen years to be exact. She paused, then she started again. "It may seem strange to you that a teacher like me would react to a nigra woman like I once did, but since then I've talked with a lot of people about it, and it's a more common occurrence than you'd think. I'll never quite forget the second it took place. It was an ordinary morning and I was coming out of the shower when suddenly I saw that nigra woman. There were several showers and she was standing there, drying herself. She had just come out herself (I thought about that later, you know) and we were probably taking showers at the same time. Anyway, she came out of hers just a few seconds before I came out of mine. When I saw her I didn't know what to do. It was as if I'd seen the Devil himself, or I was about to face Judgment Day. I felt sick all over, and frightened. What I remember — I'll never forget it — is that horrible feeling of being caught in a terrible trap, and not knowing what to do about it. I thought of running out of the room and screaming, or screaming at the woman to get out, or running back into the shower. My mind was in a terrible panic; I thought of everything I could do at once, but I felt paralyzed. I felt like fainting, and vomiting, too; it was shock, like seasickness; it took hold of me all over and I wondered whether I was about to die. My sense of propriety was with me, though — miraculously — and I didn't want to hurt the woman. It wasn't *her* that was upsetting me. I knew that, even in that moment of sickness and panic. Then I came to my senses. I realized I had to do something; but all I could do was just stare at her. I must have looked as pale as a sheet. It seemed like an eternity, though it probably was only a few awkward seconds. Finally, I jumped back into the shower and stayed there, listening for her to go and thinking about it all where I *could*, because I felt safer. It was awful.

"When I came back to my room I felt as if I had been through a terrible nightmare. I felt exhausted; and then I actually found myself crying. It wasn't the way you cry when you think about something or somebody, and then get sad and cry about it; it was just a flood of tears that suddenly came upon me. I only realized I was crying when I started feeling the tears on my face."

She apparently was shaky for hours after the incident. Even today she can recall the emotions — disgust, anger — she initially felt toward the Negro woman for causing the crisis. Those emotions were soon followed by shame: that she, an educated woman, had behaved so irrationally. She eventually concluded that the reason she didn't say anything to the Negro but fled was that words were irrelevant, whereas action at least extricated her from an "ugly situation." It was an explanation suited to her long-standing belief, held before she ever left Georgia and still very much in her mind, that feelings about race are deep and silent parts of a person. They do not respond to laws, but only to new experiences. "Words and explanations about race don't mean much," she explained to me. "It's what the person's life has been over the years. I was almost trembling then, and nothing a rational mind could offer — to myself or that Negro woman — would really have made sense of it to *either* of us.

"Of course, over the next few days I became more and more ashamed of myself. Finally I tried to put myself back in the shower room, but I promptly became clammy again. I was sure that if that nigra lady came in I would do the same thing again — flee. Mind you, I don't think I was prejudiced then, any more than I really am now. We grow up with certain ideas, and you can't shake them in a second."

Though she found it difficult to go back into the bathroom at all, she did, every day. She found herself dreading the time the Negro would return. She would be washing her face, and might picture the Negro staring at her after she cleared her face of soap. She would be in the toilet closet and think of the Negro opening the door and confronting her. For the first time in her life she found herself looking at Negroes more closely on the street. She noticed the clothes they wore, or whether they appeared in a movie or restaurant. "You never give some things a thought until you've gone through something like that, then you find yourself suddenly aware, even if it's out of fear.

"I can't tell you how much that split second in my life affected me. Sometimes I have to remind myself that it was *only* a split second, because it's lasted forever, in a way." She told me that one day when we decided to resume talking about her experiences in the North. "I didn't actually see the woman so that I could recognize her, though I kept on thinking that she would remember me and somehow catch up with me. I knew I wouldn't be able to pick her out in a crowd. To be honest they all look alike to me, unless I know a particular one. For a while I thought of going to a hotel or getting an apartment, but I knew that was absurd; and besides, I was more ashamed of myself than anything else.

"After a while I realized that there was more than one Negro in that dormitory; and so I'd better gird myself or do *something* to settle the matter once and for all, though I didn't know exactly what. I noticed them in the cafeteria. I looked at each of them — there were five or six, I think — wondering which one was *the* one. Of course, none paid me the slightest attention. I kept waiting for some trouble to happen, some scene to occur suddenly. It was ridiculous, I know. After several days I could sit in the cafeteria and watch them calmly. I seemed to be getting it into my system that they were just like anyone else. I had just about convinced myself of that fact when two of them came from the cafeteria line one day and sat down opposite me. I can remember the meal to this day. I had veal — breaded veal cutlets, some lima beans and mashed potatoes and rice pudding. I looked at them, and I thought I was going to have to get up. I felt sick again, really just like before. I tried to turn away. I was afraid — not only of what I felt, but afraid for them to see me. I don't think they ever had any idea what was happening, and I'm not sure I did for a while. I just sat there for a few minutes. Then I realized I couldn't eat to save myself. So I got up and left. I think I turned and smiled at them, though, almost as if I were excusing myself from the table to them. It was terrible. I was shaking all over inside; and most of all for fear they'd know what was happening. But I knew after I had left that they couldn't have noticed anything. It had all happened inside me."

What she eventually learned to do that summer was sit with Negroes and eat with them, and shower in the full knowledge that next to her, in the very next stall, there might be one. "It was hard for me myself to believe that I'd done it by the end of the summer, but I had. When I came home I wouldn't tell anyone. I didn't think they would understand. At that time people would have thought one of two things: I was crazy (for being so upset and ashamed) or a fool who in a summer had become a dangerous 'race mixer.' (Things may have changed here in the last few years, but it's *only* in the last few years.) When I came back I felt as lonely as I felt up there. Oh, today it's almost fashionable to talk about Negroes, at least among some of the middle-class people here. We've become such a Northern city, with business moving down and all those companies and their employees. In a way this is New York for all the country people who move in here from south Georgia or Alabama. They try to become sophisticated, if they make some money. They try to be like they think 'everyone' is. I don't mean to criticize them too harshly, though it does trouble me at times. I just don't approve of attacking our region, the way some of our own Southerners do now. They all laugh at what they call the 'rednecks' or the 'poor whites.' Well, I think we've *all* shared in this problem and done our share of wrong — so we've all got to take the blame for the wrongs done. I think the way to start is to be positive, accept the best of our Southern kind of relationship with nigras, then work to change all the negative things.

"Most of the children I teach come from well-to-do families, and they've been brought up to say the 'right' things about tolerance, but I wonder if they really believe their own words. I know children in the poor sections of the South who *don't* say the right things, but they are capable of real softness and kindness to nigras when they're not in school with them, in *their* [white] school. I don't mean to be hard on our middle class here, but sometimes I fear we'll lose the best in the South, and end up with another Northern climate, where people don't care about one another, regardless of race. I've seen whites ignore and insult Negroes up North the way many segregationists down here would never think of doing. I know we're paternalistic, but we do care for one another. We'll have to learn to have different kinds of caring, but I hope when we do it will be our very own kind."

When desegregation was imminent she indicated, discreetly but firmly, her interest in teaching a desegregated class. Those who could not do so, who would not do so, had been given a chance to say so. Their superiors did not wish to enforce a collision of reluctant, angry or fearful teachers with nervous children, whites for the first time with Negroes as well as Negroes with whites. "I had my doubts about integration," Miss Lawrence recalled. "Not because I didn't favor it, but I think I tend to be cautious, and I felt that perhaps we should wait a while, and educate our nigras more fully, and prepare our white people, too. I suppose I was still reacting to the experience I had up in New York. I kept on wondering what I would have done had those Negro women I finally got to know been different. What if they had been less tactful and understanding; I could have become annoyed and angry with *them,* instead of being ashamed at *myself.* When people are tense, their minds do funny things. I'm setting up a double standard, I know. I'm asking the nigra to be better than we often are. Isn't that part of the problem, though, to get us to understand one another? We made them worse, and now we expect them to be better. Yet, you have to start with human nature somewhere when you're planning a change like this. I don't think it's realistic to assume that all people are going to be able to deal with their emotions so intelligently that they can cope with some of these things easily. That's why I was so much in favor of going slowly, and carefully educating both us and the nigra for change. On the other hand, once I actually started teaching a desegregated class I wasn't so sure. I came to disagree with my own earlier attitudes." The two Negro children learned from her, one for a year, one for two years. They were the first Georgians of their race to study with a white high school teacher in a white school.

"We were as nervous as they were." I heard several teachers say the words almost as if they had all rehearsed them. Miss Lawrence described the first day of desegregation briefly: "You could hear a pin drop. Those children just sat there and they looked as if at any moment a frightful disaster, a tornado or something, might come upon them. It was obvious that none of them wanted to sit near the Negro child, and yet they were so curious you could read it all over their faces. I'll have to admit it, I was, too. How were we to know what might happen? After a while you realize that we *should* know, because we're the same old people, the same old teacher and children, in the same old room; some scattered dark faces don't make it any different. But you have to go through it to know it, or we did. No one else ever had in Georgia."

She felt that she had never faced so strenuous a year. Before school even opened she found herself aware of the loneliness the Negro children would experience, and the fear and confusion the white children would feel. She briskly started her first class with a firm declaration of her wish for "order"; she would insist upon it in her classroom, and everyone must know that, and not forget that. Then she outlined the year's work before them. She wanted them to realize they had come *together, to work.* She wrote the three words on the blackboard; she then underlined them slowly.

They did work; she made sure of that. She allowed no non-sense. She never had in the past, and this was hardly a year to start doing so. Work, she reasoned, would unite them. It would dampen the tension in them, and thwart the stirrings of hate and violence. She had always watched her students closely. In fact, until this year, she had grown tired of the mechanics of teaching. There was just so much that one could do with the same books, the same stories, year after year. What saved it all was that she had never tired of watching adolescents. They grow in so many different ways. This year she expected to see more growing than she ever had before.

The first weeks were filled with apprehension and uncertainty, with more of both in the teachers than the children; or at least more that she could recognize. "We are so much more fixed than they are. We can't help it, we're older. We've lived with segrega-tion as a fact of our entire lives. Take lynching; lynching was hardly protested when I was a girl. Our children may oppose integration, but it's a fact of their young lives, not something strange and impossible, the way it seemed to me for so long. I really don't think any of our young people will run away nearly screaming from a Negro in a college room the way I did."

Miss Lawrence read constantly. In the early morning she would rise to enjoy the best hours of her day, relaxing over coffee and jellied toast, and reading "Mr. McGill." Often she talked to me of Ralph McGill. "I read Mr. McGill like the word of the Bible. He's not as popular down here, you know, as I think he is in the North. We've been calling him names for years; my closest friend does. She'll read a column of his and then call me up to tell

me what a terrible person he is, how he's against all things Southern. In my opinion, Mr. McGill should be declared a college, a
one-man fully accredited college, by the Association of American
Colleges. I've wanted to write him that for years, but I'm shy at
such things. I think all of us have been prodded by him, even
those who keep on calling him ugly names. He has courage, and
he has a sense of timing. He doesn't say something and then
forget it. He knows what a teacher knows, that you have to
repeat and repeat, and not despair when your students seem
apathetic or even resistant. He's been doing that for years,
patiently saying things that the rest of us were afraid to say, and
maybe even became angry at him for saying — I suspect as much
out of shame as anything else. He never got too far ahead of
us — that's what I mean by good timing — and he never left us
impatient or in despair. I think all this means that I feel he really
is one of us, and he knows what's happening here. I don't resent
the Northerners who come down here and preach at us, or write
their books after a two-week tour of a couple of Southern cities. I
just don't pay any attention to them. People going through what
we are going through have to learn from themselves. Mr. McGill
is of us, and he writes for us."

All that year she kept watch over what her children learned at
school: "I've never kept my eyes so fastened on a class." She kept
scrutinizing herself, too. "How can you plan some of these
things?" she asked herself and me one day. "You can plan all day
and predict until the world ends, but there's no way for anyone to
be sure about how children will act. Some of the children I would
have thought least likely to approach those nigras have done it so
nicely and casually, while others I thought their potential friends
are afraid to lift a finger, or risk a shred of their 'reputation.' The
first thing I learned was kindness and decency didn't have anything to do with I.Q. scores or grades. There's the matter of heart
and compassion, and say what you will about intelligence, I'm
not sure it has all that much to do with sensitivity. What I mean

is that the very broadest kind of intelligence will include sensitivity; but I'm thinking of a very able student of mine — he gets almost all A's. He cares much more for his own memory and how well he can use it to get a high mark from me than for what is happening around him, to white people or black people, to any fellow human being."

The teachers talked to one another, comparing experiences and attitudes much as their students did. Miss Lawrence did this not only in her own school but with friends she had in other schools. All her friends agreed upon the need for outward calm and firm discipline, regardless of the turmoil in the students. Some wanted to go further, help bridge the silence and hesitation between dark and white students. Yet, any move in this direction required planning. The pulse of the class had to be carefully estimated day by day. The image was Miss Lawrence's and she continued it with the remark, "You can't treat a condition until you take stock of it.

"It's like anything else, what happens in the classroom will depend on us and the children both." She was evaluating the progress of desegregation, and emphasizing some of the variables. "I've been collecting stories this year, because each school is different, and even the classes in them." She gathered obvious pleasure from telling about teachers in one school peeking into a classroom during the first days. "I can just imagine what the parents or children would think if they saw that scene, a group of teachers behaving like children looking in a store window. Well, it was quite a novelty, and we're human like everyone else. Look at all those TV people who came around the first few days, and the reporters, too." Then she liked to mention the incident with the psychological facet to it: "I think you would be particularly interested in what happened to another English teacher. She was no integrationist, just a hard-working teacher. The first week she assigned a theme which was to be titled "My First Week at School," or something like that. She has been assigning that topic for years, and so have I. Would you believe that out of all her classes, with all those children, she received only a small handful of themes which even mentioned desegregation in connection with the first week of school? Imagine that, with all the police and the nationwide publicity, with all the coverage on television, those children were simply afraid to mention the subject. They ignored the most important thing to happen that week, or that year. It shows you what the mind can do. I've often wondered whether it was a deliberate thing, whether they were simply frightened, or whether it was unconscious and they really forgot. I suppose those children reflected the atmosphere around them: everyone was holding out on everyone else; no one really dared to say what he thought, or no one except a very few outspoken segregationists. Even they were quiet at first, at least in school itself. Those were crucial times, those first weeks. All kinds of attitudes were set, or for that matter prevented, by the policies we teachers adopted."

She felt that about her work generally, that teachers can do a lot. She was proud of her profession. "It all depends upon what you want, I mean what the teacher wants. The first thing, as I keep on saying, is that children must learn; nothing must be allowed to interrupt that. After that, it's almost a matter of what the teacher decides to do, of what her goals are. I know two history teachers who teach the same course. One of them sticks to facts and events; the other is concerned with ideas and ideals. Isn't that the same alternative that faces all of us in this situation, too? I teach English — grammar and composition as well as literature. Yet, I don't think a day passes that I don't have some opportunity to draw some moral, some more universal message from our work together in class. I've always done that, telling them how important order is, in punctuation or driving on the road, to preserve us from chaos. Of course, when we read *Macbeth* or any of the novels they select, from Dickens to Conrad, there's unlimited chance for talk about personal freedom, tyranny and what have you. Sometimes I wish we adults could see things the way some of these youngsters do. My purpose, as I see it, is to encourage the best and curb the worst in every class I teach. I know I can do it. I believe it's as much a matter of the teacher's desire as anything else, at least in a school like this, in what you might call a middle-class area. With very poor children I think it's only natural for teachers to lose a lot of their interest and concern. It's so hard to fight hunger and the bitterness it produces.

"In our school a teacher can play it as safe as she wants. She can let the children know that she cares about facts only, or she can take an interest in them as human beings. It has to be both, I believe. If I see *any* child lonely or terrorized, I feel that if he is going to learn, something must be done about his terror as well as his answers in tests. If I see a brute or bully at work, I've got to help him, too, or he'll flunk more than my examinations. I don't believe in all this psychology, this psychological approach, they call it. I believe in *teaching*. They have fancy new names for all that we do today, but any teacher worth anything always has known a lot of these things intuitively, don't you agree with that?"

She would pause, then launch into examples: about how she helped the two Negro students speak up, by calling upon them firmly but sympathetically; about how she sensed real fear in a white girl and consequently spoke with her after class, telling her that she herself, a grown woman, a school teacher who had traveled far in America, and beyond, too, had gone through some moments like that in the past, moments of tension and irritability and a sense of being *cheated*. "I said to her that she felt tricked, that was the word I used, and I could see her face respond — she knew that I was telling the truth, because I had supplied a word, an accurate word, for her confused feelings."

Miss Lawrence characterized the first two years of desegregation in Atlanta as "the two most exciting years" of her teaching career. "I've never felt so useful, so constantly useful, not just to the children but to our whole society, American as well as Southern. Those children, all of them, have given me more than I've given them. They've helped me realize that some unpleasant times in my own life were not spent in vain. That's a privilege, to be able to have your life tested and found somewhat consistent, at least over the long haul. I guess I grew up there in New York, and used the strength from it down here later on. I was just another teacher up North for the summer, but it made me a better Southerner, a better person, for a long time afterward."

2. *Closer to My People: Martha Simpson*

"Why should I encourage children to do something when I know if they go ahead it'll mean my job; and worse, the children will soon lose all respect for us. They'll forget all we've done for our people; and what a strange twist that will be. For generations we have tried to keep some hope going. We tried to keep educating our people even when they were right to ask us what difference any education made, except for the few educated Negroes the white world was willing to accept. But we kept on saying, come on to school; learn your reading and writing — no matter its use — just learn so that your children can have something to hang on to, a shred of self-respect. They listened, too, even if they laughed at us all the while.

"My grandma once asked me, 'What you want to teach for?' I told her that I wanted to keep children on their toes so that one day when we're free we'll be able to appreciate our freedom and do something with it. She understood that. She said to me, 'Girl, you have faith, talking like that; you do.' I still remember her saying those words. I was thinking about it the other day, and I'm not sure I do have faith any more; because I'm real torn up between what my head knows is right and what people say my skin should tell me to believe, so to speak. I feel in danger. It's like someone who has been leading all along; suddenly he sees people are running out in all directions away from him, and he's all alone, wandering and ignored."

Those words came as a surprise to me, and I think to her also. We had been having weekly talks for several months, and at first she was quite guarded, enough so that I completely misjudged her. I had been noticing her carefully chosen words, without exception assembled in short and neutral sentences, so that when she made the above remarks I had a hard time realizing that the vivid, flowing speech was actually hers.

Like our talk until that moment, her apartment was correctly furnished, everything blending, dust nowhere evident. When I once complimented her on the view from her parlor, and added how nice the room was, too, she responded rather directly: "Yes, I like the room. The sun shines in it most of the day, so it is always bright; and I try to keep it as clean as it is light."

She herself is a rather light Negro. When I met her she was twenty-nine, though she seemed older to me, perhaps in her late thirties. I was to learn that by her twenty-first birthday she had lived a full life. She was born in Mobile, her mother a house-keeper to a well-known lawyer. She was named Martha, after her mother and her mother's mother, Martha Simpson. She knew who her father was, and one day — two years after I first met her — she showed me his picture, the lawyer's brother. She was shy about the matter, a shyness strongly related to her respect for the institution of marriage: "You must know how common it is in the South for Negro women to bear white men's children, though we're all illegitimate of course, regardless of what any couple might wish, because interracial marriage is against the law. Then they call us immoral when we don't marry one another. It's too much for me to make any sense of it all."

Her mother was a tall, very dark woman of obvious beauty. In pictures the upward angle of her head, the direct, open look in her eyes communicated her pride. "Even when I was a little girl I remember noticing how much assurance she had about herself. There she was, waiting on people and cleaning up after them, but there was something about her that made me think she was once a queen, if there is such a thing as migration of souls. I remember asking her when I was six or seven if she wasn't really white, somehow. I don't know why I did it, I mean what made me say that; but I did. She became cross with me. Even now I can recall her giving me a hurt look and telling me to go do something to get me out of her way. Later, when she was putting me to bed, she brought it up herself. She told me about my daddy being white, and she said that you can be proud of yourself regardless of how others see you, that what you know about yourself is as important as anything you can see in the mirror. I can see that mirror today — see it better than my own furniture. My mother nodded at it while she was talking.

"We lived in that house in Mobile until I was fourteen. There were just my mother and me, and we were very close. We shared the same bed and we did everything together. She insisted on walking me to school every day until I was ten or eleven. All the other kids laughed at me, but I was glad. They used to tell me my mother acted like she was white, and that I did, too. 'You two think you're special'— I must have heard that once a day. If it wasn't that, it was 'high yellar' I was being called. (For a long time I didn't even know what that expression meant.)

"I think I started becoming a teacher when I was in the fourth or fifth grade. I did very good work, and the teacher asked me to help her with the slower children. I was very honored, and studied even harder at home to make sure I would be able to equal the teacher and keep on working for her. My mother wanted so very much for me to go to college and be a teacher. I think it became the one ambition of her life, that I not do what she was doing, that I become a leader, a teacher. To her the words were equivalent."

When she was twelve her mother's boss died of a heart attack, and soon afterward his widow closed their mansion. "I can't forget. I had just become a woman. I remember my mother cried. She was 'packing us up,' as she put it, and on top of it all she had to attend to me and my sudden bleeding. I think she connected the two things, because I recall her saying: 'God never closes a door but he opens another.' "

They moved to Atlanta because they had relatives there. "My mother had four sisters and her favorite one lived a few miles outside Atlanta. We were originally from Alabama, though, near Montgomery. My mother's daddy worked a farm on shares, a sharecropper as it's called. He had work enough to hold his sons — he had four of them; but the daughters no. My mother and her two older sisters went South; she went to Mobile, Aunt Hattie to Pascagoula, Mississippi, and Aunt Lorrie, the oldest, to New Orleans. It was Willi-Jean, the youngest, who went to Atlanta and married a postal man. He is a college graduate, my Uncle James. He majored in chemistry and wanted to be a scientist; but you know how it was then, twenty-five years ago. No matter, though, he had my aunt go to high school and graduate. Then she went to college, and she graduated there, too, the first one in the family. I'm the second. She's a teacher now in Macon, Georgia. They moved there five years ago to be near his daddy when he was dying, and they decided to stay."

Slowly she told me about her stormy adolescence in Atlanta. The city seemed to work some evil magic on her, or so she now sees it. Yet, at the time she saw her arrival there as the signal of her freedom — it was as if she had finally reached the North. The liberation was to be from her mother.

She enrolled in a junior high school, and was quickly seen for the bright and attractive girl she was. In Mobile her mother would take her to a library used by Negroes and sit beside her while she read books. She recalls protesting to her mother that the main library was much finer, and had more books. Her mother pointed out that she was guessing, since Negroes were not allowed inside the building. In any event, until she had read every book in the segregated library the issue of comparative facilities mattered very little, or so the mother insisted.

In Atlanta, where Negroes could use the main library, the girl began to pay no attention to books. She was put in a special section for bright girls, but gradually lost interest in study. She was constantly surrounded by admiring boys, and she grew to depend upon that fact. "As I look back it was almost like a drug or something like that. At first you don't particularly find it pleasant; but it grows on you. Before you know it you can't do without it."

In her own words, she went "boy-crazy — just wild boy-crazy." It was a long spell of craziness, too — three years. She barely stayed in school. Her mother all the while worked as a domestic and prayed hard. "She used to tell me that one day the Lord would have time to notice my behavior and get me to stop it. I thought she was being silly, talking that way, but I was probably scared, too. I've always believed in God."

In point of fact she became pregnant by one of her classmates when she was a junior in high school. She had to leave school and stay at home while she carried the child. At once the whole troublesome period of rebellion ended, as if its purposes had been accomplished. "I felt fulfilled," she said. She felt her mother's equal, grown-up, and uninterested any longer in boys or parties. She started reading hungrily again, often going to the library in the morning as if she worked there and staying until it closed.

Her pregnancy was uneventful, but her child was delivered with great difficulty. Most first babies come slow and hard, but hers was apparently an exceptionally complicated case. When the baby girl was born the doctors were fearful that she had suffered some brain damage, and their fears eventually proved justified. Miss Simpson gave her complete attention to her child, but as the baby failed to develop normally, failed to walk on time and talk on time and show appropriate coordination, the mother became

sad and bitter. "'I'm the child's grandmother,' my mother told me
one day, 'and I want you to let me take care of her part of the
time and you go back to school.' So I did."

She graduated from high school at nineteen, an elderly valedic-
torian. She had studied hard upon her return, and her old interest
in books (all books, not just school texts) had been revived. "I
sometimes felt I had to read for two people, because I knew my
daughter wouldn't be reading herself." She was offered a full
scholarship to Atlanta University's Spelman College, and she
accepted it. "I decided to become a teacher. My mother always
wanted that and suddenly I decided I did, too."

The mother had found an evening job washing office floors so
that her daughter could go to high school. Together they divided
up the day and the care of the baby, one coming home at three,
the other working from four to midnight. The baby remained a
baby, making her physical care dishearteningly similar from
month to month.

By the time the girl was four both her mother and her grandmother realized she would have to be placed in a home for
retarded children; yet both hesitated, and neither was able to
take up the subject openly with the other. The child had intermittent convulsions, the kind of epilepsy that so frequently afflicts
such children. She also tended to fall ill easily, suffer cold after
cold and a succession of pneumonias. "Every time she had a fit, or
took sick with a fever, I thought she would die. My mother and I
took such good care of her, we couldn't understand why she ever
became sick. I tried to teach her, too. I certainly learned patience
doing that, and you have to have patience if you are going to
teach."

The girl died one day, victim of a lung infection that simply
would not yield to a series of antibiotics. Two months later, in
December, the child's grandmother collapsed at work, was rushed
to a hospital and pronounced dead on arrival. Her daughter
asked for an autopsy and learned that her mother had suffered a

major stroke. The following June — 1955 — their one survivor received her college degree. "I recall just standing there, all by myself. I was twenty-three years old, and with no one to turn to for a smile or a handshake. But I had my degree, and I decided right there I'd live faithful to my mother and to my daughter: I would teach and I would teach children who can learn to appreciate what a gift it is just to be able to go to school and find out about the world. I suppose that's why I'm such a hardworking teacher; my life is in the job."

I met her because one of her students was soon to attend an all-white school in Atlanta, and I wanted to know what she thought about his ability to manage the challenge. Moreover, she had sternly advised him not to make the choice he did. "My best teacher told me not to apply," were the words that first brought her to my attention. "She said I shouldn't go to the white schools and plead with them to take me in and maybe one or two more Negroes, when I can study real hard where I am and in the long run prove to them that we can succeed without their help."

When I heard that I was surprised. It had frankly never occurred to me that an able Negro high school teacher would strive so hard to keep her children out of white schools. Up to that time I had been working with an embattled Negro community in New Orleans, one that was unanimous in its will to persist in the face of the mobs. The Negro teachers I knew in New Orleans were solidly in favor of desegregation, perhaps because they were so outraged at the sight of such little girls being so relentlessly harassed. One of them told me quite frankly that she knew she would lose her job, were full integration eventually to occur, "but I'd rather go back to washing laundry the way my mother did than see our children kept in these terrible buildings. I don't think I would have felt as I do, though, if it wasn't that I actually saw how far those mobs would go with our little girls. I'll have to admit that from a selfish point of view many of us Negro teachers don't want integration. Some may fool themselves and make up excuses about how much better it is for the child to stay with his own kind. I used to say that, too. I told my husband that it's easier to lose a job and money than self-respect. I couldn't live with myself if I tried to prevent desegregation just because I make a profit from it; not after seeing what those four families went through."

Of course in Atlanta there were no mobs, and there was in fact a strong case to be made for advising youths of fifteen or sixteen to finish the last year or two of their education in the same (segregated) school system they had been attending for years. It is asking a lot of a young man or woman nearly through with school to give up friends, familiar routines and all the pleasures of a graduating year for the sake of a lonely, fearful career as a Negro in a white high school of the South.

Not all Negro teachers in Atlanta argued as Miss Simpson did against integration. The youth I was interviewing told me one day: "You should go see Miss Simpson. She teaches us English and when she wants to say something, she sure gets it across. She's the one who almost made me change my mind; not my mother and daddy, but her. She just told us all those reasons one after the other, and you have to fight to keep your own mind against hers."

I took his advice and eventually called upon Miss Simpson, the first of a series of Southern Negro teachers I would eventually get to know. In time I came to know the story of her life, came to know and understand how hard she has fought for her present position, how proud she is of it, how reluctant to see it lost. Yet, more than selfishness prompts her to tell children they should prefer "their own" schools to the white schools. She knows and believes in the virtue of self-improvement. She also claims that she knows white people: "White people won't change until we've forced them to see us differently, because we *are* different, we've *become* different."

I expected her to change her mind eventually, though I did not expect to see the day; her taciturn and abrupt manner made me feel that each visit should be the last. Slowly, however, she talked more easily and as she did her honest interest in schoolchildren became apparent. I began to see how hard it was for her, caught between her own interests, the everyday truth as she saw it in the classroom, and the historical interests of her race. Long after we first met she reiterated her position on school desegregation, and finally I felt able to challenge it by saying quite openly what I thought accounted for her attitude: "Miss Simpson, I think maybe if you weren't a teacher in a Negro school you might have a different viewpoint." She looked right at me and replied quickly: "I know you think that, and it's true of many Negro teachers in Southern schools; but I honestly believe I feel the way I do because of my life and not my job. My mother brought me up to be proud, not just of my race, but as a person. I think when a child goes to a white school and is told he's not wanted, and has to demand his rights, but then be afraid from day to day, he loses his pride, his sense of self-respect. I think it's a fact that we're not welcome, and the only way we can change that fact is by developing ourselves so fully that the whites want to come to *our* schools."

We spent much of our time discussing that viewpoint. She argued resolutely. She acknowledged right off — before I dared say it — that to some extent her ideas resembled both those of Booker T. Washington and those of the Black Muslims: "It's ironic that I seem to sound like the so-called Uncle Toms and the Black Muslims. We're so anxious to 'integrate' that some of us are willing to lose ourselves, to disappear. I don't believe in denying our own culture and our own heroes. My children may look down on Booker T. Washington when they start in my class, but not when they're through. Why should we criticize a man *now* for what he said generations ago. You could do that with George Washington, too, or Jefferson or Lincoln. We Negroes are so defensive. We're willing to give up everything we have, and sometimes I wonder for what. To go to school with rude, nasty children who insult us and show how uncivilized *they* are. Of course I don't agree with the Muslims, either. They make separation a virtue, and not a sad fact of life. What I am arguing for is that we look at what we're up against and do what is actually best for us. I don't think we should confuse what we want with what we have to do to get it. I feel we want genuine equality. We want acceptance from others for the people we are. I tell my children that equality must be gained by our own efforts as well as by changes in the law, and right now because of our history I don't think we *are* equal. When I talk like that the people in civil rights get all upset, and shout 'Uncle Tom.' But a fact is a fact. Our schools have been awful, and our children very badly educated. You say you've seen Negro children do well in white schools regardless of that fact; yet I really wonder about it. Our children may be frightened enough to study hard and keep on their toes all the time, but is that really a fair way or a good way to get an education?"

What she wanted was a large-scale effort on the part of the Southern states and the national government to improve the quality of Negro education. She was as strict in her criticism of Negro schools as she was in her appraisal of the value of desegregated education. She took me on several tours, showing me a succession of terribly crowded classrooms, where too many children were learning very little from frustrated, angry teachers. The buildings themselves were old, the corridors dark and all too often swollen with children. "You see," she said once as I commented on the short periods for each subject, "we shuffle them around fast, almost from minute to minute, so that they don't get bored or impatient. Most of these children know as well as we do that they're being cheated, just like their parents were. I believe that before they go to white schools they should have respect for what they're *leaving* as well as what they're going to. After all, how can a Negro really be free if he hasn't come to terms with

himself and his own people? The children we send to white
schools are now coming back to us, and they tell us how poor we
are — how badly taught they were, how inadequate our books,
our athletic equipment or our laboratory facilities are. They're
right, too. But you can't flee from your troubles and have them
vanish. It'll take several generations and a lot of doing in desegregated housing to get school desegregation for even a majority of
our children. So I think it's very wrong to have millions of Negro
children left to second-rate schools, or first-rate schools they *think*
are second-rate — which is the attitude I think some Negroes
would have now toward the best school in the world, so long as it
was Negro. If you teach children that it takes white children to
make their education sound, you are letting in prejudice, the
worst kind, too — prejudice against yourself."

She didn't hesitate to say what she thought to her children and
to other teachers. She scorned those teachers who opposed desegregation because they feared the loss of their jobs. She would
refuse a job in a white high school: "I couldn't turn my back on
my own children, not when they need me more than ever." As I
watched her teach I realized that she would never turn her back
on *any* responsibility. She worked at a high pitch all day. She
rarely went out at night. She shunned even a social life with her
fellow teachers. An attractive woman, she continually turns down
dates. She may go to the movies on a Saturday afternoon, or to
lunch, followed by shopping and a visit to the library or a
bookstore. In the evening she watches television — news, docu-
mentaries, carefully selected movies; or she reads, corrects school
papers, prepares for her classes. She is a devout Methodist. She
attends church regularly, and is an active member of a number of
religious organizations. As a matter of fact she is quite vocal
about the role of the church in Negro life today: "It is sad, the
way everyone says we should forget religion, because it was part
of the way we were kept in tow. They ask us to give up our faith,
our emotional attachments, our devotion. What will we have left?

The vote? For a few who can afford it, the company of white
people in a restaurant? A few hours a day with nasty white school
children? Is that a culture, something you can fall back upon and
pass on to the future? Is that right, to tell people that their
praying and singing and fellowship are all old-fashioned or Uncle
Tom? What will our children have left? That's what I ask myself
every day now."

She wants reform, drastic reform. She wants Negroes to be "on
their toes as never before and more Negro than ever before." She
wants an end to bureaucracy in the schools, an end to the endless
"accreditation" procedures and "credits" required of teachers —
which mean that degrees are evaluated rather than human beings
and the actual teaching they do. "In the Negro schools the worst
of the white world becomes the vogue: everything commercial
and senseless, the television culture. We should try to be free of
that, as well as free to vote or go in restaurants."

She would often describe her day to me: the dark, teeming
halls; the countless rules and regulations which become the chief
concern of inadequate teachers, or of first-rate teachers who are
nevertheless overwhelmed by the enormity or the impossibility of
their task; the ledgers to be filled, the reports to be written in a
fine hand by people at least able to be proud of that accomplishment.

"It may be unfortunate," she reminded me in one of our last
talks, "but we *are* the leaders, and if you don't think so, you don't
know the real heart of our communities. The civil rights workers
come through, they call us 'reactionary' and 'Uncle Tom,' and
then they're gone. The writers do the same. They give us the once
over, then tell us how needy and godforsaken we are — to the
point that I suspect them when they're most sympathetic. They
see no good in us at all. Meanwhile we teachers work hard every
day with our people. Most of them are just beginning to get an
education and we're the ones who have to help them at it, in
school and out. (I have a lot to do in neighborhood and commu-

nity work, with parents' groups and church groups. It's almost another job.)"

In the last talk we had before I left Atlanta she told me how troubled she was. "Our work as leaders is being ignored. No planning is made for what we have to offer. It is as if we are to be thrown to the winds. That will not help the Negro or the cause of integration. It will deprive him of his own people who can help him, and encourage him to feel that his salvation comes only from others — from whites, from outside himself. To me, integration means accepting yourself and *then* feeling able to be comfortable with others, or even confident with them. Yes, I suppose we need pioneers to go into those white schools, but we should never turn our backs on ourselves. It's not my job I worry about, but my people. Perhaps it's not very modest to keep on saying so, but for all our faults as teachers we have been leaders. For that reason, I believe that our trouble is part of a larger problem facing our race: self-acceptance. As Negro teachers we're not a used-out part, belonging in a wastepaper basket. We are a hardworking, educated segment of our race who are finally tasting freedom. And I believe that if we are simply rejected and dismissed by society, Negro as well as white, the so-called progress responsible for it will really prove to be a disguised form of injury; that's it, another wound. And we have had so many. Every time I think of my own difficulties I don't feel hurt or lonely but closer to my people, as if there are a lot of them standing near me, telling me not to feel too bad because we are all in this together."

VI

THE PROTESTERS

W E COME to the "sit-in movement." The very words present a problem; they are so familiar, yet so inadequately descriptive in view of the enormous variety of actions and deeds — of movement within the movement. Since 1959 I have watched one or another kind of protest, demonstration or march, as well as the conflicts and tensions that inevitably preceded them and followed them. For several years I hesitated to say anything, for fear it would be rendered antique and useless by an incredibly swift and hard-to-follow pace of events. I myself was so caught up in what was happening from day to day or — at the most infrequent interval — week to week that any other kind of perspective seemed both fake and disloyal.

I still have no "larger perspective" to offer. For one thing, I am no historian or political scientist; for another, I am not sure it is yet possible to see how the civil rights struggle — and other struggles that have become tied to it — will be resolved. What I can contribute are the following observations; they are, in turn, a medical report, a psychiatric report, and a writer's description of certain people in the movement. As I heard one of them say: "Some of us drifted to this, some of us were born to it, some of us could hardly wait for it; and some of us want to get out pretty fast, and some hate to leave, ever; and some get stalled while some push everyone with them, so no one can be still very long."

1. Fred

"You know as much as I do how I started becoming a jailbird. Public enemy number one, that's my ambition." It was banter, as good a way as any for him to deal with his anger and hurt. He had just been released from jail, his eighth confinement, and I noticed the sarcasm, the forced gaiety, the boasting, all common in youths like him. Yet, at heart Fred was confused; when he was growing up he never planned to be in and out of jails at age seventeen.

As he said, I did indeed know how it all started. Fred was one of hundreds of youths in Atlanta who in 1961 decided to seek entry to white schools. His father worked in a clothing store, a new and attractive one serving the city's growing Negro middle class. "My dad never even wanted me to go to an integrated school, let alone join the movement. He kept on telling me it would only mean trouble. He was so proud of that job that I think he couldn't see anything jeopardizing it. We had a big fight, because he wouldn't sign the slip, to give me permission to apply for transfer to the white schools. I told him he was hypnotized by those gray flannel suits he was selling, and the silk ties with the 'Made in England' stickers on them. I told him I wasn't going to spend my life fooling myself. My mother was on my side. She always used to say that you can't hide your shame behind clothes. My dad agreed with her, underneath he really did. I can't blame him. It's a good job he has, the best he's ever had, and he was lucky to get it. There must have been a hundred men trying for it. His answer to my mother is that clothes do more than hide things; they make you feel better, more of a person.

"Anyway, my mother said she would sign for me. My dad asked what she would do if he got fired. She said she would go to work again. Then he really exploded. The day she could stop taking that bus across to her white lady-boss was the biggest day

in our life. It happened two years before I went to the white
school, about a month after the store opened and my dad got his
job. He came home one day and said: 'Give those people notice.
Tell them you're going to stay home and take care of us. Tell
them you've had enough of cleaning other people's homes, so
you're going to take care of your own.' A little later he was so sure
about the future that he was talking about hiring a maid for *us*.
That's what my mother and I couldn't take. My mother asked him
how he could talk about the mean whites, then try to be just like
them the first chance he gets. He didn't have much to say back to
that.

"The next thing you know, though, we were having the same
kind of argument, this time over my going to a white school. Dad
didn't want to risk anything, or get any bad publicity. Sometimes
I think he really wants to be like white folks, only a poor, scared
version."

Fred did apply, because his mother gave her consent. More
than that, she encouraged him strongly; and when he was chosen,
she rejoiced. During his long ordeal as one of three Negro
students in a new high school, located in a distinctly well-to-do
suburban neighborhood, it was his mother's attitude — as I saw
it — that really made the difference. When I asked him where he
obtained the will and endurance he displayed, he would shrug his
shoulders and shake his head in silence, or say that he didn't
know or wasn't sure, but that I might find out if I asked his
mother.

An important clue to the source of his stamina came out when
we were talking about his childhood, not his racial attitudes. As a
child Fred suffered polio, and the muscles of his legs were
particularly affected. The disease might have been more crippling
were it not for Fred's stubborn character, much encouraged by
his mother. Together they did the exercises prescribed by the
doctors with a regularity and intensity that earned Fred a bit of
fame: "I was taken around the ward. They showed me to all the

patients, as an example of what you can do to beat polio. After a while I began to feel like I was on stage."

That was the way he felt at school, the white high school that was his while a senior. It was quite a change for him. The contrasts were everywhere to be seen, heard and experienced. The building was modern, with wide windows and spacious classrooms. The desks were to him like antiques — strong, usable, yet a little forbidding. ("They're so good to look at, I hate to use them; I might mark one up.")

The school was located on a hill. From it one could see fine houses separated by trees and still intact meadowland. Fred had seen the countryside of Georgia before — his grandfather had a farm — but this was different. "Those trees and the land look somehow *pretty* to me. I never used to think of trees being pretty. They were just trees; they were there to be cut or to protect pastureland from the wind. But I catch a glance out the window every once in a while and I think to myself that it's as if they arranged it all, the trees and the brook and the hill we're on, almost as if they gave the school makeup after they built it, lipstick and powder and real shine."

Inside he admired the science laboratories and the "language rooms" with their individual headgear and record machines. The cafeteria had the air and appointments of a first-class white restaurant. The school had a splendid auditorium — to him it was like a theater. Then, there were his classmates, his rich classmates. "That's what I keep thinking. They're rich. They're rich. They're rich. You are sitting beside millions of dollars."

Actually, he went to school that year with the children of his mother's old boss. He went to school for a while in a police car, then on the same bus his mother used to take to work. He and his mother shared stories about the scenery, the talk he heard and the people he saw — and the cars that brought the other students to school. "Those cars, every one of them is new and a lot of them are foreign. I never saw so many cars in all my life, not owned by people my age."

He often joked with his father about the clothing his classmates wore, the expensive yet casual shoes, pants and shirts. "They spend ten dollars on a button-down shirt, then they roll up its sleeves and treat it like it was a sweat shirt, or my old work shirt. They even wear work shirts to school — with ties. You never could get away with that in a Negro school. They would think you'd lost your mind."

Of course, when they wanted to, when the occasion demanded or suggested it, they could — in Fred's words —"dress to kill." In fact Fred once suggested that his father come to school with him as an observer. He could learn a lot about high fashion in men's clothing, then use what he learned in his store.

As the year moved along Fred gradually lost his sense of surprise and awe at what was about him. He had to study hard to keep up with his classmates, and though they were generally but not exclusively polite — in contrast to the behavior of many white students in the city's more modest high schools — they were also increasingly hard for him merely to notice and accept.

"I'm getting tired of them," he told me after the Christmas holidays. He had been away from school for two weeks, and upon his return felt critical and short-tempered. "They think they're God's gift to the human race. For a time I thought how lucky I was, being with them in class and being spared all the trouble other Negroes have gone through during desegregation. I don't think I could take the behavior of white trash. But you know in a way I'm more nervous here than I would be if I had to walk through a howling mob and fight my way down the corridor every hour. It's not even race that's the trouble. It's the fact that my classmates think they're above everyone — white or black."

He became increasingly interested in how other Negro children in Atlanta were faring, not only the handful in white schools but the many thousands still in Negro schools. Though for a long time he had wanted to be a lawyer, by Easter of that year he abandoned all interest in the law, or any other profession. He was developing an interest in violating the law rather than studying it. Just before the end of school he told his parents that he wanted to defer college for a while.

About that time he and I had one of our longest talks. I had been sensing all along his rising dissatisfaction with what he called "rich livers" at school. Unlike his sister, who is two years younger and who at that stage wanted to be a model (later she became interested in commercial art work), he showed less and less interest in "success." He spoke very bluntly to me: "Success, that's what my dad has been talking about all my life. The poor guy, he doesn't see how ridiculous his talk is. He thinks I can be 'successful,' when actually I'll be lucky if I can vote, and be treated better than a dog every time I go register my car, or try for a driving license, or go buy something in a store. They say I'm lucky; I'm going to the best high school in Georgia. Well that's about what success is for a Negro: being alone; being the exception; and knowing every second that the top for you isn't even enough to make you feel safe on the street, because it's the bottom for everyone else."

In addition to his sister, Fred has three younger brothers — at that time they were in elementary school. He didn't want to set the same example for them that their father did for him. It was an example, he felt, of surrender, of acquiescence. Perhaps with a bit of nervousness in my voice I asked him what he *expected* his father to do. "You don't think I don't wonder myself," he replied with some resignation. Then he stared at me. He was suddenly aware that I was willing to extend a good deal more "understanding" to his father than he was, at least then. It wasn't what I said. It was the tone of my voice, the look on my face.

I myself didn't realize how fully I had communicated my thoughts to him until he told me: "You're all for trying to feel sorry for him, I know. So am I sometimes. I say to myself: 'Look,

Fred. He's over forty, and he has a family, and he's only trying to do the best he can. So why give him a hard time? Do you want him to go join the sit-in movement, and picket the State Capitol, so that the colored man will get a better deal? If he did, what kind of a deal would you get, and your sister and your brothers, and especially your mother? She would have to go back to work, and though she might say that wouldn't bother her, if it had to be done, I don't think it would be fair to push her that far.' That's what I say to myself. But I have an answer, too. My dad has his life. It's not the same as *his* dad's. Unlike my grandfather, my dad was lucky. He came here to Atlanta and stayed with an uncle of his. He got himself a high school education. Then he fought in the war, and so afterward he could pay for some college time through Uncle Sam's help. He still had trouble keeping a job down until lately. But now he's got a good one, and he forgets how lucky and unusual he is. My grandfather used to tell him that he was wasting his time going to college, that Negroes could go to college for twenty years, then be fortunate if they found jobs in the post office or the Pullman trains. That was the truth my grandfather knew. My father proved him wrong. So you see, everyone has to figure out what's right for *him,* and that depends on his age. I'm angry at my father now because he wants me to be like him. He had his ambitions. I have a right to mine."

When he had finished talking it was late, near midnight. Fred still had work to do, study that he himself had decided to put off, study that meant increasingly little to him. As I left he smiled and shook my hand, as always. Then he started talking again. "Your children may not always go along with you, just as I'm not following all my father's advice; but there's a difference, too. You are white and I am Negro. If I don't join the movement and try to change things here, *my* children might just as well not be born. It's that bad." It was the first and last time I would ever hear him explicitly refer to my race.

Fred's disenchantment and his progressive involvement in the student protest movement came precisely at a time when he seemed best in command of himself and his work. He was nearing the successful end of a unique and hard experience. He had every right to be confident, even self-congratulatory. Instead, his mood turned dark, even sour. He became increasingly critical of his classmates, picking out their faults with almost indiscriminate zeal. When I mentioned to him — as gently as I knew how — that everyone had some annoying characteristics, he replied immediately: "Yes; but that's not what bothers me about them. It's the way they treat me as a Negro, regardless of who they are and what they're like otherwise. The nice ones act like royalty out slumming. The unfriendly ones stare, and you can see the hate in their eyes. Sometimes I try to forget it, and just imagine that I'm one of them. I'm not, though. I don't really know whether to blame their attitudes or mine. I know I get upset, too, apart from what they do."

Clearly he distrusted not only his classmates, but himself. It is easy to say that he felt "guilty"; that as a result he could not allow himself to enjoy a triumph that had other implications to him: "I'll graduate, and some people at the ceremony might even forget I'm a Negro. I'll probably never feel whiter than I will that day."

Yet, more was at issue. Yes, he was tempted. Yes, he wanted to disappear, to be reborn. On the other hand, he had personal, only indirectly race-connected reasons to reject a world he finally had seen and experienced. His mother had done that, done it gladly and emphatically. A year after he had graduated from high school I talked with him in Mississippi, where he was working in a voter-registration project. We were by then old friends, and able to relax rather well with one another. Moreover, he was now a man, on his own, working hard in a hard world. He liked beer; when he had it in him he liked to talk and reminisce. I had attended his graduation, and now he wanted to talk about that; about the tuxedo, and the roses the girls carried, and the band,

and his parents, sitting there in the audience: "All my classmates were straining their necks to find their parents; a lot of them couldn't, there were so many people. I was sure lucky then; I could spot mine so fast it wasn't funny."

We lingered on that scene, then in a flash he changed the subject: "You know, no matter how beautiful and nice it was there, I was glad to get out. I felt like my mother did when she came home for the last time. She threw her coat down — I can remember her doing it as if it just happened. Then she said: 'They've been squeezing me dry, telling me to do everything, expecting me to smile all the while, and give every ounce of my energy to their kids. I'm so glad to be home to stay. I'm afraid that tomorrow I'll wake up and it won't be true. I'll probably be pinching myself for a few days.' She said more; it was a long speech she made. I've never heard my mother talk so much, before or after. Until she stopped working she never had time to talk. She worked two days every day; one started at five-thirty in the morning and the other at five-thirty in the evening."

He continued to talk about his mother and her routine. He had watched her more closely than even he himself knew. He had seen her leave home strong and come home weak, depart in good spirits and return bitter. It was only now, when he was away from home, that he could look more closely at his mother's life, and at his own shifting emotions during that year of "integrated" education: "Since I've been away from it all I've been able to see that my mother didn't come back in a bad mood just because she was tired. It wasn't only the work she did for white people that got to her. I'm sure that part of her problem was leaving our broken-down apartment to go to that mansion. I never realized what the change was like until I saw those homes myself, and went through the same kind of experience she did. You watch it all on television, the way they live; but you can't really believe it's real until you see it. She must have been glad to get away from us and spend a day in that place, and she must have hated to come

back and face it all at home, the mess in the house, with everything old, secondhand or cheap compared to things out there. I
guess she couldn't admit how she felt herself, any more than I
could. You feel you're a traitor. You feel so low and bad. I realize
now that it's inevitable, being so split up, but I sure didn't then."

Like his mother, he reacted only when he safely could; like her
own, his was a reaction of both nostalgia and outrage. Both of
them, I thought, were as loyal to the white people they knew as
they were contemptuous of them. Fred could describe his
mother's mixed feelings much more readily than his own: "She
was glad to have it over, going to them, but I think she was sad,
too. Now all she had to do was be at home, and it wasn't that big
home with all those fine things. I could tell. It's like a drug. You
get hooked on it, and it won't let you alone, even though you
know it hurts you. I began to see how much she missed her work.
She would say how handy the money would be that she used to
make. She would ask me how the bus ride was, and whether the
trees were in bloom. She would try to figure out how near I came
to her old boss's home. I could tell. Even Dad could tell, and he's
not tuned in to anything but his work. He would tell her to go
back to work, because she missed it. I think he knew it wasn't
only the work."

For both Fred and his mother, integration, real integration,
meant achieving for themselves a life each of them had tasted,
but recognized — and guiltily disavowed — as still not theirs.
"I'm doing this," Fred told me once shortly after coming out of
jail, "because I don't think a few like myself should go into the
white world, leaving twenty million Negro people standing outside, scared and hungry as they always have been."

Fred spent two years in Mississippi, the first one when there
were very few like him in the state, the second in 1964, when
students came from all over the country to assist "field workers"
like himself. From the beginning he lived in constant danger of
death. He moved into a particularly tense racial district, and set

to work encouraging Negroes to secure the vote. Many of them thought him crazy and feared his presence more than that of any white man. Had it not been for the help of two Negro farmers who fed and kept him, he would have been run out of town by his own people as well as the sheriff. For a long time he expected to be killed. He wrote a letter to his mother that told her of his love, that explained his work to her. He put it in the hands of one of his local friends, to be mailed after his death. He lived expecting each day to be his last.

His mere presence in the town was a living symbol of defiance to both whites and Negroes. He lived because the sheriff wanted to outlast him, see him leave. The sheriff told him so several times. Every day he drove by Fred's home, usually waving to him as he did with that mixture of politeness and scorn that certain Southern officials can express toward Negroes. Once or twice a month he would take the youth into custody for what he called "a heart-to-heart talking." I heard about the content of one such encounter from Fred.

"'What you want here, boy,' the sheriff said. Then he poured me a cup of coffee even though I didn't ask for one. I don't drink coffee, and I certainly didn't want any of his, but I took it. I don't know why; probably I was afraid, and I knew he was testing me so I wanted to show him I *wasn't* afraid — to take it when he offered it, and show him I felt his equal. It even flashed through my mind that they were poisoning me. (I've watched too many television programs.) Anyway, I kept on drinking it. Once I had it I was glad to have it; I had something to do while he talked.

"At first he tried being the kind plantation owner. He wanted to know how I was getting along. Did I like the county? Was I planning to stay long? They always liked tourists. They liked for them to be right at home. 'Now boy, you feel free to come here any time you want, and let me know if there's anything I can do for you.' That's what he said, and he started toward me with his coffeepot. Suddenly I had to go, or see if I *could* go. He asked me whom I was going to see. I didn't answer, because I knew it meant trouble for anyone I mentioned; and besides, I really didn't plan to see a soul that day, just write my weekly report for the Atlanta office, and maybe a few letters. When I didn't reply for a few seconds he blew up. He must have been looking for an excuse. He put the coffeepot down on a table near me, slamming it real hard. Then he moved closer, still holding a cup in his other hand. I didn't know what to expect. I thought to myself: 'This is it. He'll put the cup down, and then he'll reach for his gun.'

"It was a funny thing. He didn't say anything, not a word. He moved closer and closer, until he was practically on top of me. He kept staring at me. I can see his eyes right now; they were light blue, and I think a little watery, as if he had a cold. I couldn't keep looking into them. I was afraid, and I was worried that if I kept staring he would get angrier than he was already. So I looked halfway down. I could see his thick leather belt, loose around his stomach — he had a tire of fat. I was too scared even to look at that. I thought he would resent my noticing his flabbiness. He didn't seem flabby then. In fact, I thought he was going to be the man who killed me.

"It's funny what comes to your mind in moments like that. I pictured my mother sitting with us in church and praying. She was doing the praying and I was just sitting there, watching her lips move and looking at her face, and then the Bible she was holding. For some reason I remember her gloves. She had on a pair of white gloves. She used to wear them every Sunday to church. She called them her church gloves. My sister could play with her shoes or her pocketbook, but not those gloves. Then I went blank. I heard him telling me to 'git.' He repeated it several times: 'Git, boy, git before you become too welcome here, and we decide to make you a trusty. We need one or two, and you look the right man for the job, a smart nigger who knows enough to do what he's told, or else. So git, and I mean from the county.' I especially heard his last words. It was after them that I looked at

him, right into his eyes. I didn't say a word and moved toward
the door. He turned to his flunky and said, 'Show the goddamn
nigger to the street, and let him know that the next time he comes
here it'll be for a year or two on bread and water!' "

Fred went through such "visits" repeatedly before he was
arrested for the first time — for exceeding a twenty-mile-an-hour
speed limit. He denied the charge: "I drove so carefully I was a
menace; I kept my eyes on the speedometer all the time." In any
event that was the beginning of a series of imprisonments, six of
them in a matter of months on similar charges — speeding, being
a "public nuisance," talking to high school students and thus
"contributing to the delinquency of minors."

Ironically, with the arrival of Northern students for the Summer Project of 1964, he and the sheriff found themselves, for
once, in agreement. The sheriff started preparing for an invasion.
The town was put on alert; people were encouraged to arm themselves; and the paper talked as if the final moment of truth was at
hand: resistance or death. Fred was also fearful, and for his own
reasons resentful. Who were these youths, and what would their
sudden, naïve, white presence do to the hard-won trust he had
earned from increasing numbers of Negroes, even from a few
white businessmen and the sheriff himself? "I was against this, as
well as for it," he told me just after the students started coming
into the state, ten of them to his town. "We need help, God
knows we do. Maybe the whole country will get to know our
problems as a result of this project; but meanwhile I don't know
what we're going to do with these volunteers. They don't know a
thing about living down here — how to get along with Negroes
or whites or anyone. Yesterday I found myself thinking like the
sheriff and his police and the white people. I thought to myself:
'Who are these outsiders? Why do they want to come here? Why
don't they clean up the mess in their own backyards first?' "

Much later, toward the end of the summer, he learned the
value of the project, and the reasons for his fear and suspicion.

He had good reason to be afraid that violence would be wide-spread once the students arrived. He also had reason to be envious of them. In comparison to him they were rich, well educated and influential. It was *their* work in the state that captured the nation's interest and concern — the attention started even before they arrived. When they did arrive, even though he recognized them to be the diverse group they were, all of them roused tension in him: the able and effective workers because he felt their occasional arrogance; the hesitant and fearful ones because he recognized their incompetence and the burden it placed on everyone. Those who got on easily with the Negro families prompted his jealousy. Those who were reticent or embarrassingly ingratiating with Negroes earned his misgivings and scorn.

In the end, though, he was sad to see them leave. "I've come to like them, and I can see now that they probably made me feel insecure. I'm glad that two of them are staying, and especially that it's the two I like best. They've all done a lot, not just for the people here, but for me. It's been like going to college; I've met different people. I've got to leave here myself one day, when this is all over and we've won."

One year later he did leave, to enter college. At this writing he seems solidly directed toward the law as a career. He wants to be a lawyer so that he can continue to work for the rights of his people. He wants to be a lawyer because he will have a profession, be a person respected and called upon for advice. He wants to be a lawyer because he is faithful to his father's lifelong dream that his children will surpass him and attain the favored if still emaciated ranks of the Negro middle class. He wants to be a lawyer — most of all, he thinks — because "my mother used to say to me that if I became one, I could fight for my rights, and it would be legal." He used to think of his mother when he went from home to home in Mississippi urging people to vote who were sometimes even reluctant to listen to him. "I finally would have to tell them about my mother, and it worked if anything was going to work. I'd say my mother felt the way they did. She just followed orders all her life and was glad even to be able to have the orders to obey. Then one day she got tired of it and stopped.

"The next thing that happened was that I was going to school with her old boss's children. Now don't you believe that Georgia and Mississippi are sister states, and the same can happen here? That's how I'd always end, with that question."

Sometimes they wouldn't listen to him. Sometimes they would only listen. Yet sometimes, in his words, he "scored." Most often it would be the young who joined company with him, the young who had the approval of their mothers. "I could see their mothers giving them the silent nod. They must have felt my mother's voice coming through to them, saying just what she always used to say to me: 'It's time; maybe not for everything, but enough to start in the direction of everything. Starting is harder than fighting to get what you want after you've started.' When I left Mississippi I felt that my people had begun. They were trying to register, even before the Congress passed the voting bill. After it was passed, they could really respect themselves for their own work, for starting before Washington had. They got me started, too. When I went back to college, I knew why I was going, and I knew where I was going. I told them I would keep coming back, and one day I'll come back a lawyer. If they need one, I'll be there, or someplace like there."

2. *Larry*

He thought he might have appendicitis. The pain in his stomach had persisted for a day, then moved vaguely to the right side of his abdomen where he felt it intermittently. He had no appetite, and he thought he might have a fever. He waited for another day, then became worried enough to seek out a doctor. The pain seemed to have settled deep in him, and he feared that the next event would be rupture, and a belly full of poison. "For a while I thought I'd be going to medical school next year," he told me after outlining his symptoms in an orderly and precise fashion. He was then a senior at a first-rate Eastern college. He was bright, well spoken, intensely idealistic, very much determined to reach Mississippi and be of service there. "Even if I do need surgery, I'll be able to get down there within two weeks, won't I?" he both stated to me and asked me as I prepared to examine him.

Though I couldn't be certain, I did not think that he had appendicitis. I told him so, and also told him that we should keep an eye on his pain and his general state of health. Then I asked him how he was managing at the orientation sessions. (It was the summer of 1964 and we were in Oxford, Ohio, for two weeks before going into Mississippi.) He said that things were going well, but his manner — the impatient legs, crossing and recrossing, the averted eyes — told me to let the subject drop. I asked him to come back in twenty-four hours for another examination.

He was back that evening, after a service had been held for the three missing civil rights workers, later found dead in Philadelphia, Mississippi. His stomach seemed better. For the first time in two days he had eaten a full meal. Now that the threat of surgery was gone, he was in good spirits. "I dreaded the idea of spending the summer in the hospital and not in Mississippi," he said almost immediately. I told him that even had the worst been the case, an appendectomy was no longer the serious matter it used to be. "You would have certainly arrived South by mid-July."

For a few moments there was silence. I wanted to ask him, again, how he was feeling, how the orientation sessions were going. He was less restless and apprehensive than he had been, and I decided to ask him how he happened to become involved in the project. He gave me a quick glance, as if to say that he knew who I was and what I had in mind; moreover, knowing it, he was not interested in the kind of casual talk I only *seemed* to have in mind. I expected the awkward spell of quiet that fell upon us to be followed by his departure, when suddenly he spoke: "Do you think it will do any good? I've been asking myself that more and more. I know it's good for us. We'll learn a lot about the South. What about the civil rights movement though? How can a few hundred students change Mississippi?"

The questions were unanswerable at that time. We both knew that only events themselves would provide the answers. I asked him his major and it was history, with a minor in American literature. I suggested that it was hard to evaluate history as it was happening. Inconsequential incidents may be significant beginnings. Elaborately planned uprisings may come to nothing. We talked in such generalities — banal generalities — and he became more relaxed and more talkative, that day and on the other days we met.

"I expected to be in Europe this summer. My cousin and I were going there. My brother is studying at Oxford, and the three of us were to travel in England, then go to France and Italy, and maybe Greece. Then this happened. I wasn't really very interested in civil rights. My parents were always much more involved in that kind of thing than I was. To tell the truth, for a long time I was bored with the whole subject. I remember that a couple of years ago I asked my father why he never seemed to get tired of all those 'causes.' One after another he takes to them, and each time you would think the whole world stands or falls on what happens. We had quite a fight. He said I was pretty casual because we had money and I said he was pretty tense because he didn't trust his own success; he constantly feared someone would take his job away. I suppose I was unfair to him. Actually, I think he's a very sincere man, and wants to help when he can. The only way he really helps, though, is with money. That's what used to bother me. I saw him write the checks, then look satisfied with himself when he was finished. He would tell my mother to be sure to address the envelopes and mail them right off the next day. I could see the look of satisfaction on his face. He had done his generous deed and he wanted my mother to know it. He was almost distrustful of her, as if she might take away his glory by not mailing the check. I had never read Freud then, but I used to wonder why he was so worried that somehow his checks wouldn't be mailed.

"I still don't know exactly when I decided to go South instead of to Europe. I read of the project and heard that students were being recruited. I went to a meeting — a question-and-answer meeting — because there were no movies around that I hadn't seen. I think I really went for the same reason you're probably here: I wanted to find out what kind of people would be there. I noticed right away that they weren't the ones I expected. I thought they would be the politicians, who always work up a storm over one issue or another. Instead they all seemed to be like me, and more were there than I expected.

"We heard a few speeches. I almost left in the middle of one of them. A Negro kept on telling us how rotten America was; how rotten every white man was. I wanted to stand up and ask him why he was asking for our help if we were so damn 'corrupt' and 'hopeless.' No one dared say anything though. I knew some people felt like speaking out but couldn't. You feel guilty, to blame for it all. You also feel that the man who is talking has been so hurt and beaten down that he's no longer rational. So you excuse him, as you would anyone who has had a rough time.

"I think I first thought of joining up when I heard another Negro talk — this one from Mississippi. Unlike the first Negro, he stumbled and paused; at times it was even hard to understand him. He was the real article, though, as genuine a person as I had ever seen. He really got to me — standing there and asking us so politely to come down for the summer, as though we were future guests of his. He offered to put all of us up, even if he and his neighbors slept in the woods. Someone finally had the nerve to ask him what we would do. I wondered about that, too, but I was afraid to ask. I thought it might offend him.

"He didn't hesitate for a second. He knew exactly what we could do. 'You can live with us and give us some of your strength, and maybe then the white people of Mississippi will stop and take a look and remember that colored people aren't alone any more.'

"I remember feeling that I *had* to go shake his hand. All I could do was look at it — a huge, big black hand it was — and they were lined up shaking it. I left after my turn — I wanted to get some distance on my emotions. If I had stayed I would have joined, because of that man.

"It wasn't easy to forget him. A few days later I still found myself thinking of him. I could hear his deep, strong voice. I pictured him standing there, all that way from home, and in an Ivy League college. He was the first person I ever met who made Faulkner seem real to me; I used to think he was just a romantic writer. Now I had met the kind of real person who inspired him.

"Two of my friends decided to go down there, and I began to feel that if I didn't go I would feel lousy all summer. I pictured myself going through a museum in London or Paris and feeling like a worthless coward. I talked to my parents about it, and they said I should go to Europe; there would always be summers to spend on civil rights. (What do you think of *that* for a long-range view of things?)

"They were trying to be helpful, I know. They sensed that I *did* want to go to Europe, but that I didn't want to admit it to them. I also sensed that they were really afraid of what would happen to me if I went South. I asked them whether that wasn't. No, not at all; they wanted anything I wanted, so long as I turned out to have a 'happy' summer. I work hard at college, they reminded me. I deserved a rest. Each person makes his own contribution toward a better world. You can't compare lives. I could do a lot for civil rights just by doing well at school, then going to law school and doing well there. Eventually I would be able to help as a lawyer with civil rights cases. That's where the real victories would be won, anyway. And so it went, one argument after another. I kept on wondering what that poor Negro farmer would make of us: my father trying to have it both ways by giving money but taking no risks and preventing me from taking any either; my mother always ready with an excuse in the form of a reminder that there are many roads to Rome. For my own part, I was excited less about civil rights than a particular Negro who makes Faulkner's writing come alive.

"I didn't *decide* to go South. I simply couldn't get myself to buy that ticket to Europe. When I finally called my parents to tell them that I was going South, they said no. Since I was under twenty-one, I had to get their written approval. They refused it, and we had the fight of our lives at home.

"I've never seen more truth come out in a shorter time. My father tried several strategies. First he told me that he was sympathetic to the project's aim, but opposed to *my* involvement. To that I didn't even have to reply. With a look I confronted him with his hypocrisy. Then my mother tried another tack. She wanted me to wait a year, *'just* a year.' My father agreed. They insisted that I would 'have more to offer.' I told them they were trying to buy time, on the assumption that in a year I would lose interest; and I admitted that I might. Yet, the more I heard them talk, the more I wanted to go, then and there. My father's temper eventually got the better of him, a good thing in a way, because he is always more honest when that happens. He shouted, 'You can't go, period.' He paced the room, and in a few minutes it all came out: we were fools; the Negroes in Mississippi should leave and come North; a few hundred college students can't fight a whole state, with the police and the courts against them; they would jeopardize the Negroes and risk their own lives, all to no avail; it is selfish and romantic to try being a hero when a complicated political problem requires — as he put it —'other approaches.'

"I knew there was no point continuing the argument that day. I also knew that if I were going to get any place, it would be through my mother. She didn't say much after my father exploded. She just mentioned that she was afraid for my safety — and I respected her for saying so. It was the one honest moment we had.

"I let a few days go by, and then I asked my mother very casually one day whether she would give her permission. I had the form with me, and a pen. I said, 'Mother, just sign. I won't get hurt. If you don't let me go, we'll fight all summer, and we'll all be hurt worse than anybody in Mississippi will be.' She looked at me for a second, and said she thought I was right; then she signed.

"For weeks my father refused to talk to me when I came home. He flushed, or gave me a look that meant he was arguing with me inside himself. He's a lawyer. It's his job to argue. He does it all day, and half the night. He doesn't know when to stop.

"I made my plans as if he had given his approval. I went to the preliminary meetings, and my mother's signature was accepted as sufficient by the leaders of the project. Meanwhile, Mother slowly worked on my father, without telling me what she was doing. She bought a few books on the South, and read them. She left them around for my father to see: Lillian Smith's book, *Killers of the Dream; Segregation* by Robert Penn Warren; and Ralph Ellison's *Invisible Man*. He read them — I later found out — in that order. It was a good way to get into the problem — reading what two white Southerners had to say, then a Negro who lived in the South.

"Lillian Smith really moved him. He broke his silence on the subject by asking me questions about her and her book. Was it all true, or was she a writer, someone who exaggerates or is always dramatic? Why did Negroes stand for the treatment they received? (While you may think some of his questions naïve, they show how hard it is — even for someone who is *trying* — to understand what is happening down there.) In a few weeks he was no longer curious. He talked as if he had lived in the South for years. He insisted that there had to be change down there, fast change. He signed my application without a word of protest — and here I am. I'm not sure now that my father isn't more confident than I am about what this project will accomplish. It's going to be a harder summer than I thought."

During those days of orientation I saw the fear in Larry. I also realized how unwilling he was to talk about his fears. "Sometimes it's best not to think," I heard Larry — and many others — say as the orientation period ended.

During the summer I met Larry several times. We spent a week together when I had occasion to stop traveling about Mississippi and stay in the "Freedom House" he and eight others occupied. All along, from June to September, I tried to learn how he was adjusting to the rather special kind of life he was living. By the end of the summer it was quite clear that he had survived a difficult time rather well. As I proceeded to take stock of my observations — and his, as we recorded them on tape — I realized how various his moods and feelings had been during that relatively short, if eventful, span of time.

Two days after he arrived in the rural cabin that was to be his summer home I found him more confident and unafraid than he would ever again be in the South. He was staying with a large farming family. He was determined to be open and friendly, and immediately so. He saw in his hosts his own attitudes: they were warm, indeed more hospitable than any people he had ever known.

On the day of his arrival he started teaching, concentrating particularly on elementary schoolchildren and their reading problems. He wanted the twenty or so children in his class to have a summer rich with words and stories. Three of his students

came from the home where he stayed. Their mother packed
lunches for them and for him. She herself ate at her "white lady's
place," where she had spent time and worked since she herself
was a child, at her mother's side: "Then we didn't much go to
school. We learned about life tagging after our mother, and if the
white folks were good, they would teach us something now and
then. My mother can't believe it, the children going to school so
regularly, and now a white man from the North staying with
us."

The second time I saw Larry he had been ten days with her
and her children, but felt much worse about matters. He had
tried very hard to be friendly, so hard that he could not very well
recognize the nervousness and fear he inspired in the Negro
family — and felt himself. He could, however, acknowledge that
he didn't like the food served him, and often found talking with
Mississippi Negroes awkward: "I try and try to get them to call
me by my first name, but either they won't, or they get around it
by not using my name at all. I'll work up a sweat making
conversation, but it's hard to keep it going. I'm used to talking
about ideas and events, or about people, writers or politicians,
men in the news or in history. They talk about what's happened
during the day, or what they're going to do in the next few
minutes. I know they want me with them and like me, just as I
want to be here and like them; but it's difficult being together —
I know that, too. It's not only the race barrier that gets in our
way; it's the social differences, from the world of upper-middle-
class New England to the poor South."

What kept him going, indeed kept his spirits high, was his
work. He was so obviously doing so very much, and so very much
that was worthwhile. The children adored him, he could see that:
"They may find it hard having us around them at home, but they
love coming by our school, and they at least relax *here*." In the
beginning he was appalled by the children's faulty grammar.
Sometimes he had trouble understanding them at all. After a few

weeks he decided that the problem was his as much as theirs. Many of the children spoke the strong, forceful, active language of the Negro farmer. Perhaps he should let that be, rather than fight it; perhaps — instead of dwelling on the grim history of slavery — he should try to teach the children pride in their race's history, in its survival against odds no other people in America have faced, in its ability, despite everything, to produce a distinctive culture: "I think it's important for these kids to know what is really outstanding about Negro life, its writers, singers and artists; its men of science and learning. I didn't know about those people myself until I got involved in this project. All I knew was that the Negro has been nearly destroyed by slavery and persecution. It never occurred to me that he had really built a very significant culture of his own here, even in the South. I owe the fact that I did learn such things to the people who got this project going. They made sure right away that we didn't try to turn these children into pre–Ivy League types. Despite their warnings, it took me a few weeks to appreciate the more positive forces working in the lives of these boys and girls."

A week later — his fourth in Mississippi — I found him relaxed with the Negro community but increasingly concerned with the white people of the county, of the entire South. Until then he had hardly noticed them; suddenly they were on his mind every day. He went to several church services and coffees, only to find himself ostracized. Instead of welcoming him, people glared at him. The only words he could elicit from people were harsh and critical ones. Twice he was asked to leave the church. He refused. He never before had found it necessary to defy others in front of a church, to claim (against their wishes) his right to worship. When he went to the drugstore or the post office he met up with the same opposition, so much so that he found ordinary tasks like mailing a letter or buying razor blades and toothpaste extremely difficult: "I'm *afraid* in the evening; they might dynamite us or snipe at us; but it's shopping I *hate* — meeting the whites and seeing the murder in their eyes."

As he talked one could feel how lonely he was, and conflicted. He was sensible enough to see that the white townspeople he dreaded — but was drawn to — were not mad, not especially evil: "They make me wonder what I would do if I were in their shoes. I've never been in a situation where I would be ruined socially and economically for trying to live up to my moral code. Their code is supposed to be like mine, Christian; but I guess we just don't read those words in the Bible the same way."

At times he simply wanted to see white people, to be with them rather than argue with them or speculate about their predicament. "A day will pass — or two and three — and I won't see a white face. I even forget for a while that I'm white. I'll see another white person and register shock. Then I'll go downtown and feel like an explorer who has been away a long time and finally has returned."

The split between the Negro and white world that he was noticing every day became a decisive emotional experience for him, marking off in his thinking the past from the present and future. He felt that he never again would be able to take certain things for granted. In a sense he felt a break with his earlier life; something had started in Mississippi that was destined to affect him long after he left the state: "I feel I'm taking advantage of these people in a way. I'm living with them and being fed by them; and even if I'm teaching their kids, they're teaching me much more. I'll never again be able to take even the ordinary things of life for granted. It took coming down here to realize how privileged my life has been. I knew it in the abstract, from reading books and taking sociology courses, but now I've learned lessons about people and their problems that a million books and courses couldn't get across to me. In fact, I'm afraid to go back to those books and courses."

That last sentence, spoken in the middle of the summer, would be repeated by him again and again. He found himself thinking of his return to school with mixed pleasure and dread. He missed the movies, the dormitory and its comforts, the social life of college. He wanted to swim, play tennis, or simply take a drink without worrying about sheriffs and dynamite. "I have to admit, every once in a while I just want to fly away from here. I picture myself stretched out on a sandy beach, sipping a gin and tonic. A few seconds of that and I feel ashamed. It's the truth, though, not an idle daydream: we can always leave here when we wish. We know it, and I'm starting to realize that the people in the town do, too — both Negro and white."

He spoke like that to me during the week I spent doing medical examinations on the children in his class. While the summer was far enough advanced to justify a return North, he now found the possibility of that return both haunting and ironic: "So long as I can go, I've never *really* settled in here."

We spent long hours that week talking about degrees of "involvement" and "commitment." How fair is it to come down, spend two months, then depart? How hard should one like Larry try to communicate with white people? Is there really the trust between him and his Negro schoolchildren that he hopes for, or imagines to be? How well, deep down, was he getting along with his "family," the Johnsons? What would happen when he came home, when he saw his parents, his friends, their style of life, their concerns that were once — still are?— his concerns? Could he take memorizing and studying for multiple-choice exams in order to get good enough marks for law school? (More and more he thought of being a lawyer rather than a doctor.) Apart from an occasional moment of nostalgic, boastful recall would he forget the whole summer within a year, perhaps even less?

He was gloomy as well as fearful of the future, or at the very least speculative about it. He felt like a frivolous, privileged intruder upon the lives of the Negro children he taught, and certainly upon those in the civil rights movement who were giving the struggle more than a summer of their time. While he was angry at the state's white people, he also was newly sensitive to the charges they had leveled at him and his kind. What he imagined the Negroes thought about him confirmed what he had heard angry whites say, and what he now — in his cheerless, doubtful spells — believed to be true: he *was* an outsider; it was indeed only a summer's effort for him; in a few weeks there would be the same old and terrible confrontation of impoverished dependent Negroes and whites with at least power if not widespread affluence; and, above all, he knew that he wanted to leave, even as he wanted to stay. He knew that even were he to stay a year or two more he would still have his departure in mind upon occasion. That fact, that option if no other one, made him a privileged person among the needy.

One night we talked through to dawn, and I heard him express a good deal of his guilt and confusion. If he felt a bit easier for having done so, I was more than a little troubled when we had finished. True, some of what he said was familiar to me before I ever set out for Mississippi that summer: as a psychiatrist I knew the strains felt by many youths as they obsessively wrestled with questions of freedom, authority and social custom. Yet, the conflicts Larry now had were grounded in the harsh truths of a political and historical struggle. They were not primarily private conflicts. Nor were they simply personal tensions masked by participation in a social cause, or finding symbolic expression in that cause. Before Larry ever became involved in the civil rights struggle he felt both loyalty and defiance toward a number of people, from his parents and teachers to his friends. He was unsure of his major, unsure of what profession he would choose, unsure of his standing with girls he successively dated, even unsure which friends were in fact his close and lasting friends. His uncertainty was not, however, asserted by "symptoms," by the various disorders of thought, mood or body that bring some youths to psychiatrists. It took a summer in Mississippi for him to become enough upset and alarmed about his torn feelings — his doubts and misgivings — to want to talk with me about them.

Regardless of how appropriate I thought his nervousness to be, he had his doubts: "I wonder what's coming over me. I used to be pretty calm about life. I knew what was going on; I always read the papers and magazines. But I never let current events rub off on my *personality*. I never became tense, just because the world is tense. Now it's different. I wonder whether I'm becoming sick. Everything that goes on here bothers me inside — makes me sweat, or makes me lose my appetite, or get a headache, or lose sleep. Sometimes I think I'm going nuts, but then I see it happen to others too, and I figure that it's not imaginary things getting to me, not in the least. So I talk to myself. I say, 'Larry, it's right to get worked up. If you didn't you'd be a fool, or a louse; if you didn't *then* you'd be sick.' That helps — while I'm here. What about when I go back though? What will happen then? Will I just forget the whole thing, chalk it up to a nightmare, or even worse, a kind of summer-camp experience — exciting, even dangerous, but no longer a part of my real life? That's the kind of possibility that scares me more than the segregationists do; because if that happens I will really have become one of them — in my own New England way, one of them."

We had our last talk in Mississippi two days before he left for home, then school: "I can't believe I'm still here, when I think back to my first few hours in the town. I was so scared I couldn't even allow myself to know I was scared at all. I kept on telling myself how wonderful everything was, the people, their attitude, their life. When you asked me how we were getting along, I said, 'Great.' I can remember saying it — exactly where we were when I said it. The answer stuck in my throat, but I didn't know why. It took time for me to see how scared I was and how scared the Johnsons have been all their lives, and how scared a lot of white people are down here, including the sheriffs, who have guns."

Larry's departure from Mississippi was as touching an episode

as I saw in my work in the South. As at graduation time in high
school or college, there was a succession of events — suppers,
informal picnics and dances — to mark the occasion. On one
evening Mr. and Mrs. Johnson made a large supper for Larry and
his students, for neighbors and other civil rights workers, and for
a few visitors — a lawyer, a minister, myself — whom they called
the "older generation of Northern help." It was actually a community celebration, and was held in the Baptist church. Larry had
been arrested twice during the summer, once for "speeding," once
for failing to halt (at least long enough to satisfy a waiting
policeman) at a stop sign. Each time they had emptied his
pockets, removed his watch, and held him in jail for what they
called "the processing" of his violation. Each time his watch was
returned damaged. The second time he refused to take it back.
Before supper the Johnsons gave him a watch. Mr. Johnson said
very little: "Larry, this is for you from us. We're proud to know
you, and we thank you. I don't know what more to say, except
God bless you."

A year afterward he would still recall the event as if both he
and I had not been there, and needed a detailed description of
what happened. "It was late afternoon, not evening. They eat
early, because they rise early and work long hours. (It took me
time to get back into the swing of things up here, supper at seven
instead of five.) They came together quietly, in the church. They
don't talk too much. They can be silent without feeling nervous
or inadequate. They handed me the watch and thanked me for
being with them, and for doing what I could that summer. Mr.
Johnson handed me the watch. Then Mrs. Johnson asked me if
she could help me put it on — and that about broke me up.
There wasn't a dishonest moment the entire time. She wound up
the watch and strapped it down on my wrist. They clapped, but
only for a second or two. Mrs. Johnson announced that she had
made some delicious fried chicken. She asked us all to eat it
before she had a chance to get at it; if we didn't do so, her hands

would pick up one piece after another, her dress would stretch and then split, and that would be more than she could bear, or afford either. I never ate so much in my life, and I never felt so good. I told the Johnsons that since many people work fifty years for a watch, I was getting away with a lot. Mrs. Johnson didn't wait a second to reply to that: 'We're giving you a freedom watch, not a slavery watch.' "

Larry left very early in the morning, and he left quickly. The good-byes were kept down to a minimum. They all pretended — or believed — he would soon be back. As he drove North he never doubted that he would see the Johnsons again, but he did doubt his capacity to resume life at college. "I kept on wondering how I could face it: the silliness and emptiness; the instructors who think they're God because they've read a few books and can sit and talk about 'ideas'; the ivy that doesn't only climb the buildings but grows up the legs and into the brains of both teachers and students. What would a football game mean to me? A spring riot over nothing? A rule about wearing a tie at breakfast? I could hear all those instructors telling me how 'complicated' everything is, and how 'practical' you have to be, and how more 'research' has to be done; and I knew I would do one of three things: cry to myself, scream at them, or just smile."

After he had returned and settled into his studies some but not all of his bitterness left him. He began to realize that it was not very sensible to compare school in the North and life in Mississippi. They were different, almost incomparably so. He kept up a continual and spirited correspondence with the Johnsons, and with several of his students. At Christmas he returned to see them. The more he realized that he could keep in touch with the South and with his friends there, the less he had to insist upon confronting his college with Mississippi at every possible turn. Just before he went South a second time he had this to say: "I'm settled back here, I guess. I'll never be settled back the way I was before, but I'll stay and graduate. I don't hate college the way I did when I first came back; I think I really appreciate it more. I want my friends in the South to have what we have here. They even have a chance to have more than we have here, by avoiding some of the mistakes we've made.

"Anyway, I think I'm going to law school. Whatever I decide to do I'll never forget the civil rights issue, and its meaning — for me as much as the Johnsons. That's what happened last summer; I learned that the struggle was mine as much as theirs. I told them so just before I left, and they laughed. They apologized for 'giving me trouble.' I said, 'That kind of trouble I need.'"

3. *After Joe Holmes*

I was born in Reform, Alabama; that's between Birmingham and Columbus, Mississippi. My daddy worked on shares — cotton and some tobacco. We had our own garden, too. (I can remember the first time I ate tomatoes from a store, and corn from the can. I thought they tasted real strange.) There were us seven children who lived (we lost some before they were born and some after they were born) and my mother took care of everyone, including keeping my daddy going in the fields, and keeping an eye on his mother and her own mother; though, naturally, both grandmothers helped out a lot around the house.

It wasn't so bad growing up as some in the movement like to picture it. They don't know what hurts you and what doesn't. To listen to some of them you'd think a colored boy in the South is born in hell, and when he grows up he's entitled to get a diploma that says he's been there. I'd as soon live on an Alabama farm as be in New York or Chicago. As a result of being in the movement I've got to both places, on fund-raising trips, and it's really like hell up there: cold, so cold no one can relax his limbs; and the way people live there, it makes a coffin in a cemetery down South seem like a mansion.

Back home we had our bad times and our good ones, but I

never used to divide them like that: it was just life, moving
along, and me, living. You know how it is: you're not like the trees
or the rocks, so you keep doing things and more things, and you
know you're "you" even if most all the time there's no reason to
think about things that way. When I was eight or nine I once
asked my mother about that; I said, "Momma, tell me how it was
decided I would be me, and someone else would be them, like
Mr. Jameson's boy Andrew." You know who Andrew Jameson
was? He was the mayor's son, and my age. He's become a lawyer
now, like his daddy. My mother used to go help there sometime, not regular though — if they had extra laundry, or a
party to give. ("He's the bossman of the whole county, Mr.
Jameson is," my daddy would say proudly, "and your mother has
gone to work for him.") Well, anyway, my mother didn't have a
very good answer to my question. She said, "Son, you can't know
about things like that. The Lord, He's the only one who knows,
and He don't tell until we gets to meet Him, which is you know
when." I hadn't given up on my mother's Bible faith then, so not
only did I hear her, I was satisfied with her explanation.

Looking back, I was satisfied with everything in my life until in
church one day a man stood up and said we were going to
rewrite the history books in our lifetime. There are always a few
people to speak out on Sunday, but mostly it's Scripture they will
read, or a lesson from it they have received that they feel the urge
to tell. Suddenly Joe Holmes, he just stood up and said his television set was speaking the Lord's will. Every day it showed
pictures of what the colored man was doing, and how he was
coming into something, at last. "It must be God's desire," Joe said,
and then he wanted to know if we were all ready. "Are you ready
for the Day?"

I thought he meant Judgment Day, just the way it's always
meant that; but he was talking of something else. He must have
known we were confused, because he explained himself before
we could ask him to: "There'll come a time not too much away

when we'll have to say to the white man that it's over, treating us bad, and we are as much citizens of the country as everyone else has been all along." I remember him talking as if that day was tomorrow, or next week at the latest. I never had heard anything like it.

We just didn't ever think like that, let alone speak aloud such thoughts. You grow up and take things for granted the way they are. If the rich take them for granted, so do poor folks. Why should they think it will ever change, the world where colored people have to be below the white man? My daddy's reaction was to say that poor Joe Holmes was always funny in the head, and now he had gone and lost his head. My mother said his head wasn't bad and it wasn't lost; it was just that he didn't know when to keep his mouth shut. He kept on saying out loud things no one can say, unless he's bound straight for the penitentiary — and plenty of us go there every year. "You just forget that kind of talk." I recall those words from my daddy. But my mother said, "Don't forget them, but don't let them fasten on to your tongue, or there'll be no end for you but the chain gang."

I forgot about Joe Holmes and his speech until a few weeks later I heard that Joe Holmes was beaten up near to death by the police. Some students in the Birmingham civil rights movement were going from county to county trying to get us all organized, to start school desegregation and get better streets for us, with lights, and get us some jobs maybe. Joe went to a meeting they had, and they started coming to see him at home. We heard that he said they could even use his house, come live there. I guess the sheriff heard the same thing. One night they were waiting for Joe on his way home from town. We knew they were watching him. ("It's a matter of time, only time," my daddy kept on saying.) They must have followed him until they could get him in secret, on the long, empty stretch of road going North. He was beat so bad they must have thought he was dead when they left him. It was a white man who saw him, lying near the road, and he drove to our cousin Mac's house to tell him that a nigger was sick on the road and needed help fast. Mac said he knew what it was that happened even before he started his car to go find Joe. The white man said it looked from the distance like a stroke or something, there being blood; but he must have been a stranger, a salesman or something. Mac knew, and any *white* man from Reform would have known, too.

Mac and two others, they drove Joe to Birmingham. They called the civil rights people to tell them ahead what was coming. They had people waiting outside the city on the main highway, and they worked a long time on Joe, the best doctors they could find. It took a week, but Joe died. His head was hurt so bad he never woke up, and probably without the doctors he would have been gone in a few hours.

We heard the news right off, as soon as Mac heard. His wife sent word over with Jean — she's their little girl. My mother started crying. She and Joe grew up together, and she used to kid daddy that Joe was too much like a brother for her to marry, but if not she would have. My daddy was upset, too. He started to say that Joe got what he deserved for being so bold, but he thought better. He looked at my mother and I guess he changed his thinking. He said that the time was when colored people could be killed to suit the whites, but no longer. Then he got nervous, for having said what he did; he warned us kids not to let it happen to us, not to become like Joe Holmes. I could see that he was afraid, and that he was mad, both at the same time. He kept on repeating that colored people used to be murdered all the time, but that it was different now. I wasn't sure he *believed* it was different, any more than I was sure that I did, either. My mother, she didn't say anything; she just cried, then she stopped, then she started again and stopped.

Whenever she cried I felt like crying, too; they're like an alarm clock in you, your mother's tears. I didn't cry though. I felt too old to cry, being a man. (I was fifteen then.) Anyway, a few days

later I found something better to do. The civil rights people came
to town, and they came to our door, asking if we would help
them. They said we couldn't let Joe Holmes die for nothing, not
in 1961 we couldn't. They said they were going to hold a meeting
in a church if they could get one, or outside Joe Holmes's house
if they couldn't get one, and would we come. My father said he
couldn't; it wasn't safe. He said there was no point making extra
trouble, and causing more people like Joe Holmes to die. He said
they didn't know what it's like in Reform, Alabama, the civil
rights people didn't. "This isn't Atlanta, nor even Montgomery,
and don't you forget it," he told them. They had an answer for
him right away: "We know. But they talked like you in Atlanta
for a long time, and in Montgomery a lot of people still do talk
that way; it isn't until they stop talking defeat and start acting
victory that there is any change."

My mother didn't say anything until they were about to leave.
She asked them how we could find where the meeting would be.
They said they would come back with slips of paper that would
tell us. My daddy said not to bother. My mother said nothing.
After the civil rights people were gone my mother and daddy
took to fighting, as much as they ever did in their lives. Daddy
said we weren't going to get into any trouble. My mother said she
agreed, only you can't blame someone for wishing it was a fair
world, and not so hard on us, and trying to bring things about so
that we always aren't so down on our luck. There wasn't more to
speak about after that. Daddy asked us all to forget the whole
thing. He said Joe Holmes would ask the same thing, after what
happened, because Joe didn't believe in people getting killed for
nothing, himself included.

I kept on thinking maybe I should do something more, being
younger. At school the teachers said we shouldn't talk about it,
even if it was the only thing on our minds. They said we had
learning to do, and that was that. When they buried Joe, a lot of
people must have said the same thing. They just didn't show up.

I know, because I went without telling anyone. My father would have punished me good if he knew.

I couldn't get Joe's wife and his kids out of my mind, nor what the minister said at his funeral. He said that it wasn't only the Lord who wouldn't turn his back on Joe; *we* had to keep him in mind, too. No one said anything about the white people that killed him, but the minister did say that as bad as everything all was, a lot more people were joining our side than ever before had, and Joe Holmes was probably the most famous man in our county now.

When we left the church the rights workers were there, handing out slips of paper, to announce the rally they were having the next day. They were holding it in a field near the church, and we were all invited to come. Some were burying the paper in their pockets, and others were throwing the paper away, as if someone were watching them. I decided I would throw mine away, so my daddy wouldn't even see it, and then go to the meeting anyway.

And that was how it got to me, finally. I heard people my age, or not much older, speaking up the way I used to think and not ever dare tell my own mother and my own father that I was thinking. They said we have taken it long enough, being killed and killed and killed, after being worked like horses and beaten like dogs, and everything bad. "Amen," we all said, and "Amen" I said to my taking it any more. I signed up with them, even though I knew it would cause trouble for me.

I went home and told my mother what happened. She told me to keep it quiet for a while until I was able to finish my schooling and maybe get a job someplace else. She was afraid for my father, and what would happen to us. She was afraid for me, too. She told me I was right though, right as could be; only you have to be careful to stay alive.

Things happened so quick though. The civil rights people didn't up and leave us, the way we thought. They opened up an office and moved in with us. They started holding classes for those who wanted to learn more, and they started visiting us at home, even if some were afraid to have them come. Then everything changed, all over the county, so that we knew we had more friends than ever before. Every night you could see on television that it was all changing, even in Alabama. So after a time my daddy said I could stay and not leave town, and work in the movement. "You can even keep the rights people here if you want," he told me, and then he said that he wished he could have had the chance when he was my age; but he hoped I wouldn't think he could have done anything then, no matter how hard he would have tried: "They killed us all the time then."

That's how I became one of the leaders here in Reform, and how I got to go to Selma, and up to Washington. It was Joe Holmes who did it, and the students who came here and stood by him at the grave and stayed with us. Sure, the sheriff gave us a lot of trouble, but he never dared beat anyone else, let alone kill anybody, and now with us getting the vote and all, they say he will retire when his time is up. But how it got to me, finally, was hearing a colored boy my age speaking better than any white man I ever heard. I told myself that's no boy, he's a man, and since he's about your age, you can be just like him, which after a while I did become.

4. Not Easy to Be a Southerner: Jim Porter

"People up North give us the rough time we deserve, but sometimes I think they enjoy doing it — and they go pretty far. They talk as if every white man in the South is some kind of criminal; as if we're different from others. When they talk with me they're very kind; in fact they're kind to the point of being insulting. They let me know how special I am, and how glad they are for such exceptions to the rule down here. They look at me as though I was a strange animal whose kind heart somehow survived all the badness we have.

"I'm tired of being thought peculiar. First of all it's not true, and also it's unfair all around. I'm as loyal to the South as any segregationist. The word itself is confusing. Everyone thinks it applies to all white Southerners, but in many ways it applies to only a few. Most of us in the South are closer to Negroes than any other white people in the country. Not only don't we hate them; we love individual Negroes as you can do only when you live near them and work with them and get cared for by them. People laugh at that and say it doesn't mean anything, because we keep them out of our schools and restaurants, the real test of equality. I agree I'm in the movement to end every kind of segregation; but there are some kinds we've ended down here long ago, at least a lot of us have. If people can't understand how we can be so unjust to the Negro, let them at least try to understand how for some of us being real close and friendly with the Negro is as natural as can be."

He is a tall, very blond boy from Tupelo, Mississippi, and he is an active civil rights worker. He is twenty, a junior at an old and respected Southern college that has yet to admit Negroes. The year is 1963. His job is to recruit Southern white students for the movement. There are a group of students like him, and their work is as difficult as any I have seen: to convince the region's white people that the legal and social changes in their society are morally right. I have known him for a year now, and we are in the midst of a long talk. I have in my mind — and he knows it, because I have told him so — such questions as: Why him? That is, what in his life and background made him take up such an effort? Is there anything a psychiatrist can learn, listening to a youth like him, that goes beyond the truth of a particular life — in itself a truth hard enough to encompass?

"You ask how different I am from others my age. I don't know how to answer that. I know that my life has been fairly average. I mean that I was never the village oddball who has finally found a place to fit — with others like himself. I was born in West Point.

Figure 1
Ruby by Ruby at age 6

Figure 2
A white girl by Ruby at age 6

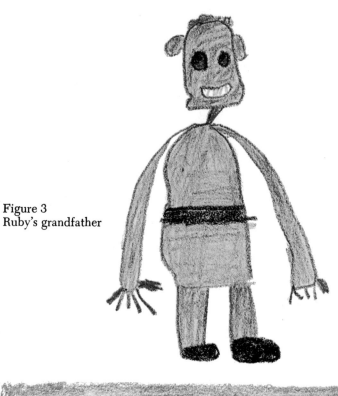

Figure 3
Ruby's grandfather

Figure 4
Ruby's landscape

Figure 5
Ruby by Ruby at age 7

Figure 6
Jimmie by Ruby at age 6

Figure 7: A Negro boy Jimmie's age by Ruby at age 6

Figure 9: Ruby by Jimmie at age 7

Figure 8: Ruby by Jimmie at age 6

Figure 10: Ruby in school by Jimmie at age 7

Figure 11: Ruby in school by Ruby

Figure 12
Negro friend and white classmate, by Johnnie

Figure 13: Allan draws the difference between Negro and white

Mississippi, but I grew up in Tupelo. My father is a lawyer. He originally comes from near Vicksburg. His father was also a lawyer, and a county judge later in life.

"Our family has been in Mississippi for a long time, as things go in the state, for I think they settled on a farm in the middle of the nineteenth century. They went west from North Carolina. At that time Mississippi was really 'west.' My mother comes from Mobile. Dad and she met through mutual friends; he was visiting them, and they introduced him to mother. Mother was born on a farm, not too far north of Mobile, and she was the first in her family to get a proper education. She fought her daddy real hard for it — being a woman, and of farm people. She won though, like she usually does when she wants something.

"My mother brought us up to respect people. She never told us to respect only whites. We had to be obedient to Harriet, the maid; we had to mind her as if she were another mother of ours. When I was a boy I remember my mother and Harriet talking over the menus for the day, and deciding what we were going to wear, or how we were going to spend the day, if it wasn't a school day. Harriet used to come with us to church. We went as a family, and she sat with us, as part of us. That's hard for people to understand who aren't real Southerners. The Yankees who move down here to live (a lot of them take up the segregationist cause as if they were converted) say that they like the cheap wages in the South. They hire as many Negroes as they can get their hands on, and they treat them like *servants,* the way they used to up North. I admit Harriet was a servant, too, but she was *more* than that — and as much as anything else it is the "more" that makes for what is Southern.

"We had Harriet with us, and I mean with us to love — that's the only word I can use. When I hear a politician 'ask for nigger blood' (that's what we call a certain kind of election speech), I think of Harriet and her family. We used to visit them; sometimes my mother would go to *their* church services, too. I know it sounds like we were special, liberals or integrationists; but that's not true. We were ordinary people — I suppose you could call us middle class, and maybe among the better educated in the county. But every county in Mississippi has people like us, and most of them never thought to call themselves 'integrationists' or 'segregationists.' They were just people, living with the 'nigras' (as we call them) in real closeness and friendliness.

"They call it 'paternalism,' but there's more to it than that; I say that even though I am against the whole system now. It was exploitation but it was also a lot of real closeness across the race line, and it started disappearing *before* the Supreme Court decision or the civil rights movement.

"You talk to most Southerners in cities like Atlanta or Charlotte — I'm not talking about the Yankees who have moved down here — and you won't have to go back far to find their origins. They likely as not were born on a farm, and came to the city to get a job. If they weren't the ones who did so, it was their parents who did. We've been witnessing the end of the pastoral life down here, the small-town life — where people know one another. They may keep the Negro in his place in those towns, but it isn't the place a Northern Negro has. I want you to know that."

It wasn't the first time I had heard his Southern pride expressed, and it would not be the last. I have noticed that when we talk more than a few minutes, he takes to a defense of his native soil — even when I am agreeing with him. Again and again I have tried to find out why he has set upon the hard job of persuading his fellow whites to want what they increasingly realize they must reluctantly accept. As I press him to make the explanations he gives for his often risky, certainly iconoclastic actions he resists with all his might: "I'm not some strange character, or a neurotic, or a special case. I'm an ordinary guy, who was brought up to be as decent as he knows how, to both white and colored. For my generation, this is one way to do it, to be true to what you've learned from your parents and in church by showing that you can live with new laws or customs. It's as simple as that in my mind."

He is brave. I have watched him move into a strange town, a town whose police and leading citizens are unfriendly to his every purpose. He has not even had the protection of the Negro community, of the Freedom House that Negro students can establish in the home or store of a local Negro. While there may be a white family that will nervously shelter him, or a minister who will allow him to stay in his home or the basement of his church, or a nearby school whose dormitory he can use, often he has no alternative but to camp out. Outgoing and direct, he starts knocking on doors and talking with people. He has a shrewd sense of whom to approach, and how. "I don't go charging into people with my ideas. That's not why I try to have ideas, so that I can attack other people with them. I begin telling them about myself and my life, and how it's not easy to be a Southerner today — I mean a white Southerner. Then I tell them what I'm trying to do."

Though I was aware of what he was trying to do, I asked him the question again because, as he and I both knew, he has not always had the same goals in mind. When I first met him he was, as mentioned, a student at a well-known, still segregated university. He had only recently become involved in civil rights activity. A Negro church nearby had been dynamited and he joined a delegation of students that walked the several miles from their campus to the scene of the damage, to protest the deed and to extend sympathies to the minister. That experience "changed" him, or activated him to what he called "new thoughts on the race problem." He started thinking more carefully about the Negro's condition, and noticing how the Negroes he met as he went about his everyday business lived and got along with white people. "I assigned myself a job: to find out what life is like for the Negro — apart from what I *thought* it was like." Although he moved from that self-appointed task to other, more active and decisive ones, he always returned to his initial experiences when talking about the purposes he had in mind: "You ask what I'm trying to do. Every time I meet someone and start talking with him about 'race' I'm hoping to get him *thinking*. That's what happened to me when I saw the ruins of that church. I started putting things together. I already knew a lot of what I was putting together, but I was finally making *sense* of what I knew. I saw that a burned church could be rebuilt, but millions of burnt lives were beyond any repair.

"When I meet someone — I mean a white person, of course — I try to speak about our responsibilities, as the people who run the society. Sometimes it jolts them to hear it put that way, just as it did me when I first realized it. We overlook our power; things go along every day, and we forget who owns property, and who votes, and who has a say in what happens. I remember what that minister said, standing near the ashes of his church: 'It's our position in the world, to suffer; even our buildings have to learn that. We don't have anything, so we have to take what comes our way, and pray.'

"I became angry all of a sudden — that he should take it on the chin so willingly and show so little anger about it. I asked him whether he didn't think Negroes should stand up and say that it *isn't* their 'position in the world to suffer,' that it's un-Christian for one group of people to make another suffer, from generation to generation. He gave me a long glance — I can recall his eyes looking into mine. He must have thought I was a civil rights worker, or some strange breed of white man. Maybe he thought it was a trap, that I was trying to trick him into saying something 'radical.' All I could see was how guarded he was, no matter what I said. He nodded in response to my remark, but that was as far as he would go. I think it was his behavior as much as the burning of the church that made me stop and think. A Negro can't trust even a friendly white man, not right off, anyway. He isn't even free enough to welcome the support he desperately needs. He isn't free enough to shout out his anger or his indignation; or at least that minister wasn't that free, and a lot of Negroes still aren't nearly that free. I think I was that free when I turned six or seven, but there were limits — I now realize. The white man in the South isn't as free as he may think. That's what I try to show white people when I talk with them. I try to tell them that perhaps the minister was *confused;* he probably wondered later about that white boy who thought he could talk like that and get away with it. Sometimes I wonder myself — who I was when I started talking like that, to the minister, and then to my friends. It didn't just 'happen' though — suddenly, because a church burnt down. As I see it, my reactions at the church and with the minister were to some extent those of a typical white Southerner, of a certain kind. I admit we have other kinds down here, but they do everywhere."

When I have tried to find out why, in the first place, he chose to march in protest of the church-burning he has been quick to answer: "A lot of us marched, about a hundred or so; more wanted to, but didn't because they're not the marching kind — for anything." When I have pointed out that among the hundred he stands alone, the only youth to commit his energies so long and hard to the cause of integration, he has been rather consistently self-effacing: "I don't know why that is. I don't think it's because I'm much different from any of the others, or even because my views are different. Maybe what I've done can be compared to being a school dropout, or joining the Peace Corps. Some students have a need sometimes to get away from books, or from the safe, predictable life, in order to see a little more than they could otherwise. When I began to get involved with civil rights work the Peace Corps was just getting going, so it wasn't available; and college deans frowned upon leaving school for any reason, no matter how conventional. I think the church-burning made me stop and think about a lot of things, about right and wrong. One thing led to another, and I joined the movement. I've always remained loyal to my own life though — to my background. I've asked myself the same questions you have, and I keep on coming back to my parents, and the real affection they taught me to feel for Negroes. When white people say to me 'Who are you?' with that suspicious look in their eye, I reply 'I'm Jim Porter, and I'm a white Southerner, too.' Then I try to find out whether they, too, were reared to have respect for Negroes and to feel grateful for all they've done. I meet enough kindred souls to keep going — to make me think the South has a fighting chance. Can you say more about any other region?"

5. *Down from Chicago*

You want to know what makes me tick, how I got involved in all this. I can tell you, it's easy to say: I was working, trying to keep working, going from one job to another, so that I could go back to college. I started college right after high school, but after the first year I was broke, and my family was broke, too. There wasn't the scholarship money around then that there is now; so I had to go out and work.

Not that work was strange to me. I started working at seven or eight, helping my father. He took care of buildings; he was a janitor. My brothers, even my sisters, used to help him. He had more buildings than five men could properly take care of, but he never dared raise his voice in protest. We lived in Chicago, in the Black Belt of Chicago, and any job was a status symbol on our block. What do you think of that — of a man working day and night, for about thirty dollars a week, and thinking he's the luckiest man that ever lived? That's freedom for you.

My dad actually spoke of freedom. He would tell me that so long as we weren't on relief we were free — even though he could have loafed and collected as much in unemployment compensation or welfare money as he made on his job. My

mother worked, too. For a while she was a maid, then she lost
that job because the people moved away. She had to settle for
washing floors and dusting desks in an office downtown. In the
evening when we all had our supper and were watching television, she left. My father did also — it was either barrels, or a
fuse that blew, or a leak. So we were alone at night.

I was the studious one. My older brother kept on telling me I
was crazy. "You're wasting your time. You're wasting your time."
That was the way he talked; he repeated everything he really
meant. The teachers tried to knock it out of him, and my mother
and father told him he'd better stop doing it; but he stuck to his
guns, and to this day he repeats himself at least a few times in
every talk we have. When I joined the movement in Chicago and
decided to go South he said to me: "Now you're a winner; now
you're a winner, brother."

I was the first one in my family to graduate from high school.
My brother kept saying I'd never graduate, but I stuck it out for
exactly the reason he said he couldn't: there was nothing else to
do. I saw him hanging around the house, then moving to the
street corner, and I thought I'd rather be in school than on the
street. He took up liquor, and then it was drugs. He started
falling apart right before our eyes — especially mine, because we
always slept together, he and I and my two younger brothers. So
I was right in there at the beginning, when he fell into bed stink-
ing drunk with cheap wine; and later, too, when he seemed to be
staring all the time, or dreaming — and, I'll tell you, talking
poetry, too. I never have forgotten that, how much poetry was
in him, and how it came out with drugs. People say a man like
him, he's a waste, a waste or a burden on society, but it kills
me most when I think of him talking under the drugs, because
then you could really know what was in him that was dying,
every day dying.

You ask if I remember what he said, but that's hard. I don't
remember the exact words. It's more the mood I remember. I

would be going to sleep and he would come home, talking to himself, but not like when he was drunk and didn't make any sense. We didn't dare say anything; we were scared. At first my father wanted to throw him out of the house; but my mother felt different about it. She said it would make him worse. She said if he went she would go, too. "He's our blood and he's gone wrong, but it's not only him who has, or his friends, either. It's all wrong, everything." That's what she said, and I can remember it word for word, because it's *all* she said about my brother and she must have repeated it a million times while we were growing up — and my brother was getting from bad to worse.

So he stayed, and he talked to us — it was almost like going to church every night, only more of the psalms or the poems than we used to hear in church. He even brought God into his talks. He'd be lying there, half dozing, staring up at the ceiling, and my brothers and I would be hanging on every word he said. Once I remember he spoke about our mother and God, and how both of them must cry in secret because they make life and see it wiped out so quick and there isn't a thing they can do, not a thing. He started talking to me and my brothers that time — I guess he assumed we were awake listening, or maybe he didn't care but just wanted to have an imaginary talk between himself and us.

"You guys, you're still alive, so I'm speaking to you from the grave, from the grave. They buried me a couple of years ago; it's just the dirt that hasn't covered me yet. Maybe we'll all meet someplace and it'll be better then, not like this life, where you try to hang on but there's nothing to grip, nothing to grip." He must have said that "nothing to grip" ten times.

It upset me more than anything else, because it struck home, that phrase really did. It said everything there was to say about the world we have. I told my English teacher what my brother said, because he was on my brother's side, way down, I knew it. (He would tell how rotten things were, and how we had to learn, but whether it would make any difference was another question.) I told him, and he didn't answer for longer than usual. Then he said my brother was right, but he was wrong, too, because there had to be a better answer than slow suicide. He told me to tell my brother that if we clenched our fists and offered them to one another, then we would have something to grip — one another's clenched fists.

There were some rumors that he was a Black Muslim but now I know they weren't true. He was the only teacher we trusted, and the one Negro teacher who didn't keep telling us how good the white man is. He was a civil rights leader, that's what he was, and I think it was he who first got me thinking there was something to *do,* some way to *act.*

It happened in his classroom during Negro History Week. Every year we had one of those, and they bored us as much as learning about George Washington and all that. He used to give us compositions to do in class. He would write the topic on the board, then give us half an hour to say something about it. That week he wrote "Negro History Week" on the board, and we thought that would be the subject. I remember lowering my head to think what I would say and then hearing the chalk moving some more. He underlined what he had written, but then went on to write more, underneath it: "I Have Had Enough."

Even today I can see us in that classroom. We looked at each other as if the poor teacher had finally lost his mind. No one dared say anything, not because we were afraid to, but because we were embarrassed for him. I don't know about the others, but I didn't even try to connect the two things he wrote until he decided to do it for us. (He saw how nervous we were. Some laughed, and others just stared at him.)

"Okay, get going," he said, and then he gave us a long speech. He told us that not only people had their limits but a race. He said we were Negroes and so was he, and it was about time we stopped thinking how great it was that a few Negroes were poets or teachers one hundred years ago and start doing something to make us more than a half-cut above slaves.

What happened was that he wanted us to tell him that we've

had enough, too. I wasn't sure *what* he had in mind then. I sat there — I can see myself now in that room — and suddenly I just wrote on the paper what he did: "I Have Had Enough." It became the title of my composition.

You're right, it would be interesting to read it now. I never saved anything I did in school though. Mostly it meant nothing to me, my work there. It was a waste of time, doing the work, but better than what was happening to my brother. (I always thought of that, and I think I stayed in school because somehow I felt it prevented me from taking to his kind of life.)

That's what I said in that composition. I didn't save it, but I didn't need to; my mind kept the words together. I can remember what I said almost word for word today. It's probably the only thing I ever did in school that I *can* remember, that ever stuck to me. I wrote that my brother was in a bad way, because he tried to find work and couldn't, and turned to taking too much drink and then the drugs. So he has nothing now, except what he imagines. How's that for really having nothing? I remember I asked that question, and then I answered it by saying that most Negroes have nothing — even those who think they have a lot. I wrote: "As long as we are kept out of places everyone else doesn't have to think twice before going into, and as long as most people treat us as though we were a cross between a dog and a human being — because we look like men, but deserve to be kept like animals — then we don't have anything, anything that matters." Then I ended it: "I have had enough, just as the title says. There is only one way to stop having nothing, and that's to demand your share, and tell the world to stop treating you the way it has. When you tell the world you've had enough, you may begin to get someplace." It may not have been that, word for word, but it was pretty close, I'm sure of it.

He gave me an A, the teacher did, and put my paper on the bulletin board, all alone. I never felt so big. I almost felt like trying to be smart like that every day, and maybe get into a college. I could hardly keep my eyes off the paper, so I didn't hear much of what went on in class the rest of the week — until the last day, Friday, when the teacher said he was going to take my paper down, but we should all have memorized what it said by heart.

He read out loud my last sentence, just to make sure we all kept it in mind, and then he handed me the paper. He said I talked and thought the way the civil rights people did down South — Martin Luther King and the people who belong to CORE.

That was news to me; but the more I thought about it that weekend and the next week the more I decided to look into the civil rights scene. Then I talked to my brother about it. I told him what the teacher said, and how he liked my composition. He wanted to see it, but I couldn't find it. I must have thrown it away with the other papers — arithmetic and history and such — as I did every day. He got angry, real angry at me. He said that was typical, a Negro boy throwing away the most important words he ever said, the one thing of all his school work that meant something. He made me tell him what I wrote — word for word, he wanted it. Then he told me I should finish out my high school course and go South.

"Go South?" I asked him. I didn't know what he meant. I had a picture of myself getting on a bus and telling the driver to let me off when we were in the middle of the "South." He said when I was ready to go, I'd find out where and how, and in the meanwhile we should forget the subject.

I did — for two years; but not really. I saw those freedom riders on television, and would have given anything to be with them. That's where I disagreed with some of my friends. They said they were wasting their time down there, staying in Mississippi and Alabama and trying to get things changed there. They should come up North — to Chicago, for instance.

"That's a laugh," I said, and I showed them how wrong they

were, not only about the South but about up North. It's comical
seeing Negroes in Chicago think they've got a better deal than
their brothers in the South. I knew it then — the way I sure know
it right now: that it's all the same; that maybe it's even better
down South, because there's no ghetto like up North, freezing
cold and with rats to sing you to sleep every night.

So I graduated, even though I didn't really care by then. I told
my brother I would graduate, even though he said I wouldn't —
even though he told me I should, regardless of what he said.
("Don't try to make sense of what I tell you," he used to say.) I
never even went to the ceremony. It meant nothing to me,
nothing; nor to most of us. We knew school wasn't leading us any
place but to the end of a dead-end street. I didn't mind walking
it — the only choice was that or my brother's kind of street — but
I wasn't going to *celebrate* the whole business, as if it was
something good all by itself.

To tell the truth, I didn't want to join the movement. I wanted
to get a job. I had a girlfriend, and she wanted to get married.
She kept on saying I could get a job if only I wanted to bad
enough, and I believed her. I did get one, washing dishes in a
cafeteria, then doing the floor, wax and all. They gave me sixty
cents an hour, and called me lazy every time I wasn't working
full speed. They wouldn't give me their food — they threw it out
rather than let the help eat it, and we heard them talking about
how "niggers" steal and loaf if you don't keep a real close eye on
them. I couldn't take it. I decided I'd sooner steal, if it came to
that, but not from them. I quit.

I flunked my physical — they said I had bad teeth and spots on
my lung and my bones weren't good, so I must have had
tuberculosis in the past. They told me to go see a doctor. I felt in
good shape, so I figured they were giving me some line. I didn't
want to go into the army anyway.

I was lost then, for a few months, and going downhill. I could
tell myself I was lost. I started liking beer too much, and mixing

it with stronger stuff, even in the morning. My brother really laced into me; he was afraid I was walking his road. "Stay off my turf," he said, over and over again. He only *sounded* angry; I knew he wanted to spare me his misery. I was lost, that's all you could say about it; like a lot of guys my age in the South Side of Chicago.

I was lost, but then I found my luck. I heard about some work in Louisiana, real work that meant taking a chance on getting hurt and not getting much pay but keeping your head above water. "Don't drown," my brother used to say to me, and when I heard they were signing people up to work in the South, I thought it would help me as much as them down there, which turned out to be true.

I had some relatives down in Louisiana, so they accepted me as a worker. I could go live with them and encourage them and their neighbors to try to register to vote and stand up for their rights all along the line. That's what I've been doing since I came down here, and it's been my luck to have had the chance. I started college here last year, and I think I'll spend the rest of my life in the South. I write home sometimes and tell them they should come back. They think I'm kidding, or nuts maybe, but that's because they don't know how bad they have it, compared to what you can do down here — by fighting for your rights, I'll admit, by fighting. So they won't listen to me; but my children, they'll be Southerners, and probably better off than anyone in my whole family up there.

6. *How Long Do They Last?*

In a number of psychiatric papers and general articles[1] I have tried to discuss the fate of civil rights workers. I say "discuss" because I do not believe that my clinical impressions can precisely describe the fate of those workers. It is not every century that has looked — without apparent embarrassment — so closely at the motives that urge people on and influence the character of lives. Perhaps there are times when it is enough — and more than enough work — simply to observe, and record what has been observed. Yet, I want to make sure that I am not read as an observer of "the" civil rights movement, as an expert on the *general* subject of activist youths, or as a psychiatrist who knows about a new — the political — dimension to what textbooks in adolescent psychiatry call "activity-passivity."

I have tried to present five youths, not quite as I would at a clinical conference, but with the same purpose — to make them as individuals come alive. In doing this I have used their words and mine, their observations and mine. (Even when the words are only theirs, my editing has its influence, not to mention the questions I long ago and repeatedly asked to elicit the responses set forth here.) Whatever illumination is supplied by these youths — and my acquaintance with them — has come from the success with which the truth of their particular experience is revealed, rather than from any (and futile) attribution of universality to that experience.

As a matter of fact I have found psychiatric and psychological generalizations hazardous enough to warrant combining all my doubts: there is no one kind of student — of either race — who typifies the activist. An enabling historical moment progressively came into the lives of all sorts of youths: the rich and the poor; Northerners and Southerners; Negroes and whites; the well-educated and the barely literate; thinkers and doers; the rebellious, the controlled, the anxious, even, I might add, the fearful. After I interviewed, say, my first ten students, I had seen enough idealism and fanaticism, timidity and belligerence, innocence and wary sophistication, to make me see that whatever characterized such youths as a group had to include more than the sum of its members' individual characteristics. When I put the problem to one of them he said: "Well, we're together, down here, that's the answer you need."

What has distinguished civil rights workers from others in their generation and in some past generations is the *purpose* to which they have applied both their energies and their conflicts. Their struggles (to "grow up," to be "free" and independent, to achieve some effort or way of life that they can call their own) to the child psychiatrist are, finally, rather pedestrian. What emerges as unusual, as extraordinary is the ethical context chosen for the struggles — and allowed, even encouraged, by history. What indeed activates a youth's ego, causes him to generate an idealism of deeds as well as of thought? The mind's relentless, ever-present past? History's arbitrary encouragement, granted almost indiscriminately? Or an almost exquisite — defying questions and questionnaires — blend of the two?

By and large these young men and women have fared well psychiatrically. The success of their day-to-day activity has not required from them a particular kind of goal or childhood. Moreover, just as they came South (or exchanged one kind of Southern life for another) in a number of ways, they left for a number of reasons. I wish I could match the entrances with the exits, thereby giving the reader (and myself) a certain sense of predictability about at least this aspect of human existence. Yet the natural history of participation and eventual departure — with all the trials that characterize both — has varied widely in these youths.

In several psychiatric papers[2] I have tried to give what coherence I can to the adjustment of civil rights workers, their manner of survival, the problems (internal as well as external) they have faced, and the eventual resolution to those problems achieved by most of them. There is no doubt that they go through certain "stages": periods of fear that give way to times of calm and competence; episodes of moody doubt that suggest to the volunteer that he leave; once gone, moments of nostalgia that urge him to return. There is also no doubt in my mind that the lives of these youths together teach the clinician what he should all along remember — he has been taught it — from his first days in medical school: human beings are a diverse lot, and very often avoid or succumb to disease in hard-to-predict fashion.

Again and again I have found myself confounded at the seemingly limitless endurance of one youth, or the precipitate and surprisingly inexplicable collapse of another. Anna Freud and her co-workers[3] studied heroic children, boys and girls who were moved to save the lives of others, and found them so "ordinary," "sane," or without psychopathology that they did not warrant special psychoanalytic investigation. Though some of these civil rights workers have eventually sustained enough duress to suffer from it — and justify clinical treatment for the symptoms that they have reported — their heroism has also been somewhat "ordinary"; that is, the heroes are not readily characterized by the particular qualities of their "personality," or by any chosen style of action. There is an additionally commonplace quality to such "heroism"; it has not been a matter of specific deeds done, but of an everyday willingness to go about one's business under vague, continual, and in a flash dangerous hostility.

In general it seems hardly surprising that the most tenacious have frequently been those most aggrieved by background, or most strenuously involved by virtue of temperament or psychological makeup. ("Once I get involved, I get involved," I heard from a young lady whose involvement was hardly in question.) The least resilient have sometimes been the most ideological: the fair-minded idealist or intellectual who feels compelled to demonstrate — to himself as much as others — his "practical" or "realistic" side. Ironically, it is better for him — so far as his survival in the South is concerned — if he is shy, stubborn, and sentimental in addition; though not any of these to any great excess. In my experience the really cold, confident and arrogant ideologues have tended to stay clear of Southern sheriffs. In any event, almost any character trait —"good" or "bad"— can become a lever to grasp and hold. Those who do so build contemporary survival on what was, perhaps, the outcome of an earlier failure.

In example here is a youth from a Midwestern farm community explaining how he managed to keep going: "I just do. I keep going and keep going, every day I just keep going. It's what holds me together. I try not to think about what and why, just keep working, from one thing to the next. The police drive by, or I hear a suspicious noise, or we get a phone call telling us we're all going to be dead in a half hour — I try to ignore things like that and keep working. I suppose I'm like an ostrich, sometimes; but I can't let myself dissolve into a puddle of nervous sweat, and that's what would happen if I didn't shut my mind to a lot that goes on.

"In a way I've always done that. When I was in the fifth grade the teacher called my mother in for a talk, because she would call my name in class and I would be so engrossed reading that I apparently wouldn't hear her. She thought there must be something wrong with a child who does that. My mother told her that I had always been a child with a one-track mind. I would get hung up on one thing, and then block out everything else. So I guess down here I'm reacting true to form.

"It's strange: when I'm working in the Freedom House, even if it's only helping with the food or cutting something out for the bulletin board, I'm absolutely convinced that nothing bad can happen. It's as if there's something in what we're doing here that can make any dynamite the Klan might try to plant harmless. The same goes for the teaching: when I'm sitting with those little children, trying to teach them history or a few words of French, I feel I'm immune to fear or nervousness. The children are so anxious to learn, and by trusting us more than we trust ourselves they *give* us trust. We're one of their few lifelines to a better kind of world, and they know it, even if we sometimes have our doubts. They look up to us, smile at us and work for us as if we were offering them a fortune to study a few hours a week. Every time I face them in that classroom we've built I feel I've received an injection of courage.

"Yes, there are other things that keep us going. We have our singing in the late afternoon. We assemble in a circle on the lawn with the children and their parents, and we sing freedom songs. I think they could be dropping bombs on us and we wouldn't run then. I never thought a few songs could mean so much, could give so much strength to you. I heard some of the songs before; I even owned a few records that feature them and I used to play them before I came down here — 'to get in the spirit of things.' That was different though — much different. It's not only that we're down here, or even that we're singing; it's that we're singing together, with enemies nearby. Enemies make you stronger; they make you find ways of pulling close to others, and feeling their support.

"In addition to singing I should mention the letters we write and get. Everyone back home knows how important it is to write us, to keep our morale up; but I wonder how many of them realize how important it is for us to sit down and write to them. I find that when I write a letter to my brother, just a friendly, folksy kind of letter, I let myself think more openly about the dangers here, and I settle — in my own mind — how I feel more than at any other time. Even if I don't write everything down — I wouldn't want to, anyway — I find myself calmer and quieter for having written what I have.

"So letters count, and news from 'outside,' too; news that tells us how we're getting across to the rest of the country. It's hard for people to realize how isolated these rural communities are. It's not that the people *here* are so isolated; with television they see more than they ever have — too much, in fact. *They* know how bad things are for them, and they see what the rest of us are getting just by tuning in on the programs, day or night. It's the people up there who are isolated. They're the ones who don't know what's going on. Even if you read the *New York Times* you practically have to wait for a disaster — a shooting, a dynamiting or a riot — for some of the 'background story,' as the reporters call it, to come out. That's why we hope our activities down here at least will get across to the people we know, and to their friends' neighborhoods. When we find that a local paper is reporting something about life down here, about the facts of life these people have to face — even if it's because we're here, the white civil rights workers, the hometown boys and girls — we feel stronger. I told someone who called up here the other day threatening us to go right ahead — kill us. I said that everyone in the country would read about it, and then I asked him what he thought would happen to his 'way of life' that we are 'destroying.'

"Well, that's about how we make it here. Mostly, I'd say we fall back on ourselves. A person like me shuts things out. Someone else will talk, talk, talk, and analyze everything, until he's convinced that we can't get into trouble because the *segregationists* have analyzed the risks and figured out it doesn't pay to hurt us. Then you'll see the overactive type: the kind of girl who doesn't only teach, but cleans up everything in sight, and gets the children to do the same. She worries about how neat the Freedom House is, so that we don't set a bad example for the children. There's no point trying to stop her — she's letting off steam, letting out fear — we know. It's always easy to figure out how the *other* guy is protecting himself from fear.

"One thing we've decided about our fears is that it's a poor idea to talk a lot about them, or analyze them. We have long talks, bull sessions that help us share thoughts and feelings; but we always seem to gravitate away from introspection, from making one another self-conscious, and as a result paralyzed. We try to keep the talk oriented to real problems and what we can do to solve them. There's plenty to keep us busy, without hitting at one another with 'observations,' and as a result falling apart. (I suspect that if we fell apart as a group we'd soon start falling apart individually.) You learn how to talk together and what to say to help one another without ever realizing you're doing it."

What further comment — elaboration or explication — is necessary from one like me? The lives of such youths reveal how intimately and variously the mind's past lives with the present. Established traits and old styles of behavior obtain new relevance, or indeed fail to do so. It comes (or should come) as no surprise that almost any quality of thinking or mode of behavior derives its "value" from the social and cultural context in which it takes place: the criminal's murder or the fighting soldier's courage; the limitless and isolating suspiciousness of paranoia or the hungry and finally rewarding doubt that characterizes a good deal of the best scientific research; the aimless yet determined defiance of the suburban delinquent or the precise toughness of the well-to-do youths who have left Northern campuses to express — and live out — their kind of defiance.

When these youths have "collapsed," given way to uncertainty and to an exhaustion that eventually takes hold of them rather than urges them on to further effort, the "explanation" ought to be at least as subtle as the complicated development itself is. Whatever the term "battle fatigue" means — and it clearly has many degrees of meaning, from "simple" exhaustion to extremely knotty disorders that in fact are the culmination to a lifetime of unhappiness and fear — I do not think the particular kind of despair and weariness I have seen in these youths properly qualifies as "war neurosis." I say so not to quibble over terms (or with my own previous reports) but in order to make sure that the psychological state that falls upon many of these students with some regularity be understood for what it is: the result of a grim, hard-won awareness of the world — one that at last allows the mind to make necessary adjustments of perspective and purpose.

I have seen exhaustion in these youths come and go, and of course had to treat some very definite physical and psychological symptoms: relatively minor aches of one sort or another — head-

aches, stomachaches, backaches; more severe physiological dis-
turbances undoubtedly related to stress, such as the appearance,
or reappearance, of ulcers, asthma, various forms of colitis and
crippling migraine; those symptoms that skirt the borderland of
psychiatry and internal medicine — insomnia, appetite loss (or
extravagant gain), irritated eyes and so-called "spontaneous
tachycardia," that is an inexplicable speeding up of the heart's
action. Finally, of course, there has been the roster of psychiatric
complaints, from mild anxiety and moderate fear to every clinical
stage of depression.

In contrast to (or in addition to) these complaints many
students show a kind of "collapse" (often followed by their
departure North, to school, or to other work in the South) that
has a quality all its own. It is not that their guard is down, forced
down by duress, by the jailings, beatings and threats they have
experienced. Nor are they simply tired and frustrated, reason
enough for any number of symptoms. In fact the specific "breakdown" I have seen in them is likely to occur when they are most
rested and under comparatively little strain. Often — though I
intend no tidy generalization here — the young man or woman
will get into a minor automobile accident, or slip and fall, or be
hurt in a game, thereby tempting me to say that they are "working something out unconsciously," or are "accident prone." That
may be — and often is — the case. Yet these youths are struggling with more than the tension of unconscious wishes in collision with the mind's conscience and its sense of awareness. There
is an outside world pressing upon them as inexorably and
urgently as that most inner of worlds, the unconscious. If we all
have to make peace — or at least some arrangement — with our
secret hates and temptations, some few of us, apparently, face
unusual, lonely and extreme confrontations with the most public
and evident of those emotions — the murder in a sheriff's look,
the generous blandishments of a society that asks only to be left
unbothered.

I asked Mary, a twenty-three-year-old, devoutly Catholic girl from Texas what "went wrong." Perhaps because she was experiencing what I was merely observing, but also perhaps because she was not tied down to any particular psychological system or viewpoint, her mind could draw rather striking conclusions about its condition, and state them — I thought — with definitive candor.

"I didn't smash into that car because I was in a daze. It was much worse. I was driving along and I was thinking how hard it is to change things, to really change them. Until that time — or a few days before — I just worked and had faith. We also did a lot of talking and analysis of what was going on in the community, and we had our down moments about our effectiveness, but we never related what we were doing to the larger picture — I mean to more than the civil rights picture. Somehow I think most of us believed that the people we were 'helping'— if you want to put it that way — were going to get a better deal out of life, *in our time*. It took me much longer to realize that my work was *devotional,* almost an act of faith, religious faith. It was work that meant more to me than to the people I was staying with; I mean it was work that probably would help me more than them.

"Not that we aren't doing some good — or that I expect the world to change overnight, or in my lifetime. It's just that I came down here expecting to help make concrete changes, in voting eligibility or in the education of young children. What I see now is that even with the Civil Rights Bill and Operation Head Start, let alone our work in the community, the effects of this kind of social system — a rural, caste system, centuries old — won't go away so easily, no matter how hard one talks and pleads and teaches, and tears one's heart out.

"Some of my friends get cynical and say money will do it, or giving more power to the poor. When I say it's more than that they say it's my 'latent Catholicism' coming out. But I think it's more than that; it's that I've gradually been able to see how hurt and scared and beaten a lot of people down here are. Just as they're not beyond hope — I know that, too — they're also not perfect or without scars. (They wouldn't be human if they weren't injured, and in need of hope as well as help; and it takes people longer to know what to do with hope than with money or work. Not that these people have money and work yet, either.)

"Well, anyway, I think I crashed the car because I knew all this and was getting ready to leave. I knew I had to *do* something in order to leave, to make my good-bye through an *act* rather than an *explanation*. I wasn't looking for an injury, or trying to punish myself out of guilt. I was getting ready to go. My friends were joking with me. They said, 'Mary, you're going to latch on to something, and then you'll be able to leave.' They know. You say: 'I'll stay until the start of the next semester in college, or until we complete a particular project down here, or until we finish building the community center.' You're not depressed. You're awakened, and you know you have to go away, to fall asleep a little, so you can live and bear it, the prospect of a few more decades up there, not just weeks or months down here. So you search for a way to go that will be *tactful,* not because you want to be polite, or escape your own guilt or the criticism of your friends. It's more complicated than that. Hope is a fragile thing. You don't want to see it injured when it's trying to grow — and you've helped it a bit yourself. The Asians would understand. You have to leave in such a way that 'face is saved': yours, but also the other people's — and most of all, the face of hope."

She was much less depressed than her words on tape sound now or read. She was fulfilling every psychiatrist's wish, being eminently "realistic": it was time for her to go back to college. I think she was also doing more than punishing herself for wanting to (and preparing to) leave. The conflict she had was all too clear to her — as was the need for a polite departure. A few minutes later she said it again: "I have to go in a way that won't offend and discourage my friends here. I never planned to hit another car, but in the flash of that yellow light I kept going and didn't stop. I had been thinking that maybe soon I'd have a minor accident — you always think it'll be minor, of course — and then leave."

At the time I wrote in my notes that "she possesses awareness with a vengeance . . . she now seems almost too sophisticated, both about the rural South and her own mind." That was the point — though I did *not* see it then: her mind was not only unconsciously conflicted and driven but unusually and exquisitely in contact with both its own dilemma and that of the world around it.

I asked Mary just before she left whether she minded if I called her a bit depressed — perhaps fatigued by several years of battle, of social struggle. "Yes, I do. I'm not depressed, and I'm not 'denying my depressions,' as you people say. I'm not suffering from a 'neurosis of war' — I've read about them. I'm weary, and maybe a little 'resigned,' the way Kierkegaard uses the word — you've faced life, and you're tired from doing so. That's not a depression, or *only* a depression." I think she is right. The vicissitudes of the strong and willful are not adequately described by a language that hopes to document the pains of the ill.

7. Back to Chicago

"I feel like some of the Negro sharecroppers must have felt in the thirties. There's nothing to do down here but feel useless and unwanted; so it is best to go North. I don't say that to feel sorry for myself. I think I *should* go North. I think we did what we could do when we could do it, but now it's for the Negroes themselves to work at the problem, with as little interference from whites as possible, no matter how friendly they are.

"I'm going home then, back to school in Wisconsin. After that I'll work in Chicago, where I grew up. I'm sure I'll find some kind of job to do in civil rights or that so-called 'war' on poverty. I don't mind leaving, even though the South has grown on me — more than I ever expected. Even that drawl that I used to detest, it's not so bad now; it even sounds better than the Northern accents I remember. I notice *them* now, probably the way Southerners do."

She was soon to leave Mississippi when she indulged that nostalgia, and now she is gone from the South, by her own estimation "probably for good." She misses the region now more than ever, as one might expect. Listening to her one senses an almost uncanny mixture of sorrow and rationalized acceptance. I suppose the word to describe her mood is "resignation." She didn't want to leave, but she felt it was right to go. She had ideas and projects in mind, but others thought they should not be suggested or implemented by her, or her kind.

When asked, she was forthright: "Yes, it's harder for whites in the movement. Everyone knows that, even we know it, the people who have worked here all this time. I guess it had to come. It's not racism in reverse, it's the natural development of a feeling of community and power among Negroes."

Yet, a while later in a different mood she could speak her regrets. "There *has* been some racism developing among Negroes. I've seen it build up — in the people we've been trying to help as well as in the staff. A few years ago we were all relaxed with one another, not completely so, but much more than now. It's not just that we're psychologically tired, more on edge, although that's also true. It's the racial tension. If you're a Negro, you can only hate a governor or sheriff so long. Eventually you have to have a more immediate person to let go against. If you're white it's the same thing: the Negroes you meet are apathetic or sullen, or they resent you for bothering them, or stirring things up and getting *them* in trouble. (You can always get away, and they know it.) I think we've all tried too hard to ignore a racist society. We've pretended that *we* could love one another, even if in the world blacks and whites are either enemies or they couldn't care less about each other. I guess in the long run it finally hit us, too."

Did she mean by "it" racism?

"No — and yes. I mean that racism *affected* us. When you fight something, you have to think about it and look at it and argue with it and after a while it becomes almost a part of you — or something like that. I don't know exactly what I mean, but I think an enemy has power over you when you're fighting him. Just as we have power over the segregationists — they're scared of us, and they have to scream when we act, which means in a way that they follow our lead — the same holds for us when a racist governor or a police chief starts bearing down on us. We have to react; we have to fight back; we have to spend time and energy. We get angry and scared, usually both; and I'm simply saying that when all that happens, day after day, year after year, there is an effect on us, and *part* of the effect is that we become like our enemies. Don't misunderstand me: I don't mean we become segregationists, though we may for moments, or even longer. I'm talking more about our mood. Maybe this is how to say it: if you're fighting a stubborn, crafty enemy, and he fights you at every turn, and keeps on frustrating you by letting you know that he has all the power, and you can't *really* get any of it away from him — just a few tidbits here and there — then after a while you either surrender (and some of us have done that) or you develop his tactics and learn from him in order to beat him. What else can you do?

"I think nonviolence was *our* tactic; it had roots in our history, the white intellectual's as well as the Negro's. For us whites it was an ethical form of protest; we had read about it in the writings of Tolstoy and Gandhi and Thoreau; it meant something, particularly to a generation brought up to fear that the whole world might be destroyed by atomic violence. For the Negro nonviolence was part of his history. He never really had much choice in the matter; it wasn't anything intellectual or ethical, just a terrible fact of life for him. When the white man has the guns, and he's likely to kill you at the drop of a hat, you believe in nonviolence — or the dignity of suicide, I suppose, as an alternative.

"Anyway, we've been nonviolent, and since we're still a minority — as everyone reminds us — we'll continue to be nonviolent. We haven't been treated nonviolently though; and because of that we don't feel very nonviolent. I think in the beginning we did. We were fresh, today we might call it naïve. We had faith, if not in the segregationist whites, at least in a lot of other whites — the 'average man' as he's called. Most of all we had faith in ourselves, in what *we* could do.

"After a while we realized that it wasn't working, *our* nonviolence by itself. We had to do all kinds of other things: develop contacts with the press, and Northern people; use every kind of economic and political leverage we could find. In this country a nonviolent leader is likely to be killed — there's so much violence here. Kennedy was killed. Malcolm X was killed. James Meredith was shot. They've hit Martin Luther King. A really charismatic leader runs risks in America that he might not in another country. Furthermore, the enemy is too 'complicated' or 'spread out' to define precisely and then put under pressure. It's not like King George III, or the Czar, or the British Viceroy. (I admit they were only symbols, too; but they *were* symbols, and there isn't the same kind of symbols, personal symbols, for us to attack. A governor here and there, yes; but there's no one man who sits on top of the whole social system.) So, it's been hard on us, and eventually I think we've become hard on one another.

"I think right now the development of black nationalism is a final attempt to keep the movement going. It *is* a movement: we're on the run; we're trying to move people; we have to keep ourselves and the people going, on the move against the status quo. Unless we find some way to capture the imagination of the poor, frightened Southern Negro, he's going to continue to live as he does, for all practical purposes in slavery. The presence of us whites hasn't made those people less afraid, maybe just the opposite. The new federal laws have barely touched them where it really counts, the pocketbook and the police station and the courthouse. That's why they need power — enough money and influence to make people listen to them rather than beat them up.

"That's why the Negro civil rights leaders want to work by themselves. They don't want us any more, with the promise of 'integration'; they want to show — themselves and the people they're trying to reach — that the black man can do it himself, organize himself and make himself heard and felt. At least that's what I make of the changes in the movement now. There are going to be less and less of us around, people like me."

VII

THE INTEGRATIONIST
SOUTH

THE civil rights struggle has furnished an obvious rallying
ground for Negroes; but the white Southerner has been the
Negro's companion in at least one respect, he also has inevitably
had to respond to that struggle. One white man supports the
Negro's rise; another stands in terrified opposition to it; still another feels petulant annoyance that may even shift to a dazed,
reluctant admiration.

"They're leading us around. Everything they do, we have to
think about. Who says the nigger is on the bottom? He's calling
the tune, and we run to hear it: this place, that place, everywhere, it seems." He is a police officer in Alabama, and so
perhaps more sensitive than some other people to the Negro's
recent deeds. I told him that, and he replied good-naturedly:
"Maybe. But you go talk to any white man down here and ask
him about it, and see what he says. Pick them from all over; it
doesn't make any difference if they be dumb or smart, or rich or
poor, or what their opinions are. They'll have to agree, we're
being led these days by the nigger."

Some of the following people may feel more like leaders than
followers. I suppose the policeman would say that the white
leaders, too, have been led — by the protests and demonstrations
of Negroes. It is a familiar riddle: how far can a leader go on his

own? Does he reflect what others want, or bend them to his own desires? How much does the white Southerner respond to the Negro? How much do his actions express his own desire for change?

1.   *A Yankee Went South: The Professor*

"My father was a Yankee, and he went South. I mean, he came South. Sometimes I talk as if I'm still up there; and I know why. I feel like going up there every few weeks for a rest."

He teaches history in a small private liberal arts college in Alabama, and for years before the Supreme Court's 1954 decision he had urged desegregation upon his colleagues, to no avail. "I wasn't treated badly then, in the forties and early fifties. People thought I was quaint, a kind of village eccentric, a nice guy who had strange but harmless ideas."

As the issues became increasingly grave and freshly charged with controversy, he came to recognize the turning point facing him: "I remember one morning back there — it was around 1955 or 1956. I woke up and told my wife that we had a decision to make. For the first time in my life I would have to weigh every word I spoke. Mind you, I wasn't suddenly becoming aware of Southern intolerance; I was becoming aware of something new — the region's last-ditch struggle to say no to desegregation, when yes was as inevitable as it could possibly be.

"My wife is an optimist, and she said that I was exaggerating. 'They'll take it — from you — they always have. It's not as though you were some new convert, an integrationist who suddenly appeared in town, or an outside agitator, as they're now calling them. Everyone knows what you think, anyway. You've been saying for years that people deserve equal rights, and you've been telling the president that they should take in Negroes, qualified ones. So why should you become afraid now? I think people will actually start listening to you for the first time.'

"She said a lot more, most of it along those lines, but I told her she was wrong, dead wrong; and I turned out to be right. About a month after we had that talk at breakfast we had to have another one — this time after I came home from the college, and a talk with the president. He told me I had to stop talking about equality and integration. He said he meant it, too; if I didn't stop I would be asked to leave."

When he talked about those years, the middle and late fifties, he gave himself little credit for the survival he had managed at the college. To his strict conscience even that survival could be counted evidence of compromise. In fact, he had become discreet, though for a long while his reputation as an outcast was secure: "They needed me then. When I kept quiet they heard my *thoughts,* and reacted to them. You have to hate a person, not just an idea. What a lot of people in the North don't know is that the Negro himself isn't an enemy enough, once bigotry and fear really get going. There have to be a few white people around — to be punished and persecuted; otherwise, it becomes hard even for the ignorant to believe that an obviously weak and downtrodden people are conquering an entire region. So the friends of the Negro are eagerly sought out — the white fellow travelers, we're called, or white niggers. Niggers are niggers, but a white nigger is a nigger lover, the most awful person around."

All that he once said to an apparently indifferent, even bemused community had not been forgotten: "It was as if they were listening all along, silently listening in the forties, but waiting for a time to let me know what they thought. For years I kept my promise to the president that I would refrain from speeches or public statements of any kind. What surprised me was how totally unnecessary and futile that promise was. They remembered, and what they didn't remember they made up."

To the credit of the college he was not fired. The president asked him whether he wanted to leave, and volunteered to help find him another and better job. He refused the offer. He decided to stay — it was his form of nonviolent protest. "Talk about passive resistance; all I had to do was keep quiet and go about my work to wage a real struggle, not only in the town but the state. The governor told them to get rid of me. The trustees were tempted to oblige him, though eventually they didn't. I think they realized that if they gave in to such political pressure, from either the town people or the state government, the cost would be too high. They would be rid of me, the nuisance I was to them, and the pressure that others were putting on them; but for once having yielded they would forever be susceptible to similar pressures. That's how you find protection sometimes: it hurts your enemies more in the long run to punish or sacrifice you than it does to stand by you; so you're protected by a 'balance of forces' rather than for ethical reasons."

Though his job was thus "protected," he had good reason to worry about his life, and his family's safety. From 1954 not a year passed without at least one cross-burning on his lawn. He tried to protect himself from threatening phone calls by securing an unlisted number, but to no avail. Small-town telephone operators are amiable, and it is not hard to secure the information they possess. When I first met the professor in 1961, he was a man who every day thought — and was told — he might be injured or killed; yet he felt compelled to tell me apologetically that he was afraid to speak out what he truly believed. "I'm a coward, really. I'm living off my reputation as an integrationist, but right now I don't say a word more than anyone else in town on the subject."

"Is anyone else here having a rougher time of it than you? Is anyone else being shunned and threatened?"

"No, no one; but you have to remember I'm not earning the reputation I have, I'm living off it. I have a hard time justifying my silence. Sometimes I think that I'm alive because there's a silent agreement between me and those who harass me. So long as I don't say anything *more*, anything *new*, they will make life hard for me but go no further. It's as if they need me for an enemy, a visible one, so they won't cause me any harm; but they have their limits, too — as they remind me every day.

"I remind my wife sometimes of the irony to all this. My father came South to get the sun, to help his heart recover. He was a young minister, but with rheumatic heart disease. He disliked and feared the winters up there, though he never could have simply gone South for a rest, even if he had the money. He heard about a position in a Montgomery church, and he decided to apply for it. When he went South to look at the church, and be looked at by the vestry, he fell in love with the South. They liked him, too, the people in Montgomery did. Those were quiet, peaceful times, and a Yankee could add a bit of polish or interest to life. So my parents moved South — in time for me to be born in Montgomery. What a stroke of luck *that* was for me. At least I can say I'm a native Alabamian, an issue that comes up almost every day. I never, never bring it up myself by reminding people where I was born. It's bad enough bowing to parochialism; I'd hate to stand accused of cultivating it."

I learned about his Northern ancestry in the course of taking a routine medical history from him. He seemed at first acquaintance rather healthy, a big reddish-complexioned man who at fifty-eight looked forty-eight and moved about or took exercise as if thirty-eight. Yet he suffered severe attacks of migraine, and I wanted to know whether his difficult social situation had brought on the disease, or made it worse.

No, he had always had migraine, or at least had it as far back as his youth. His father suffered from that disease, too, and the Southern way of life, slower and quieter, made no difference. Perhaps they both shared some inner, unappeasable wrath; or perhaps their genes inevitably destined them for pain. "I don't know whether it's constitutional or not. Now my doctor says it's psychosomatic, caused by the trouble I've been in. When I remind him that I've always had migraine, and my father before me, he smiles at me as if I'm a fool, who has to be gently suffered.

He knows it's my nerves, and my stand as an integrationist. Sometimes, though, knowledge can trick people. If that doctor weren't so sure he knew what the latest theory says about migraine, he would listen to me more carefully, and even remember some of his own observations. He treated me for those headaches when everybody liked me and forgave me my views. *Then* he said they were inherited from my father's Yankee blood — a kind of penance deserved by Northerners of every generation."

Whatever caused the headaches he and his father had to endure, I feel sure that the Yankee minister who went South prepared his son for the dangerous and bold stand he eventually took when a grown-up professor: "Some of my friends ask me why I believe what I do, as if I must be crazy or I wouldn't. Other friends are kinder; they want to know what keeps me going, how I get whatever it takes to put up with the hecklers and the threats. I don't have an answer for either group, but I think it's my father's influence that makes me worry about the rights and wrongs of the world, and I know he was a strong person. He may have given some of his strength to me."

"Did your father talk much about Southern customs, in contrast to those up North?"

"No, not very much. When I was a child Southerners weren't so defensive about the South, not, at least, as openly as they are now. I don't recall my father hearing what my children hear all the time: if you're not born here, you're an outsider and you have to prove yourself by being more militantly segregationist than most people — 'out-seging the seg's,' we call it."

"How do your children manage? It's a small town, and they're both nearing high school age?"

"That's been one of the hardest things my wife and I have had to face. The boys are split somewhat, too. One of them supports me wholeheartedly; he even tells me to be more outspoken. The younger one is more frightened; in addition he and I don't get along as well as his older brother and I do. Sometimes he speaks up at supper, tells me he wishes I didn't bring so much trouble down on him. He also will argue with me about the Negro issue. He feels they're inferior. 'They don't only look different, Dad. They're slow-moving and hard to teach. They should be kept separate, most of them. I don't say all of them; but most of them, yes.'

"Then we'll argue it out. He keeps referring back to a time when he was nine or ten. He tried to teach the maid some lesson that he had just learned in school. She couldn't remember from day to day what he had taught her. So he decided she was stupid. I remember when it happened. I remember telling him that maybe Ruth was bored, or too tired to pay attention to everything that excited *him*. He wouldn't accept that: she was stupid, and he would prove it.

"I forgot about the whole matter for a while until I found out from my wife that he was making Ruth's life quite impossible. He asked her to remember this bit of history and that bit of geography. He even tested her out on reading. Naturally she wasn't as eager and sharp as he was about learning. I think she tried to humor him along though — she was probably afraid to do anything else — until, finally, she came to my wife and asked her for help.

"We were confused at first, but the more we looked into the matter the more we realized that the boy was really hounding Ruth, making her feel nervous and deficient every day. I called him up on it and he didn't hesitate; he wanted to argue. He was trying to convince himself and me that he had been right all along — Ruth was stupid.

"We realized that the best thing to do at the time was let the matter drop, or deal with it obliquely rather than in head-on fashion. I'm no expert on child-rearing, but I could see that both our children were put in a spot by my position on race, and if one handled it by being an overenthusiastic supporter of mine, the other had reason to try another tack. Then my wife got drawn into the question. She is *pure* Southern — without a drop of Yankee blood anywhere in her lineage. Her family are fine people and basically feel as we do, only quietly so. The worse things have become down here, the less tolerant her family have become of my stand, not my ideas. They don't know it, but they're taking out a lot on me that they really feel toward Alabama's segregationists. I had my say a long time ago, and when I did they were surprised, but pleased. It's the climate here that has changed. I've even gone along with it by keeping silent whenever possible; but somebody has to be the enemy — and the representative of what is coming. My father-in-law feels I'm exposing the family to danger, risking our lives and welfare. Yet what he really is upset about, and can't dare acknowledge, even to himself, is not me but this town and the panicky people in it, including himself, and I guess at times me, too. As I keep on reminding him, I've been consistent and, lately, quiet; it's the attitude toward me that has changed."

"Including your wife's?"

"Yes, including her attitude. I was getting to that. For instance, she said that maybe Ruth *was* as stupid as my son Jimmie claimed. Mind you, Ruth had been working for us from the start of our marriage — she took care of both boys from birth. My wife always used to sing her praises. Suddenly she was calling Ruth dense and slow. I remember her words: 'You can't blame the boy for being impatient with her. He's so bright. She must frustrate him. He's a born teacher, like you; and any slow learner annoys a teacher.'

"We never settled the problem of Ruth. She left us while we continued to argue over her. She may not have been able to remember where all the cities were that my son pointed out, but she was smart enough to see a divided, troubled household bearing down on her as a symbol of its difficulty. We left the next maid alone. I think we all realized that there was no use starting another round of argument at a poor Negro woman's expense.

Once my son began to ask her whether she could point out where London was on his map. I called to him and asked him to go for a walk with me. I've never been angrier, but I tried to control myself. I glared at him, and then I told him that if he tried that again I would tear up every map he had — and give him the beating of his life, too. I'm sure he never saw me like that before — or since. We looked at one another, and I think the message got across: the maids were to be left alone.

"I remember that on the walk my boy started asking me why I 'favored nigras so much.' I told him that I didn't 'favor' them, any more than I did whites. I just thought people were people. He wouldn't let that pass. He said that even though people were people, Negroes weren't treated as whites were in Alabama — and, if I didn't mend my ways, we wouldn't be treated as whites either. I couldn't answer that very easily. I told him that was the way it would have to be."

I often asked the professor *why* it had to be that way, why he didn't shift his position just enough to protect his everyday safety and comfort. It would have been easy: a few well-publicized words; a guarded or ambiguous plea for "understanding" and "caution" instead of his former bluntness; a new insistence upon what is "practical" rather than what is ethically desirable.

He himself was at a loss to explain his behavior. He was in many ways a loner. He belonged to no organizations, and drew little support from others of his kind. He spoke as a teacher, a minister's son, his father's son. The longer I knew him the more I realized how powerful and sensitive his conscience was. In a curious way his migraine headaches signaled not tension but the absence of choice. Once when telling me about the pain he suffered — both in his head and as a citizen — he commented upon its significance. "The migraine I get doesn't come with tension, it comes when I'm tempted to escape tension, to give up the whole cause. It's at those times I get my worst headaches —

you might think because I want to surrender my ideals, but I think as a warning to me that I shouldn't."

I think his mind has struggled all along with both of those alternatives, but the pattern of his headaches suggests that he may well be right. He gets them not when faced with imminent danger, with personal harm, but when confronted with contradictions and ironies in his own life, and especially his family's, that threaten to weaken his clear-cut position: the fears of the children, his wife's hesitations, his loyalty to friends he likes but whose particular adjustment to segregationist pressures he scorns. His increasingly severe and recurrent migraine reflected the ambiguities of social existence as well as the anxieties of a man often facing real threats. Indeed, by the mid-sixties his headaches came less often. The South had shaken itself loose from enough of its past to make his views seem unconventional only by virtue of their age. In 1966 he gave me his latest count: "I'm down to about one a month, just the number I always had before all the trouble down here started."

2.   *"I'm the True Southerner": Mrs. Trumbull*

In many respects she is the most explicitly Southern person I know. Her name is Southern, Flora (Searcy) Trumbull. Her speech is as soft, her accent as honeyed as any in the South. In her bones — they are slight and she is a thin and small woman — she is the delicate Southern lady the region continues to venerate and make a show of defending. Her family background is unblemished: in the early eighteenth century her ancestors came to Virginia, then moved down to South Carolina, to Charleston. "That's where they were during the American Revolution," she once told me. In that same conversation she rather quietly and wryly reminded me that she was a daughter of both that revolution and a later one: "Sometimes I tell my own daughters they're going to have to choose when they're twenty-one — either they'll be a Daughter of the American Revolution or a Daughter of the Confederacy."

Mrs. Trumbull lives in Mississippi on a plantation, "a smaller one," she apologetically says. Her husband was a lawyer as well as a farmer, and his death, in 1957, revealed to her how very much she had become a Mississippian, and a planter's wife.

"I was born in South Carolina, and I expected to die there. Do you know that both my parents made a point of telling my brother and me that they never had put a foot out of that state. They claimed distinction for that, and even said that their parents hadn't either — though I think each of them had something on the other in that respect. I later found out what: both sets of grandparents had traveled out West, and my father's father had gone to Washington, even to New York — 'on business,' he insisted when I confronted him with what I had discovered."

She knew that laughable as the determined and boastful parochialism of her parents was, they were living quite intimately with history, with the temper and style of their generation's South. "It was fashionable for Southerners to stay home then, or travel only to Europe. They would even justify their travel to London or Paris by reminding themselves of the great sympathy felt for the Confederacy in London or Paris. It may seem absurd to you, but that's the way many of our present-day leaders were brought up to think. I don't frankly know how I managed to free myself of such blindness. In a way, it was coming to Mississippi with my husband that did it. I realized that after he died. I went back to Charleston on a visit — alone this time, and so more exposed to people and their views. I found old friends of my age still talking about the wonderful, mystical South, unblemished by Negroes except in the cotton fields or our kitchens. Those friends are young, too, if you think being forty-five is young.

"One evening I went to a party, filled with youthful conservative segregationists. They knew the South they wanted was gone forever. (I don't believe it ever existed.) Four years after 1954 they must have known history was moving in the opposite direction. Yet, there they were, talking like my parents, only sounding harsher and more absurd. Suddenly I understood what had happened to me. When, as my mother put it, I went 'West' to Mississippi I went from the frying pan to the fire; but I also went away, to a different state with different customs, even if staunchly segregationist ones. (People forget how very different each Southern state's history is.) It was geographic distance and a new social situation that gave me a real chance to see what nonsense and cruelty I had overlooked all my life — indeed even accepted as fair and honorable."

I first met her in 1958, shortly after her husband had died. I was living in Mississippi at the time, and a doctor I knew told me I should go see her: "Mrs. Trumbull is the most outspoken integrationist who has ever managed to stay alive in this state. She's a well-to-do white lady, unquestionably a Southern lady, and the mother of four daughters. She has gray hair, and she's a churchwoman, a devout Methodist. Maybe for all those reasons no one has shot her yet. One thing I know, there isn't anyone else in the state — white or Negro — who would dare talk the way she does — without expecting to die in twenty-four hours."

When I approached her house I felt disrespectful for doing so in a car. The home, the trees, shrubbery and flowerbeds around it, the cotton fields nearby all suggested an earlier, quieter age: columns in front of the fine, white plantation manor; high ceilings and antique furniture bought in the shops of Royal Street in New Orleans; delicately scented rooms where one is sent to be "refreshed"; warm air that must not be cooled, as Mrs. Trumbull puts it derisively, "artificially"; fragile china and carefully brewed tea served by the strong hands of a tall, confident young Negro servant; a sense of timelessness. We sometimes take authors to task for being "romantics" when in fact they do literal justice in describing people like Mrs. Trumbull and homes like hers.

During the two years I lived in Mississippi I gradually came to appreciate how astonishing her leadership was. In subsequent years, while living in Louisiana and Georgia, I continued to visit her, or watch her in action at a committee organized to insure peaceful desegregation of schools, or at meetings of human relations councils — groups dedicated to what Mrs. Trumbull delicately called "improvement for all the people of the South." Her voice would ever so gently yet firmly emphasize the word "all." As she put it once: "You have to pay respect to the possibilities in language. Perhaps we in the South have produced so many writers because everyone, from the intellectuals to the ungifted, has to learn the subtleties and indirections of what my husband used to call 'race talk.' Even outspoken segregationists who seem capable of nothing that is refined so far as the Negro is concerned will resort to euphemisms and pretense under certain circumstances.

"I remember a friend of ours who screamed 'treason' just because I used the word 'Negro' instead of 'nigger.' (I think I was probably the first friend he ever heard do so; and he took a long time to get used to it.) Yet, when he went hunting he wanted company, and the company he most wanted and enjoyed was that of his 'nigger boy,' James. They were friends, anyone who cared to look closely could see that. They enjoyed talking about work to be done on the plantation, about everything from the weather and the state of the crops to hunting. They hunted together, too; only the Negro had to go as 'help.'

"Well, I saw them going and coming back, and they were companions. They even drank together. The Negro was his boss's age, and they had known one another since they were both children. They had grown up together. For a while when boys they called one another Jimmie and Ted; but soon Jimmie became James, and Ted had to be called Mr. Theodore, which still makes James privileged, a 'house nigger,' as men like him are called — in 1960, mind you. The others, field hands or more remote servants, have to say Mr. Stanton.

"Anyway, one Sunday I saw Ted Stanton and James coming back; half drunk they were, and as happy and familiar with one another as could be. I asked my husband how Ted could do it, do it in his mind so that James and he got along the way they did. I'll never forget what he said: 'There's not very much logic to human emotions. People do contradictory things, and there's no explaining why. It's just in their nature to do so.'

"I disagreed with him then, and I do now. It's the one thing we never agreed on, to his last day. I believe that when Ted Stanton talks about needing 'help' from James he is behaving in a very logical, predictable way. When I first asked my husband how Ted could do it, I meant that I was surprised at the man's ability to miss the logic of his own behavior. Ted wants a friend's company, but he has to call for his 'help.' That means Ted, despite all his money and influence in our community, follows the rules rather than makes them. He thinks of himself as a leader, but he talks like a follower. It's not that his actions are illogical, it's that he protects himself from the truth that would explain them."

Mrs. Trumbull willingly talked with me about her reasons for being extraordinarily committed to so unpopular a cause. She, like Ted Stanton, had grown up close to Negroes, had been cared for and "helped" by them. Her mother had been a sick woman, intermittently confined to bed with tuberculosis while her three children were growing up. Mrs. Trumbull has two older brothers, both lawyers, both in Charleston, both in her words "conservative and segregationist, but not indecorously so."

"Why you and not them?" I asked her — and, as we got to know one another, she asked herself out loud. If she had been a boy she would now have the same social and political attitudes her brothers have, or so she was inclined to speculate: "I've thought about all this vaguely. You have to think about what you're doing when it's so unpopular. It's hard to do it though. You don't want to discuss your motives too much with those who are taking the same risks you are — if you start doing that, you'll soon stop doing anything else. So you talk to yourself sometimes, in front of the mirror while dressing; or when you should be reading and your mind drifts; or after one of those calls, telling you your life is about to end.

"I never come up with a real answer. Right now I'm 'too far gone,' as my friends tell me rather angrily at times. To them I'm sick, mentally ill. They wouldn't even believe *you* if you told them I was sane. They would say you're crazy, too. That's how they dismiss anyone whose thinking they don't like, or they fear. They call the person insane, or they say the ideas he advocates are crazy ideas. Sometimes I find myself going along with them, thinking just as they do — about myself. I'll remember the quiet life I lived as a child in South Carolina, and ask myself what in those years ever made me the way I am now. (Isn't that what you're trying to find out?)"

"To some extent," I replied. "Though I don't think we can fully 'explain' someone's contemporary behavior on the basis of specific childhood experiences. I think we can look back at a life and see trends in it — of cruelty or kindness, of concern for others or self-absorption, of indifference or continuing involvement in one or another problem or activity. Yet, such trends — they are patterns of thinking or acting — come about for many reasons, some of them apparently innocuous, or inconsistent with one another. There may have been a cruel parent who inspired compassion in a suffering son; or a kind parent whose child for one or another cause grew to confuse easy-going toleration with indifference, or gentleness with weakness. Then, as you know, events in the world, and in one's later life, bring out things in people, or for that matter, prevent people from being the kind of people they perfectly well might have been. So, I think a lot happens in childhood that either helps make us what we are, or prevents us from becoming what others are; but each person's life — entire life — has to be considered very carefully before 'explanations' are offered for his or her willingness to take an unpopular, a very dangerously unpopular stand in full public."

Once she gave me a long letter she had written to herself. She had been told by the sheriff of the county that he could not be responsible for her safety, for her life, if she continued her advocacy of "race-mixing." This time he not only said so, but wrote her a letter telling her so. She started her letter of reply in direct response to his, but soon felt impelled to wander through her past.

"Of course I have always known that one day a vulgar threat on my life, or my family's safety, might become much more, a nightmare become real. I have discussed the dangers with my daughters, and though they are more fearful than I — they have more living ahead of them, more to lose — they support my position.

"What is my position, according to you so likely to cause me 'serious harm'? I simply believe in the law of the land, in the obligation that every American citizen must assume to obey the courts and the decisions of Congress.

"You, sir, may find me simple-minded for insisting that Mississippi is one state in the United States, and as much subject to the Constitution and its spirit as any other state. You address me as if I were in peril. You write to me as if I were a confused outcast, causing trouble, but also deeply in trouble with herself, and in need of what you call 'wise counsel' before it is too late. My 'eccentric position,' you tell me, will 'ruin' me and my children. We might very well die, you say; or at a minimum, we will be destroyed socially and psychologically. Fortunately I have enough money to resist economic pressure. If I didn't have enough I am sure you would have mentioned the likelihood of *that* ruin, too.

"I want you to know why I'm doing what I am; why I am 'risking my life,' as you have described it, 'in order to get a few niggers into a school, and change everything around against the will of the people.' Until you understand that fellow Southerners, and not simply 'outside agitators,' want to abandon segregation as both criminal and wrong, you will be as confused about me as your letter was insulting to me.

"As you know, I am from South Carolina, and I dare say as Southern as you or anyone else in this town. Perhaps it is because I am a woman that I feel the way I do, a woman who grew up with two brothers who constantly made light of what I could do or be. Instead of being their pet younger sister, I became someone they could bully, and call weak. My mother and I were close, though, and in her eyes she was weak, too. She believed that all women were weak because she believed my father, and he said so — often. He was a rich man, partly through money he inherited and partly through money he made in law and investments. My brothers worshiped him, and my mother obeyed him. She was the 'Southern woman' you sheriffs are always talking about; the one who is so wonderful and beautiful and fragile and delicate and in need of your brute force to protect her against — of all things — the nigger-lust in every Negro's body and soul.

"Actually my mother was silently strong; and my father was noisily weak, so weak that he had to scare everyone around him to compliance, submission, agreement, or at least a pretense of such behavior. Thus, neither of my brothers ever had a chance to be anything but lawyers, and anything but intolerant — about the poor, the North, Negroes, foreigners, and in a way, women.

"My mother and I were supposed to mind the house, the garden, and ourselves. I remember my mother waiting until my father left the house to read his newspapers and magazines. She used to go to the library to read books — there. 'Your father wants us to breed and decorate the world, but when someone is lynched I feel a child of God has been killed against His will, and my instinct as a mother is aroused.' She told me that when I was about ten or twelve. I suppose I must remember that women then had only recently been able to vote, let alone object to murder.

"When I was a teen-ager my mother wanted to join a group of Southern churchwomen who had organized to protest the wave of lynchings that periodically took place over the South. My father absolutely forbade it, and she gave in immediately to his decision. At least she pretended to do so. That's where she and I have always differed. I believe that women and men have to respect one another. When I was engaged to my husband he promised me that he would never treat me as a child because I was a woman. He never did, and I will never be able to forget his kindness and fairness. To my mind, the Negro is treated like a child by nervous white people, who feel safe so long as they have someone to step on and generally abuse — women and Negroes, not to mention children! When I was fifteen I told my mother that — long before I read books by historians or psychologists. She smiled at me and told me not to get too 'thoughtful,' as she put it. That was her way of admitting how impossible it was sometimes to look at certain problems. Of course, I think my mother would be different now. Women have become much more independent, even among the sheltered rich or middle class.

"I came here to Mississippi because it was my husband's home. His family has been here for a long time, and they are fine people. They are now troubled and frightened by my stand. They worry for my life and even for their own, since the Klan does not discriminate in its hate; a family is a family to them. I don't say my in-laws go as far as I do, even when we talk in the privacy of our own homes. They try to make up for the historical record, for the cruelty that the Negro race as a whole has suffered in the South, by being unusually generous with their tenant farmers and household help. They have even offered to help them go North, and pay them a yearly wage *there* until they feel settled. None of the Negroes want to leave though; they are as devoted to my husband's family as they were ten or twenty years ago.

"I argue that it's still paternalism. My sister-in-law and my two brothers-in-law say that *their* generosity is not paternalistic. It's hard to settle the point, but I think we all agree that the *system*, apart from exceptions, is paternalistic, at best. I would rather have a few favored Negroes on their own but poorer, and the rest finally free. My husband always agreed, but he never would say so out loud, and his brothers and sister are like him today, silent about what they think.

"Since he died I've been the one who has taken the risks, gone out on a limb by writing letters and helping form committees, in order to *declare* what some know in their hearts is right — and others feel is dead wrong. For doing that, speaking my mind, I have been ostracized and threatened as if I were a murderer, or a foreign agent. Even those who agree with me think I am crazy — "emotionally disturbed," one of them told me after two martinis. Those who disagree with me are trying to find out how much I'm paid by Northern emissaries, or government people. It would all be funny if it weren't done at the expense of a whole race of people, who have about lost their patience with such antics all over the world.

"People have asked me to wait. 'This thing will take generations. Why do you want to take the whole burden on yourself — and your children?' (They always wait before they add the last few words; and they smile, so as to conceal their nastiness with a veneer of friendliness.) Of course I thank them for their concern — especially for my children — and tell them the simple truth: they want nothing done; I want to do something; that is that.

" 'Are you afraid?' they ask. There would be something wrong with me if I weren't. But I'm no more afraid than they are. At least I know why I'm afraid, and what I fear. They're so frightened and suspicious they've lost their common sense. They talk of 'conspiracies' and the like. They get nervous at every whisper, every news story, every rumor, every hate-mongering voice they meet up with. Yes, I'm afraid that one day I'll be shot at. I've settled my affairs in case it happens, and I'm ready to go.

Meanwhile, I live every day as my conscience tells me to do, and as a result I feel content with myself, if scared at times. What about my friends, who wish me so well and keep on telling me to talk with a doctor or minister for 'counsel'? They're angry, distrustful, shrill and hateful — and getting worse in all those respects every day. Most of all, they're guilty, and they don't know it. Who needs the 'counsel,' I ask you?

"There is one more matter I would like to bring up. I have been asked by everyone from the police to members of my family why I have 'chosen' (as they put it) to be so 'different.' The truth is that I was brought up to feel as I do. My mother taught me most of what I say. She may have feared saying it in public — and sometimes even at home when my father was present — but if she were alive today she would be proud of me for doing so. My husband might have disagreed with me, but he never would have tried to silence me. We would have talked it all out — and perhaps changed one another a bit in doing so. Now he is gone, and I must do what I feel is right, without his advice or views. I miss him when some of those threatening calls come, but I can't dishonor his memory by buckling under to those calls because he isn't here to protect us. I told my daughter the other day that we owe it to his memory to be strong — to prove that he truly *gave* us his strength, that we have it in us, to use and rely upon. So long as I can think back and see my mother and my husband, I think I'll be able to keep my courage up. I know they would be happy for what I'm doing. They would be afraid, too; I know that. If they were alive they might be so afraid that they wouldn't do what I'm doing. I know that, too. But they are gone, and I am here. Perhaps I'm too loyal to them — still — but I feel somehow I can make the best of them live on, in honor."

Mrs. Trumbull never mailed that letter to the sheriff. Instead she sent him yet another curt note, reproving him for his "illegal, unconstitutional manner of law enforcement." She had kept a diary for years, and told me she intended to make the letter a part of it.

I felt lucky to have a chance to read the letter, but at a loss to answer her question after I had finished. "Does this explain anything to you, about why I've taken the stand I have?" I said yes, it did; as much as such things could be explained. Her reply to that was quick in coming and a surprise to me: "I think explanations don't settle an issue, they only make way for more questions. I've asked myself a lot of the questions you've asked me, directly or indirectly, these past years. After I answer them I still don't feel at rest. There are other women who have had mothers like mine, and have lost husbands like mine. I could have done other things with my memories, or my loneliness. It seems that I couldn't though. That's the only explanation I've ever been able to find for myself that sets my mind to rest."

3. *Working for a Change of Mind: Tom*

"The difference between us and white students in the move-ment is that we're students first of all. We're trying to work with other students — white students, that is — and on the campus, not the streets. To be honest, most of us don't know much about Negro life, at least not the way white students do who go to live in Negro communities and join in their protests. We believe that our job is different — I guess *we're* different. We work for a change in other students, in the young white people of the South."

In 1962 I first met with this young man, Tom, and several of his friends. They were all in college, all born in the South, all white, and all interested in bringing about social and economic change in their region. Yet they were not like other white students I had met in the movement. They knew that, and wanted it to be that way. They had their own particular goals, and their own hard-ships to face, also. As one of them put it to me: "At first I thought

I should apologize for not risking my life or going to jail, the way some white students have. They've left school and placed themselves right on the firing line. I've never really been able to imagine myself doing that; and to be honest, I don't think it's out of fear, either. (I mean fear of the police or of going to jail.) I guess I'm just not like the civil rights workers — or at least the real front-line fighters."

Tom was brought up in Virginia — and in a home where Negroes were employed, but not hated. His mother paid their servants the average wage, then each year secretly gave them a series of gifts and "bonuses." He very much wanted me to know the quality of his family's relationship with Negroes: "People outside the South, and even many people who live here, don't know — or don't admit to knowing — a lot that goes on in the region. There's the public attitude, the obligation everyone has to obey segregationist laws or customs; but on the other hand there are people, millions of people of both races, who can't help being natural with each other. For some of them it's a matter of being naturally hateful and mean, while for others it's trying to forget the neighbors and the police, and being naturally friendly.

"I don't mean 'friendly' the way bosses are with their workers. One of the first memories I have is being punished by my mother for ordering our maid around. She hit me harder than she did when I disobeyed *her*. She told me I was never to get the idea I could push anybody around, regardless of their job or color or age, or anything. She repeated herself many times on that score — I can hear her now: 'girl or boy, baby or grandparent, black or white, rich or poor, we are put here by God, to live together for a few years and then depart. We are not put here to bully one another, but respect one another.'

"That's how she still feels, though I have to admit she's been afraid to speak out. My father is a doctor, and when he did make the slightest move toward joining a human relations council, organized to further desegregation, his patients started complaining and threatening to leave him. They heard about it before he actually went to a meeting. It's a small town we live in. At that time people were so afraid they didn't want to be caught going to a doctor who might become known as an integrationist. One person phoned another, and they all called my father — more worried about themselves than him. Several patients said that if my father was called an integrationist, they would deny ever having known him.

"I was in high school then; and I learned about political science firsthand, by the 'case method' my professor now talks about. My father and mother both felt they had no choice but to keep their feelings quiet. My father denied he intended to join the human relations council. He said he had only expressed 'curiosity' about its purposes. He withdrew from all political life in the town. He even resigned from the board of health. I remember that for a time he didn't want to read the newspapers. He just couldn't bear knowing about the bombings, the murders and the mobs.

"My mother supported him. What else could she do? They told us — in the privacy of the home — what they believed. They even told us that they were afraid, and unwilling to risk isolation, financial disaster and possible danger from the really wild segregationist crowd. My sisters and I used to be confused when they told us their fears. It was almost as if they were confessing to us. We didn't know what to say, or do. Sometimes I guess we were mean. We would tell them that they should stand up for what they believed, and not be so afraid. We told them that *we* weren't afraid. *We* didn't care where we lived, or whether we had the money to go to college or not. I can see now that it was almost as hard for them to deal with us as with the Klan.

"When I graduated from high school my father was particularly happy. He knew I was not only leaving the town, but the state. He also knew I was going to a good, liberal Southern college, where there was a long tradition of free speech and forward thinking. The day I left, he told me how lucky I was:

'This used to be a quiet town, and it still is on the surface. Underneath, though, there's a cancer at work. You're lucky to be going away — and especially to Chapel Hill. You'll be spared the hypocrisy and the hate here.'"

Of course Tom wasn't spared either hypocrisy or hate. Colleges cannot isolate themselves from serious social conflict. Colleges get money from state legislatures, or are under the authority of trustees or directors. "I learned that most students were like my parents in the clutch: they meant well, but they were afraid to say anything or do anything that would be controversial, and get them into trouble with the deans or the trustees. I'm not saying I wasn't afraid — for the same reasons they were. There was a difference though. My parents really brought us up to believe in the *equality* of the Negro, even if we didn't dare work for his *integration*. Most of my classmates really believed that the Negro is inferior; they were brought up to believe it. When things are tense and oppressive they're certainly not going to disagree with what they already are inclined to go along with anyway."

It was the theme of "equality" that he and his friends first picked up and tried to highlight. They spent weeks discussing the purposes of a proposed campus organization. They decided to concentrate on what I often heard them term the "rational" side of the race question. Particularly in a university setting they felt able to discuss the Negro's inherent equality, as a human being and citizen, in contrast to what they called "the social problem of integration." They wanted integration, too — but their aim was to work with Southern white people who showed no sign of welcoming what the region was in fact gradually accepting under the pressure of demonstrations, court orders and congressional action.

"We are trying to persuade, to work with our own people so that they will really understand what is happening to them, and in the long run see how helpful it is going to be for them, too. My father is a doctor, and for years has been afraid to say what he believes. The white people of the South are afraid of everyone —

the Negro, outsiders, the government in Washington, the Klan, students from Harvard and Berkeley, but most of all, one another. They're constantly trying to figure out what the people next door think — and they're afraid to find out what they themselves think.

"The South has not only kept itself segregationist, it has paid only lip service to the old separate-but-equal doctrine. My father said he could always score a point with his friends by pointing that out. They had to admit it, and they became guilty the more it was discussed. So we have a leverage point, as I see it, a way of getting people to talk, and feel sympathetically involved."

Once at a meeting Tom told his friends what he had told me — the memory he had of his mother's admonitions to him as a child. He had learned his lesson, and he was sure that he could teach it: "She told me a Negro is a person, a human being, as much so as anyone else. I believe we can approach the white people of the South that way, rather than with a direct integrationist appeal."

One student spoke his impatience and his scorn: "Why should we organize at all? What is the point of doing so, if we're so frightened ourselves that we don't dare say what we believe? I don't see how we're going to influence a single white Southerner if we disguise our every word and goal. We'll be talking the way they do already, the way my parents do: you have to give the nigra good schools, and pave his streets, and treat him well enough so that he'll soon stop the bellyaching he's been doing these past few years. My father is even ready to let them vote. He says maybe we should improve their restaurants and movie houses out of public funds, so they won't try to get into ours.

"We want the white people of the South to wake up and realize that *Plessy v. Ferguson* is dead, that it won't work to catch up with an outmoded nineteenth-century doctrine when we need to adjust to the twentieth century. Isn't that why we're trying to go out and meet people? Or are we trying to fool ourselves *again?*"

Tom replied quickly. "I agree with you, but I don't think you understand what I'm trying to say. You and I have no disagreement on all this, but what about the very people you mentioned, your parents? And what about a lot of people in the South — the majority of the white people — who would consider even your parents radicals for what they say and want done? I presume we either write them off, or we try to reach them. At least that's what I think we're here to discuss: whether there might be some way for us to do our own kind of civil rights work, not in the streets or even with Negroes at all, but with our own people, who need looking after and encouragement, too."

Eventually they consolidated themselves into a group of about ten, with Tom their leader. He went to other campuses, enlisted additional supporters. He became as efficient an organizer, as active a worker, as any of the student demonstrators I met in the South. During summer vacations he and others moved into a neighborhood, obtained work, and practiced a subdued kind of Christian witness. When I asked him to tell me how he went about his work, and what his goals were, he became almost proudly evasive.

"There's no telling what we're going to do until we're faced with a situation, an actual chance to do something. We pick a town because one of us knows it; maybe there's a relative there, or a friend. We find a place to live, an apartment or some rooms in a house; we've even camped out. We get jobs. Then we just live. That's all you have to do, settle in a place, and start living: work, go to the movies or a restaurant, buy gas, go on a picnic to a lake or the ocean. You meet people. You start talking. In about ten seconds 'the subject' has come up: the nigger is trying to do this or that, and it's terrible; the nigger has got to be stopped; there are too many niggers and Communists coming down from the North, getting our good niggers all excited and uppity. On and on it goes.

"We listen, and we add our opinion. We do not try to provoke arguments, or even get into them at all with people who seem really looking for them. On the other hand, you'd be surprised how often people say things they don't really believe. That's been the greatest discovery we've made. I'll be buying some clothes or having gas put in my car, and the salesman will make some wisecrack about niggers, or the Kennedy brothers. He'll look at me for a reply, and I'll make a quiet remark, disagreeing. He might say something like: 'The niggers are going to be sleeping on our front lawns, next thing you know.' I might say: 'Well, they've been fixing our food with their hands and working to keep our bedrooms and bathrooms clean, so they might as well get a taste of our grass.'

"There are some who will give you a hard look, and start to get angry. They might think you're a little softheaded, and not aware of the implications of your own words. So they'll make a stronger remark, and look at you to see what you'll do then: 'Oh, they can take care of my grass, but if they try to eat in my kitchen, they'll have the fight of their lives.' I try to be as cool and casual as I can be when I reply: 'They've been in our kitchens since we had them. They helped build them for us, then they helped grow the food we ate in them, then they cooked it for us and served it to us and cleaned up after us. Their hands fed us as babies and prepare our food now — in the back rooms of restaurants and in our kitchens at home. It's almost funny, how we say we have to keep them away from us, then forget how close they are to us, as close as people can be to one another.'

"By that time the fellow is looking at me rather carefully. His eyes may look away, because he's angry but doesn't want to admit it, or because he's afraid to get into an argument with a customer who talks as if he's obviously lost his mind. Some people stare right at me though. They want to know if they can really believe what I said, if they can trust me — or if I'm taking them for a ride, in the South a dangerous ride.

"I've had strange reactions at this point in the conversation; it's the moment of truth. A few will get angry and tell me they don't want to carry the conversation any further. You can tell by their look where they *would* carry it if they felt free to do so. Others just stop talking. They don't seem particularly angry. They just clam up. You can see what is going through their minds. They don't want to get involved in an argument, any argument that will affect their job, their business, their popularity, whatever it is that all three mean: their daily living and their 'position' in the community. They've been talking about 'niggers' and 'keeping niggers out' because they've learned to — with many it's almost like saying 'good morning' or 'the weather is lousy today' or 'isn't it tough, the drought we're having?' Now someone comes along who seems to be putting a wrench in the machinery; he makes them feel self-conscious or nervous about remarks they make all the time without thinking, so they want no part of him.

"Then there is another group of people who never cease surprising me. As soon as they see that I mean business — that I mean to show how foolishly and unfairly we treat the Negro — they change their tune completely. I've even learned to divide such people into two subdivisions: those who sense my attitudes, then automatically comply with them, whether they actually agree with what I've said or not; and those who have secretly shared the same feelings all along, and are relieved and happy to find a friend.

"The first kind of person is much more common than I ever dreamed. Often he's a Willy Loman. He believes that his job is to please the customer, at any price to his own beliefs. In fact, you get the feeling that he has no beliefs, that he's like a sail: he's waiting for the wind, no matter from what direction it comes and where it is headed. For a long while I found people like that the hardest to take. I almost preferred the wild segregationists, who were at least willing to state their views and even stick to them when it paid to change them. Now I've come to realize that whatever makes people ready to shift positions so quickly can't be considered a Southern problem. In a way there's hope for us, at least on the race issue, if people will switch their opinions on it because they think it pays, or it's the popular thing to do. (I admit, in the long run the whole country may be worse off, because too many of us are like that, without real values that we really believe in, and will fight to keep.)

"What has surprised me, though, is the number of people who are like me, or at least like me before I started doing this kind of work: they think one thing and say another. My mother once told me that a lot of Southern people are afraid to say what they really feel. I was in high school then, and I thought she was fooling herself, as she often does. She wants to believe the best about people and the world, so she manages to find the best, forget the worst, and even imagine the good when she can't ignore the bad, or find very much that *is* good.

"I would say about a quarter to a third of the white people I meet are ready to agree with me — and mean it — as soon as they see that *I* mean what I'm saying, and have dared say it out loud to them. It shows how people can become silent, afraid to reveal their own convictions. I've come to know a lot of such people, and they tell you some strange things: how they were children and liked Negroes, and have never quite learned to give up liking them, but feel they must, as grown-ups; how they still feel sorry for Negroes, and even want to help them, but are afraid that other people might be able to sense it, or notice it because they don't make the necessary number of segregationist jokes or remarks; how they have friends like me, and sometimes they all get together and tell one another their true feelings — you get a picture of the South being full of undergrounds, networks of people afraid to reveal themselves or their views, but troubled enough to get together with one another."

For several years I watched Tom move into one Southern town after another during his summer vacations. Eventually he devoted a full year to the job. In every place he lived he would meet the various people he describes so shrewdly, yet — still — with a certain surprise and bewilderment. I have watched him go about his work, and often wondered at his initiative and purpose.

"Where do you get the energy, Tom?"

"I don't know. For some things I have no energy at all. But I like doing this. Actually it makes me feel I'm helping myself. I don't want my children to go through what I did, and I don't want to have to talk with them the way my parents did with me. If I can spare myself and them the lies I learned, I'll have a better life, and so will they, and so will the South. I want to stay here and live here. This is my home, the South, and I love it enough to work for changes in it."

4.   *Esau and Jacob: An Alabama Doctor*

I first met James Butler at a medical conference in Birmingham. He is one of the city's leading citizens as well as a doctor interested in the quality of the city's medical and psychiatric services. That day a number of public health officials were discussing the grossly inadequate pediatric care received by poor children, and James Butler was there to hear what they said, to offer to do what he could.

On initial acquaintance he is a quiet, serious man. I remember his shyness when I first met him, and his unassuming, almost deferential manner. In time — we talked at monthly intervals for three years — I came to appreciate how genuinely he stood in awe of people: "I grew up almost in seclusion. We lived on a large estate, and for most of my childhood the only people I knew besides my parents and my brother were the Negroes. Later I was tutored for a long while — my parents thought it the best and 'least hazardous' way to learn. What they meant by hazardous was any significant exposure to the outside world. There weren't many private schools in the South, and public school — as my mother used to put it — 'meant risks.'

"She wanted us to keep our own company. We were aristocrats, I'll have to admit it, not fading but in full bloom. Our family tree is well sprinkled with governors, senators, Confederate generals, and in the beginning what we call 'tidewater Virginia names.' My father didn't sit back thinking about the past though. He was a very successful businessman and lawyer — an industrialist I guess he'd be called today in the North. We still don't use the word much down here. We've never had enough industry to make us give a special name to the owners.

"Every day my father would be driven off to work, and I recall that about the time he left the tutors would arrive for me and my brother. My brother was two years older than me, and very bright. Often his teacher and mine would combine us into a foursome for certain subjects like geography or history. Even then my brother wanted to be a teacher and a lawyer, both; only he thought a choice had to be made. Now he's a professor of law and a determined segregationist. We get along, but never discuss race.

"When we were children we loved Negroes, that's the only word that does justice to our feelings. They took care of us, and they loved us, too. I can remember every one of them the way you can with people in your childhood. Especially Ruth: she was our mother, really. I found that out when I was psychoanalyzed."

He had been psychoanalyzed when he was thirty-five, and one of the public changes in his life had to do with what he learned about his feelings toward Ruth. He became increasingly concerned with the Negro's condition in Alabama after he learned how much Ruth had meant to him as a child.

"I knew she had taken care of me. I even used to say rather casually that she brought me up. What I had to forget was how much love she had given me, and how much love I felt toward her. When I finally was able to see that, I tried to talk to my brother about it. That was a mistake. He flew into a rage. He told me I was coming out with nonsense, crazy nonsense it was. I could tell by his excitement that I had hit upon a sensitive nerve, but I also realized it was foolish of me — and maybe mean — to expect him to understand in a moment what had taken months for me finally to see and, more important, *appreciate*."

From the beginning he told me how painfully alienated he and his brother had become, as a result of the very psychiatric treatment that had enabled him to feel closer to his brother.

"One part of my analysis helped me to relax with my brother and get over the tension and rivalry I used to feel when I was with him; but the more I began to change my racial attitudes — also because of the analysis — the worse he and I got along. For a while it was as if our old antagonism was shifting to a new level of expression, centered on race. I told the doctor that I wasn't getting over anything; I was switching the subject of the argument, not stopping the argument."

Apparently the doctor agreed with his patient's appraisal for a time, but then changed his mind.

"He said it was my brother's problem, not mine. I was trying to be as friendly as I could with my brother, but he couldn't take either that or my racial views — it's hard to know which of the two bothered him more, my new warmth toward him, or my talk about the Negro's right to vote or his need for social justice."

When I met James Butler he and his brother had already agreed upon a truce: they would be friendly to one another, but avoid any discussion of politics and race — the two being inextricably bound in the Alabama of the 1960's. It was a truce that was agreed upon before a war.

"In 1958 I wrote a letter to the Birmingham papers, saying that as a doctor I felt an obligation to *all* people, and as a citizen I could feel no different. I never once used the word Negro — here in the South there's no need for that. I said 'all people' and the message was clear. I was Birmingham's 'citizen of the year' then, and I thought it was an appropriate time to talk about the rights of citizens, all citizens, under the law.

"Frankly, I never expected what happened. You might have

thought I was talking treason, the way people reacted. We were almost overwhelmed with telephone calls and letters, almost all of them telling me I was a Communist, a spy, a traitor. I was threatened with death so many times that I began to take it all as a joke, until one night someone shot into our living room. No one was hurt, but our window was shattered, and a bullet lodged in the wall, right near a portrait of my grandfather. (He fought the Klan in Alabama, but he also despised the Yankees who said we don't treat colored people right.)

"One day — I'll never forget it — the mailman came to the door because there were too many letters for our box. We had known one another for years, and liked one another, too. He looked at me as I took all those angry postcards and notes in my hands, and then he couldn't resist saying something: 'Dr. Butler, you never should have done it, never. People can't say those things you said in public. I agree with you, but I couldn't say it out loud — not even at home, I couldn't. One of my children might go repeating it, outside, and then I'd be in for it, too.'

"He was trying to console me, but he helped me in another way. I suddenly realized that it wasn't just the Negro whose freedom is unfairly restricted, but mine, and the mailman's, both of us white. I told my wife that and she agreed, but she also felt I was getting myself into more trouble than she or I or anyone else in Alabama could take. There were our three children, the rest of our family and our friends, and my work. One mistake was enough to jeopardize everything; a second one, showing that I really *meant* what I said, would ruin everything. As one of the threatening letters said: 'You may have just forgot yourself or been confused. For your sake, we hope so.'

"Actually, I never did repeat myself so openly. I had to decide how I would handle my own opposition to segregation, and for me it involved weighing a lot of things carefully, and taking each step as if I were on a tightrope — as I was. My wife agreed with my views, but worried about the children. The children were young — in 1958 they were twelve, ten and six. Of course they agree with me, but they had their friends and classmates and teacher to contend with. Then, I had my parents to worry about. They are still alive, in their eighties. My father didn't fight the Klan to achieve integration. He simply disliked violence done by whites. In Negroes he condones anything — murder, rape, robbery. He is a racist, you see, like most everybody of his generation was; and I regret to say my generation, too — in Alabama."

Since 1961 I have watched James Butler risk his comfort, his reputation, his family's security, even his life (if those who threatened him with death were to be believed) for the sake of one integrationist effort after another. Yet, at all times he was discreet enough to avoid the notoriety of outright identification as a "race mixer," a term of special condemnation reserved for more outspoken whites. Between 1960 and 1964, as Alabama increasingly had to accept at least a token of desegregation, he never signed public petitions urging compliance with federal law. Nor did he go to any interracial meetings, often enough watched by police and threatened by Klansmen.

"I wasn't afraid for my life; it was my *way* of life I tried to keep going. I did keep it going, too — until the worst was over. I took my particular stand, my risks, when it was much safer to do so; and yet I suffered more than I ever expected."

In 1965, after the Civil Rights Bill was passed, he took the lead in suggesting that the two hospitals on whose staff he served desegregate their facilities. He also publicly signed a statement of support for the new federal law — it was now the law of Congress, not the Supreme Court — and he agreed to serve on the board of a human relations council. (As he put it, "in the South that is a polite way of describing the goals of a group devoted either to desegregation or integration.")

He became ostracized. His true colors were emerging to people who had suspected them all along. Among those people he found his brother, his cousins, his friends, and most of the doctors with whom he worked every day.

"I became a radical to people hungry for one. In a way I think they were very grateful to me. It can be a relief to find a real human object for all your hates and fears. The Communists under the bed, in the shadows, up in New York and abroad stop satisfying even the most paranoid person's sense of reality after a while.

"The worst part of it was my brother's reaction. We were never exceptionally close, but neither were we unfriendly. The strangest part of all this is that I was our Negro nurse's favorite, and only realized that fact during my analysis. Our mother was very fair — impartial, really — with us, the way a mother can be when she doesn't have to sweat out the everyday tensions of her children. The nurse was really our mother, until we were sent off to school after twelve. Naturally, my brother went to school first, being older. He would come home on holidays full of jokes about niggers, how stupid they are, and animal-like. I never connected his attitude then with the fact that I was alone with Ruth, and he away from her. In his heart he must have felt the way I did when I finally did leave — homesick, and more for our nurse Ruth and handyman John than either of us dared admit to ourselves, let alone anyone else.

"When my brother became so angry at me, and started calling me a 'god-damned nigger lover,' I asked him why he was so excited, just because — in 1964, mind you — I was advocating what the United States Congress had long since proclaimed to be the law. He said I'd always been 'soft on niggers,' and I had a stubborn anti-Southern streak in me, and maybe I should go North where I seemed to belong. I couldn't get him to talk any more rationally than that, and he is a lawyer, an Ivy League-trained lawyer.

"One of the advantages of psychoanalysis is the vision into yourself and others you *keep*, not simply catch for a year or two, then forget. I'm not saying that people like my brother and me take sides on the race issue because we had different childhood experiences with Negroes. It's not as simple as that, or complicated. (What can be harder to determine than the real truth about a person's early years?) A lot of us in Alabama shout at niggers because we're afraid *not* to shout, or because it's like owning a car or a house or something: you feel you're *somebody* when you can do it, or join others who are doing it.

"But there are choices, even here, even in a closed society, and especially among the well-to-do. That's where I think individual psychology comes into the picture. Some people hate Negroes the same way they hate their parents, or their husbands and wives. There's a real intensity to their hate; it's *personal* hate, underneath. They don't just oppose Negroes in general, as a group, or oppose them because they're trying to upset the familiar ways we all grow to depend upon. They oppose because they *need* to oppose; they need an enemy.

"That's what I finally said to my brother. I wasn't going to be one of those armchair psychiatrists. I just said to him: 'Why don't you leave me and the niggers alone? That's all I ask you, leave us *all* alone, and find some other enemy.'

"That stopped him, those words. They didn't stop some kids from heckling my kids. They didn't stop some of my doctor friends from avoiding me. They stopped my brother though; and enabled me to keep my strength up. He's never said another harsh thing to me. He keeps his hate to himself and his friends, away from my ears. I can take a crank's threats, but it's too painful at my age to see old wounds still unhealed, still giving pain. I mean personal wounds, family wounds, not only the racial ones everyone knows we have here in Alabama."

5.   *Stay Home or Go to School?*

The first children I came to know in New Orleans were Negro children, and for a while it appeared that they would be the only children in the two schools the four little girls were attending. As one of them reminded me in a talk we had after her first few days of school: "I don't see anyone but the teacher all day. They said I would be seeing the white kids, but none have come yet, and the teacher, she says they may never come — all on account of me. But I told her they will."

In point of fact several white children were almost always at school during her long ordeal, though it took her time to become aware of their presence. For a time she *was* the first grade of a fairly large school, while a fluctuating handful of white children constituted the remnants of the other grades, the second through the sixth.

Two of these white children came from minister's homes, one Baptist and the other Methodist. Four of them, two boys and two girls, came from a third home, a Catholic one with five other children, headed by an accountant.

"We are eleven, so we're a mob, too," the wife of the accountant and the mother of their nine children once told me as we stood in her kitchen and looked at an angry crowd outside and not far away. She was counting those on her side because she knew those on the other side had become her enemies.

She lived near the school, near enough to see it from her backyard; near enough to see and hear the crowds from her front window. She was born in Louisiana, as were her parents, and their parents. She and her husband were "ordinary" people, or at least so it would once have seemed. That is to say, they lived with their children in a small, lower-middle-class area, their home like thousands about it, their life distinguished by little except its daily routine of care for one another and the children. They were both high school graduates.

Just before the crisis which came upon their city they had no interest in politics and were against school desegregation. "We never really thought they would do it, and then we found that not only did they mean to go ahead, but ours was slated to be one of the schools." That was the way she summarized her surprise, her previous attitude of mild or unexcited opposition to what the newspapers less indifferently called "mixing."

In a matter of weeks this mother and her children were being subjected to a degree of danger and intimidation which rivals for violence any I've seen in the South. Her house was assaulted, its windows broken, its walls stained with foul inscriptions. Her husband's place of work was threatened and picketed. It became necessary for the police to protect her children as well as the little Negro girl whose lone entrance precipitated disorder in the streets and sporadic violence destined to last for months. In watching this Southern white lady walk through those mobs with her small children, one could not but wonder why she persisted. Why did she take on that challenge, and how did she endure it?

After years of interviews with her, I have had to guard against tampering with my recollection of this woman, against making her into someone she wasn't at the time she made the various choices — choices which in turn helped make her into the person she is *now*. This is a problem psychiatrists must always keep in mind. It is possible to forget the truth of the past when the present, with its visions and formulations, is the vantage point from which the conclusive determination is being made.

Here is how — word for word — she once described her attitude when the conflict of school desegregation, hovering over the city for months, settled upon her children's school.

"I couldn't believe it. First I became angry at the nigras. I figured, why don't they leave well enough alone and tend to their own problems. Lord knows they have enough of them. Then, I thought I just couldn't keep four children out of school; not on one little nigra girl's account. So I thought I'd just send them and see what happens. Well, the next thing I knew, mothers were rushing in and taking their children out; and every time they did it, they would get cheered. The end of the first day of it there wasn't much of a school left.

"The next day I decided to give it one more try. I was going to stay away, keep my children away, but to tell the truth the idea of having four children home with me, squabbling and making noise and getting into trouble, was too much for me. So I thought I'd just stick it out and maybe things would quiet down, and then we'd all forget one little nigra and our children would go on with school.

"The crowd was there the next day and they were more of one mind now. They started shouting at each white mother that came to the building, and one by one they pulled back. It was as if the building was surrounded and only the police could get through, and *they* weren't doing anything. The mob let Ruby (the Negro girl) through, because they said they wanted her to be there alone. They screamed when the minister brought his girl, and I decided to withdraw. Well, I was walking back home, and I saw the back door to the building. They were so busy with the minister and shouting at the reporters, they weren't looking at the rear. So I just took the children there and let them go in. At that moment I thought, 'It's better than their being at home, and better than their listening to those people scream all day from our porch.' It was bad enough *I* had to hear it, and my baby too young for school.

"The *next* day I really decided to join the boycott. I couldn't see fighting them, and they weren't going away like I thought. Well, my husband stayed home a little later than usual, and we talked. I said no, no school for the kids, and he agreed. Then he said maybe we should try to move to another part of the city, so that the kids could continue their schooling. Then I said I'd try *one more day*. Maybe the mob would get tired and go away. After all, they had their way — there was only the children of a minister or two left out of five hundred families. I snuck the kids in, and later that day one of the *teachers* called, to ask me if I was sure I wanted to do it. She sounded almost as scared as me, and I think she would just as soon have had the whole school closed, so she could be spared listening to that noise and that filthy language.

"That night, I think, was the turning point. A few of the mob saw me leaving with the children, and started calling me the worst things I'd ever heard. They followed me home and continued. Thank God the police kept them away from the house, but I had the sickening feeling on the way home that I was *in* something, unless I got out real fast. In the morning I couldn't send them, and I couldn't *not*. One woman came here instead of to the school, to swear at me just in case I tried sending the children off. I guess she thought that just her being there would take care of me. Well, it did. I became furious; and I just dressed those children as fast as I could and marched them off. Later that day those women from the Garden District came, and they said they'd stand by me and help me and even drive the children the one block, and I guess I soon was a key person in breaking the boycott.

"But I didn't *mean* to. It was mostly, I think, their language, and attacking me so quickly. I didn't feel any freer than the nigra. I think I gained my strength each day, so that I was pretty tough in a few months. After a while they didn't scare me one bit. I wouldn't call it brave; it was becoming *determined*. That's what happened, really. We all of us — my children, my husband and me — became determined."

Of course I am giving you one section from hours of taped conversations. I knew her quite well when we had that talk, and it was not the first time she had given me an account of those experiences. When I listen to her voice today I can almost feel her drifting — precisely that — drifting — and then coming to terms not only with her own past but with history itself. Choice was required: at some point her children either had to stay home or go to school. Each alternative had its advantages: a home without restless children, or a home unbothered by restless and angry outsiders — calling at midnight to predict death and de-struction, shouting similar forecasts in the daytime.

We are still left with the matter of why this woman chose as she did, and how she managed the strength to make her choice stick fast so long.

Surely we may call that unassuming strength her courage. Not everyone, even among the so-called "mature," will take on the possibility of death day after day with evident calm. In this woman's case her commitment, her course of courageous action developed through a series of "moments" or "accidents." Step by step she became an important participant in a critical struggle. Indeed, in looking back at her life and the situation she faced we may forget that a historical event was once a crisis by no means settled. Had the boycott in New Orleans held fast, the forces at work there for segregation would have become stronger, perhaps decisively so for a long time. That is what I heard from people on both sides of the struggle as it was occurring.

Our "Southern lady," like Conrad's Lord Jim, slipped into an important moment that became a determining force in her life as well as her country's history. Not only her views on segregation but her participation in community affairs and the goals she has for herself and her children are far different now than they "ordinarily" would have been. "I met people I never would have," she said to me recently, "and my sights have become higher. I think more about what's important, not just for me but for others; and my children do better at school because they're more serious about education."

What can one say about this woman's choice? Certainly there was no one reason that prompted it. I have talked with enough of her neighbors to realize the dangers of saying that her past actions or beliefs might easily differentiate her from others. Many of her nearby friends are decent, likable people. Before a mob they simply withdrew themselves and their children. This woman had also planned to do so. Yet she never did, or she never did for long or for good. She drifted. She tried to resolve the mixed feelings in her mind. She weighed her fear of a mob against her annoyance at her children's loss of schooling and their bothersome presence in the home. She was a hopeful person and she assumed — wrongly indeed — that the riots would end quickly. She is a sound, stable person, and once under fire she did not waver. She is the first one to remind me that her husband's employers stood by him. Had *they* wavered, she is certain that she would have quickly withdrawn her children from the school. For that matter, were her husband different — that is, more of a segregationist, or generally more nervous and anxious — she might never have dared stand up to a mob's anger.

In sum, there were a number of reasons which helped this woman's courage unfold, each of them, perhaps, only a small part of the explanation, though each necessary. I suppose we could call her — in the fashion of the day — "latently" courageous. A crisis found her strong, and in possession of certain ideals. Those ideals gained power through a cumulative series of events which eventually became for one person's life a "point of no return." She puts it this way: "After a few days I knew I was going to fight those people and their foul tongues with every ounce of strength I had. I knew I had no choice but that one. At least that's how I see it now." It was an impressive experience listening to her tell her story, and watching her realize — often only in the telling — what had actually happened to her feelings and her goals.

VIII

LOOKERS-ON
AND THE LAST DITCH

E VEN when an entire social system is in convulsive transition there are many who neither try hard to resist change nor lift a willing finger to bring about a new kind of life. From people on both sides of the struggle one hears summoned the "ordinary" man, the "average guy," the "typical person" as potentially friendly, vaguely supportive, fitfully antagonistic, or somewhat — but only somewhat — alarmed. Such descriptions, inevitably tentative, ambiguous or open-ended, reflect the uneasy truth known to ideologues and just plain idealists of all persuasions: many people, perhaps most people, are content to live in society rather than commit themselves to its alteration, let alone transformation. Among those so content are numbered the discontented as well as the reasonably well-to-do. Just as I have found all classes represented in both the sit-in movement and the various segregationist organizations, I have found among a wide range of people in both races an essential determination that their lives — in the words of one (Negro) citizen of Georgia — "not be bothered by all the trouble around."

1. A Store Is a Store

The more I watched sit-ins and other demonstrations over the South the more interested I became in the specific psychological effect they exerted. What happened to white people (or Negroes) as youths or ministers quietly, solemnly marched before them, or toward them? During a long — perhaps too long — interview with a tired, angry, still nonviolent Negro youth in Atlanta I heard him suggest an end to our talks, and a beginning for another series of conversations.

"I can see how you might want to know how someone like me keeps his head from splitting in all directions, but I think you're losing a real opportunity. You should go speak with those white folks — the ones who look at us, and stare, just stare without giving a clue what's going on in their minds. Or you could go talk to the store owners we picket. Some of them look as if they're ready to go mad, not get mad. One came out yesterday and begged us to leave him alone. He said he didn't care one way or the other what happened. He just wanted to make a living and mind his own business — I mean *really* mind his own business, without us bothering him. We told him he could. All we wanted was to help him make *more* money, by serving us. But no. He said the white people would stop coming, and he'd go broke or have to move to a Negro neighborhood.

"To tell the truth, I felt sorry for the guy. I don't know how he feels about segregation and integration, but he didn't strike me as very different from my own parents. They want to stay alive, and when given half a chance, they'll keep quiet and do just that, stay alive. Now the trouble is, a lot more Negroes have trouble staying alive than whites, so a lot more of us are moved — moved to *do* something, get involved in the *movement*. But there are plenty of Negroes, even the poorest — maybe especially the poorest in some towns — who don't want to get involved. They say leave me alone, and after you've tried to get them to join you, and they've said leave me alone again, only louder, you know they mean it."

I went to talk with the very storekeeper he mentioned, and eventually came to know him rather well. The Negro student knew him only as a demonstrator does a man of property who repeatedly refuses what is asked of him. I soon learned, however, that the nonviolent student was a shrewd — and in a way compassionate — judge of human nature. Eventually I was able to tell the middle-aged merchant how the Negro youth had appraised his position and his attitude.

"He's right. I want peace and quiet, and I want to go on making a living. If he knows that, he knows that he's wasting his time trying to preach to me or demonstrate. The way I see it, he and I are together. Neither one of us made the world the way it is; and all I want is to stay alive in it, just as he does. At the rate he's going, he'll spend most of his life in jail, and I'll go broke. What does *that* solve for either of us?"

I found him to be a stubborn but pleasant man, a native-born Georgian, in turn a high school graduate, a soldier in the Second World War, and the recipient of a degree in pharmacy. He bought his drugstore with a large loan, and worked for years to own, really own, his business, located in a small town that is really a suburb of Atlanta.

He and his wife grew up together, and fitted together very well. He tended to be serious, even somber. She had a light touch to her voice and her everyday mood. He worried about money and the marks each of their three children brought home from school. She was a devout Baptist and *believed* in faith: "I tell my husband and my children both that it matters not what things of this world we have, so long as we pray for God's grace." (She would often exalt her sentence structure when reproving what she called "the excessive worldliness about us.") They received me cordially into their home, and talked as openly with me — I became convinced — as they did with their neighbors or, for that matter, between themselves.

Sometimes, particularly when under pressure, her husband fell back upon her outlook. Indeed, one day I heard him, and not her, talk of God with such feeling that I at once sensed I was hearing not only his strongly held opinion but perhaps the (hitherto secret) inspiration for his wife's piety.

"Who ever stops to figure out why we live the way we do? Those nigra students come and try to talk with me and the other businessmen on the block. They tell us they're going to sit in, they're going to picket, they're going to do this and that to embarrass us, and shame us, and make us lose money, until finally we surrender to them. They ask me: don't you feel guilty, don't you feel ashamed for all you've done, all your people have done to us? They say if I don't give in, they'll *make* me — by marching up and down, and being nonviolent, and letting people spit on them, and shout at them, or getting the police to arrest them.

"For a long time I tried to ignore them. First I thought they would get tired and go away; then I thought the police would take care of them, or my customers. But they didn't get tired, and it seems that the more they're arrested, the more they want to come back.

"My customers were the ones that became tired. They told me they just couldn't keep on coming in and out of the store, past those nigra students, with their signs and their songs and their slogans. Some of them made a point of shopping downtown, though the drugstores and restaurants there are being picketed, too. Some tried to cut down on their shopping trips. They would save up things to buy, and come here once instead of twice a week.

"I had to close the counter. Who wants to eat with those people trying to move in and eat beside you? I lost money that way, but there wasn't any choice. Every customer I had would have left me if I hadn't done it. White people won't eat with nigras, and the sooner those students find that out, the better it will be for everyone."

I asked him at that time what he felt about the students. Did they bother him as little as he had been saying, or was he trying to "forget" — at least in our conversations — how troublesome they actually were to him?

Yes, it was true they bothered him, though he wanted very much not to take their actions personally. That was the clue to survival, he felt: "I've seen other businessmen knuckle under. They get so angry at the nigras that they close their stores or they start fighting them, and make all their white customers afraid to come near, for fear of violence. Or they try to make a settlement with the nigras, and lose all their white customers that way."

Why did those customers leave — out of fear, distaste, outrage, resentment, shame? Again and again we came back to that issue; he was obviously interested in discussing it, and I felt that the more he talked about his "average" customer, the more I came to know the contradictory substance of *his* views, not to mention the customer's. They were earnestly held views, but easily abandoned ones. Over several years I watched a changing social and political situation utterly undermine some of those views, and make others seem antique or irrelevant even to the man who once proclaimed them. Yet again and again he did come back to certain principles that *were* consistent.

"Say what you will, people run a store to make money. You offer things to the customers, and you hope they'll buy what you have to sell. Now this race thing has suddenly come up; I don't know from where. All my life I've lived with nigras, and not treated them bad, nor them me bad. We've got along — and recently a lot of them have come to me and told me how sorry they are for what I've gone through. Like with most white folks, a lot of the colored just want to live and let live.

"That's my philosophy: live and let live. You can't make a rich man the equal of a poor man. Even in Russia that guy Khrushchev has villas and big cars and all that, while the peasants live the way our tenant farmers do, or worse. The same holds with race. The white man is different from the nigra, all over the world he is. They say we in the South are unfair to colored people. All I want to know is where do they really give a nigra the same acceptance a white man gets? In Boston, or New York? In England? (I've been reading how they have their problems there, the same ones we do.)

"You go into a nigra's home in Atlanta and you'll see them eating well, and wearing good clothes. They have cars, bigger ones than I would ever buy. They have radio and television, and everything else. I've seen their drugstores. They sell the same things I do. They have what the country has to offer. Isn't that enough?

"They try to tell me no — that they're treated inferior. They try to make me feel as if I'm persecuting them, as though I've done something wrong to hurt them. One of them said to me the other day: 'Don't you feel that in turning us away you're being un-Christian?'

"I say no to them every time. I don't see what Christianity has to do with politics or the customs we have. I don't want to hurt them, and I don't want them to hurt me. It's as simple as that. They're trying to make me into a slave owner, or something. I can see that, and I told them that once. I told them they weren't going to get me angry or excited, the way some people get. They want that to happen. It gives them satisfaction. It makes them think that they're right — that we'll lose control and give in after a while.

"I went to see my minister and talked with him about this. He said that I had to examine my conscience and pray. I told him I have, and that I can't see why I should have to make up for whatever troubles the colored man has in Georgia. I'm just an ordinary person. I can barely depend on enough money to pay my bills. I can't subsidize an integrated cafeteria in my drugstore. Soon it will be segregated again — all black.

"The minister told me that the problem was larger than both of us. (Our church has no colored in it.) He said we both faced a lot of trouble these coming years, through no fault of our own, but because the society is changing and the average man has to adjust himself to it. I told him I was as flexible as anyone — I'm just waiting to see every other drugstore — and church — in Georgia 'adjust.'"

A year later (1963) he was no longer the besieged storekeeper. He had won his battle, and kept his store white. The Negroes eventually tired of demonstrating in front of his store. He continued to fear their renewed interest and attention, and out of his experience he developed an interest in what they were doing elsewhere. He often talked with his customers — and his minister — about "the problem."

"You know, it is our number-one problem today, *the problem*. I'm like you — I have to be in my business. I want to know what people think, where they're headed in their thinking. To be truthful, I think we're slowly going to settle this thing. We already have nigra children in the schools, and it's only a matter of time before they'll be back here asking me for coffee and Cokes. I ask some of my customers what they think, and I can hear them being as annoyed with the whole thing as I am. They're no longer as shocked though — any more than I am. When those colored boys first came here last year I thought they were crazy. Then I thought they were hoodlums pretending to be nice and Christianlike. Now, from what I see on television, they're the younger generation of nigras, or at least they're *some* of the younger generation. I still think a lot of nigras don't care one way or the other. Like most of us whites, they want calm. You only live once, and you don't want to spend your days fighting."

His drugstore was desegregated in 1965, after the Civil Rights Bill was passed. He was nervous and fearful when it happened, but also relieved: "They finally got around to me. To tell the truth, I thought they were overlooking me as not worth their while. I told my wife I felt hurt. When I saw them come in I shuddered again, just like before. They weren't the same nigras, and I thought they might get tough or violent. But they didn't. They just moved in on those counter chairs and asked for coffee. My countergirl looked scared, and confused. She turned to me and asked me with a look what she should do. I didn't say a word. I just nodded to her. She knew what I meant. She started pouring. They didn't seem to want to stay long. They drank a bit, then they got up and left. The three white people at the counter just sat there. They had stopped drinking *their* coffee out of curiosity. We all looked at one another, then one of the customers said to me: 'A store is a store, I guess; and you have to serve whatever walks in from the street.'

"That wasn't the way he talked last year, I remember. But I guess it wasn't the way I did either. It's changing down here, that's what's happening, and the man in the street, he has to keep up with it, even if he doesn't always go along with it. I suppose that comes later, agreeing with what's already happened. Some of my friends say that if we had fought this battle harder, the integration people never would have won. I tell them that we did fight once, and lost. No one ever let us vote on this. We're all segregationists, the white people of Georgia; or most of us are. But we've got caught up in something that's bigger than us, and we've got to live with it, the way I see it. There's no choice. When I say that to them, they agree with me, no matter how much they talk of killing every nigger in sight. So I guess most people make their peace with things as they are."

2.   "I Want No Part of All This"

I have heard those words continually from Negroes in the South, not only from the alarmed parents of sit-in students who were risking their lives in protest, or from those teachers with vested interests in a segregated school system, or even from the very poor, the very vulnerable, the very scared. Almost every time I spent a long evening (which invariably faded into morning) listening to civil rights workers discuss their goals and tactics, the subject of apathy eventually came up. For some workers it was quite simple: the Negro has been persecuted so long and so hard that widespread apathy is inevitable — and anyone who is surprised at its presence is naïve, while anyone who complains too bitterly about its effects is demanding and presumptuous. I have seen those who *don't* complain — those whose patience seems to defy comprehension — eventually succumb to despair and weariness.[1] To such intelligent and idealistic youth the price of understanding comes high. Rather than be annoyed and angry that their efforts are ignored by large numbers of Negroes they turn on themselves in resignation, and then gloom.

In a number of instances I have had to stop being only the interested observer of such developments. Individual civil rights workers have wanted treatment for anxiety or depression. More than any other *external* trouble, the Negro's apathy or indifference bothered those workers, whether Negro or white.

In the midst of one talk with a Negro student-activist in Louisiana I decided to make a point: "You talk as if the segregationists, the sheriffs and their police don't bother you much, or not nearly as much as a Negro reluctant to join company with you. Do you really think that is how you feel, or is it easier for you to let loose your frustration and anger on voteless, defenseless Negroes — who, after all, are afraid first, then apathetic — than on powerful segregationist politicians or highway patrolmen?"

He would have no part of my explanations, put forth in rhetorical questions. At last, however, he *did* express some of the disenchantment and near hopelessness he had been carrying around inside himself for so long.

"Well, that's not so. I mean, there's more to it than that. I know it's easier to take out your dissatisfactions on yourself and your own people than the enemy, especially when you can't fight the enemy head-on because he has all the power. But I think we get frustrated by the work we do, and even if the police were helping us, not fighting us, I think we would be frustrated.

"Let me tell you, it's not only the poor people in the Delta. When they tell you they haven't got a penny to their name, and would be killed in ten minutes if they signed their name to *anything*, you have to believe them, and respect them. It's the people who are comfortable, and could easily join you. I don't mean the Uncle Toms, the people who make a living by begging off the white man. I mean the Negro who says he wants to vote, says he wants to be able to go into the public library, or send his children to the white schools, but then tells you he doesn't want to 'shake things up,' or 'get ahead of everyone else,' or 'do something rash.'

"A lot of them have spoken like that to me, and I know they're not speaking out of fear — at least not the kind of fear *you* have in mind (and I did, too, in the beginning). They're just afraid of rocking the boat — the one they're riding in. They don't even want to risk discomfort, let alone danger. No matter how much they complain about white people, the truth is they don't want to do anything to change things. One of them the other day said to me: 'Look, I'm only here on earth this one time. It may be bad, but it's not so bad I want to disturb my whole life. If things will change, that's to the good, but if they don't, well I'm lucky to be alive, and we have enough food and clothes to keep us, and our own fun, even if there is segregation.'

"That man is a lawyer, a lawyer! He won't touch a civil rights case, though he tells the *white* civil rights workers he's all for us. When they get wise to him they call him Uncle Tom or dismiss him as part of the 'black bourgeoisie.' Then the next day they'll go recruiting help from the poor — ninety per cent of Negroes. They'll go into a town, or a rural community — say, in Tennessee or in New Orleans, where today [1963] things are fairly safe, certainly for work at community organization. They'll start knocking on the doors, and one after another they hear the excuses and the pauses; and they see the obliging, smiling faces. They know they have to be persuasive, so they *work*. They talk and argue — it's a good sign if they can get an argument going. Mostly they just talk and talk, and get smiles, or yeses, one after another, yeses. The ones that frown and say no, I know they'll be the ones who will join us. They've got some honest doubt, or critical sense left in them. The others, they're friendly but beaten."

I wanted to know how he accounted for this. Was it a *Negro* phenomenon? After all, large numbers of white people fitted the description he gave me of Negroes. They, too, are often self-absorbed, unconcerned with social and political issues, content to make do with what (little) they have, regardless of how unfair their condition may be when it is placed in the context of this nation's overall wealth. What about the millions of poor white people, or not-so-poor white people, who don't lift a finger to organize themselves, to combine and fight for their interests? If they are apathetic, too, the problem becomes American, a social and economic one that transcends the racial problem.

"It may be; it may be that we ask too much of one another, we Negroes do — at least when we're in the civil rights movement. Our lives *are* different though — worse than that of any other American group. You would expect enough dissatisfaction on that basis alone to generate a protest movement. And I guess there *has* been that — enough dissatisfaction to get some change. But you always wonder. What if it hadn't been for the Russian threat, and the rise of the African countries, and television, and all the things that have helped us? What if some of the segregationist politicians had played it smarter than they did, and not behaved so bad, so ridiculously bad that the whole country was aroused against them? What if we had different people running things in Washington — different Presidents than Kennedy and Johnson? We've screamed at both of them, but we always know they're listening, and ready to help us when the chips are down. The same holds for a few federal judges. If it hadn't been for Skelly

Wright in New Orleans, and Judge Wisdom there, and Judge
Tuttle in Atlanta, I wonder how far we would have moved, even
with all our protests."

He was putting so many hypothetical conditions in his way,
and the Negro's way; he was speculating so gloomily — all the
"if's" postulated a worse world than I could bear to imagine —
that I felt impelled to bring up what *had* been accomplished, and
ask how he accounted for so many achievements in so short a
span of time.

"You are impressed by too little," he replied with barely
subdued scorn. "We've moved, but we've only begun to move.
We've obtained some concessions, but they are minor ones. Most
of my people are still poor, and even worse they are still very
frightened, so that they can't even take advantage of the concessions we've supposedly won. That even goes for the well-
educated, comfortable ones, the middle-class Negroes, who are so
scared of the white man in the South, and so anxious to imitate
him in the North, that it makes you want to cry in desperation."

I wondered whether the fearfulness and the ingratiation he
described were the race-bound phenomena that he felt them to
be: "Many middle-class people of all races and nationalities tend
to be conformist, nervously compliant, set in their ways, unwilling
to take large or unsettling risks."

"That's right," he said, "but there's the big difference that with
us Negroes we have more *reasons,* objective reasons, to be dis-
satisfied and politically active. We've been a caste in America,
not a class. The wealthiest, best-educated Negro has been a
nigger to any white man walking down the street, and not only in
the South."

I didn't think that the Negroes he was criticizing saw things
that way. "They see their own lives, and apparently find them
comfortable, or — the reverse — insecure enough not to want to
do much about social change. Perhaps many Negroes have yet to

find a program that speaks to them, makes them feel whatever they risk will be worth it."

He agreed, but disagreed. "I think you underestimate the apathy in the Negro. It's different from the apathy you describe in whites. It's much greater, and much more paralyzing."

We continued talking that evening, and on many others we resumed the same discussion. I pointed out to him that in fact the white Southerners had been rather remarkably apathetic themselves: in large numbers they had failed to organize against the civil rights workers, and had failed to respond to those segregationist groups that had organized. I played for him the taped interviews I did with several segregationists.

I had in mind one portion of one tape. A Mississippi policeman I knew quite well — going back to the years I lived in the state, before I had been a student of the civil rights movement — was talking about the attitudes of his friends and neighbors: "People say they can't stand what the nigger is doing, pushing all the time to go where he doesn't belong. But do they do anything to stop him? The way I see it, not half what they could do. They join the citizen's council, then sit back and watch. The white people are the majority here, though you would never know it, the way things are going. They can send troops down here, the way they did the *last* time, but they couldn't really get any integration going if we really got ourselves organized to fight it. That's the trouble, we're lazy. Each man is for himself, and to hell with his neighbor, or the rest of the state, or the South. When someone starts bellyaching to me about the uppity niggers and what they're going to try next, I tell them that the nigger will push his way into the White House, and heaven, and every other place in the universe unless we stop him; and I don't see any evidence that we're going to try. We say the nigger is lazy; well, I'm beginning to think he's learned it from the white man. We let anyone push us around, the way it seems."

The situations are not comparable, or so the civil rights worker said. He was interested in the parallels, but he insisted that an oppressor's lethargy (understandable) is not similar to a victim's apathy (terrible and almost incomprehensible). He felt that I should talk with "ordinary, apathetic Negroes, not just civil rights workers."

Of course I maintained that I had been doing just that. Many of the parents whose children initiated school desegregation in the South had not chosen such a role for themselves or their boys and girls. They were as "ordinary" as any people are — though I soon saw what extraordinary circumstances can sometimes do to ordinary people. As I heard those mothers and fathers describe their lives and the events that led to their involvement in the conflict over desegregation, I usually found the same (previous) apathy that in other families are *all* one can (presently) see.

I played another tape for the student, this time recorded in the home of a Negro family in New Orleans. Their daughter was a pioneer, a leader in the city's school desegregation, and they were describing for me — yet again — how it all came about: "They chose her, the school board, without us really expecting it. We thought they were going to let all the colored children into the white school, not just three or four. To tell the truth, I can't remember everything that happened. All I know is that one minute life was going nice and quiet and peaceful for us, and the next minute we thought we'd be killed any minute. If I had it to choose again, I'd never choose what we had to take. But we didn't have a say; it just came upon us, like a big accident or something, and we just had to go along, and fight as hard as we could. And to be honest, a day doesn't go by that either my wife or I don't wish we could somehow have stayed out of this, and let others lead the way. That is the truth."

In any event I followed the advice of the civil rights worker — of many workers — and sought out several Negro families who preferred to remain on the distinct sidelines of the South's social conflict. One family owned a store, and in many ways their problems ironically complemented those of the white storekeeper just described. Two other families were poorer, but none the less resistant to what they again and again — and derisively — called "involvement."

The storekeeper — in one of Georgia's medium-sized cities — said to me at the end of our talks what he said in the first minutes of our first talk: "I want no part of all this." I heard the same words — with or without the word "all," depending on the particular speaker's inclination — from many Negroes throughout the South. Their actions — or the lack of them — attested to the conviction with which they all spoke.

"I want no part of all this," the storekeeper said. "I run my store, and try to do the best I can. I try to please the customer. I give them what they want. I'm even a step ahead of them. (You have to be to keep in business today.) I go out and get things, because I know they'll be watching television, and then coming in here and wanting them. I'm not worried about being colored. Why should we get all upset about what we are? Those people come around telling you to march, march, march. They don't work themselves; they just want everyone else who *is* working to go put their necks out, and get them cut off — I'll tell you, cut off real clean.

"They came around and at first I listened to them real carefully. They wanted me to take the lead, and try to go with people to white stores for coffee, and all that. Now imagine, leaving my own store to go get coffee in someone else's. Then they said I was scared. So I told them I should be. Then they told me it was because I had money and property, and I was middle class. So I told them to go talk with my customers, and the poorer the better. Let them tell you how I keep them going on credit, and how sometimes I forget the credit they've used — it becomes so much they owe — and they start in all over again. I said they should get all the tenant farmers and all the poor colored people in the town, and see if *they'll* march with them.

"Well, they tried, and they didn't get very far, from what I can see. So is it my store that makes me scared? No, sir. I'm trying to do the best I can for my family, and I want everything I can for the colored man — of which I'm one. Is that being selfish? I ask my wife that sometimes, and she says no, it's being like any other person, white or black. So that's it: we just don't want no part of all this."

I found him two years later quite willing to send his children to a desegregated school. They would face no danger then. The issue had been settled by others, in other cities of that state, and in other states. He still wanted no risks. He would go to no meetings: "Those outdoor meetings become free-for-alls." He would move as fast and as far as — in his words — "the country seems to be going." I asked him how he knew the country's direction, its policy and the speed of its change: "I just do. You can tell, from the papers and the television, what's going on. I tell those civil rights people: you can't get ahead of yourself, that's bad."

In Mississippi I visited a tenant farmer's home. He and his wife lived in the Delta, and worked its soil as long and hard as anyone else in the region. Intensive efforts were made to persuade him and others to "sign up," to register to vote. A few did; this family — like most others — refused. I wanted to know what made for the difference. Those who *did* join hands with civil rights workers spoke about the indignity and inhumanity of their condition. Those who didn't spoke of the futility of protest. They remembered other, previous attempts to obtain this or that improvement. They often smiled: "Yes, we could stir up quite a thing this summer. Then you'd all leave, and we would be here to get paid — in the hide — for what we said; or we would have to go with you, that's for sure, if we wanted to get off free."

I found it very hard to make psychological generalizations about these people, about why some of them resisted involvement in civil rights work and others took up the dangerous effort willingly. Neither money nor brains necessarily determined which choice was made. Some realized the impossibility of their life, and seized an opportunity to change it. They had nothing to lose, or so they saw it, but their lives. Others gave rather sharp and poignant justifications for inaction. They valued their present attachments and involvements — what others did they know? — and they doubted that the region could sustain much change. They feared the losses of protest: death or injury; a move — to where? — and a loss of whatever continuity and day-to-day certainty they knew. As one farmer put it to me: "They say all the bright niggers go North to Chicago, or join up with the civil rights people. Then I hear the rights people say it's the same up in Chicago, only worse, and so they leave us here to go up there. (So I guess we were 'bright' to stay here, after all!) Meanwhile, say we have joined up; and the white people, they've been sitting back and waiting to get us. The rights people are a thousand miles away, and no one hears us being beat up, or docked an extra dollar a day for being too smart for our own good.

"That's why I want no part of all this upset. You see it one minute, then it's gone, all the civil rights business. Meanwhile, we're here. If you're going to *be* in a place, you have to see things the long way around. You don't just catch a side look at things; you're *in* them."

3. The Last Ditch

On August 5, 1964, a press service story quoted an FBI agent who was working in the area of Neshoba County, Mississippi, where the remains of three civil rights workers were found: "I wish I could have a psychiatrist examine whoever did this right now and see what they'd be thinking now that we've got the bodies."

I had heard a similar remark several weeks earlier from an agent in McComb, Mississippi. A house occupied by several "integrationists" had just been badly damaged by dynamite, and while I was looking into some of the medical problems — two students were injured — the officer was trying to find out who was responsible for the explosion. Standing near the debris with soda pop in our hands we talked about the details of the incident. The officer assured me that it was a serious attempt at murder rather than a mere effort to warn and frighten, and then he turned his attention to explanations. Why would people want to do this? He asked it, then I asked it, both of us less curious than appalled. Yet, slowly the curiosity rose in him, and well after we had finished our talk he came back to the question. Why would anyone have nothing better to do in the middle of the night than plant dynamite? He was clearly suggesting that only an unhappy, a disturbed person would be awake so late, preparing that kind of deed. Perhaps, he suggested, I had some thoughts on that matter.

We each returned to our work, though I found myself ruminating about how indeed I might have explained to him exactly what my thoughts were. As I tried to lay that challenge to rest I kept on coming back to the chief capability we have in psychiatry, the case history. Perhaps if we had had the time I would have been able to show him what I felt to be the answer to his question by telling him about a particular segregationist's life, including of course the life of his mind.

This man did not murder the three civil rights workers, or plant dynamite in that home in the terror-stricken McComb area of Mississippi; but he has committed appallingly similar acts, in company with many others. He has been in mobs and will not deny having seen Negroes assaulted and killed as a result. I am sure he would satisfy those agents and all of us as a prototype of the bigot who is a potential killer. I thought of him immediately that morning in McComb, and again when I read the report of the government agent's dismayed call for psychiatric help in Philadelphia.

I first met John, as I shall call him, while he was protesting the archbishop's decision to admit some children who were Negro but also Catholic to the parochial schools of New Orleans. It was a warm, faintly humid early spring day, a Saturday too, and the next year's school opening hardly seemed a timely worry. Up and down he walked, picketing, tall, husky from the rear, an incipient paunch in front. He wore a brown suit, slightly frayed at the cuffs, and on its right shoulder rested his sign, wrought and lettered by himself: "Fight Integration. Communists Want Negroes With Whites." His shirt was starched and he wore a tie. He had brown eyes. He was bald but for the most meager line of black hair on his neck — baldness must have happened early and fast. His face was fleshy and largely unlined, and I thought, "Forty or forty-five."

Several of those in the picket line seemed unaware of the gazes they attracted. John, however, was the most engaging and communicative. Looking at people directly, he would talk with them if they showed the tiniest interest. He moved faster than the others, and seemed to be in charge, now signaling a new direction for walking, later approving or suggesting luncheon shifts.

We moved along the pavement side by side, he and I. Would I want a sign — he had several in reserve? I would rather talk with him; I was very much interested in his opinions. I felt it important that he, that they, not be misunderstood, and I would do my best to record fairly what he thought and wanted. I am a physician, I told him, a research physician specializing in problems of human adjustment under stress. A little amplification of this, and he laughed — it *was* a strain, the police and the scoffing people, and those reporters with the sly, obviously unfriendly questions. He would talk with reporters, any of them, so long as they were not niggers, not Communists, because he wanted to be heard. It was important to be heard or nothing could be accomplished. He wanted to do something, not merely have his say, and so he would surely talk with me if I were a teacher, if I wanted to report the truth to the educated. They needed the truth. I agreed. He was visibly impressed with certain credentials which, in my nervousness, I had offered: cards, pieces of paper which I now know were unnecessary for his cooperation. We began that day, later in the afternoon, signs put aside, over coffee. I arranged to meet him regularly, weekly, for several months at his home, or over coffee in a diner. He gradually told me about himself and his life, about what he believed and how he came to see things as he does.

He is a passionate segregationist ("you can put down the strongest, the strongest it's possible to be"). He has plans. He would like to exile most Negroes to Africa, perhaps sterilize a few quiet ones who would work at certain jobs fitting their animal nature, itself the work of God, he would emphasize. He would strip Jews of their fearful power, sending them off also, but to Russia, where they came from and yearn to return. There are other suspicious groups, Greeks, Lebanese — New Orleans is a port city, and he has worried about them leaving their boats. Do they try to *stay* on land? Unlike the niggers and Jews, whose clear danger to his city he had formulated for some time, he had not determined his exact position on such people, or his solution for them.

He was born in central Louisiana, say for example a town like Acme in Concordia Parish. The state is split into its southern, Catholic and French area and a northern section, basically Protestant and Anglo-Saxon. Typically, his father was the former and his mother Scotch-Irish, a wayward Baptist who embraced the Roman Church (the only term used for the Catholic Church in certain areas of the so-called Bible Belt) a few weeks before her marriage. Born their second child in the month America entered the First World War, he was sickly and fatherless his first year of life. While his father fought in Europe the boy was taken with what we now call "allergies," a timid stomach which mostly rejected milk, a cranky skin which periodically exploded red, raw, itchy, and was often infected by his responsive scratches. His sister was five years older, and she remembered all this. She and her mother, still alive, have told him about his fretful infancy, and he knew it well enough to be able to pass on their memories. *His* first memory was a whipping from his father's strap. With his father home from war, a second son and last child was born. John was three. He had pinched the infant, done enough wrong to the child's skin to cause a cry and attract his father's punishing attention. That was to happen many times, though he held a special place in his mind for this earliest occasion: "My brother and I started off on the wrong track, and we've never got along with one another."

His brother is tall and thin, ruddy-faced and blue-eyed like his mother, wears a white shirt to a bank teller's job near their hometown. John, dark and short like his father, has several "blue-shirt" skills which at various times he has used. "I can build a house myself" was his way of summarizing them: carpentry, electric work, plumbing, even bricklaying.

The childhood development of the boys forked: one neat, precise, his mother's favorite as well as her physical reflection; the other, by his own description, naughty, often idle or busy being scrappy. John in short was an overlooked and troubled middle child. He resembled his father, yet had hated him for as long as he can remember. Oddly, though, his manner, his temperament sound like the father's as he describes the man and shows pictures of him, now ten years dead, a large blustery fellow, open, opinionated, rumpled, a mechanic preoccupied with automobiles — under them daily, reading magazines about them by night. He had storms within him, and they fell upon his middle child, alone and arbitrarily, the boy felt.

Once John and I had talked long and hard — it seemed like a whole day. I noticed it had actually been three hours. The length of time measured a certain trust, a certain understanding that was developing between us. I found myself knowing him, recognizing some of the hardships he had endured, not just psychological ones, but the hunger and jobless panic which must have entered so many homes in a decade when I was scarcely born and he yet a child. I felt guilty for a moment, torn between him and the simple but of course complicated facts and experiences of his life, and him as he now is, a shabby fanatic. He was feeling his own opening toward me, and with considerable emotion in his voice, lifting his right hand in a gesture which might well have been his father's, he interrupted our talk of Huey Long's racial attitudes and how they compared with those of his family: "Daddy [Southern fathers can be "daddy" to their children forever without embarrassment] had a bad temper, and I took it all myself. We had never had much money and bills would set him going, but he wouldn't touch my mother, or my brother or sister either. Yes" (I had asked), "my sister and brother both favored Ma, and Daddy, he'd feel no good because he couldn't get a week's pay, so he had to hit someone. Oh, he was for Huey boy all the way, except Huey was soft on niggers, but I think Daddy was, too. He used to say they were children, and we should protect them. But if they're like kids, they're like bad ones, and just like animals, so they've got to be watched over. You wouldn't let a wild animal go free in your home or in school with your kids, would you? It's right crazy how we forget that sometimes. Look at Harlem, and what happens when they let them go. They rape and kill our women and dirty the whole city up. I've been there and seen it. No" (prodded again), "I don't blame Daddy, because, you see, in those days we had them firm under our grip, so it was different and you didn't have to worry about them. But look at now." We did talk about current events for a few minutes, but each of us tired suddenly, and hardened.

Of course, from those old times to the present had been an eventful period for him as well as for the Negro race. He almost died twice. At seven he had a serious bout of pneumonia which — with no help from antibiotics — almost killed him. He recalled gratefully a Negro maid who cared for him through this, one of those (few now) who knew and willingly lived in her "place."

She died shortly after he recovered. Abruptly and looking still young ("I think she was around forty, but you can't tell with niggers"), she collapsed before his very eyes while preparing supper for him. It was by his description probably a stroke that took her, and she proved irreplaceable. They had paid her a pittance, but she had stayed with them for lack of better. About that time several Negro families started moving North, while others trekked south to New Orleans. Though his father had not really been able to pay Willi-Jean her established wages for many months, only death ended her loyalty and their comfort. "I got pneumonia again when I was twelve, and so did my brother. It nearly killed Ma taking care of us. She used to try to keep everything in its place, I think that's why it was so hard without Willi-Jean. With us sick on top of it, she almost didn't get through it all, she got so nervous."

In telling him of my interest in his medical history, I asked him several times to describe in further detail his fits of illness, and the care given him during those times. It seemed clear that he had, in fact, suffered badly at his mother's hands, neglected by her for his sister or brother, blamed by her for getting sick. The Negro woman's sudden death was actually a severe and deeply resented blow to him. His affections for her were hastily buried with her. He had to keep on his guard against his mother's personality, now no longer buffered by Willi-Jean. During one of our last talks he said, "You know, Doc, I think I *did* have a bad time with sickness when I was a kid. When I was twelve I almost died of pneumonia, and then I broke my leg a few weeks after that and lost that year of school." He had tried to run away from home before he contracted pneumonia, and after his recovery, too, until his lame leg made such attempts impossible for a while.

If his mother was nervous, oppressively ritualistic, and hardly his advocate, his father was a heavy drinker, temper-ridden, and fearfully unpredictable. When drunk he was moody. He also became brutal, and his middle son was his customary target.

Declaring a truth whose painful implications he could not look at too closely, John once reflected, "I never figured why Daddy picked on me. We got along fine when he was sober, but when he got liquored up, I got it first and hardest. I looked like him and helped him most in fixing things around the house, but he never remembered things like that when he was drunk." Not that his parents weren't "the nicest parents anyone could ever want." Any vision into their shortcomings, any criticism of them, had to be followed eventually by the atonement of heavy sentiment. He had long ago learned how dangerous it was to speak his mind. Perhaps his life, as we now see it, has been a quest for that very possibility. "I used to be afraid to say anything for fear it would get someone upset at home, so I just kept quiet and ran my trains." Trains were his chief hobby for a little longer than is usual, well into the early teens. He warmed while telling me about his empire of them, and he became wistful afterward. I wanted to hear of his childhood interests, and in speaking of them, he said ambiguously, "I knew trains better than anyone in town."

By the last two years of high school he had found an easier time. His mother reached menopause, surrendered in her war against dust and for order, and became cheerless and distant. His father now drank less, but had to struggle hard with another form of depression, an economic one which he shared with his country. Amid all this John strangely enough prospered. His sister married poorly, a marginal farmer soon dispossessed of his land. Slothful and malignant, he beat her regularly, fathered two children by her, and left shortly thereafter. She never remarried and has had to work hard to keep her two children fed and clothed. John's brother had trouble with learning. He left high school after one year, and for a time, nearly penniless, he drew food and small coin from government relief programs. Recently he has managed a job in a bank, but his wife is a heavy drinker, maybe worse, and they have five children. John says they "live like pigs," and apparently this state of decay set in very rapidly after their marriage. His brother's cleanest, most organized moments are at his job.

John, however, graduated from high school, the first in his family to do so, and went beyond that by securing a coveted job in the local hardware store. He had come to know its owner and his daughter, too. Always interested in fixing things — bicycles, injured cars, faltering plumbing, stray wires — he began in the hardware store as a willing and unpaid helper. The radio, new and mysterious, was his love, and he tinkered endlessly with the various models. The store had many other gadgets, and it also had his girl friend, the owner's daughter. He determined at about fifteen to marry her and did so at twenty. At the time of his marriage he was a relatively prosperous man, now wearing a white collar, regularly paid in dollars increasingly powerful out of their scarcity. ("My folks said I married real well, especially for those days.")

To hear him talk, the twelve months before and the twelve months after his wedding day were his best time. He remembers the pleasure and hope; but his nostalgia is brief, and is always tinctured with the bitterness which soon followed. His father-in-law's business collapsed, to be foreclosed by the handful of creditors who seemed to be gathering the entire countryside into their control. These provincial financiers, with their small banks all over the state, were controlled by Big Power and Big Money, both in New Orleans. Governor Huey had said so, and they killed him. John, with a wife and a boy of three months, had no choice but to try Huey's gambit — follow the Power, follow the Money. "We just up and moved. An uncle of my wife's thought he could get me work repairing radios. They were like TV today. No matter how poor you were, you needed some relaxation." John got a job and held it. He started by going into homes to repair wires or replace tubes. Soon he was selling radios themselves, all shapes and sizes on all kinds of payment plans. He was an exceptional salesman, seeing the radio as a box of easily summoned distraction for weary, uncertain people. He aimed at first not to sell but to explain, tracing with the future customer the webs and tangles of copper, informing his listener of their connections and rationale, pressing hard only at the end their whetted appetite, their need. ("Mostly they were people without cash.")

However, by the time a second world war was underway most Americans had radios, and his work slackened. In early 1942 he was the father of a four-year-old son, a two-year-old daughter. He owned a comfortable home in a distinctly middle-class area of white frame houses, each bulky, yet each a bit different. Most, though, had green shutters, high ceilings, thick walls, large, long windows, but no garage, all expressions of a warm, wet climate. More likely than not every residence had a single car so that the streets, palmy, well-paved, were lined on both sides just as from a plane's view the roofs asserted rows of radio antennae.

He still lives there, though many of his former neighbors have moved. For some the neighborhood was out of keeping with what they had recently become. They left for one-storied new houses in sprawling developments outside the city. The emigrants were replaced by others for whom the same neighborhood's value was defined by what they had just left. There are, however, a few who still prize those old houses, see their faintly shabby gentility and cherish their age and the memories they inspire. For John it is this way: "Those ranch houses are too expensive. Funny thing with a lot of the nigger lovers, they move out into the suburbs and then tell us how we should open our streets to them. I won't leave and I'd shoot to kill if they ever tried to buy a house nearby." (He cannot afford to leave. "They" are 2.4 miles away at their nearest.)

The war came as a relief. The economy was stagnant, floundering with too many unemployed. Poor people had bought their radios, and he was beginning to feel the pinch. ("Even the niggers had them. Some of them even had two.") Actually, he had sold many to Negroes in his years of salesmanship. He had collected money from them and taken showers after he came from their houses. Outweighing such services for Negroes was his participation in lynchings. He's been in two. His words: "We'd go home to see our folks, and you know in the country things are more direct, and there's no busybody reporters around. Once I heard one being organized, so I dropped by to see it." The other time was a rather spontaneous and informal affair. He noted that they "did it real quick like, the way you should. When you draw them out it makes it hard because you might get bad publicity. There are still lynchings around in farm country, I don't care what they tell you in the papers. We know how to take care of them when they get wise. We don't use rope, it's true, and get the crowds up we used to get. We may not always kill them, but we scare the Jesus out of them. You know the buckshot shootings you read about every now and then, it's the same thing as rope or fire. They know what'll happen if they get smart." Did he object at all to this? "Hell, no."

The Negroes were working for the Communists, any he would want to kill; I must know that. Had there been Communists in his town when he was a boy, during the twenties and thirties when lynchings were more public and common, some of them seen by him as a youth? Of course. The Communists took over in 1917, he knew the autumn month, but some of them had been working in this country even before that. He wasn't sure how far back, but he thought maybe twenty or thirty years, and they wanted to take this country, its free economy, for their prize. John was capable of broad, apocalyptic strokes: "This is a war between God and His Commandments and the Devil, and we may lose." I broached the subject of loss. How could God lose? "To punish us." Why would he want to do that? "We disobeyed him." Just an example or two — I was interested in them. "Nigger-loving."

In any case, he was glad to go to war in 1942, for he was accumulating unpaid bills. He yearned for the East — he wanted to go fight the Japs. He wasn't so sure about why we were fighting the Germans, who were combating the Reds, and might be our allies if we would have them. Hitler's enemies were his enemies: the Jews, moneyed, slyly alien and the main support of the Negroes, inferior lackeys who did their bidding for small reward. This was all communism, personified in those hundreds of thousands of hook-nosed or black-skinned natives who lived in New York, in Hollywood. They were the capitalists, too; they controlled publishing houses, banks and the stock exchanges. Their voices commanded a crippled, traitorous President's ear, bought the votes of errant, susceptible congressmen. "I was never against the Germans. I was proven right. Look at us now. They're our best protection against the Commies." Still, he added, the Germans would be of small help if the UN and integration took over America.

He never fought, though he helped others fight. He did his service at an army camp in New Jersey, a very small distance from Manhattan's subversion, perversion — and fascination. He went to New York all the time, to look, to see his enemy. He would always tell his friends how well he knew his New York enemies, and his friends, from what I could see, always seemed interested and stimulated by the details he supplied.

From all those furloughs to Union Square, Harlem and Greenwich Village he managed to return home alive, heavier by fifteen pounds, his balding completed. He worried about work after his discharge, with good reason. He came home to children grown older, a wife with moderate rheumatoid arthritis ("her joints are stiff all the time"). He was now irascible and sullen. His wife usually wanted to stay away from him — out of pain, out of lack of response. She was withdrawing into her narrowing world of routine care of the home and the symptoms of a chronic, slowly crippling disease. To help her she had a young Negro, a high school girl, not very experienced, but not very expensive. (The price of Negroes was rising, along with other postwar costs.) A mulatto, as thin and lissome — I gathered from pictures I saw of her with his children — as her mistress was fattening and severe, she stayed wth them for three years, five part-time days a week, until her marriage bore unexpectedly heavy demands of her own in twin sons.

During those years right after the war John found life confusing and hard; and he became bitter. He tried television-repair work, but couldn't "connect with it" as with radio. He drew unemployment relief for a while, short rations in the face of consuming inflation. Finally, nearly drowning in doctor's bills, in debt even for essentials like food and the most urgently needed clothing, his home heavily mortgaged, he found rescue in the state government, a clerk's job in a motor vehicle registration office. Now barely secure, in his mid-thirties, he was free to settle into concentrated, serious suspicion and hate. It was, after all, the decade of the fifties, when many of our countrymen would seek far and wide for subversives — and when the Supreme Court would declare segregated schools unconstitutional.

I met him, of course, well ripened in such zeal and involved in actions based upon it. From our first meeting it was clear that he relished talking, and talked well. He had found comfort for his views from his employer, a Louisiana state government whose legislature, in its very chambers, had carried on a mock funeral of a federal judge, a native son who had ordered four Negro girls into two elementary schools in New Orleans.[2] The governor was a man whose chief merit seemed to be as a banjo player and singer whose theme song (composed by himself) was "You Are My Sunshine."

John dips constantly into the literature of segregation for support. It ranges all the way from the remarks of a scattering of biologists about a purported inferiority of the Negro on the basis of a supposedly lighter, smoother brain (fewer lines on the all-important frontal lobes) to the pathetic gibberish of the insane. He reads in such allied fields as the frantic anticommunism which holds the President and Supreme Court contaminated victims, even agents. There are always such diversions from the mainstream as the menacing ability fluorides have to erode America's freedom.

One of the first questions he had hurled at me, in our early tentative moments, was about his son. The young man was contemplating marriage and, a loyal Catholic, was about to attend a pre-marriage instruction course offered by their local church. The church was hell-bent on integration, however, and John feared the worst for and of his son. Did I believe "in integrated marriage courses"? I wanted to know more about this. Well, he would kill his son if a Negro came into such a class and he, John Junior, remained. His customary composure cracked (one of the few times I was ever to see this, even when I knew him much better) and he shouted at me. I began to doubt whether he was "reasonable enough" for me ever to get to know "reasonably well." Yes, he'd kill his own son, he shouted. Would I? I thought not. Still, I told him I wanted to hear more about integrated marriage classes. Well, if I wanted to hear more, he would oblige.

The real truth was that he and his son hadn't been able to get along for many years, and for that matter he and his wife weren't now "together" as they used to be. Menopause along with arthritis had come to his wife, heightening with its flashing signals her sense of decline, pulling her from her husband into a separate bed. (He still remembered his mother's menopausal depression, and he mentioned it when talking about his wife's health.) Once scornful of even an aspirin, she now juggled and swallowed seven separate encapsulated remedies. Their daughter, *his* daughter, his great delight for years, had rewarded him with excellent school work and high achievement in pre-college tests. Yet her success in the form of a full scholarship had eventually transported her away from home. Now it was their son, an office worker by day and part-time college student by night, who was about to leave.

His family was dissolving, his marriage disintegrating. He was lonely.

"My boy is a fool, and he always has been." He became angry at first, but later appeared to regret his own remark. His son, it seems, cared little about Negroes and their threatening postures. He and his son had fought about ways of dressing, table manners and hobbies; had fought all along as the boy tried his own ways and John resisted, tried to pinion the lad, fashion him in his father's image. Murderous thoughts by a father at the shameful possibility of his son's "church marriage class" becoming desegregated were but a final expression of long-standing turmoil.

It was against a background of such family problems that John ardently pursued a world as white and shadowless as possible. His work for most of the fifteen-odd years since the war had been uncertain or dull. He tired of temporary jobs selling in stores, then became bored with the security but confinement and meager pay of his state position. About a year before I met him he had run for a significant political office, claiming he would ferret out Communists in his district, export Negroes North or across the Atlantic, deprive Jews of any local if hidden sovereignty, and keep a careful, alert eye upon Washington and New York. He lost, but polled a good vote. In the course of the campaign he met a man who shared his ideals. The man owned gas stations, more of them than he could operate by himself. ("He liked to watch the help, just like me. You can't trust a nigger out of the reach of your eye.") John, priding himself on his sharp vision, purchased one of the stations, mortgaging his house further. His wife was enraged; her arthritis worsened, a coincidence he noticed and wanted me to know about. Selling fuel was a tough but slimly profitable venture; a fortunate arrangement in some ways, however, because he was able to inform a fellow gasoline vendor, fast and angrily, about a Negro employee working for him whose child was one of the handful to initiate school desegregation. John helped organize the mobs around the city's desegregated schools. He was noisily attentive to those buildings, those nearly deserted and embattled buildings where a few Negro and white children stubbornly persisted in getting educated together. To enable the Negro attendant to lose his job was actually as heartening an experience as John had enjoyed in a long time, and he referred back to this accomplishment frequently. He liked disorder in the streets, but he was not one to pass up private spite or intrigue either.

In time, we began to understand the design of his life, how old threads appear in apparently new patterns. Remember John while very young: a dark and sulky boy whose black-haired, ill-humored father preferred his fair wife, daughter and younger son. John understood all too well arbitrary discrimination, the kind that appearances (height, build, complexion) stimulate. He was born in a state split among many lines — northern, Anglo-Saxon, light-skinned, Protestant country farmers on the one hand; southern, Catholic, Mediterranean types on the other, many of the thousands who lived in a wicked, international port city. His parents brought these different traditions together in an uneasy marriage, and the boy grew up a victim of this delicate arrangement. How accidental is it to find him years later moodily resenting dark people?

A psychiatric evaluation finds him oriented and alert, in no trouble about who or where he is — his name, the date and place of our talks. His mind works in understandable fashion. He does not hallucinate, and though we may consider his beliefs delusional, they are held in common with thousands of others, and do not seem insistently private or as incomprehensible as those in schizophrenic delusional systems. His thinking is not psychotic; it flows in orderly and logical steps, given certain assumptions that are shared by many others and thus have social rather than idiosyncratic sources.

He is intelligent, beyond question so. He grasps issues, relates them to others, takes stock of problems and tries to solve them.

He has read widely and deeply, if with self-imposed restrictions. Much of what he reads gives him real encouragement. Full of references to God and country, encouraging virulent racism, recommending violence as possibly necessary in some future Armageddon of white versus black, Gentile versus Jew, biblical patriotism versus atheistic internationalism, this "literature" seeks an America which we hope will never exist, but it also collects its readers into a fellowship. One can call *all* these people crazy, but it is a shared insanity not an individual one. John works; he has a family and friends. He is fitful, alternately cheerless and buoyant. He is not shy or withdrawn; and he is in definite contact with many people, and responds to their feelings. Can we call him "sick"?

In one of those compact appraisals of an individual person we might say that John is not insane, not psychotic in any operational sense of the word; neither retarded nor delinquent. He has no police record, has committed no crimes as his society defines them, is even careful to obey laws on picketing or demonstrations where they exist or are enforced. (*His* kind of demonstration has often been encouraged by some officials of his state.) Absurdly xenophobic, an anti-Semitic, anti-Negro "paranoiac"? Yes, along with many, many thousands in his region. A frustrated, defeated man, a sometime political candidate, a feckless sidewalk crank, occasionally irritable and only rarely dangerous? Yes, but far from alone.

Born in a region long poor and defeated, into a family itself humble and moneyless, often at the mercy of capricious economic, social or political forces, the boy at home faced those first insecurities, those early rivalries, hates and struggles which often set the pattern for later ones. White man against black embodied all those childhood hatreds, all those desperate, anxious attempts children make to locate themselves and their identities amid the strivings of siblings, amid the conscious and unconscious smiles and grudges, animosities and predilections of their parents. He was an active child, a fighter who managed to survive perilous disease and hard times. When grown he had some initial modest success at home and at work, only to return from war into a sliding, middle-aged depression, a personal one, but one that plagued his family, and some of his friends, too. (The papers talked of a "dislocated, postwar economy.") Individual psychopathology, social conflict and economic instability, each has its separate causes. On the other hand the mind can connect them together, and for many people they are keenly felt as three aspects of one unhappy, unpredictable life.

I looked first to "psychopathology" for the answer to the riddle of John, and those like him; for an explanation of their frightful actions. Rather than seek after political, social or economic ills, I chose medical or psychiatric ones, the kind that seemed "real" to me. John's life shows that it can be understood best by looking at it in several ways, and *one* of them is certainly psychiatric. Yet I have to keep on reminding myself that I have seen mobs such as he joined collect in one city while in another they were nowhere to be found. While the incidence of individual psychopathology probably is relatively constant in all Southern cities, the quality of police forces and politicians has varied, and so have their ideas about what constituted law and order. I have seen avowed segregationists — some of them unstable individuals in addition — submit quietly to the most radical kinds of integrated society because they worked on a federal air base. American laws and jobs seemed curiously more influential than "deep-rooted" attitudes.

The FBI agent who spoke to me in McComb was standing in front of a dynamited house in the very heart of the most oppressive area in the South. James Silver's "closed society,"[3] the state of Mississippi, has a long history to fall back upon, one enforced by social, economic and political power; no corner of the state had been more loyal to its past. Certainly I and others with me were frightened, though perhaps the FBI agent was not, by the hateful, suspicious attitude we were meeting at the hands of many of the townspeople. The Negroes were scared, and many of the whites had a kind of murder in their eyes. In the face of all that, the agent posed a question only in terms of illness, of individual eccentricity.

In McComb, in Mississippi, at that time, a dynamited house and even three murdered youths were not unique. There were klans, councils and societies there whose daily words or deeds encouraged the burning of churches, the dynamiting of houses, the beating, ambushing and killing of men. A few weeks after the "incident" in McComb I examined a minister brutally beaten in a doctor's office in Leake County, Mississippi.[4] The doctor — no redneck, not "ignorant"— had literally pushed the minister and a young student with him into the hands of a gang *in his own office*. Every bit of evidence suggests a plot arranged by that doctor — he knew in advance the two men were coming because they had telephoned to ask for medical help. Shall we suggest psychiatric examinations for him and for all the others in the state — businessmen, newspaper editors, lawyers — who ignore, condone, encourage or fail to conceal their pleasure at such episodes?

I wonder about the eager emphasis given private, aberrant motives by some in our society. Many ignore crying, horrible, concrete social and political realities whose effects — as a matter of fact — might lead us to understand how John and others like him continue to plague us. It is easier, I suppose, to look for the madman's impulse and make explaining it the doctor's task.

The bestiality I have seen in the South cannot be attributed only to its psychotic and ignorant people. Once and for all, in the face of what we have seen this century, we must all know that the animal in us can be elaborately rationalized in a society until an act of murder is seen as self-defense and dynamited houses become evidence of moral courage. Nor is the confused, damaged South the only region of this country in need of that particular knowledge.

PART THREE

COURAGE and FEAR

IX

THE PLACE OF THE CHILD

AGAIN and again in recent years, children have marched by their parents' side in racial demonstrations, both in the North and the South. Especially in the South the press has criticized this "cynical use" of children; but when I view their actions in the South historically and describe their adjustment psychiatrically, I have to remind myself that the very word "child" is confusing. At the turn of the century the labor movement asked for "a childhood for every child." Many of these Negro "children" still lack that "right." Is a sixteen-year-old boy who has lived in stark, unremitting poverty, worked since eight, earned a living since fourteen, married at fifteen, and is soon to be a father, a "child"?

Still, no matter how hard the lives of these demonstrators, many of them were young by any standard to be initiating such responsible, nonviolent protests, to be leaders in social change. Moreover, they were acting in a region that considers them not merely children but (as Negroes) the children of children. They have persisted in social action despite retaliatory arrests, brutalities and jailings, and without discernible psychiatric harm or collapse. Modern psychiatry must certainly ask why children subjected to such strains survive so handily; and modern history has no precedent for children directly involving themselves in an attempt to change the social and political structure of the adult. In fact, over our entire Western history only the Children's

319

Crusade compares with what is now happening, and priests both prompted and led those children.

Children have a special place in this country's culture, one reason being that we ourselves as a nation are so young and oriented toward "youthfulness." "Everyone tries to play sixteen," I heard once from a girl not very happy with that age and incredulous at its attractions for those who have long since left it. Large numbers of us are also wealthy enough to offer our young more protection and comfort than they can find in any other nation. For one thing they have more time ahead of them: while most children all over the world are born with grim odds for adult survival, the majority of our children have the assurance of our plentiful statistics that theirs will be the biblical three score and ten.

But if our middle-class young have been protected, when they become older and enter high schools and colleges they receive no immunity from criticism. Social scientists question their morals, call them "alienated" (their elders were "lost") and, in contrast to their contemporaries in other lands, "nonideological." Ironically, even in their own country some of their contemporaries, emerging from poor backgrounds, also stand in contrast to them by taking active roles in a serious social crisis, in school desegregation and in protests against unjust racial practice.

We have read of them consistently these past years. "Juveniles" some of the papers have termed them. They are called "boys and girls" or "high school students" by those who would simply describe them; or "delinquents" and worse by some of their critics. They have ranged from grammar school youngsters of eight or ten, walking hands clasped in those of their parents, to a large number of adolescent youths whose actions are very much their own. While their participation in the Birmingham demonstrations attracted national attention, young Negroes, sometimes joined by young whites, have been picketing or spontaneously conducting sit-ins for several years. I know of several towns in the upper South where libraries and drugstores were desegregated by junior high and high school children to the surprise of their own parents. The white librarian of one town told me that she never could turn children away from books, but only a few years ago her reluctance might not have been so easily indulged.

It is difficult to discover what prompted the initiative taken by these young people. A common charge is that they are "brought out" by conspiring adults. Often it is quite the contrary; nervous parents have been afraid to allow their children's participation in the initially tense months of school desegregation, let alone the more volatile uncertainties of street demonstrations. For example, half of the children who initiated Atlanta's token desegregation of its schools in 1961 had to work hard for their parents' consent before they could take on the additional reluctance of the city's school board.

It was not easy for me as a white psychiatrist to get to know such facts, let alone learn more generally the emotional ties and strains at play in Negro families. It is easier to observe the families sociologically, then to categorize them: some of them are matriarchal families whose members are underprivileged, ill-educated people, relatively deprived of (white, middle-class) cultural traditions and roots. Even descriptions of the anger and frustration common to most of these families may fail to account for the origin of these feelings in the special, grinding humiliations constantly faced. We may easily understand a Negro's instant anger before a threatening state trooper, but fail to see that from their first years Negro children must learn who they are, where they may not go, what they most probably will be and cannot be. The lessons taught by such a reality become psychological facts — accurate reflections of social and economic ones — that determine the child's sense of his worth, his sense of the power of those who define his worth, and consequently of their work. Under such circumstances, a Negro's open anger at a Southern policeman may be more of a milestone for him than we (so quick and willing to understand it) will ever know.

If the Negro child's life is one of having to learn how to

confront a future of unrelenting harassment, his intimidated
parents must prepare him for it. They must teach their child a
variety of maneuvers and postures to cope with his baffling lot. By
seven or eight most Negro children know the score, and I have
seen them draw only faintly disguised pictures of the harsh future
awaiting them. Yet although the future may look harsh and
purposeless, it can alternatively hold out some promise that the
pain endured will contribute to the eventual end of its causes. Put
another way, suffering can have its own neutrality; any physician
sees wounds from assault that resemble ones inflicted by
surgeons.

Until now nonviolent action has come naturally to Negroes,
because the only alternative has been to turn their suffering in
upon themselves, converting it to sullen despair. Negroes are not
now *becoming* angry. At some level of the mind, in its corners
that are out of both the white man's sight and often enough his
own, the Negro has always *been* angry. We are fortunate that for
the moment his anger has found constructive expression. Other,
more destructive, kinds are waiting in the wings as fierce reminders that the real alternative to the remarkable stability and
resilience in Negro children is the violence, delinquency and
addiction of some of their more injured (or exhausted) peers or
elders.

Suffering also can ignore the color line. In a sense white and
Negro children have more in common with each other than with
their parents. They share a historical moment that can be painful
to them regardless of race. We have seen white schoolchildren in
the South suffer with shame as they slowly begin to realize what
Negro classmates must endure. Even some frantic segregationists
experience guilt, an unconscious kind which sometimes accumu-
lates large enough in a particular child to change his racial attitudes. Most Southerners simply turn away, in apathy or defensive rationalizations; or they watch. They watch in surprise as
these Negro youths contain themselves under the repeated provo-

cation of hecklers. "Where did they ever learn to behave like that?" I was asked by a white girl of seventeen who watched her town's police club a Negro girl two years her junior. She went on to express her covert sympathy with the girl by saying, "I don't think any girl of her age really wants to cause trouble, even if they do."

Yet there are records of violence and antisocial behavior from children, both younger and older than that Negro girl, which go back into the Middle Ages and persist through our time.[1] Schoolchildren once were armed, and the word "truant," which I hear applied to so many Negro children trying to become American citizens, comes from a Latin word describing a wandering student. Such youths were readily accepted by many societies until their freedom slowly began to threaten the more stable order of life demanded by the rising bourgeoisie. The nineteenth century, that sober era when upper-class children were most precious and least indulged, was amply touched by juvenile crime and violence;[2] the earliest records of the Children's Aid Society of New York (founded in 1854) mention many instances of both. Across the seas student groups — such organizations as Young Italy and Young France of the 1830's and 40's — were forming the rebellious vanguard of spreading nationalism.[3] Today's protesting Negro youths, despite their supposed lack of "civilization" and their susceptibility — even if at a segregated distance — to twentieth-century liberalism, with all its supposed encouragement to lowered standards for obedience, are much less violent and wild, much more controlled or "repressed" than their nineteenth-century counterparts in Western Europe; and despite the hardships of their race's special exploitation, they seem no less sturdy.

Indeed, there are no easy correlations between parental ideology, class or race and "successful" child development. Many children the world over have revealed a kind of toughness and plasticity under far from favorable conditions that make the determined efforts of some parents to spare their children the slightest pain seem quite ironic. Despite our wealth and the advantages it promises our children, despite our constant interest in their "welfare," we so far have produced no general flowering of humanity. Our middle-class breast-beating over "juvenile delinquency" and "the self-indulgence of the younger generation" has its justifications. However, the affluent section of our society has also produced — in the Peace Corps, in the Northern college youths who have joined the civil rights movements — a remarkable kind of idealistic youth, many of whom have achieved their own virtue by rejecting their parents' often too obvious materialism. Similarly, I have come to know reliable and productive Negro children from the most desolate homes. Their parents are tired, beaten, and sometimes very unattractive in speech and action. But such parents produce their fair share of delinquent children, too.

For some time students of literature and psychology have tried in bewilderment to understand paradoxes like Dostoevski's early "traumas" and Kafka's terribly twisted childhood.[4] Lives such as theirs illustrate more than the triumph of genius over illness. They are exceptional examples of how very hard it is — or should be for us in our present state of knowledge — to define the sources of "health," "creativity," or "maturity" in many people. We see the wide behavioral variations of children from relatively similar neighborhoods. We are struck by the common cause and ethical commitment of children from widely divergent ones. Growth in children seemingly challenges as well as responds to a wide and complicated assortment of influences: social, economic, psychological — spiritual.

What has happened to children who have endured the special hells of our modern civilized world — its wars and devastated villages, its concentration camps and prisons, its two nuclear bombs? These disasters have generated a genre of books that discuss the impact of various modern barbarities upon children. The titles and their subject matter evoke the recent past: *War and Children*[5] by Anna Freud and Dorothy Burlingham, on British children under the blitz; *Children in Bondage*,[6] essays on child life in Nazi-occupied Europe; *The Hunted Children*[7] by Donald Lowrie, on the rescue of the young from the Gestapo; *Polish Children Suffer*[8] by Witold Majewski, a description of how Polish and Jewish children managed under the Nazis — and fought them hard; *Children of the A–Bomb*[9] by Arata Osada and *Children of the Ashes*[10] by Robert Jungk, describing what happened to the children who survived our most sophisticated and ruinous form of war; and there are many others.

These books tell us much about the inner resources of children. The files of American and European newspapers are also informative. Take the *Nieuwe Rotterdamsche Courant* of June 7, 1941: "Children between the ages of seven and thirteen are committing offenses against the occupying forces which must be called crimes." (Strangely familiar words to anyone who has read certain of our Southern newspapers.) Throughout Nazi-occupied Europe children shared in the Underground — the term "children's front" was used by many to describe their participation. Unlike our Negro children they were following their parents and teachers; and impressively so. They boycotted Quisling's teachers in Norway; they sang songs of protest in Danish schools; they helped derail German trains in Holland; and even murdered Gestapo agents in France. Their German conquerers imposed upon them the new and fastidious scholarship of "raceology" (*Rassenkunde*), and they outwardly submitted. But not fully, or not really; and at the first possible moment, not at all.

Many children facing war, prison life or nuclear holocaust showed astonishing resourcefulness and precocity before disaster. Fighting for survival, waifs in the wake of atomic bombs or Nazi armies, they formed gangs to seek out food and shelter, to support one another. Years later we hear them recalling their common trauma and marvel at their clear and comprehending words, at their capacity for reflection and expression of feeling.[11]

The bestiality and terror of German concentration camps destroyed young children. Yet a veteran of four of these camps writes about older children in the camps whose early emotional development was more secure: "There is another side of the coin. Those of us who were caught up in the Nazi web . . . have learned something in the camp that no other form of education could have given us. We have learnt the value of freedom and of life itself."[12] Some comfortable American youths complain bitterly that they lack such knowledge, have never learned such lessons.

We need not *recommend* adversity (there is world enough and time), but we also so far have to live with the definition of its opposite — contentment and happiness — still elusive. Nor can we forget that adversity has an ageless role in the lives of most people, and one that cannot be extracted from the context of those lives and judged by itself. We can all agree that we oppose mobs, and children facing them, but if children must face them, let us find out why, and what will happen to them if they don't. When we find out what happens to them if they don't protest, we will find out about children in daily subjection who have been asked to forfeit their freedom by the decision that they must endure tyranny rather than face "danger" or "trauma," and do so at a time when that endurance hardly seems a necessity. What can be worse psychologically and spiritually for any child? When we find out what happens when these children *do* protest, there is no neat correlation between external hardship and internal collapse. Dr. Martin Luther King has said, "Undeserved suffering is redemptive." I would merely add that I have seen precious little psychiatric illness to such redemption.

Of course, until recently we would not even be concerning ourselves with the special vulnerability of these "children." In his remarkable book *Centuries of Childhood*[13] Philippe Ariès has shown that from the Middle Ages to the seventeenth century children were weaned late, but then went very directly, at about the age of seven or eight, into the world of adults. They were often entrusted to strangers who worked or taught them and presumed them grown — little grown-ups, yes, but responsible ones, and sharing in the tasks and play of the community. We often forget that Joan of Arc was seventeen at her most notorious and adored. Romeo and Juliet, lovers at fourteen, seem perhaps older to us today. To their world they were adults, and so were the children who in the same century reputedly followed the Pied Piper as well as itinerant priests to the Holy Land.[14]

Starting in the seventeenth century, children were asked to relinquish widening shares of their adulthood to take shelter under the newly developed protection of middle-class families and schools, neither of which became full-fledged institutions in the sense we now know them until relatively late in Western history, really in the past two hundred years. These are the same centuries in which we find childhood being extended to later ages than ever before. These two centuries have also confined the child not only by narrowing the latitude of his freedom but by increasing the adult world's preoccupation with The Child.

Historians and sociologists have correlated this growth of "childhood" with the rise of complex industrial societies.[15] These societies valued property and privacy; and the new classes emerging within them were self-conscious and often sharply separated from one another. A world supported by intricately divided and specialized labor needed widespread education for some of its young, and time for this to be accomplished. However, labor and particularly unskilled labor rose in value. By the nineteenth century in Britain and in our country, children were being at once extravagantly idealized as the repository of all wisdom by writers like Wordsworth and Pestalozzi[16] and ruthlessly exploited by the economic system. Children working in Victorian mines and factories were not youthful medieval adults in pursuit of an apprenticeship but mere faceless property which their poor, horrified parents suddenly found themselves owning.

In contrast to the poor, the middle classes became intent upon fulfilling their destiny. They found in their children a significant mirror of their own identity, an element of their own lives which could be consolidated and perpetuated. No wonder the reality of childhood, and thereby its meaning and experience for many of us today, slowly changed. From *Pamela* to *Émile,* and with strong if less philosophic continuation in Dr. Spock, we have speculated with increasing intensity about how to rear our children. It is as though we believed their fate entirely dependent on us, as though perfecting our children were our only hope of immortality.

In a sense childhood has for some of our educated middle class become a focus of a final "ideology." The world is darkly threatening. God and various Utopias have been disappointing. "I don't believe in anything but my children," I remember hearing from a lawyer whose child I was treating for some emotional difficulties. The father had grown up when parents were less self-conscious about children; when children were not the last hope in an uncertain world plagued by nuclear fallout, racial disorders, middle-class delinquency, and the various confusions of a technological and bureaucratic society. True, *his* parents were immigrants, and he represented for them a kind of hope, a hope for the future, a living forecast of a new and better life, not for themselves, perhaps, but surely for their young. The boy was to become a lawyer: he would have to work hard, give up pleasures, deny himself. Strains upon children were not calculated and then lamented, perhaps because the good life was too near grasp to worry about anything but its final possession. His parents' dream and his own hard, painful effort have now become the third generation's surfeit and to some extent its ironic burden. What this father wants for his children is that they be spared, given the "best" education and protected from all kinds of turmoil. Tensions, whether they be those of private or social origin, are "bad" for children. His children's "mental health" is a source of concern to him, and also the "environment" in which they grow up. They must live in a nice neighborhood, be treated by parents and teachers alike in certain careful ways. The father, I felt, was more interested in what was good *for* his children than what good he might ask *of* them. And the particular child I was seeing did indeed have a problem: he didn't quite know, after all, what was "good" and what was "bad," what he could do and what he must not do. Once he might have been called "fresh," "spoiled" and "wild," but now he was "impulsive" and his "problem" involved "acting-out." He did have a problem; and its complex nature, I fear, is not only psychological but sociological, and ethical as well.

Meanwhile, many Negro families, in contrast to some of those in our educated white middle class, still believe in the Bible, have yet to become openly disenchanted with what very little they possess, and are still hoping for more, although with few illusions about when they will see their dreams realized, at least on this earth. Unlike immigrant groups who came to this country with hope, if no other property, the Negro has lived here all the while. His own special, native American condition has been so low, so apart that he was largely unaware that others were arriving and quickly moving upward to pass him by. Moreover, in earlier times many children died young, families were more authoritarian in structure, social controls were perhaps firmer when societies were not only more simple and compact but more isolated. Until recently, the Negro was not secure enough even to conceive of the true security of real freedom. Now he is; it is a mere beginning, but a crucial and historic one.

Negro youths I know — there are striking, well-publicized exceptions — are still surprisingly little concerned with ideology, and their parents even less so. With more success these parents and children will have the various choices that make thinking and planning appropriate. "Right now," one of them grimly told me, "I don't do much figuring, and I don't worry about what's going to happen to me. I just try to get into those lunch counters and registrars' offices. My parents, they don't much care one way or the other *what* I do. I mean they do care, but they don't know, to tell the truth, what we're doing, because it's hard for them to *believe* that we're actually doing what we say we are." Moreover, it is an ironic fact that many Negro children have had much wider latitude in street play than their white counterparts. There has been until recently much less reason for a Negro parent to restrict his child to study and discipline. This very "freedom" of the poor child whose parents do not have faith in the future has allowed some of these children to make their very spontaneous street demonstrations.

To many of these children their parents have not merely lost hope, but are deeply compromised by virtue of their long, if historically necessary, submission to the white world. If I needed instruction on the ways Negro leaders — college presidents, businessmen, ministers, political leaders — have had to truckle to their white counterparts, then go wearily homeward with their pittance, these youths have given it knowledgeably, eagerly and bitterly. In a sense these students are their race's first truly independent spokesmen, asserting a critical role — perhaps unique in America — toward the (both Negro and white) adult community similar to that played by students in other countries where education is rare and freedom is being newly sought or has only recently been won.

I have said that these demonstrations — picketing stores or courthouses and braving the subsequent white "justice" of hoses, dogs, truncheons, electric prodding poles, trials, jails, criminal records — do not necessarily cause psychological collapse or psychiatric symptoms in these teen-aged youths. Yet, when we try to evaluate their strengths we often are brought up short by our own problems. We are a generation that looks very carefully at motives. The most common interest I hear from many concerned people is one that urges a curiosity about what *kind* of person takes on a hard life of protest, of demonstration and frequent arrest. Inevitably there is an associated fear that the minds of these youths will be hurt, badly hurt, by the dangers they encounter.

Well, who are these "children" and what are their motives? They are everybody — seekers, wanderers and rebels; children who are already men, young men sometimes acting in very childish ways. How do they compare with youths the world over? They have restless energy and spells of anxious hesitation. They seek self-expression and may at moments fear it, too. Some of them are controlled and studious. Others are delighted, if a bit surprised, to find themselves *both* lawbreakers and heroes. All over the world youth is the time for riot, ranging from panty raids to political demonstrations. Even "delinquency" is worldwide, and classwide. How do we compare the youthful spirit that causes wanton destruction of property at Princeton with the youthful spirit of the young white students in Oxford, Mississippi, who in 1962 shouted their vulgar defiance of federal law? In a Northern city I recently watched a group of white youths about fourteen or fifteen years old scream various obscenities at a Negro couple moving into their neighborhood. What distinguishes their impulses, motivations and problems from those of the civil rights demonstrators in the South or North?

Some of the differences are clear. Many of those youths taking part in racial demonstrations are better integrated psychologically as well as racially. They act out of deep moral convictions and in a spirit of sensitivity and thoughtfulness. In contrast, other youths in Mississippi or Chicago are squalid, mindless toughs, acting out of careless impulse. But for many of both groups the differences are less psychological than social and cultural. Indeed, as James Silver has shown so very clearly,[17] the white students at Oxford, Mississippi, were living out their state's history. What can a psychiatric analysis of those youths tell us? Can they be called "sick" or "delinquent"? Is the issue before us primarily psychological or ethical? However we assess the psychological *motives* of either James Meredith or his persistent assailants, their respective deeds will have to be judged in the light of history; and before God, or before our secular moral sensibilities.

Southern Negro children, eager for sit-ins and marches, are not willing to accept the prevailing values of a segregated society. They are committed to action, dedicated to affirming new values. It is their actions that make them guileless and powerfully innocent, and in tune with our time; and it is this very time that enables them to strike out and claim successfully once forbidden territory. They have not been the first to dream of freedom, to want the white man's cafeteria coffee, to covet revenge. They are not the first to scorn their parents' anxiety and fear and undertake their own social action.

The chance to translate the possible into the actual enables individuals to be useful and productive. In contrast, the chief complaint of most of our mentally ill is not that life is hard, or even painful, but that it is both of these without a sense of fulfillment. The dreams of the ill seem out of touch with the reality of their lives. As psychiatrists we must help our patients understand their dreams and — as they are called — their "goals." Yet, goals must find their destiny, and this destiny will always be outside our offices, in the midst of the world and its particular opportunities — or lack of them.

Precisely what, I have asked myself, can a child psychiatrist do to help a young Negro — or white — child who at the age of six or seven throws fits in school, and steals regularly from stores? His teachers may well ignore and abuse him. His home may be crowded and a bore or worse to all his senses. The child may be hungry, may lack clothing or even a few cheap toys. If such a boy's world were different, would his actions, evidence enough of a "troubled mind," persist? I have no unequivocal answer to that haunting question.

X

THE MEANING OF RACE

SALLY, one of the Negro children I knew in New Orleans, drew heavily upon her grandmother's spirit when confronted with the hate and violence of mobs and the forced, pointed loneliness brought on by the boycott of "her" desegregated school. Like the other three girls selected, Sally (and her parents) had no idea that she would face exposure to mobs as the price for entering a once all-white elementary school. Her parents had submitted her application because many of their neighbors were doing likewise. Having arrived only recently in New Orleans, they had assumed that its attitudes were not those of the state's rural areas. So much else was different in New Orleans — its buildings that anyone could enter, its streetcars where anyone could sit anywhere, its sidewalks where Negroes could walk on the "inside" without interruption instead of retiring to the road at the approach of a white person, its stores serving *all* customers by proper turn — that school desegregation seemed another miracle to be accepted quickly as part of living in the city.

Sally and her parents were eventually to realize they were fated to challenge their city rather than quietly enjoy some of its advantages. There came a point in my observations of how they managed such a fate when I was puzzled at their continuing calm in the midst of danger. I frankly wondered — at first to myself, then aloud to them — why they did not gather themselves together and leave. Sally's grandmother gave the following explanation:

333

"If we run away, we'll fool ourselves; you can't run away from being a colored man. It don't make any difference where you go — you has the same problem, one way or another." I asked her whether she thought those problems in any way comparable to those faced by white people — for example the few white families who were resisting the mob's will, defying its boycott to keep their children at school with Sally. "Yes," she replied firmly, "we is all the same under God, so we has the same problems; but colored folk has special ones, too. It's the same being colored as white, but it's different being colored, too." Then she repeated the words, nodding her agreement with them, "It's the same, but it's different."

It may seem a bit obvious and simple-minded to insist upon putting the Negro's problems in the context of those shared by all of us as human beings; moreover, it hardly seems surprising to learn that the Negro has problems that are all his own. Still, I think research into what it means to be a Negro will sooner or later meet up with the methodological hazards involved in abstracting people on racial grounds (on religious, social, economic or geographical ones as well) and then talking about "their" feeling (in contrast to any individual's or, for that matter, those found in *all* individuals). I do not think either Sally, her parents or her grandmother established any new record of courage and endurance in the face of threats. In many ways the crowds were angrier at the few white parents who defied them by keeping their children in school. Each family — confronting similar daily odds — stood fast for its own reasons, even as they all had some purposes in common. We lose when we dwell exclusively on either the private or the shared experience or intention.

What interested me about the remarks of Sally's grandmother was that she gave me an essentially matter-of-fact explanation for her steadfastness: there was simply no alternative. A Negro cannot flee danger, try though he might. Danger is everywhere, a never-ending consequence of his social and economic condition.

Danger is written into history with his blood, into everyday customs by laws, into living itself by the size of his wages, the nature of his neighborhood. In contrast, every white parent I knew fell back upon another kind of reason for his actions. One father was a minister; he called upon his religious faith. Another parent was especially devoted to the education of her children; she could not stand idle while a school was destroyed, her children untaught. One family had only recently come to New Orleans; they did not "believe" in segregation — and they were stubborn and plucky enough to want to stand up for their beliefs, or, in this case, the absence of them. (Of course, I met a few others who put their ideals more positively; they were very much "for" integration; yet they were also "for" the safety of their children, enough so that they yielded to the prevailing storm and sought out other schools for their children.)

What all these white families revealed together was a willingness to "choose" danger in the pursuit of an ideal or goal. Each one of them would mention the possibility open to them of rejecting a role in school desegregation. One father mentioned travel, just as Sally's grandmother did: "When I saw those people acting that way, I became ashamed of the city. We even talked of moving away, to Texas or California; but then we thought we just couldn't rest easy, running away." Each one of them rejected flight from the mobs, or indifference to them. Many others, very much like them, could rationalize their disinterest in desegregation, or defend their unwillingness to oppose segregationist street violence, by pointing to the fact that even the police — let alone the majority of the white parents in the school district — were disinclined to disperse the mob.

I do not think that situation in New Orleans was unlike the general situation in our country, as it confronts Negro and white people. The stakes may usually be less grim, less distinctly defined, less dangerously at issue; but the Negro has his skin to help him establish the nature of his problems and his beliefs, while white people must grapple for other mainstays of self-awareness or faith. Children who grow up and experience the Negro's lot in our society — no matter how various its expressions — achieve at least some measure of self-definition. It may be insufficient, it may lead to ruin, yet it cannot be seen only as a burden. To quote again from Sally's grandmother: "We may not have anything; but at least we know why." She was telling me about the whites of her region, whose ability to look down upon her did little to elevate their material or spiritual welfare. Oppressors, they knew little about the reasons for their own impoverishment.

What can be said about how Sally feels being a Negro, about how her grandmother feels, or any of the other children, the other adults we have met in this book? All that has been said about the meaning of skin color to Negro children[1] surely holds for Sally — and has always held for her parents and grandparents. Sally at six could tell me rather openly that she wished she were white. Other Negro children her age deny and conceal similar wishes with great vehemence — that they, in fact, have such wishes is all too clear from their drawings, games and "innocent" or "unintended" remarks.

Still, as we grow, or live, we all want occasionally to be what we are not, or cannot really ever become. What must be done is to establish the relevance, the importance of Sally's fantasies about her skin for the rest of her life. To do so requires placing discrete psychological events (and the observations made by psychiatrists of those events) in the context of the general growth and development of the child, including, of course, the influences of society upon how he is reared and taught to regard himself.

My clinical impression — slowly consolidated over these past years of working with Negro children — is that most of the "usual" problems and struggles of growing up find an additional dimension in the racial context. In a very real sense being Negro serves to organize and render coherent many of the experiences, warnings, punishments and prohibitions that Negro children face. The feelings of inferiority or worthlessness they acquire, the longing to be white they harbor and conceal, the anger at what they find to be their relatively confined and moneyless condition, these do not fully account for the range of emotions in many Negro children as they come to terms with the "meaning" of their skin color. Sally's grandmother said more concisely what I am struggling to say: "They can scream at our Sally, but she knows why, and she's not surprised. She knows that even when they stop screaming, she'll have whispers, and after them the stares. It'll be with her for life. . . . We tell our children that, so by the time they have children, they'll know how to prepare them. . . . It takes a lot of preparing before you can let a child loose in a white world. If you're black in Louisiana it's like cloudy weather; you just don't see the sun much."

The "preparation" for such a climate of living begins in the first year of life. At birth the shade of the child's skin may be very important to his parents — so important that it determines in large measure how he is accepted, particularly in the many Negro marriages which bring together a range of genes which, when combined, offer the possibility of almost *any* color. What is often said about color-consciousness in Negroes (their legendary pursuit of skin bleaches and hair-straightening lotions) must be seen in its relentless effect upon the life of the mind, upon babies and upon child-rearing. A Negro sociologist — involved in, rather than studying, the sit-in movement — insisted to me that "when a Negro child is shown to his mother and father, the first thing they look at is his color, and then they check for fingers and toes." I thought such a remark extreme indeed, until two years later when I made a point of asking many parents what they thought of it — and found them unashamedly in agreement.

As infants become children, they begin to form some idea of how they look, and how their appearance compares with that of others. They watch television, accompany their mothers to the local market or stores downtown. They play on the street and ride in cars which move through cities or small towns. They hear talk, at the table or in Sunday school, or from other children while playing. By the time they enter school, at five or six, to "begin" to learn, they have already learned some lessons of self-respect (or its absence) quite well.

I have been continually astonished to discover just how intricately children come to examine the social system, the political and economic facts of life in our society. I had always imagined myself rather sensible and untouched by those romantic nineteenth-century notions of childhood "innocence." As a child psychiatrist I had even committed myself to a professional life based on the faith that young children see and feel what is happening in their family life — and if properly heard will tell much of it to the doctor, whether by words, in games or with crayons. Yet I had never quite realized that children so quickly learn to estimate who can vote, or who has the money to frequent this kind of restaurant or that kind of theater, or what groups of people contribute to our police force — and why. Children, after all, have other matters on their minds — and so do many adults.

I do not think Negro children are, by definition, budding sociologists or political scientists, but I have been struck by how specifically aware they become of those forces in our society which, reciprocally, are specifically sensitive to *them*. They remark upon the scarcity of colored faces on television, and I have heard them cheer the sight of a Negro on that screen. In the South they ask their parents why few if any policemen or bus drivers are colored. In the ghettos of the North they soon enough come to regard the Negro policeman or bus driver as specially privileged — as indeed he is, with his steady pay, with his uniform that calls for respect and signifies authority — and perhaps as an enemy in the inevitable clash with "whitey."

"The first thing a colored mother has to do when her kids get old enough to leave the house and play in the street is teach them about the white man and what he expects. I've done it with seven kids, and I've got two more to go; and then I hope I'll be through." She was talking about her earnest desire to "be done with" bringing children into the world, but she had slipped into a recital of how Negro mothers must be loyal to the segregationist customs of Southern towns. Still, she preferred them to the North; and so did her son, a youth I had watched defy sheriffs (and his mother's early admonitions) in Alabama and Mississippi for several years. "In the North," her son added, "I'd have learned the same thing, only it's worse, because there a mother can't just lay it on the line. It takes time for the boy to get the full pitch, and realize it's really the same show, just a little dressed up; and until he makes that discovery, he's liable to be confused. The thing we're not down here is confused."

The Negro child growing up is thus likely to be quite rigidly and fearfully certain about what he may do, where he may go and who he eventually will be. In the desegregated schools of the South, where Southern whites have had a fresh opportunity and reason to watch Negro children closely, teachers have been especially impressed by what one of them called the "worldliness" of the colored child. She did not mean the jaded, tough indifference of the delinquent — perhaps a later stage of "development." She simply was referring to the shrewd, calculating awareness in children who have been taught — worried about, screamed at, slapped and flogged in the process — the rules of the game as they apply to Negroes. She had come to realize that growing up as a Negro child had its special coherence and orderliness as well as its chaos. The children she was teaching were lonely, isolated and afraid — a few of them in a large, only recently desegregated white elementary school in Tennessee — but they also knew exactly what they feared, and exactly how to be as safe as possible in the face of what they feared.

For that matter, it is not simply that Negro children learn the bounds of their fate, the limits of the kinds of work allowed to them, the extent of their future disenfranchisement, the confines of their social freedom, the edge of the residential elbowroom permitted them, the margin of free play, whim or sport available to them now or within their grasp when they are grown. They learn how to make use of such knowledge, and in so doing gain quite gradually and informally an abiding, often tough sense of what is about them in the world, and what must be in them to survive. In the words of Sally's grandmother, "Sally can get through those mobs; she was born to, and one way or another she'll have to do it for the rest of her life."

So it is not all disorder and terror for these children. As they grow older, go to school, think of a life for themselves, they can envision a life which is quiet, pleasant and uneventful for long stretches of time, or at least as much so as for any "other" children. That is, the Negro child will play and frolic, eat and sleep like all other children; and, though this may seem no great discovery, it is essential that it be mentioned in a discussion which necessarily singles out special pains or hazards for analysis. Sometimes when I read descriptions of "what it is like to be a Negro" I have to turn away in disbelief: the children I have been working with — in sharecropper cabins and migrant camps as well as in cities — simply do not resemble the ones portrayed. Perhaps it is impossible in *any* description to do justice to the continuity and contradiction of life, but we can at least try by qualifying our assumptions, by acknowledging that they do not encompass the entire range of human experience.

"It's like being two people: when I'm around here I'm just me; when I leave and go to school or go downtown I'm just another person." A high school student in Atlanta is speaking, a Negro youth who is trying to integrate those two facets of his personality as well as himself into a white school. Yet, not even his sharp, clear-cut statement can account for the range of sensibilities which develop in Negro children as a result of their race's history and present condition.

As in all matters of human behavior, each Negro child or adult I have met has developed or is developing his or her own style of dealing with what is essentially a social experience that becomes for the individual a series of psychological ones capable of giving "significant" structure or form to a life. Some of the styles are well established in folklore and in the daily expectations of both whites and Negroes: subservience, calculated humiliation, sly ingratiation, self-mockery; or, changing the tone somewhat, aloof indifference, suspicious withdrawal, sullen passivity or grim, reluctant compliance. Again, in areas of diminished repression, where outright submission has been replaced by the possibility of social and racial disengagement or "coexistence," one sees impatience, or ill-tempered, measured distrust; indeed, in evidence is everything from irritability and barely concealed resentment to an almost numbing hatred and fury.

What most Negro children of ten or twelve have learned is a tendency, stimulated by the white man's presence or appearance, for one or (more likely) a mixture of several of these or other adaptive modes of dealing with him. The choice, of course, depends on the private life of the child, his general development of personality — there are reasons other than racial ones for being prone to good-humored supplication or to anger, despair, resignation, sulkiness, insensibility or inertia. The manner of adjustment also varies, as I mentioned, by region and by class or occupation, too.

Even though Negroes in general grow to be especially sensitive to — and on their guard with — whites, the quality and quantity of experience, hence of feeling, between Negroes and whites is not all of a kind. Some Negroes are constantly in contact with whites: taking care of their homes, waiting on them, carrying out their orders in offices and stores or working alongside them, even of late giving them orders or directions. Others live in the shadow of the white world, but really have very little direct encounter with white individuals. "They touches on us, but we don't much see them, to tell the truth." The wife of a sharecropper, she worked the land of a white farmer, lived in his house, saw him or his deputies drive by; yet, her actual, person-to-person meetings with white people were few. She and her family carried on their daily lives with that mixture of freedom and restraint characteristic of poor rural folk. Though their "inheritance" as Negroes—their social and cultural traditions—set a different atmosphere for them than, say, white sharecroppers or small farmers in the same county, the similarities of living in that county are by far more striking. Negroes tend to discount the importance of "legal" marriage, are often much more open and relaxed about breast-feeding or toilet training, and tend to keep less orderly households. On the other hand, white parents tend to be more attentive to their children as they become of school age, their individual preferences indulged where reasonable or possible. However, what both races share are similar routines, similar worlds with which they must contend. These common experiences fashion a common attitude toward education, food, clothing and other people in contrast to those of one's own family.[2]

In the ghettos, or the all-Negro middle-class areas of our cities, a somewhat similar pattern holds, of random association with whites in the midst of an ordinarily exclusive relationship with one's own people. Naturally, class differences obtain, it being one thing to try to imitate the white middle-class world (and to have the means to do it) and quite another to live the uncertain, hand-to-mouth existence characteristic of any slum. Yet even in Atlanta, where there is a Negro residential district of matchless elegance (if compared only with other Negro districts), the experience of crossing into contiguous white areas demands its recognition, a recognition not unlike that in the Negro who leaves the same city's ample slums on a shopping trip or to look for a job downtown.

The word "caste" only partially explains such shared feelings, which persist in the North regardless of class, even among those

Negroes — their number is obviously increasing now — who live predominantly in the white world. For that matter, in the psychotherapeutic or psychoanalytic relationship — where presumably troubled *individuals* are consulting *doctors* — psychiatrists have commented on certain general problems which arise out of the difference between the patient's skin color and the doctor's.[3] Regardless of their particular symptoms, Negroes and whites in the psychiatric office have a special problem to face, not necessarily difficult, by no means insurmountable, but nonetheless real and rather commonly present. There is a likelihood of more distrust, more fearful hesitation, than is usually the case; and the mind of both the Negro and white person — whether doctor or patient — will find it difficult to refrain from noticing and responding to the various symbolic and emotional meanings of color.[4] They are, after all, part of our entire culture, and certainly significant in the childhood and adulthood of Negroes in America.

When I lived in Mississippi I had a home in a small town. The people I knew were intelligent and kindly — all of them white, middle-class people who were born in the state, brought up from their first days by Negro "mammies." I recall their weekly trips to "nigger town" — they were adults now, and there was laundry to take there, or a favorite servant's birthday to remember. After I became interested in how young Negroes lived and got along with whites, I went with a doctor and his wife one day to the colored section of our town. They had always ignored laundromats, would not think of buying a washing machine; Louisa had been washing and ironing their sheets and shirts for years. Louisa and her mother had taken care of the doctor's wife when she was a child: "She fed me as a baby. I was the first baby she cared for; she learned from her mother how to do it — I don't remember much of it; I just remember Louisa smiling and helping me choose a dress to wear for a party at school, and maybe a game or two she played with us." Later that day this very sensitive woman told me of an experience she *did* remember, and quite clearly: "I think I was seven or eight, and I went with my mother to a five-and-dime store. It was one of those old ones; I can still see the counters, and the fans going. They hung in rows from the ceilings. . . . Anyway, we were walking down the aisle, and I bumped right into a nigra woman. I said, 'Excuse me, ma'am,' and right in front of her my mother told me never to use 'ma'am' with the colored. It was okay to say 'excuse me,' because that showed I was a well-mannered girl; but 'ma'am' was different. . . . I had trouble making sense of that, and I asked my mother her reasons for being so against using 'ma'am' with the nigra. She tried to tell me that it was the way we did things in the world, but it never made sense to me. . . . I think what *did* make sense to me was that I had to obey my mother's wish. Then you grow older, and you stop trying to make sense of things like that. You just know that there are things you can do, and things you can't, and that's it. My brother once tried to get my parents to explain to him why he had to wear a tie one place, and not another. It was the same thing. My daddy just said, 'Jimmie, that's the way it is, and that's the way we have to do it.' "

Looking back at all the conversations I have had with individuals like this lady since that day, it has been a rare person — even a rare "poor white" — who has not mentioned similar memories. The confused and tortured intimacy of white and Negro people in the South has been described by writer after writer.[5] Yet to be confronted by it comes as a challenge to anyone interested in just how the human mind deals with the inconsistencies and contradictions of social existence. That woman today — in spite of her ordinary civility and even graciousness — is grimly opposed to any change in the way Negroes and whites get along with one another. She feels that others, "outsiders," are imposing strange and unsettling demands upon her. The strangeness of her own childhood, of her own relationship to Negroes as a child, no longer troubles her. Yes, there are memories, and if she is not pressed, not questioned with any intent to argue or even interpret but simply to learn, she will reveal them to herself as well as her listener. All in all, though, her present anger at Negroes and her long-standing sense of them as beyond the bounds of her politesse combine to exact a price: she cannot really feel comfortable with some of the best moments in her own childhood; she must work hard at denying them in order to keep her present attitudes properly charged and effective in her daily life. There is no romantic indulgence in Faulkner's descriptions of the passion that fuels the hate of white Southerners for Negroes, particularly those white yeomen hard-pressed by hunger, self-doubt and loneliness, whether in comparison to other Southerners or (as even well-to-do Southerners often feel) in relation to their countrymen in other regions.

If the white man must often deny his early, increasingly confusing friendliness with Negroes, the Negro has little choice but to come to terms with his early, equally confusing awe, envy and hate of whites, and his friendliness with them. "Keep your fear of the white man, I has to tell it to every child all the time until they knows it for themselves." I asked this poor, uneducated wife of a former sharecropper whether her children had *only* fear of whites. She shook her head. "They be jealous of them. Sometimes they might want to see how they live; so my husband drives them over and picks me up from work." (She worked as a maid in a comfortable Atlanta suburb, and her daughter was now at school with children who lived in that suburb.) "I told her, we can have all the rights they have, but you can't feel easy with them so fast. . . . I just make sure my kids know to be afraid."

The "ma'am" that the white child learns to drop the Negro child learns to say — say fearfully, say anxiously, say reluctantly, say eagerly, say out of habit, say with conviction, say and mean, or say with reservations that surely include a wide range of bitterness and resentment. Doubtless the experience of a Negro growing up in Boston is different from that of a Negro in the Black Belt of Alabama, but I think the common need persists everywhere in America for Negro youth to gauge their relationships to white people warily. While the white man loses part of his own life history, his own kindness or good will when he isolates his present self from his past feelings, the Negro loses part of his own life history, his natural self-protective assertiveness, his confidence with others and ease about himself, when he learns to separate his past experience of surprised indignation from his present sense of what the world expects and will demand. Just as we can compare white people by how easily they submit the occasions or psychological moments in their "private" lives to the judgment of social and cultural imperatives, so I should imagine Negroes differ in their willingness to deny and surrender themselves in order to curry the favor of the white man.

One of the most thoughtful and careful investigators of how Negroes endure their lot in American society has asked in one of his papers:[6] "Why do not all Negro men become schizophrenic?" The very fact that such a question can be formulated suggests at once some of the problems facing both Negroes and social scientists. We do not know for certain the cause (or causes) of schizophrenia; but we do feel that consistently disorganized, brittle, tense, fearful parents in some way influence its development in their children. It does not seem fatuous, therefore, to inquire why *all* Negro men are not schizophrenic. A number of observers, from several disciplines,[7] have remarked upon the serious psychological problems facing large numbers of Negroes who live impoverished lives, in a social and cultural climate which commonly rejects them, and in families often enough unstable, disturbed and split apart.

Of course, it is obvious that millions of Negroes survive such special strains — if not handily, then at least with no crippling mental disease. As a matter of fact, what is puzzling to those of us who have worked with the more penniless, "backward," rural Negroes is our continuing sense of the remarkable sturdiness and

poise in many of them. Many others, of course, are tired, apathetic, almost lifeless; though even people in this latter group
show a striking capacity to come alive when exposed to the
momentum of social and political change.

The privation, the domination and oppression of the Negro in
this country have been all of a special kind. It is futile to compare
it to the intermittent excesses of colonial powers, or to the
sadistic regressions to bestiality characteristic of totalitarian
regimes; for that matter, I am not sure there isn't a real difference
between the way persecuted minorities once lived with their
oppressors in the various European countries and the way
Negroes and whites have lived in the South. Likewise, the caste
systems in Asia are not quite like ours. Despite our flaws, we
claim ourselves a democracy, and have almost torn ourselves
apart for a century working to justify the assertion. In addition to
holding the Negro first a slave, then isolated legally and socially,
we have also lived side by side with him, blended our blood and
skin with his, shared our homes and names with him, entrusted
our children to him, and in the South, scene of his longest and
most dismal affliction, nevertheless and coincidentally joined him
in poverty and suffering, given him food and clothing and even
affection. It may not be very easy these days to consider the
kindness and warmth over the generations of many white Southerners toward Negroes[8] as anything but condescension, or a
peculiar refinement of an exploitative social and economic system.
Nevertheless, for many years such living habits, and particularly
the emotional climate that accompanied them, have constituted a
very definite psychological inheritance for millions of Negro
people — setting standards for their behavior, giving form to their
individual feelings. I don't know where else in the world, when
else in history, two groups of people have had quite so wide a
range of relationships — spread over time, involving all the complicated and often conflicting social, economic, political and
psychological influences at play in our nation, our South.

When I first started interviewing Negro children and their parents my chief concern was with the hard life they faced, the special stresses they met when seeking entrance into a society often only grudgingly willing to greet and welcome them. My chief task — as I saw it for a long time — was to document carefully and precisely the specific psychiatric toll such personal hardship, such social repudiation exacted from these individuals.

Though in no way do I deny what Kardiner and Ovesey[9] have called the "mark of oppression" (in fact, I have ample evidence to add further confirmation of just how cruel, enfeebling and unsettling a brand it can be), it remains equally true that alongside suffering I have encountered resilience and an incredible capacity for survival. To travel about with migrant workers, to stop with them as they visit their sharecropper brothers or cousins, is to realize how tenaciously and sternly they persist, as well as how unequipped they are for our white, middle-class world. Moreover, I will risk being called anything from a fool to a sentimental apologist for a dying order by insisting upon the fun, good times and frolic I daily saw in these people. Of course, they have downcast and sour moments, too — often brought on by the presence of white people. Yet, as one man reminded me, "We can always forget them when they're gone, and most of the time they're just not here to bother us — we know they're always on our back, but it's when they get in front of us and try tripping us up that we get upset." I watched his angry petulance, his artful self-abasement with the white foreman on the farm he helped cultivate; I also saw how very pleasant and even sprightly he could be at home with his wife and children. "We has it rough, but we knows how to live with it, and we learned it so long ago it's second nature; so most of the time it's not so bad; tell the truth, it's only once in a while things get bad . . . so long as you keeps your wits and doesn't ask for but your rights." Even in segregated, impoverished rural areas there are "rights" in the sense that the social system is not erratic, chaotic or inconsistent with its own (if peculiar and arbitrary) traditions.

I have, for instance, seen migrant farmers cut a farmer to the quick, refuse to appear on his land, because he has gone "too far," screamed too loudly at a worker. Sheriffs can use electric prods and shout to a pitch of frenzy at Negroes demonstrating for the right to vote, but they will often hardly so much as raise their voices with other Negroes "going about their business," even if they are thoroughly annoyed at how badly or ineffectively that business is being done.

In general, I have been trying to indicate that I find the task of talking about "the Negro" difficult indeed, the more so because of how many individual Negro men, women and children I know. Even their common suffering, a suffering that has cursed all Americans since the beginning of this country and has yet to be ended, fails to bind them together sufficiently to cause them to lose their individuality, a fact that may be sad for zealous social scientists but is ultimately hopeful for America.

There is undeniably a concrete reality in being an American Negro; millions of people are tied down to it; some of them are driven mad by it; others are frightfully torn by its prospects; the spectacle of what its consequences have been for this nation is not yet completed; in its grip people have faltered, cowered and pretended; from its grip people have fled and battled their way; and finally, the worst and best in mankind have emerged.

I hear talk about the Negro's childlike behavior in the face of a culture that so regards him. I hear that he is a symbol of this or that to nervous, sexually troubled whites; or that he is himself foolishly, childishly wanton and bold, or fearfully thwarted and stunted. I hear that he has his special black soul, mysterious and wonderful, defying description — the very attempt to describe it being a characteristic of the white soul.

Who can limit by any list of attributes the nature of any person, the possibilities in any group of people? We cannot forsake our informed attempts to do just that, particularly in the case of those kept so long outside us while so deeply and sacrificially within us. I would only hope that someday soon the Negro will achieve an order of freedom that will make our descriptions and categories no longer so relevant — indeed, not only out of date, but out of order. It may not now be impertinent for a psychiatrist to talk about "*the* problems" of "*the* Negro," but I surely hope it soon will be.

XI

THE MEANING OF PREJUDICE

IN the past chapters I have tried to look at lives which, though different, nevertheless faced a common set of circumstances: the decline of one kind of political order and the uncertain but steady emergence of another kind. "It's a new life we're fighting to get born here in Atlanta," a Negro youth told me in 1963; but in that same year, in that same city, an old lawyer, a well-known segregationist lawyer, could still say: "They want to change things around on the street, then they think they'll be different inside; but they won't be, because they're born niggers, and that's the way they'll die."

The last generation of psychiatrists has done much to make understandable the mind's willingness to hate and envy others, uncritically and en masse. It is a tragedy of our time that in the face of continuing wars and racial hatred very little remains *un*known about why and how people grow to be prejudiced — against themselves as well as others. One does not have to agree with every aspect of Freud's original drive-bound theory, or even the later modifications applied to it by the so-called "ego psychologists,"[1] to see how bluntly psychoanalytic observations confront us with certain facts of everyday adult behavior, not to mention the demonic and generous capacities that live side by side in the nursery. When he wrote about man's apparent inability to stop hating others and waging war against them, Freud made it hard for any successor to build a one-sided "philosophy" about our essential nature — its "goodness" or "badness."[2] To obtain love requires assertion, the demonstration of willfulness; while a display of anger may be rooted in nothing more sinister than timid yearning or devotion.

What does psychoanalysis have to say about the various racist doctrines, and the hate or even wars openly proclaimed in their name? To summarize an extensive literature, psychoanalysts have emphasized the *possibilities* for racism that emerge as the child grows up. Children learn to accept themselves (predominantly) or they learn to loathe themselves because others show them little love or respect. Children learn what is forbidden about the world, and even their own bodies. They learn about the black-brown parts of themselves — the "waste," the good-for-nothing — that must be ousted. They learn (and joke) about the dark, smelly corners and crevices of their flesh. They learn about differences between boys and girls, between older and younger people, between big strong people and little weak people. They learn about *others,* about brothers, sisters, playmates and class-mates — all of whom set in motion rivalries and envies as well as affections. Children learn the shifts and displacements that time demands, and if some of them gain strength and competence thereby, others never cease longing for what was — and hating whomever or whatever caused them to be dislodged.

The mind's way of dealing with its own desires and the world's will or its rules makes for all kinds of contingencies and devious psychological developments. One child can hate by hating a Negro, his brother, his sister, parts of himself. Another child can endow a Negro with the lure of pleasure, the joy of defiance, the triumph of the forbidden. Neighbors, or distinctive (and darkly unequal) strangers, inevitably invite comparison with the most familiar people the child knows, the men, women and children of his family.

I am repeating what is (or should be) common currency in a world decisively affected by psychoanalytic knowledge.[3] The scapegoats that the Bible described Freud showed to endure in everyman's unconscious. They are also given sanction by entire social systems. In no century has man been without his Souths and his wars. The conceptual problem that faces any psychiatrist is how and whether to use what he knows about behavior, about the potentialities (for love, for hate, for courage, for fear) in the child as they are progressively fulfilled in the individual adult to explain complicated political and historical developments.

Perhaps we psychiatrists had to go through a heady, exuberant stage when eager theorists used psychoanalytic principles in a game of leapfrog, jumping over this concept or that into any territory available, from literature and the theater to biography and politics. We took the fearful, nasty, spiteful, voracious elements from dreams and fantasies, from the backyard, the playing field and the schoolroom, and converted them into explanations for the widest range of social questions or historical puzzles. The therapeutic value of analysis soon became a serious consideration not only in child-rearing but in social planning. If only more people could be analyzed! There was talk of a treated and "cured" elite that would lead us out of ignorance and wrongdoing. The same logic and reason that finally had glimpsed the workings of the unconscious mind would take control of the body politic; the same insight that at last had characterized and defined the shadowy, unmentionable forces at work in the family would now set straight man's racial, religious and national tensions. Such thinking may have lost much of its glow for the intellectual community, but its influence persists among psychiatrists, despite the fact that rancor, hurtfulness and an assortment of prejudices and snobberies can be found among the analyzed, and even among those who analyze — whose "schools," cliques and dogmatic, arrogant postures are a noticeable if waning part of contemporary American life.

If a psychiatrist is appalled by the grandiosity and narrow-minded foolishness of some efforts to take clinical observations even a short distance outside the office or the hospital, how can he proceed to do so himself, once he has done some work that tempts him in that direction? The dangers have been pointed out in the past century by Tolstoy, Freud, Erik Erikson and Bruno Bettelheim, among others; so at least there is some recourse to the protection that well-spoken good sense offers. In his two epilogues to *War and Peace,* Tolstoy labors hard with the polarities of "chance" as against "genius," the numberless incidents affecting millions of people meeting up with the one person whose life seems to have a design and a law of its own. "Why did it happen in this and not in some other way?" Tolstoy asks that question,[4] and it is one I have heard Negro and white Southerners ask for many years. "Did they have to let it happen this way?" little Ruby once asked her mother after a particularly hard day of it with a mob on one of New Orleans's streets. Her mother replied: "Maybe if it didn't come like it has, it never would have come at all, and then we'd be even worse off than we already are."

Tolstoy answers his question as inscrutably as his wisdom will allow: "Because it happened so!" Then he lets history speak: "Chance created the situation; genius utilized it." Yet, one question's answer leads to further riddles. "But what is chance? What is genius?" Here is his reply to those questions — hauntingly pointed and direct, and still so very fitting to our dilemmas:

"The words *chance* and *genius* do not denote any really existing thought and therefore cannot be defined. Those words only denote a certain stage of understanding of phenomena. I do not know why a certain event occurs. I think that I cannot know it; so I do not try to know it and I talk about *chance.* I see a force producing effects beyond the scope of ordinary human agencies; I do not understand why this occurs, and I talk of *genius.*"[5]

In a section of his famous letter to Albert Einstein, Freud writes tentatively, as if an intimate of Tolstoy. He prepares the reader for some of his recommendations by telling him that "our mythological theory of instincts makes it easy for us to find a formula for indirect methods of combatting war." He goes on to suggest that the forces that bind men together be encouraged, but he is not sure exactly how that can be done, and he is discouraged: "An unpleasant picture comes to one's mind of mills that grind so slowly that people may starve before they get their flour." He is talking about methods that "promise no rapid success" in preventing war. "The result, as you see, is not very fruitful when an unworldly theoretician is called in to advise on an urgent practical problem. It is a better plan to devote oneself in every particular case to meeting the danger with whatever means lie to hand."[6] Where he hesitated some of his followers cut capers.

Freud's theoretical mind was willing to share a great novelist's hesitations before the awesome spectacle of history — and the wars, the hate and the destruction that go to make up so terribly much of it. In recent years, for all the tiresome refusal of the public as well as many in the social sciences to accept Freud's own definition of his theory, and the range of its usefulness, encouraging progress has been made by those analysts willing to do precisely what "the first psychoanalyst"[7] recommended: devote themselves pragmatically and flexibly to particular cases and situations. This Erikson has done in a notably successful way in his study of Luther as a man and a figure in Western history,[8] and this Bettelheim has done in his moving studies of the bearing that prejudice has upon social change — a follow-up to his personal experience with the institutionalized murder and madness of the Nazi concentration camps.[9]

Erikson has avoided the reductionist tendency that bridges the gap between an individual psychology and a theory of history by merely transferring the language and concepts of one to the other. Instead he tried to make as much sense as he could of Luther's life both from what is known about him and from what he himself wrote, then look for the reasons why history granted Luther the immediate response he received. The psychoanalyst and the historian must share with one another, give and take, and thus achieve at least a common ground of experiences and thoughts — a convergence rather than the false harmony of an agreement that denies what should be affirmed and enjoyed: the existence of two different modes of thought.

In discussing the relationship between the bigot and his society, between a man's prejudice and the world he lives in, Bettelheim also emphasizes reciprocity: "As long as there are personality structures which remain poorly integrated — first because of upbringing and later because of too much tension created by insecurity and frustration — and as long as the individual's upbringing prevents him from acquiring adequate controls, for so long will society have to offer outlets for the discharge of hostility. On the other hand, as long as society continues to permit or to condone such hostile discharge, the individual will not be forced to integrate his hostilities, or to control them."[10] It goes without saying that poor people and persecuted people may well have a hard time being relaxed and hopeful parents, so that their children may well for that reason alone stand a poor chance of feeling cheerful or confident, even at three or four, in the "privacy" of their homes. It also goes without saying that societies do not often plan the "outlets for the discharge of hostility" we daily must witness: the acts of violence by sheriffs, the mobs that are overlooked by police or even sanctioned by authorities, the inflammatory rhetoric — in word, in print — of the fearful and the hateful. As one Negro youth from Alabama explained to me: "I used to think it was all figured out, the way a colored man is treated. I asked my father once when it was that the whites decided how we were going to live. He told me to stop being silly. He said it just happened that we live the way we do. They took us over here, and they've always had the guns, and we've had the muscle to work for them, and that's it. So there's no figuring it out, just knowing we're on the bottom and they're on the top, and once you know that, you know a lot — I guess everything there is to know."

When I asked him whether he thought both his oppressors and his own people could make a switch and get along as equals, he had a psychological view that rather matched his historical and social one: "I suppose yes, I suppose we all could. As I see it, you can do almost anything if you have enough reason to, and especially if you know you've got the company of others in doing it. When I was a boy, I didn't think a colored man was anything but one of God's castoffs. Now, I think my skin is as good as anyone else's, from high yellow to white and back again. My grandmother, she used to say we would only be saved if we learned to change our skin color — and only God could do it, later on when we died, if we've been good. My mother said no, but she couldn't figure out a *better* answer when I asked her, except for me to shut my mouth and mind her and work when I grow up. But me, I think I can see the answer: it's for people to have to mind one another the way I used to have to mind my mother. I mean it's for black and white to mind one another equally, or else get punished the way I used to be. Then, you'd be surprised — the two colors, they won't mean so much, and keep people so apart any more."

Words like "dark" and "black" or "light" and "white" have a number of connotations — biological, social, psychological and symbolic. The night, with its sleep and dreams, is dark; and there are the long, cold nights in winter, not to mention the longest night of all, death. Blindness, and its solitude, is continual darkness. The clouds darken the sky, keep away the sun, bring thunder and lightning. Dirt is dark, and summons in hygienic middle-class minds all sorts of fears — germs and illness, contamination. Man's waste products are dark, and if they are not eventually expelled he grows sick. Sex is so often associated with the night; and we cover ourselves with clothes, keep ourselves in the dark, for modesty's sake. Sadness and gloom are dark states of mind and in the shadows and the dark corners of the mind and of life itself lurk secrets, mysteries, confusion and danger — the unknowable or at least the unknown. The devil is dressed in black; and the evil of our sins is dark — a stain upon our good conscience. We are tempted by black serpents — though if we repent our slate is wiped clean again. Indeed, a little Negro boy — uninterested in this kind of discussion — was describing the good work he did that day in school: "I walked up to the blackboard when the teacher told me to, and it was empty. Then I just picked up the chalk, and the next thing I knew that board was full of what I had to say. The teacher said I really knew my stuff; but I said no, it was the chalk."

There is a difference between black and white, and a distinction between the races and the sexes. Certainly Southern white men talk a lot about protecting their women (presumably weak and in need of protection) from the Negro, who is also weak and ruled — if not protected — by the white man. Certainly several generations of Southern ladies (by definition white) have labored to help the Negro in a number of ways. As Lillian Smith has shrewdly pointed out,[11] the vigilant and sometimes frantic championship of white ladies by their Southern husbands, brothers and fathers has fallen just short of giving those *women* — who, after all, are more than ladies — a kind of nervous custodial care. It seems that the purest white — the delicate flesh of the fair sex, the weaker sex — is especially vulnerable (and susceptible?) to the predatory appetite of the downright black, the dark race, the weaker race.

Children, of course, want everything almost indiscriminately, and certainly want what they cannot have, often for reasons hard to comprehend. They slowly learn though — learn why, or simply learn that there is no why — that they must obey the arbitrary law of their parents' whims, fears or "attitudes." Children also are immensely self-absorbed; it takes months for the infant to recognize and know particular people, and we all know that some people (the inordinately "narcissistic") never get very much beyond that "level" of development. In most people (the "normal" as well as the troubled), self-concern and self-criticism are present in various and perhaps unique mixtures. The way we are progressively treated — the manner of our acceptance or rejection at home, in the nursery, on the streets, in school, at work — shapes our sense of self-respect or self-loathing, polarities which are not meant to be timeless, implacable categories, to be measured and fixed without reservation upon people, but rather a manner of describing trends or developments. In some individuals self-concern has managed to advance from an acceptance of the self to an interest and delight in others; in others self-criticism, necessary and important in itself, has been so relentlessly encouraged and experienced that a firm disregard of the self eventually becomes congealed into hatred that may easily be expressed toward others rather than accepted as an "inside" state of affairs.

Children thus grow and develop so that racism can fit in quite easily with the mind's need for this or that form of expression or aversion. The blond child may like herself enough (but not so much) that a "tall and dark" (but not too dark) man seems, also, "handsome." Then a blond child may seek after dark (and sometimes very dark) men because she does not have very much use for herself. The different, or the "other," can be desired, feared or envied — and in any case often given possession of what is wanted but forbidden or not wanted but all too at hand. The mind is at least as devious as the world.

"White" and "light" have no more simple a time of it in our everyday language or in our unconscious. While we turn "white as a sheet" in fear, blanch with horror, pale with alarm or worry or illness, we also strive for the pure clean that white implies. The doctor in white is a healer — and is unstained by the smears and smudges that the rest of us (not only Negroes) would provide by our mere presence in his operating room. The first-driven snow is virginal, but doomed; and virgin soil is rare, too — so what is clean, unsullied and untouched is in danger, or at least destined for other things. We grow old, grow white and hoary; yet, somehow transcendence is possible, because a white heat is the hottest one of all. Even Snow White was tempted, and I suppose that every "woman in white" one day abandons her medical or nursing preoccupations to become a "lady in the dark." In our time night and day as well as the races of mankind are not so distinct or separate, with electricity and the atom, with "darkness at noon," and with a supposed understanding by many of other cultures, such as the Chinese, who mourn in white; though some would argue that we in the West may be whistling in the dark so far as history goes, for precisely the reasons Conrad indicated in *Heart of Darkness*, our own unremitting and exploitative self-centeredness.

What in daily life gives actual and sometimes monstrous import to the symbolism of white and black? In America the children of light and the children of darkness that the Bible mentioned live on, though skin color was hardly what St. John or Paul the Apostle had in mind when they made the distinction. In the dreams of my middle-class white patients I once heard occasional references to the Negro — his skin prompting the same imagery that writers use more elegantly; and so now with the dreams of poor Negroes. It may be interesting to me that skin color can become "libidinized," a launching pad for all sorts of associations, a target for displacements, projections — in sum, the lot. I may know that nervous, insecure, "traumatized" whites fight off desires for the Negro body, only to surrender unwittingly to the power of those desires by night — and in so doing come to terms with an issue that ironically has to do not with the Negro, but their own childhood. I may know or find out that Negro children hate what they are, and hate what they want to be instead, and hate themselves for all their hates (and preferences). Eventually I may even find out that it is quite possible for a white person and a Negro person to love one another or hate one another for reasons no different from those inspiring or plaguing anyone and everyone. Such knowledge — stated in the abstract — deserves its own respect, but also requires some fastening down to particular lives. If very few of the psychiatric formulations I have just made came directly to the minds of many people I observed — or even to my own mind — in the course of a rather long time of acquaintance, then we are indeed up against a problem familiar (sometimes) to both clinicians and historians: generalizations provide a collective frame of reference for individual lives and incidents; they do not, however, account for all that goes on, nor for a lot that doesn't. Psychiatric generalizations in particular are at present ways of making *some* concrete sense about frequently scattered bits of evidence.

Let me again fall back upon some of the individuals whose words are clearer than mine because they have been wrought in daily experience. I have just asked a white man whom I have known and talked with for three years in Mississippi whether the Negro's entry into his daughter's school worried him because — as he himself had once said in passing — "they are animals, mostly, uncontrolled animals." He hesitates only briefly, then speaks as if he knows both what he means to say and I am likely to be thinking: "I'm a lawyer, not a psychiatrist, so I don't know what you do about all this, but I don't think you can jump from what we say and believe in our hearts to what makes us oppose school desegregation or the sit-ins. I know my daughter isn't going to be harmed by one or two little colored children in her school. I'm not fighting *them.* So help me not once have I thought that little Susan will get into trouble with a nigger. If Susan were twenty, and a sitting duck for some wild nigger, I still wouldn't be fighting to keep them out of school — not for that reason, I mean.

"In school, they're where they shouldn't be, where we were brought up not to see them, ever. You go and talk with every white parent in Mississippi, and they won't tell you it's sex and all that they want kept out of our schools. It is, of course; it's their lower mentality and everything that goes with it, including sex, I suppose. But it's more than all that, too; it's like anything you've grown used to, and depend upon or believe in: if it's going to be changed right from under you, against your will, you'll be angry, and you'll try to do something about it.

"Take an Englishman or a Yankee came down here. We get as angry at them as the niggers; frankly, we get more upset, and not because they're trying to force all those colored people down our throats. It's their rudeness, and interfering arrogance, I'll tell you.

"I can't argue with you, I know, because you can say it's all 'underneath,' and we just don't know what's really at the root of things. I hear that in court all the time from the alienists they bring in from Jackson and New Orleans. All I can answer is that we're brought up to expect niggers to be in one place and ourselves in another. Now, if that is changed, I'll bet we go on having the same fears underneath, but we'll come to expect them in the schools, like it or not. What will happen then? Will we get over our fears, after desegregation? I doubt it. Our houses are desegregated — they live in them and take care of us, and we still don't want them playing equal to us when they're *not* equal. That's the point: we don't see them as our equal, as intelligent as us, or as *like* us; and I don't believe it's any one thing in the mind that's responsible for our attitude, any more than I think any one law will change it. When people have had a custom for hundreds of years, and different kinds of living, that's a reason for an attitude, a mental attitude, as much as anything else."

I can know why in general men hate, and why in one instance a man hates Negroes; but why that man takes to the street one day against Negroes requires quite another level of analysis. Since we are only just beginning to take a look at *action* and *deeds* — in contrast to *motivation* and *symptoms* — the individual life (not seen as a case history) requires a kind of study that foregoes the glee and pride of large-scale answers.[12]

XII

THE PLACE OF CRISIS

I ONCE asked a Negro youth involved in the sit-in movement whether the intense commitment he displayed could be explained satisfactorily by his sensitivity to the social and economic injustice he saw everywhere. We had been over the territory often before, and he knew where to begin: "Not completely, I guess. There's always something else going on — in your *own* life, I guess. Isn't that what you keep on coming back to, every time we talk? I was thinking, though, the other day: there's a *lot* going on in everybody's life all the time. What makes people respond to what they do — rather than respond to something else? I mean, I have a million complexes and hang-ups, and each one of them might be pushing me in a different direction. So why do I finally decide to follow one lead, and not another? It isn't necessarily how strong you feel about something that makes you go do it. If that were the case, I'm surprised I didn't go on a rampage years ago and pick a fight with every white man around. I remember hating every white man in sight, without knowing a thing about them. I must have been nine or ten when I first remember feeling like that.

"It must be that something makes sense to you at a time when you need it to make sense, and then you go do it. (For a lot of reasons it makes sense, and then you have something to do that satisfies all the reasons.) It has to be something you *can* do though; that is, unless you want to waste your life by going in for the useless or the weird — you can *always* do those — that will change nothing and no one will notice."

Certainly a lot of people were noticing what he and others like him were doing — including the lawyer from Mississippi just quoted. I do not think that my curiosity had much to do with initiating their curiosity. In the midst of change they wanted to talk about its causes, and about the motivations of those who were opponents — fighters and resisters. Again and again I have had to remind myself — and be reminded by those I was "study-ing"— that my job was neither the clinician's nor the contempo-rary historian's nor the political scientist's, but some hard-to-define and often confusing mixture of them all. If the people I knew were mostly "like everybody else" (that is, not sick) they were also different because of their public activity, their partisan-ship, or their mere existence — that is, the time and place they were fated to live and, as one Southerner put it to me, "stand by and see everything change so fast you can hardly keep yourself from getting dizzy." While some may wonder whether in truth — and in the long run — there was or will be that much change, the vertigo of that Southerner has been shared by others all over the region, whatever the shade of their opinions or skin. As a matter of fact an impatient and outraged Negro youth in Mississippi told me — in 1966 — that "it's *all* in the mind, what's happening here. We get excited and have our marches and stir up dust and become elated and then feel as lousy as can be, and nothing really changes in the end. A few more people are registered. A few schools have one or two black faces. That's all, and that's nothing, really — except for you to study and see what happens, to us and to the children, I guess."

It must be clear by now that the closer we look at human behavior, the more nonpsychiatric influences must be summoned to "explain" what turns out to be a rather complicated and not always obvious connection between the life of the mind and the life of the world. Those two lives, be it remembered, are but convenient abstractions to aid our thinking about an *intensely shared continuity* that actually exists. You will remember Ruby (see Part One, chapter II). Her father once said to me: "They say it's not us, it's the poverty; then they say, it's not the poverty, it's the way we are, and our bad family life, so if we were different, we could shake it all off, the poverty. To me it's all the same package and the same rope with a big knot tied around it. You can touch the knot there and say that's the cause, but it's the whole knot, and then it's the rope, and then the package — and the package, it was made for the rope, it was shaped so it doesn't know what to do without that rope. So that's how I see it. The rope and the package, they're together, just like this house and the backyard mean so much to Ruby, as you can see in her pictures." Perhaps his metaphors are mixed and ambiguous; they are also more subtle than the substance of some theories of human development.

Whatever Ruby and her father may think about race and poverty, a series of historical changes eventually became for them a trial and a chance for personal effort and advance, or collapse and disaster. I have not shirked reporting Ruby's symptoms, or those of her race's older leaders. Yet it must be said that under grave stress she and they have somehow done more than persist, more than endure. They have prevailed in the way that Faulkner[1] knew they would by summoning every bit of their humanity in the face of every effort made to deny any of it to them. In so doing they have become more than they were, more than they themselves thought they were, and perhaps more than anyone watching them can quite put to word: bearers and makers of tradition; children who in a moment — call it existential, call it historical, call it psychological — took what they had from the past, in their minds, out of their homes, and made of *all* those possessions something else: a change in the world, and in themselves, too.

Of course the example of these lives can mislead us, and there are many who are all too eager for just that to be done. No matter how precise the language used to describe these people and their deeds there are those who will take any words, any lives as grist for one or another propaganda mill. Say that certain children under certain circumstances have shown courage and survived danger impressively well, and you are suddenly a bland advocate of all sorts of tribulations for children. Or you are an optimist — deliberate or naïve. Perhaps, worst of all, you may be labeled a propagandist, kept by any one of many groups to rationalize suffering, or to rob heroism of its dignity with one more revelation that what is, after all, can only appear to be.

In one of his papers on identity[2] Erik Erikson says: "In order to find an anchor point for the discussion of the universal genetics of identity, however, it would be well to trace its development through the life histories or through significant life episodes of 'ordinary' individuals — individuals whose lives have neither become professional autobiographies . . . nor case histories. . . ." That is what I have tried to do.

We live in a time when Negroes and the rest of us have come into possession of new slogans and phrases: "the Negro family" and "black power" are two examples. Each generation has to assert its own destiny, through language among other ways. It is certainly possible to see how thoroughly familiar the meaning of either of those expressions was to earlier generations. When the impressively literate social scientists of 1930 or 1940 did their work — in Chapel Hill,[3] in New Orleans,[4] in John Dollard's "southern town,"[5] in the "deep South" of Davis and Gardner[6] in the midst of the "cotton culture" once described,[7] the "mill villages" of Herring[8] or the Negroes Odum and Johnson[9] heard singing "workaday songs" — they all spoke again and again of the mean, harsh living that the Southern poor had to endure, and particularly the Negroes among them. As sociologists and anthropologists or psychologists, these writers did not confine themselves to a careful description of poverty; they consistently showed what it does to fathers and mothers, to children and grandchildren. Fear, hate, hunger and utter separation from the rest of the community establish an atmosphere that inevitably affects the child and the parent every day and profoundly. That it is controversial or comes as a surprise to anybody in America that the Negro family has had its special horrors to face — and has paid a high price in doing so — is perhaps the most interesting revelation to emerge from the "new" discussion of the Negro family. The arguments about the Negro family or "black power" show again how the obvious can become the controversial: every Negro family has to come to terms with the distinct fact of the Negro's relative powerlessness in American society; and political facts become psychological ones when a jobless man tells his hard-pressed wife that their hungry rat-bitten children will simply have to keep on living that way — and perpetuating such an inheritance over the generations. At least we might admit that the real problem is not whether Negro families have to endure and suffer special strains, or whether Negroes need more — much more — power, but what our political system can (or cannot) do to solve the hurt and weakness some of its citizens not only feel, but possess as a reliable, unalleviated curse.

I want to emphasize one observation I have consistently made in the South: in the region where he is still most numerous, most humble, isolated and poorest, the Negro has shown remarkable adaptive resiliency and assertiveness, given the right social or political circumstances. I have seen enough Negro children over a long enough time to realize that their family tragedy starts not in the first years of infancy and early childhood, but in those later years when the world's restrictions become decisive antagonists to the boy or girl — saying "no" to them about everything, teaching them finally to transform those refusals into a judgment of their worth as individuals and as citizens. As Erikson[10] pointed out a long time ago, however impoverished and lowly their position in American society, Negro mothers are generally warm and affectionate, almost desperately so. Even among the poorest tenant farmers, even among families who couldn't be living deeper in the ghetto, infants receive the constant attention of their mothers — while young boys and girls are kept close and watched hard. I am not arguing against the practice of birth control by the poor, but I wonder how many of us understand what the presence of a new child means to many of our poorest mothers — indeed to the men in their lives and to their other children.

A woman who recently arrived in Boston from Georgia speaks too sharply for me to delay putting her words into print: "They came telling us not to have children, and not to have children, and sweep up, and all that. There isn't anything they don't want to do to you, or tell you to do. They tell you you're bad, and worse than others, and you're lazy, and you don't know how to get along like others do. Well, for so long they told us we couldn't ever go near anyone else, I suppose we should be grateful for being told we're not going to get near enough if we don't behave in the right way — which is the sermon I get all the time now.

"Then they say we should look different, and eat different — use more of the protein. I tell them about the prices, but they reply about 'planning'— planning, planning, that's all they tell you. The worst of it is that they try to get you to plan your kids, by the year; except they mean by the ten-year plan, one every ten years. The truth is, they don't want you to have any, if they could help it.

"To me, having a baby inside me is the only time I'm really alive. I know I can make something, do something, no matter what color my skin is, and what names people call me. When the baby gets born I see him, and he's full of life, or she is; and I think to myself that it doesn't make any difference what happens later, at least now we've got a chance, or the baby does. You can see the little one grow and get larger and start doing things, and you feel there must be some hope, some chance that things will get better; because there it is, right before you, a real, live, growing baby. The children and their father feel it, too, just like I do. They feel the baby is a good sign, or at least he's *some* sign. If we didn't have that, what would be the difference from death? Even without children my life would still be bad — they're not going to give us what *they* have, the birth control people. They just want us to be a poor version of them, only without our children and our faith in God and our tasty fried food, or anything.

"They'll tell you we are 'neglectful'; we don't take proper care of the children. But that's a lie, because we do, until we can't any longer, because the time has come for the street to claim them, to take them away and teach them what a poor nigger's life is like. I don't care what anyone says: I take the best care of my children. I scream the ten commandments at them every day, until one by one they learn them by heart — and believe me they don't forget them. (You can ask my minister if I'm not telling the truth.) It's when they leave for school, and start seeing the streets and everything, that's when there's the change; and by the time they're ten or so, it's all I can do to say anything, because I don't even believe my own words, to be honest. I tell them, please to be good; but I know it's no use, not when they can't get a fair break, and there are the sheriffs down South and up here the policemen, ready to kick you for so much as breathing your feelings. So I turn my eyes on the little children, and keep on praying that one of them will grow up at the right second, when the schoolteachers have time to say hello and give him the lessons he needs, and when they get rid of the building here and let us have a place you can breathe in and not get bitten all the time, and when the men can find work — because *they* can't have children, and so they have to drink or get on drugs to find some happy moments, and some hope about things."

It is interesting that the controversy about the Negro family has centered hard upon the absence of the father in so many Negro homes. I would add to the analysis given by Glazer and

Moynihan in *Beyond the Melting Pot*[11] (considerably expanded by Moynihan in his famous report[12]) the clinical observation that against awful odds the Negro mother has probably done as effective a job at child-rearing as any mothers anywhere. Very young children, anyway, can survive handily without too much of their father's presence; certainly they do in other societies, and in our own upper middle class. It is the schoolchild in our country who looks especially to his father, who looks for new leaders, authorities and guides — which brings us back not only to the Negro father, wandering aimlessly among the jobless, but the schools, the street corners, the stores that Negro children frequent. I have watched the way Negro children are introduced to drugstores and food stores, let alone schools. I have seen them make their first acquaintance with money and power and property. They come as petulant, fearful boys and girls, very much lacking the confidence, even the brusque assurance and boldness one sees so commonly in suburban markets. (I cannot help contrasting the way my own young son talks to the grocer or the druggist.) At five and six one already sees the early social differences later to emerge as statistics on delinquency, gang behavior, riots, addiction — in sum, all the psychopathology no biologist is likely to prove transmitted by genes, even race-linked ones.

When Tolstoy had finished with *War and Peace* he added his epilogues, and in them indicated how hard it was *ever* to finish what he had tried to do — come to terms with the very nature of history. He also had a few words to say about the purpose of psychology: "To define the limits of freedom and dependence is very difficult, and the definition of those limits forms the sole and essential problem of psychology."[13] We might today congratulate ourselves on how many *other* responsibilities we have placed on the psychologist's shoulders, but I am not sure we recognize what makes for free children, or for "dependent" ones — nor what enables some boys and girls to feel cheerful while others are grim and sad before they even know how to give those emotions verbal expression. Dreams, life's events, the obligations and character of the neighborhood, bodily "drives," all of these involve or influence the child's mind, his unconscious mind as well as his state of consciousness. Resort to polarities like "deep" and "superficial" simply fails to "explain" the intricate problem of man's *nature* as it effects his *behavior*. For a long time psychiatrists had to fight hard to establish the reality of the unconscious in the face of opposition from a world that did not want to look "too deep." Yet, what is unconscious today in anyone's life might well have been all too conscious and decisive in the past. We sometimes forget that the unconscious, too, has a history. A psychology major, a Negro, a college student taking part in the Mississippi Summer Project of 1964 said: "Those books keep on talking about the really important, unconscious forces in you and the 'superficial' ones. It seems that the lower down you get into the unconscious — like a mine I guess — the more important material you find. I told my professor that my mother died of tuberculosis, and I saw a neighbor of ours lynched, and all the time when I was a child they took us to jail and beat us at the drop of a hat, and kept many of us near hunger. Now tell me, how important is all that for the development of my unconscious mind? It seems you're only interested in one kind of 'trauma'; but I don't see how you can separate these things in life."

I told him that sometimes we *had* to make separations and distinctions; that sometimes we had to make divisions of labor, in the academy as elsewhere. However, there are times when it is unwise to make virtue of necessity.

To quote Tolstoy again: "Undoubtably some relation exists between all who live contemporaneously, and so it is possible to find some connection between the intellectual activity of men and their historical movements."[14] That "connection" is often more obvious to *anyone* than to those whose job it presumably is to know the mind's activity, intellectual and emotional both. As for a "relation" the Russian novelist said exists between everyone alive, the South's rich white and poor Negro people can attest to that; and so can those "in between" of both races; and so can all of us who have observed the region from increasingly shortened distances — until, at last, we see its problems for what they are, our very own.

At an important psychiatric meeting I heard a colleague of mine talk unhesitatingly about the sexual fears that have prompted so much of the racism and segregationist defiance of federal laws. What he said was true, but he was quite unconcerned with other very influential causes of bigotry, so much so that it seemed clear to me that he looked at the whole problem of segregation as if it sprung out of something that might be called "the childhood of the segregationist." Not once were historical events mentioned. No remarks at all made reference to the problem of power, to the delicate and complicated issues which surround its institutional consolidation or disestablishment. Social and cultural "factors" were mentioned, but they were not specified and certainly not related to the psychological forces at work in individual lives — except perhaps as inert "conduits" for conflicted instinctual energy. Not a word did I hear about money, jobs, unemployment and how *those* "factors" touch the lives of people. Sometimes, in similar but more generous discussions, I have heard "economic" thrown in with "socio-cultural"; but the grim and intense daily meaning of those words to people scarcely comes across, because the "factors" are always that, parenthetical whispers of men impatient to get on with some other order of business.

It has been interesting to hear many school officials in the South formulate their plans for school desegregation with the following premises in mind: young children are especially susceptible to the influence of being at school with Negroes, and for that reason their parents are much more likely to be enraged enough to boycott schools or form mobs around them. One educator in one of those cities put it to me in these words: "The children are young, and they play together so intimately in the schoolyard; and their parents see it, and know how important childhood experiences are, and they get angry. So we decided to start with the high school grades, so as to stir up less irrational fear. You know how parents identify closely with young children; well, if they see a Negro boy of six playing with a white girl of six and they happen to touch one another, they might get hysterical. With teen-agers, that won't happen."

This man was sincere, and by no means a fool. He was trying to make a token plan for school desegregation work, and he was afraid of violence against even that much integration. We can smile at his talk as naïve, or dismiss his explanations as mere rationalizations, but I wonder whether we can deny that his way of looking at the behavior of children reflects an influential and pervasive mode of thinking in our contemporary culture. A Southerner, he could overlook the social and historical fact — and the psychological irony — that Negro and white children have played together at five and six for decades in his state of Tennessee with no objection from mobs. What bothers many Southerners I have met either in mobs or watching them with strong sympathy is not the fact that their children might someday play with Negro children, a common fact of life in the South more than in any other part of our nation, but the institutional recognition that hitherto "innocent" games will now become serious study, with a lifetime of social significance to it. Thus, faced with desegregation the parents of teen-agers in Little Rock were as "hysterical" as the parents of little children in New Orleans.

What is an educator to do if he is earnest and does indeed want to do anything at all in such situations? Many of them have tried to ground their decisions upon the shifting sands of theoretical speculation in the social sciences. Some have been quick-witted enough to see that whatever their decisions, they can be buttressed by a fact here, an idea become dogma there. In some cases what is educationally sensible or historically obvious, let alone morally correct, has been least heeded. I repeat what has been the obvious these past years. The history of the South's racial riots in the wake of school desegregation has been one of mobs and riots occurring when politicians and the police in a community have allowed them to occur — by maintaining a kind of "neutrality" which in fact tolerates them, or by encouraging them through various degrees of passivity, and even active support.

When I first began working with the white people of the South I saw the stress they faced largely in terms of the outward — what happened *to* them that made them respond in one way or another. Though I have tried to be evenhanded, so that my own beliefs and values do not prevent me from seeing terror and anxiety wherever it exists, I have noticed that it is easier for me to see the inner turmoil of a Negro youth asking for the right to vote than that of a white farmhand filled with almost speechless horror at the sight of a Negro doing so.

Indeed, from the very start of my stay in the South I overlooked a number of situations which at least might have puzzled me, if not set my psychiatric mind to active study. You will remember I was living in Mississippi and working there as the chief of an Air Force neuropsychiatric ward. One day as I was leaving the base I saw a group of corpsmen also walking away toward town. As soon as they crossed the base line, they split in two. I noticed that action in the casual, imprecise way we notice a lot of things, only to forget them quickly. About a mile or two down the road I heard a news report from my car radio about racial violence in Arkansas. Suddenly I realized what I had seen but not comprehended: corpsmen who worked beside one another, slept in the same barracks, frequented the base theater and club together, ate in our hospital cafeteria at common tables and took orders from one another indiscriminately, had separated into Negro and white columns as automatically as they had all been together with one another and at work with one another only moments before.

Had I been more alert I would have been interested in talking with those men about their flexibility, their ability to adapt so rapidly to the different customs demanded by each piece of territory. Most Southern segregationists, no matter how inflexible their views on race, no matter how active they are in the councils, societies and even klans of the region, are capable of the same kind of adaptive qualities shown by the men I knew in that hospital. I for one would hate to see the South become one large Air Force base to realize integration; but I think we must at least accept the fact that the problem is political and economic rather than that of the white man's total psychological reluctance or his inevitably closed mind or even heart. A century that has seen what totalitarian governments can do to the state of mind, the psychological attitudes of everyday people, will get the point of what I say and see it for the tragic and humiliating commonplace it has become.

If we condemn military and totalistic maneuvers — from any direction — can we achieve social change in the face of large numbers of people committed against it? The answer is daily coming in as yes, but the question still demands some clarification. I would say that most Southern whites are *formally* against various forms of integration; but the actual events in their lives — and the lives of other people when faced with similar issues — rarely permit Southerners, any more than the rest of us, to choose between formal alternatives like "for" or "against." White Southerners have divided themselves these past years as desegregation has pressed down harder and harder upon them. One white lawyer in Alabama told me in 1962 that "before it's all over we'll see a light and dark side to the struggle that won't follow racial lines, either." He is a "liberal," and at that time he feared the bloodshed he felt certain his own neighbors would cause. Whites would be the ones to contribute a dark side to the social conflict.

It was then, in a conversation with him, that I asked which whites he had in mind. Upset and angry, he said, "All of them." He was an exception; but there are many others. In fact I can offer three categories of white Southerners: the haters, the indifferent and the timid. There is nothing new to that — I hope you will say; but the psychiatrist faces his problem when he tries to find out why any one person he is interviewing has come to fall under any one of the three rubrics. Since hate, indifference and timidity are psychological qualities, he expects psychological explanations usually to account for their origins. Sometimes they can; but very often they cannot.

The haters are individual rioters or organized Klansmen who boycott schools or help excite mobs to "act" — demonstrate, set fires, shoot guns, threaten homes, hurt and even kill people. A few haters easily earn the labels "psychotic" or "psychopathic." I can suggest that they are "ill" and in need of medical attention, notwithstanding the fact that they would disagree with me and refuse any "help" I dared offer them. They are not all poor people; some are lawyers, doctors, clerks, businessmen or simply housewives. I have interviewed four of them, one of whom — John — you by now know a little. What I have found is what we might well predict on the basis of our present psychoanalytic knowledge: private problems have found expression in a public issue. Again and again I have heard the Negro's lowliness serve to distract the bigot from a sense of worthlessness; the Negro's proclaimed bestiality and carnality ward off the bigot's dim awareness that he, too, must deal with the impulses he decries in others; the Negro's demands, or forsaken ambitions, reflect the bigot's envies and feelings of loss or weakness. The Negro's very difference — in appearance, in the treatment he receives from all of us — symbolizes for many bigots their feeling about them- selves and their own lives, their own apartness or loneliness.

Some segregationists — they are a small number in my experi- ence — have shown considerable courage of conviction. When

other segregationists abandon the cause, when once devoutly
segregationist political leaders change their words and apparently alter their attitudes, *these* segregationists — committed
haters — are left straggling and struggling, fighting a last-ditch
battle that is pitiable and itself a reminder that suffering and
exploitation ignore the color line. As John once put it to me: "You
never can tell in a democracy how long people will believe
anything. That's why I don't like democracy. Everyone changes
his ideas too much."

We all have our hates, but most of us do not get them involved
with social and political issues to a degree that becomes frantic
and all-consuming. It is remarkable and almost frightening to see
how quickly a new generation can abandon the ruthlessly indoc-
trinated and maintained ideology of its predecessor. In the South,
as segregationist customs have collapsed, most white people have
yielded to what they once said they never could accept. I talked
with some of these people as they made the accommodation. I
call them the indifferent ones — indifferent to abstractions that
are losing the support of social approval or political power. The
indifferent ones appear to be a majority of the white people of
the South. The polls would record them as devoted segregationists. Now segregationist "ideology" has dismally failed them.
Whites have deserted it in droves. Unlike the fanatic segregationists, the "indifferents" want "law and order"; they want prosper-
ity; and when the issue is forced, they want to be at one with
their country.[15]

It can be quite unnerving to talk with these indifferent people,
because one's whole view of the "normal," the "average," the
"moral" or "ethical" is called into question. In Mississippi I have
watched certain white people for nearly a decade, and I truly
wonder even today just what they *do* believe in. In fact, their
beliefs are often less important to them than the comfortable
continuity of their lives. When *that* comes under a shadow,
they respond — and so do their beliefs. Those beliefs have

seemed flexible enough to accommodate a wide spectrum of social or political changes, so long as they are changes that at the same time promise to stop short — of what?

In 1961 a lawyer in Atlanta answered me: "I was born a segregationist, and I'll die one; but I was born a lot of things and right now I think my family and job mean more to me than keeping a few niggers out of a school or a restaurant. Yes, last year I wouldn't have said that, but they weren't breaking down our whole economy and threatening to lose us so much. I would rate myself the strongest kind of segregationist, but I think of other things, too."

Two years after he spoke those words to me he was calling a friend of his "eccentric" because he *still* believed and worked to uphold what both of them only recently said they would believe until their dying days: total, unyielding segregation. His friend was becoming an outcast. The definition of the "normal" or the "average," as it has so many times in man's history, was again changing. Even the definition of "right" was becoming involved. In another talk I heard this: "It's just not right to let your private views get so fired up that you block what's coming anyway. It's like saying you know more than the whole country. The mayor and governor tried to fight this thing, and they saw the handwriting on the wall. I think the few that can't see it now have something wrong with their heads — don't you think?"

I have always been glad that I never had him or his newly "eccentric" friend as a patient. As we hear the complaints of our patients and listen to them describe their behavior, psychiatrists have to make reference to the standards of the community. When a society like the South's is going through rapid change, it is a hard job to match the behavior of individuals with the "norms" or "standards" or "everyday practices" of the world. Even in "stable" areas of this nation there is good reason for us, the doctors, to look hard at our own beliefs and values as we estimate the excesses, idiosyncracies and abnormalities of others.

I must relate a story I heard from a Negro woman in Louisiana. She had faced mobs and risked death enough times to smile quietly about it all as she talked. Her daughter was one of the little Negro girls who pioneered school desegregation in that state. She was telling me about the *privilege* all that suffering had been: "I never had the chances my children are getting. I just grew up and picked cotton, and so are my brothers' children doing that right now, today. But we came to the city, so we got into all this. Well, as I see it, you have to think like you're growing flowers. We always grew flowers near our house after we came home from the fields. My momma said that the flowers were ours, no one else's, and prettier than cotton. Well, I told my girl she's going to be a beautiful flower, and so she has to fight off all the weeds — the people who don't care but for their own selves. And I told her not to be a timid plant, because they die; and it's no good, to want to be something and then fail and die." I asked her whether she thought the mob we had seen that day were weeds. No, she knew exactly what she wanted to say: "The weeds are just there. I think those mob people are like a tornado or a flood. They aren't part of the ground at all. The weeds, they'll be around always, no matter how much you cultivate; but some plants are timid and some aren't. That's what I mean: you have to stand up to the weeds — and the tornadoes, and anything. You have to lick your fear and not be timid."

She had defined her enemy and also focused sharply upon the tragedy that afflicts the third category of so-called segregationists I have met: those who in their secret heart aren't segregationists at all. They are people who want to grow, to be on the Lord's side, as they so often see it and put it, but who have not developed the necessary psychological or economic strength, boldness, organization of mind, power of conscience to risk the social ostracism, the possible loss of money, ease, coziness and cheer which accompany such a stand.

So they lie. Unlike the indifferent they suffer, often quite long and hard, because they know what they are *not* doing. They try the rationalizations used by the indifferent, only to feel worse. Here is a lawyer in Georgia talking: "I feel as torn and divided as it's possible to feel. I know I should be out there taking a stand, like some of the white people of the South have; but I can't. It means ruining my practice and losing everything I've worked a life to build. So I just nod with them, and to tell the truth, if the conversation gets to a point that I have to commit myself, I go along with them. Later, when driving home, I talk to myself and say, 'You're a coward and a liar.' But I think I'd be calling myself worse, a damn fool, if I destroyed my whole life and *still* didn't accomplish anything. Yes, sometimes I just want to move out of here; it's so painful."

Again and again I am struck by the distinctly different kinds of psychological adaptation a political crisis can bring into being. I submit, for instance, that we all have moments similar to what that lawyer described as his daily, yearly kind of dilemma. We are all sometimes hateful, sometimes indifferent. The three categorizations I have made about segregationists are thus limited ones; they apply to everyone's daily life. For that matter, *Negroes* can be divided into hateful segregationists, indifferent or apathetic citizens, and timid, would-be fighters for ideals which at times they betray. Though these categorizations are not exact or even altogether serviceable, and I was often hard put to fit them to particular people, I do think the three categories of segregationists represent three valid types.

We outside the South may find it convenient, or even important to think of its white people as psychotic haters, sexually maladjusted psychopaths, impossibly ignorant vigilantes or moral idiots. This way we can saddle them with the most profound kind of emotional attachment to segregation, one perhaps curable only in a lifetime. In so doing we ignore the facts of history. As Mr. C. Vann Woodward has reminded us: segregation came quickly and recently in our history, and in a definite political and economic context of that history.[16] Yet, why bother ourselves with vexing information like that? Why not worry about our poor, ailing semitropical neighbors? If we label them as sick, we may respond with tactful "help," with our "guidance." But so long as *that* is all we give them, it is a good question whether in fact the blind are not leading the blind. Must we persist in applying rigid categories of "sickness" and "health" to social problems — and to people?

James Agee once wrote a sentence as relevant to a doctor in his office as to the tenant farmers of Alabama who inspired the words: "All that each person is, and experiences, and shall never experience, in body and mind, all these things are differing expressions of himself and of one root, and are identical: and not one of these things nor one of these persons is ever quite to be duplicated, nor replaced, nor has it ever quite had precedent: but each is a new and incommunicably tender life, wounded in every breath and almost as hardly killed as easily wounded: sustaining, for a while, without defense, the enormous assaults of the universe."[17] I am glad that, finally, I could begin to learn what Agee knew.

REFERENCES

CHAPTER II

1. August Hollingshead and Frederick Redlich, *Social Class and Mental Illness* (New York, John Wiley, 1958).
2. Leo Srole, et al., *Mental Health in the Metropolis* (New York, McGraw-Hill, 1962).
3. Alexander H. Leighton, *My Name Is Legion* (New York, Basic Books, 1959).
4. An example, August Aichhorn's *Wayward Youth* was first published (as *Verwahrloste Jugend*) in 1925 by the Internationaler Psychoanalytischer Verlag, Vienna. In Boston, William Healy published *The Individual Delinquent* in 1915, and in 1926 (with Augusta Bronner) *Delinquents and Criminals — Their Making and Unmaking*. What they were doing at the Judge Baker Guidance Center was work in a pioneer field — child psychiatry.
5. Some of the work is reported in "Neuropsychiatric Aspects of Acute Poliomyelitis" which I coauthored with Jimmy C. B. Holland, *American Journal of Psychiatry*, Vol. 114, No. 1 (July 1957).
6. Anna Freud, *Normality and Pathology in Childhood* (New York, International Universities Press, 1965).
7. See my chapter "Serpents & Doves: Non-Violent Youth in the South," in *Youth: Change and Challenge*, edited by Erik H. Erikson (New York, Basic Books, 1963), for a discussion of one such incident in a Louisiana jail.
8. Oscar Lewis, *The Children of Sanchez* (New York, Random House, 1961).
9. See, especially, "Racial Problems in Psychotherapy," *Current Psychiatric Therapies*, Vol. VI, Jules Masserman, ed. (Grune & Stratton, 1966), and "A Matter of Territory," *Journal of Social Issues*, Vol. 20, No. 4 (October 1964). Also see "Southern Children Under Desegregation," *American Journal of Psychiatry*, Vol. 120, No. 4 (October 1963), and "Social Struggle and Weariness," *Psychiatry*, Vol. 27, No. 4 (November 1964).

CHAPTER III

1. Anna Freud, *The Psychoanalytical Treatment of Children* (London, Imago, 1946). Also, *Psychoanalysis for Teachers and Parents* (Boston, Beacon Press, 1960).

2. See Margaret Mead (with Frances Cooke), *Growth and Culture: A Photographic Study of Balinese Childhood* (New York, G. P. Putnam's Sons, 1951). Also *Coming of Age in Samoa* (New York, New American Library, 1953); *Childhood in Contemporary Cultures,* ed. by Martha Wolfenstein (Chicago, University of Chicago Press, 1955).

   Also, see *Six Cultures, Studies of Child Rearing,* edited by Beatrice Whiting (New York, John Wiley, 1963).
3. Anna Freud, *Normality and Pathology in Childhood* (New York, International Universities Press, 1965).
4. René Spitz, *The First Year of Life* (New York, International Universities Press, 1965).
5. A recent book is a valuable exception: Wayne Dennis, *Group Values Through Children's Drawings* (New York, John Wiley, 1966).
6. Sigmund Freud, "Dostoievsky and Parricide," in Vol. XXI of *Complete Psychological Works* (London, Hogarth Press, 1961).
7. Ernst Kris, *Psychoanalytic Exploration in Art* (New York, International Universities Press, 1952).
8. Henry Murray, *Explorations in Personality* (New York, Oxford University Press, 1953).
9. See the following as examples, among many others written in the past few decades: Percival Symonds, *Diagnosing Personality and Conduct* (New York, Century Co., 1931); John E. Bell, *Projective Techniques: A Dynamic Approach to the Study of the Personality* (New York, Longmans, 1951); Robert Allen, *Personality Assessment Procedures* (New York, Harper, 1958).
10. In example, chronologically: Bruno Lasker, *Race Attitudes in Children* (New York, H. Holt and Co., 1929); E. L. Horowitz, "Racial Aspects of Self-Identification in Nursery School Children," *Journal of Psychology,* Vol. 7 (1939), pp. 91–99; Mary Ellen Goodman, *Race Awareness in Young Children* (Cambridge, Addison-Wesley, 1952); K. B. Clark, *Prejudice and Your Child* (Boston, Beacon Press, 1955).
11. R. Coles, "Racial Problems in Psychotherapy," *Current Psychiatric Therapies,* Vol. VI, Jules Masserman, ed. (New York, Grune and Stratton, 1966).

CHAPTER IV

1. Anthony Lewis and The New York Times, *Portrait of a Decade* (New York, Random House, 1964); Benjamin Muse, *Ten Years of Prelude: The Story of Integration Since the Supreme Court's 1954 Decision* (New York, Viking Press, 1964).
2. Anna Freud and Dorothy T. Burlingham, *War and Children* (New York, International Universities Press, 1944).
3. See my reports: "Southern Children Under Desegregation," *American Journal of Psychiatry,* Vol. 120, No. 4 (October 1963); "Racial Conflict and a Child's Question," *Journal of Nervous and Mental Disease,* February 1965; "The Desegregation of Southern Schools: A Psychiatric Study" (issued by the Southern Regional Council, 1964). See also *Ten Years of Prelude: The Story of Integration Since the Supreme Court's 1954 Decision,* by Benjamin Muse (New York, Viking Press, 1964).

4. See his well-known sections on "identity" in *Childhood and Society* (New York, Norton, 1950 and 1963), and *Young Man Luther* (New York, Norton, 1958); see, especially, *Identity and the Life Cycle* (New York, International Universities Press, 1959).

CHAPTER VI

1. "Serpents and Doves: Non-Violent Youth in the South," a chapter in *Youth: Change and Challenge*, edited by Erik H. Erikson (New York, Basic Books, 1963); "A Psychiatrist Looks at Young Rights Fighters," New York *Herald Tribune*, June 21, 1964; "Social Struggle and Weariness," *Psychiatry*, Vol. 27, No. 4 (November 1964); "A Matter of Territory," *Journal of Social Issues*, Vol. 20 No. 4 (October 1964); "Young Americans in a Social Crisis: The Mississippi Summer Project," *American Journal of Orthopsychiatry*, October 1965; "A Psychiatrist Joins 'The Movement,'" *Trans-Action*, January–February 1966; "The Two American Traditions," *Counterpart*, Vol. 1, No. 1 (January–February 1966); "The Search for Community," *New Republic*, February 26, 1966; "Sickness and Rebellion: East and West," *Dissent*, May–June 1966.
2. "Social Struggle and Weariness," *Psychiatry*, Vol. 27, No. 4 (November 1964); "Young Americans in a Social Crisis: The Mississippi Summer Project," *American Journal of Orthopsychiatry*, October 1965.
3. Reported in a seminar at the National Institute of Child Health and Human Development, October 13, 1965, and published by National Institutes of Health.

CHAPTER VIII

1. See my article "Social Struggle and Weariness," *Psychiatry*, Autumn 1964.
2. Under the title of "Parents Stage Demonstration" the *New Orleans Times Picayune* of November 24, 1960, carried the following dispatch:

   "Parents and children from integrated New Orleans schools bore a miniature black coffin, containing a blackened effigy of U.S. Judge J. Skelly Wright, into the Louisiana Capitol.

   "Rep. Daniel Kelly, New Orleans, called House attention to the white parents and their children squeezing into aisles in the House open to spectators. Photographers had a field day.

   "The House stood up and with a long roll of applause, saluted the parents. The legislature last week by resolution urged white parents to boycott the two integrated New Orleans schools.

   "As the demonstrators moved into the legislative chambers, one woman in the group shouted, "the judge is dead, we have slaughtered him."

   "Some of the group feigned weeping and mourning, others laughed.

   "The blackened doll inside the yard-long coffin wore a black suit. In its pockets was a small gavel.

   "A small wreath of white flowers rested atop the coffin. Three pallbearers were on each side. Men, women and children were in the demonstration.

   "Large and small black flags and some Confederate ensigns were carried by the demonstrators. Some women wore black veils.

"A little girl carried a black cross.

"Placards said, 'Thank God for the state legislature' and 'Davis our children's protector, thank God.'

"Chief villain in the eyes of the legislators Wednesday continued to be federal Judge Skelly Wright who issued an order for integration of four Negro first graders into New Orleans schools.

"Legislators still seethed over Wright's action in enjoining the Legislature from assuming control of the Orleans parish public school system.

"In the Senate, Sen. B. B. Rayburn of Bogalusa introduced a resolution calling for removal of Judge Wright. It called upon the congressional delegation to launch the action.

"Both the House and the Senate convened at about 10 A.M. Wednesday. There was little action in the Senate, which prepared to move over to the House for the joint session.

"Another resolution, approved by both Houses, called upon Judge Wright to recuse himself, 'because of his bias and prejudice against Louisiana.' "

3. James Silver, *op. cit.*
4. Under the title of "Cleric and Student Tell of Attack in a Mississippi Doctor's Office" the *New York Times* of August 2, 1964, carried the following dispatch:

"Two civil rights workers, one a minister, were beaten in a physician's office where they were seeking medical care, it was disclosed today.

"The Rev. Edward K. Heininger, of Des Moines, Iowa, 45 years old, was said to have been injured severely by a gang of whites who attacked him in the presence of Dr. A. L. Thaggard Sr., who operates a private clinic in the Madden community near here."

CHAPTER IX

1. Marc Bloch, *Feudal Society* (Chicago, University of Chicago Press, 1961); also Johan Huizinga, *The Waning of the Middle Ages* (New York, Doubleday, 1956).
2. Wayne Gard, *Frontier Justice* (Norman, University of Oklahoma Press, 1949); C. C. Rister, "Outlaws and Vigilantes of Southern Plains," *Mississippi Valley Historical Review,* Vol. XIX (1933), p. 537; Charles A. Ellwood, "Has Crime Increased Since 1880?", *Journal of the American Institute of Crime and Criminology,* Vol. I, No. 3 (September 1910); C. L. Brace, *The Dangerous Classes of New York,* 3rd ed. (New York, Wynkoop & Hallenbeck, 1880).
3. For what one nation's "youth movement" came to, see: Walter Laqueur, *Young Germany* (New York, Basic Books, 1962).
4. Max Brod, *Franz Kafka, A Biography* (New York, Schocken, 1947); Heinz Politzer, *Franz Kafka; Parable and Paradox* (Cornell University Press, 1962).

Also, see Kafka himself in *Dearest Father* (New York, Schocken, 1954).
5. Anna Freud and Dorothy T. Burlingham, *op. cit.*

6. *Children in Bondage: A Survey of Child Life in the Occupied Countries of Europe and in Finland* (published for the Save the Children Fund, London, Longmans, Green & Co., 1942).

7. Donald Lowrie, *The Hunted Children* (New York, Norton, 1963).

8. Witold Majewski, *Polish Children Suffer* (London, F. P. Agency, Ltd., 1944).

9. Arata Osada, *Children of the A. Bomb: The Testament of the Boys and Girls of Hiroshima* (New York, Putnam, 1963).

10. Robert Jungk, *Children of the Ashes* (New York, Harcourt, Brace & World, 1961).

11. Arata Osada, *op. cit.*

12. Eugene Heimler, "Children of Auschwitz," a chapter in *Prison*, a symposium edited by George Mikes (London, Routledge and Kegan Paul, 1963).

13. Philippe Ariès, *Centuries of Childhood* (New York, Knopf, 1962).

14. Steven Runciman, *A History of the Crusades*, 3 vols. (Cambridge University Press, 1951–1954).

15. Max Weber, *The Protestant Ethic and the Spirit of Capitalism* (New York, Scribner, 1958).

16. Johann H. Pestalozzi, *Extracts from Letters on Early Education* (Liverpool, G. Smith, 1828); *How Gertrude Teaches Her Children* (Syracuse, N.Y., C. W. Bardeen, 1915).

17. James W. Silver, *Mississippi: The Closed Society* (New York, Harcourt, Brace & World, 1964).

CHAPTER X

1. See Mary Ellen Goodman, *Race Awareness in Young Children* (Cambridge, Mass., 1952); K. B. Clark and M. Clark, "The Development of Consciousness of Self and the Emergence of Racial Identification in Negro Preschool Children," *Journal of Social Psychology*, Vol. 10, No. 4 (November 1939), pp. 591–599. K. B. Clark and M. Clark, "Skin Color as a Factor in Racial Identification of Negro Preschool Children," *Journal of Social Psychology*, Vol. 11, No. 1 (Feburary 1940), pp. 159–169; K. B. Clark and M. Clark, "Emotional Factors in Racial Identification and Preference in Negro Children," *Journal of Negro Education*, Vol. 19 (1950), pp. 341–350. Eugene B. Brody, "Color and Identity Conflict in Young Boys," *Psychiatry*, Vol. 26, No. 2 (May 1963), pp. 188–201; Eugene B. Brody, "Color and Identity Conflict in Young Boys, II," *Archives of General Psychiatry*, Vol. 10 (April 1964), pp. 354–360; R. Coles, "Southern Children Under Desegregation," *American Journal of Psychiatry*, Vol. 120, No. 4 (October 1963), pp. 332–344; R. Coles, "Racial Conflict and a Child's Question," *Journal of Nervous and Mental Disease*, Vol. 140, No. 2 (February 1965), pp. 162–170.

2. I tried to illustrate the development of such attitudes among the rural poor in "The Lives of Migrant Farmers," *American Journal of Psychiatry*, Vol. 122, No. 3 (September 1965), and *The Migrant Worker*, a pamphlet issued by the Southern Regional Council (Atlanta, Georgia, Fall 1965).

3. For example, H. R. St. Claire, "Psychiatric Interview Experiences with Negroes," *American Journal of Psychiatry*, Vol. 108, No. 2 (August 1951), pp. 113–119; Viola W. Bernard, "Psychoanalysis and Members of Minority Groups," *Journal of the American Psychoanalytic Association*, Vol. 1, No. 2 (April 1953), pp. 256–267; Walter A. Adams, "The Negro Patient in Psychiatric Treatment," *American Journal of Orthopsychiatry*, Vol. 20, No. 2 (April 1950), pp. 305–310.

4. See Harold R. Isaacs, *The New World of Negro Americans* (New York, 1963), pp. 62–96, for an excellent discussion, with references, of the symbolic meaning of color to Negroes. See also A. Kardiner and L. Ovesey, *The Mark of Oppression* (New York, 1951). An interesting paper on this subject is Janet Kennedy's "Problems Posed in the Analysis of Negro Patients," *Psychiatry*, Vol. 15, No. 3 (August 1952), pp. 313–327.

5. Lillian Smith, *Killers of the Dream* (New York, 1949); W. J. Cash, *Mind of the South* (New York, 1941); C. Vann Woodward, *The Strange Career of Jim Crow* (New York, 1955). Southern writers like Faulkner, Eudora Welty, Shirley Ann Grau and Flannery O'Connor constantly return to the themes of savage hate and sly or desperate love between whites and Negroes. William Taylor's *Cavalier and Yankee* (New York, 1961) illustrates how the racial problem similarly touched and influenced writers in earlier times.

6. Eugene B. Brody, "Social Conflict and Schizophrenic Behavior in Young Adult Negro Males," *Psychiatry*, Vol. 24 (November 1961), pp. 337–346.

7. For example, Allison Davis and John Dollard, *The Children of Bondage* (Washington, D.C., 1940); Gunnar Myrdal, *An American Dilemma* (New York, 1944 and 1962); Kenneth B. Clark, *Prejudice and Your Child* (Boston, 1955); Marie Jahoda, *Race Relations and Mental Health* (Paris, 1960); Group for the Advancement of Psychiatry, "Psychiatric Aspects of Desegregation," Report No. 37, 1957; Kardiner and Ovesey, *op. cit.*

8. John Dollard, in *Caste and Class in a Southern Town* (Garden City, N.Y., 1957), gives a close analysis to the roots of such emotions. Less analytical than descriptive and autobiographical are such books as Hodding Carter's *Southern Legacy* (Baton Rouge, La., 1950); or William A. Percy's *Lanterns on the Levee* (New York, 1959).

9. Kardiner and Ovesey, *op. cit.*

CHAPTER XI

1. In example, Anna Freud, Heinz Hartmann and Erik Erikson. See Anna Freud, *The Ego and the Mechanisms of Defense* (New York, International Universities Press, 1946); Erik Erikson, *Childhood and Society* (New York, Norton, 1950); Heinz Hartmann, *Ego Psychology and the Problem of Adaptation* (New York, International Universities Press, 1958).

2. Two of Freud's most explicit and pointed attempts to discuss war and the hate stirred up by conflicting nations are: "Thoughts for the Times on War and Death," in Sigmund Freud, *The Complete Psychological*

Works, Vol. 14 (London, Hogarth, 1962), and "Why War? An Exchange of Letters with Albert Einstein," in Sigmund Freud, *The Complete Psychological Works,* Vol. 22 (London, Hogarth, 1964).

3. See Lawrence Kubie's excellent paper, "The Ontogeny of Racial Prejudice," *Journal of Nervous and Mental Disease,* Vol. 141, No. 3 (September 1965). There is an entire "literature" on prejudice, much of it concerned with the psychodynamics of anti-Semitism, but generally relevant to any form of bigotry. For example, Rudolph Loewenstein, *Christians and Jews* (New York, International Universities Press, 1951). The psychoanalytic literature also contains numerous efforts to apply what is known about the individual mind to political questions, including war and prejudice. For example, Alix Strachey, *The Unconscious Motives of War* (London, Allen & Unwin, 1957). Also, R. E. Money-Kyrle, *Psychoanalysis and Politics* (New York, Norton, 1951). While the psychoanalytic *explanations* (Kubie and Loewenstein) are enormously helpful, the value of the psychoanalytic *applications* (Strachey, Money-Kyrle and others) is doubtful. They are in essence attempts at transfer, often gratuitously done; concepts, themselves hardly proven, are carried over from the field of child development or psychoanalytic "infant psychiatry" to explain national and international problems. In addition, there is a disturbing tendency among such writers to foreclose disagreement in advance by declaring it evidence of "resistance" or the need for further analysis in the critic — certainly an extraordinarily self-righteous and convenient way of anticipating and handling disapproval.

4. Leo Tolstoy, *War and Peace,* translated by Louise and Aylmer Maude (New York, Simon and Schuster, 1942). The question about the causes of Europe's Napoleonic Wars is asked in the first epilogue, p. 1257.

5. Tolstoy, *op. cit.,* p. 1257.

6. Sigmund Freud, "Why War? An Exchange of Letters with Albert Einstein." See note 2.

7. The way Erik Erikson described Sigmund Freud in a lecture given before a German university audience (Heidelberg and Frankfurt) on the occasion of Freud's 100th birthday in 1956. The address may be found in *Insight and Responsibility* (New York, Norton, 1964).

8. Erik Erikson, *Young Man Luther* (New York, Norton, 1958).

9. Bruno Bettleheim and Morris Janowitz, *Social Change and Prejudice* (New York, Free Press, 1964). Also, "Individual and Mass Behavior in Extreme Situations," *Journal of Abnormal and Social Psychology,* Vol. 38 (1943), pp. 417–452.

10. Bettleheim and Janowitz, *op. cit.,* p. 277.

11. Lillian Smith, *Killers of the Dream* (New York, Norton, 1949).

12. In example, Anna Freud and her coworkers studied "heroic" children, and the following account of a seminar in which she participated indicates her approach to the problem: "Child heroes — who have risked their lives to save others from such dangers as fire, traffic and mad dogs — are so psychologically normal that they have not been studied psychoanalytically, according to Miss Anna Freud, director of the Hamp-

stead Clinic, London, England. As a result, she points out, the question of what makes these youngsters risk their own lives to save the lives of others remains unanswered. Miss Freud told a seminar . . . that data on nearly 70 of these child heroes — some as young as three years of age — have been accumulated at Hampstead Clinic in interviews with the children themselves, their parents and their teachers." *Frontiers of Hospital Psychiatry*, Vol. 3, No. 4 (February 15, 1966).

CHAPTER XII

1. I have in mind characters like Dilsey and Lucas Beauchamp, indeed whole novels like *The Sound and the Fury* or *Intruder in the Dust*. Certainly William Faulkner has not been spared the intensely felt mixture of attitudes that a region in profound social change generates — among outsiders as well as its own people. In example, James Baldwin and Irving Howe find themselves admirers of his, but also critics. In Baldwin's *Notes of a Native Son*, Faulkner stands with Ralph Ellison in the author's high esteem, for truly integrating the Negro by fitting his life in with the white man's, and showing how each is involved with the other. In *Nobody Knows My Name*, Baldwin's essay "Faulkner and Desegregation" answers Faulkner's plea that the South be granted time and the patience of those who condemn it. No, says Baldwin, "the challenge is in the moment, the time is always now." Significantly, Baldwin does not try to go *back* in time, by criticizing Faulkner the novelist for his descriptions of what was, what went on, what happened between people, or by denying Faulkner's vision as relevant, at the very least, to all men, everywhere. Irving Howe, in *William Faulkner: A Critical Study*, goes through much the same moral anguish that Baldwin does. He accepts Faulkner's preeminence among American novelists in discovering about the Negro "at what ever pain or discomfort, their meaning for American life." Yet, he also brings in a historical dimension: Faulkner's view of the world cannot hold in future generations, when there will, in fact, be a different world. Someone like Dilsey must therefore be admired, but not made into "a moral archetype or model." (I am sure that Faulkner would emphatically agree.) I recommend Cleanth Brooks's *William Faulkner: The Yoknapatawpha Country* (New Haven, Yale, 1963) for the broad and sensitive treatment it gives to the much abused matter of how a great novelist deals with an issue at once historical and contemporary.

2. Erik Erikson, *Identity and the Life Cycle* (New York, International Universities Press, 1959), p. 110.

3. I have in mind the "Social Study Series" that came out of the University of North Carolina in the earlier years of this century. See in example *Human Factors in Cotton Culture* by Rupert Vance (Chapel Hill, University of North Carolina Press, 1929).

4. Published in 1940 by the American Council on Education, *Children of Bondage* by Allison Davis and John Dollard in my opinion stands beside Anna Freud's book *War and Children;* in both scientific study has been done with unashamed care and reported with uncommon grace.

The work begun by Davis and Dollard in New Orleans was continued by Rohrer, Edmonson and others in *The Eighth Generation* (New York, Harper & Bros., 1960). The children I am now describing in this book obviously come from a later generation than the original "children of bondage" or their successors "the eighth generation." The very year *The Eighth Generation* was published, 1960, was the year crisis came to New Orleans in the form of mobs, boycotts and demonstrations accompanying school desegregation. As the title of this book asserts, the city's children — along with others over the South — had to face the tests of a serious crisis in order to leave bondage; while white children had to see it all happen, and find a way through a crisis of their own.

5. John Dollard, *Caste and Class in a Southern Town* (New Haven, Yale, 1937).

6. Davis, A.; Gardner, B.; and Gardner, M., *Deep South* (Chicago, University of Chicago Press, 1941).

7. See R. Vance, *op. cit.* Going well back into the nineteenth century the Negro problem and its relationship to the South's economy, not to mention its white people, was discussed in ways not unlike those heard today from the region's liberals. For example: George Washington Cable's *The Silent South* and *The Negro Question.*

8. Harriet L. Herring, *Welfare Work in Mill Villages* (Chapel Hill, University of North Carolina Press, 1929).

9. Howard W. Odum and Guy B. Johnson, *The Negro and His Songs* (Chapel Hill, University of North Carolina Press, 1925), and *Negro Workaday Songs* (Chapel Hill, University of North Carolina Press, 1926).

10. Erik Erikson, *Childhood and Society* (New York, Norton, 1950 and 1963). See, especially, the section called "Black Identity" in chapter six.

11. Nathan Glazer and Daniel Patrick Moynihan, *Beyond the Melting Pot* (Boston, M.I.T. Press and Harvard University Press, 1963).

12. Daniel Patrick Moynihan, *The Negro Family: The Case for National Action* (Washington, D.C.: Department of Labor, Office of Planning and Research, 1965).

13. Tolstoy, *op. cit.,* p. 1361.

14. Tolstoy, *op. cit.,* Second Epilogue, p. 1320.

15. The problem of Southern "attitudes" and their "change" is much more complicated than *any* survey (or series of "depth interviews," no matter how extended, by a psychiatrist like me) can possibly indicate. Even "urbanization" cannot entirely explain the apparent shift in the sentiment of many Southerners, white and Negro — though today it is commonly offered as an explanation (and panacea). I refer the reader to Eric Lampard's excellent background paper "American Historians and the Study of Urbanization" (*American Historical Review,* October 1961). Specifically, there is Meyer Weinberg's "Aspects of Southern Urbanization and School Segregation," a report written for the U.S. Office of Education, August 1965. People can move to the city and change their behavior but not their declared attitudes; or they can merely give their attitudes a new style, a new manner of expression —

in turn *called* a "change" by those who mistake form for substance. Yet, it also has to be said (and it can be shown) that a change in form can be the prelude to a later change in substance, the process being more subtle than anyone — interviewer or respondent — may realize at any given moment of time.

16. C. Vann Woodward, *The Strange Career of Jim Crow*, 2d. rev. ed. (New York, Oxford University Press, 1966).

17. James Agee and Walker Evans, *Let Us Now Praise Famous Men* (Boston, Houghton Mifflin, 1941 and 1960).

INDEX